TCP/IP PROGRAMMING FOR OS/2

With Applications for Presentation Manager

STEVEN J. GUTZ

MANNING

Greenwich
(74° w. long.)

The publisher offers discounts on this book when ordered in quantity. For more information please contact:

Special Sales Department
Manning Publications Co.
3 Lewis Street
Greenwich, CT 06830
or
lee@manning.com
Fax: (203) 661-9018

Typesetting: Sheila Carlisle
Copy editor: Doris Eder
Design: Frank Cunningham
Cover: Fernando Gonzalez Bunster

Recognizing the importance of preserving what has been written, it is the policy of Manning Publications to have the books we publish printed on acid-free paper, and we exert our best efforts to that end.

This book contains source code which is copyrighted by the author and NeoLogic Inc. Using the base code contained and described in this book, you are free to develop your own applications for commercial or internal use, or as freeware or shareware, provided you acknowledge such copyright ownership in your application's product information dialog.

The author and the publisher of this book make no warranties of any kind, expressed or implied, with regard to the source code and documentation contained in this book or the companion disk. The author and publisher shall not be liable in any event for any loss or damages caused by, or arising out of, the use of information contained in this book or the companion disk.

Library of Congress Cataloging–in–Publication Data

Gutz, Steven J.
TCP/IP applications programming for OS/2:
with applications for Presentation Manager / Steven J. Gutz.
p. cm.
Includes bibliographical references and index.
ISBN 1-884777-17-1 (soft cov.)
1. Operating systems (Computers) 2. OS/2 (Computer file)
3. Presentation manager. 4. TCP/IP (Computer network protocol)
I. Title.
QA76.76.063G88 1996
005.7'1265--dc20 96-5959
CIP

96 97 98 99 CR 10 9 8 7 6 5 4 3 2 1

Printed in the United States of America

Contents

PREFACE vii

PART I GETTING STARTED 1

1 PREPARING FOR APPLICATION DEVELOPMENT 3

Software Requirements 3
Visual Development Tools 5
Additional Tools 6
Compiler Precautions 7
Using MAKE and NMAKE 8
Dynamic Link Libraries 10
Project Directory Structure 11
Where to Find Additional Tools and Information 12
Chapter Summary 15

2 OS/2 AND PRESENTATION MANAGER BASICS 16

What is OS/2? 16
How OS/2 is Structured 20
What is Presentation Manager? 21
How Does PM Work? 23
Goals for PM Applications 31
Common User Access 32
Other Reference Works 36
Chapter Summary 38

3 TCP/IP BASICS 39
What is TCP/IP? 39
How is TCP/IP Structured? 40
Internet Addressing 42
Common Internet Protocols 43
TCP/IP Sockets 45
Chapter Summary 51

4 CONSIDERATIONS FOR SYSTEM PERFORMANCE 52
The 1/10 Second Rule 52
Multithreading 53
Using Object Windows 57
Chapter Summary 63

PART II BUILDING CLASS LIBRARIES 65

5 DEVELOPING A CLASS LIBRARY FOR NONVISUAL OBJECTS 67
Why Build a Class Library? 67
The Question of Portability 68
The NVCLASS Class Library 69
The C_INI Class 70
The C_INI_USER Class 74
The C_INI_SYSTEM Class 76
The C_THREAD Class 77
The C_THREAD_PM Class 81
The C_SEM_EVENT Class 84
Chapter Summary 89

6 DEVELOPING A SIMPLE PM CLASS LIBRARY 90
The PMCLASS Class Library 90
Application Class 93
Basic Window Class 99
Standard Window Class 126
Child Window Class 142
Dialog Class 148
Push Button Class 154
List Box Class 156

Status Line Class 163
Menu Class 166
Slider Class 169
Toolbar Button Class 174
Toolbar Class 183
Edit Class 199
Multiline Editor Class 202
CUA Container Class 221
Debug / Data Logging Class 245
Chapter Summary 254

7 DEVELOPING A NETWORK INTERFACE CLASS LIBRARY 255
What is NETCLASS? 255
The C_CONNECT Class 256
Ping Class 272
News Class 278
FTP Class 295
Developing Other Network Classes 321
Building a Connection Manager 321
Chapter Summary 323

PART III BUILDING APPLICATIONS 325

8 AN IMPROVED EDITOR 327
Coding the Editor 327
Handling Window Creation 332
Adding Status Bar Objects 333
Adding a Multiline Editor Object 334
Sizing Up 335
Adding a Menu 336
Adding a Toolbar 339
Processing WM_COMMAND Messages 344
Loading and Saving Files 350
Adding Clipboard Interaction and Word Wrap 353
Loading Dialogs 354
Search and Replace 358
Final Embellishments 367
Chapter Summary 367

9 A SIMPLE PM PING 368

Ping Main Program 368
Getting Ping Addresses 383
Ping Product Information Dialog 387
The Ping Toolbar 390
Chapter Summary 392

10 A SIMPLE NEWS CLIENT 393

Goals for the News Client Application 393
Building a News Connection Manager 395
Starting Up a News Client 402
Listing Available Groups 420
Managing News Subscriptions 431
Displaying Message Lists 438
Viewing Articles 450
What's Missing? 451
Dealing with Code Inefficiency 452
Chapter Summary 453

11 A BASIC FTP CLIENT 454

Goals for the FTP Client Application 454
Coding the FTP Client 456
Creating FTP Connections 461
Processing FTP Commands 462
Closing the Application 465
Possible Enhancements 466
Chapter Summary 467

A NONVISUAL CLASS LIBRARY REFERENCE 469

B PM CLASS LIBRARY REFERENCE 474

C NETWORK CLASS LIBRARY REFERENCE 490

INDEX 497

Preface

I first saw OS/2 version 1.0 in 1988 after IBM and Microsoft teamed up to create a replacement for DOS. Even though only seven years have passed, it all seems like ancient history. At that time, I was a dyed-in-the-wool DOS programmer, and Windows was still too immature to be a contender for my affections. I attended a product debut for OS/2, and I remember being excited about the arrival of a real multitasking operating system for the 80x86 platform.

Looking back today, I wonder what I could have been thinking. Here was an operating system designed for the aging 80286, with poor (to say the least) DOS support, and system requirements that were well out of the reach of most users. That first version had no networking capabilities to speak of and no graphical user interface, two items high on every user's checklist of requirements for a desktop operating system today. When my initial excitement faded away, I left OS/2 for dead—although with each new release I snatched another glimpse, just in case things had improved. However, OS/2 1.x was never the development platform I wanted. Even though enhancements such as Presentation Manager (PM) and networking were added, there always seemed to be something missing.

In April 1992, while attending the Borland Developers' Conference in Monterey, California, our paths crossed once again. This time it was version 2.0, IBM's first solo version after having shaken free of Microsoft, who was now married to Windows 3.0. I remember how bitter I had become toward IBM and OS/2, and as I sat down to an OS/2 demonstration system, I had one intention—to crash it. However, I played with 2.0 for a while and quickly became enamored with its features and stability. I clearly remember uttering words like "wow" and "neat" as I moused around the new OS/2 Workplace Shell. Finally, here was an operating system that could fill my needs. It still lacked some gloss, but it was truly an operating system with the potential to replace DOS and Windows.

By November 1992, I was a confirmed OS/2 fanatic. I purchased the OS/2 Professional Developers' Kit from IBM, and devoured every word ever printed on the subject of OS/2. Early in 1994, I formed NeoLogic Inc., which specializes in improving user perception of OS/2, TCP/IP, and the Internet. NeoLogic took shareware applications I had been developing since 1992 and expanded them into a product called the NeoLogic Network Suite, which now includes several applications, including a full-featured news reader, Gopher, FTP, and mail.

With each new application, I have become more (sometimes painfully) aware of OS/2's features and limitations. I developed a set of simple C++ classes to help produce applications more rapidly and with fewer bugs. While developing my applications, it became obvious that really good programmer documentation for OS/2 is rare. There are, of course, many books "for dummies" which describe these topics from a new user's perspective, but I found few books "for technogeeks." This raises the obvious question: Are other OS/2 developers having the same problems that I faced in the early stages of my OS/2 experience?

Based on the availability and quality of OS/2 applications, the answer to this question is a very vocal "Yes." Many aspiring developers have sent me e-mail asking how to manipulate some aspect of the OS/2 API or TCP/IP socket interface. In short, people were expressing interest in how the news program was written—not because they are all that interested in News itself; rather, they wanted to know things about programming for OS/2 and how to use the TCP/IP socket interface. Although I never professed to be an "expert" on either of these subjects, I have managed to unearth more information than most OS/2 programmers. This book is the direct result of my research into developing TCP/IP applications for OS/2, and I am taking the opportunity to share this knowledge with everyone.

STEVEN GUTZ
NSTN4064@FOX.NSTN.CA

Who is the Intended Audience?

This book is intended to span the basics of developing TCP/IP applications for the OS/2 family of operating systems. I have placed emphasis on the C++ programming language and the Presentation Manager interface, although most information in the book applies equally to C and OS/2 Text Mode. Where possible, I have described the C++ code at the method (member function) level in order to improve portability to C.

Like any multitasking operating system, developing applications for OS/2 is definitely not for the faint of heart. Furthermore, if you are planning to build programs designed for TCP/IP interaction, be prepared for many headaches along the way. However, I will do my best to lead you through the process of building simple TCP/IP clients from start to finish. I will make a few side trips along the way to describe the additional complications that the Presentation Manager interface adds. I hope that by the time you finish reading this book, you will have the knowledge to attack your own PM and TCP/IP projects with confidence.

Before we begin, I should describe my assumptions of you. You will, of course, need to be an intermediate- to advanced-level programmer, preferably possessing some experience with OS/2. If you have never programmed in OS/2, Windows, or other message-based OS, then this book is definitely not for you. I will initially present a few minimal programming examples, but I will quickly ramp up to building dynamic link libraries and workable applications. I will dive right into advanced topics, like the use of PM Container controls, once we get through the preamble in the first part of this book.

I will assume that you know and fully understand the C++ programming language and the concepts of object-oriented programming. Although the applications developed will sometimes be a hybrid of C and C++, emphasis is definitely directed toward developing solid, portable class libraries. Most of the source code for the class libraries is written completely in C++.

Finally, I will assume that you have some understanding of TCP/IP, at least from a user perspective. You do not need to be a network programming "guru" by any means, but you will find that some experience with TCP/IP socket programming is a definite asset, and working knowledge of TCP/IP applications is essential. I will not delve too deeply into the inner workings of TCP/IP since there are many excellent books on the subject. Rather, I will describe the basic network source code used for the socket interface, and will require that you possess only a minimal background knowledge of what is inside TCP/IP.

How This Book Is Organized

This book consists of three parts. We begin with a little background on OS/2, TCP/IP, and the Internet, and finish with a handful of working applications and the knowledge to build your own programs. The book is organized as follows:

- Part I contains all the information you will need to get started, including a quick discussion of OS/2, TCP/IP, the Internet, and what tools you require and how to set them up.
- Part II contains lots of detailed code as we develop and examine class libraries for the user interface and for networking.
- In Part III we will create several working applications designed to demonstrate the class libraries.
- The Appendices contain reference guides for the User Interface and Network class libraries.

Conventions Used in This Book

In order to present the information contained in this book in a consistent manner, the following conventions are used throughout:

- Except where noted, commands, filenames, and extensions are capitalized (e.g., CONFIG.SYS).
- This book uses a particular notation for illustrating program objects. An object will be drawn as follows:

OBJECT NAME	
Attribute 1	Method 1
Attribute 2	Method 2
•	•
•	•
Attribute n	Method n

Object inheritance will be illustrated as:

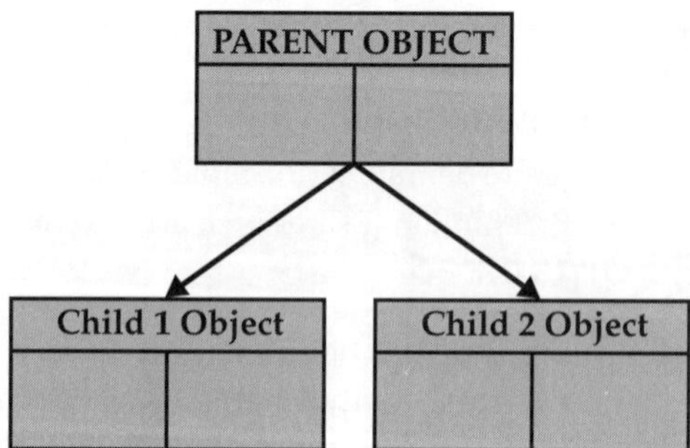

Source code in this book will follow a coding convention based loosely on Hungarian notation, originally devised by Charles Simonyi of Microsoft Corp. If you have never used this notation it might at first seem strange, but it does help write better code. The notation consists of prefix character(s) for variable names as follows:

Prefix	Data Type
c	Character
by	BYTE or unsigned character
b	BOOL Boolean type
h	Handle to windows, files, etc.
l	LONG integer
sz	NULL terminate character string
ul	ULONG unsigned long integer

When creating instances of structured data types, variable names will be prefixed as follows:

Prefix	Data Type
xs	Instance of a structure (struct)
xt	Instance of a type (typedef)
xc	Instance of a class (class)

Some additional modifiers will be used, as shown below:

Prefix	Data Type
p	Pointer to a selected data type
g	Global data

Finally, all classes, type definitions, and data structures will be defined using UPPERCASE characters, preceded by one of the following prefixes:

Prefix	Data Definition
S_	Structure definition (Example: S_USER_DATA)
T_	Type definition (Example: T_ADDRESS)
C_	Class definition (Example: C_WINDOW)

Using This Book

This book is not meant to be read cover-to-cover before delving into the knowledge you will find within it. Indeed, I certainly didn't write it from cover-to-cover; rather, it evolved as I rewrote sections several times. The class libraries were recoded again and again. Each time I added a feature to one of the applications in Part III, I realized that I had neglected to add a required method to one of the PM classes, or had forgotten to write a class completely. Since all the library code is written in C++, adding or modifying parts was usually a trivial exercise.

This is the approach I would like you to take in reading and using this book. The classes I have provided are only a basic framework, and I expect you will want to add your own features and extensions to the class libraries. You will, of course, need to add new objects to the network class library in order to implement interfaces for additional network protocols, such as mail or IRC, but you may also want to add new members to some of the PM classes, since you will likely find some omissions made either by accident or intention. The possibilities for enhancements to the classes in this book are limitless—if you are familiar with Borland's OWL or IBM ICLUI class libraries, you know what sorts of features can be added. The beauty of the object-oriented approach of C++ is that, if you decide you want your window object to do more, then you may subclass the one I have provided and add your own extensions, reusing only what you need.

About the Companion Disk

This book includes a companion disk containing all the code for the libraries and applications developed in the latter sections of the book. This will save you many hours of work when you begin developing your own applications. The disk also contains some of my favorite freeware and shareware applications, as well as copies of some of the RFCs referenced in the book.

The source code contained on the companion disk will compile with either the Borland C++ for OS/2 package or IBM VisualAge C++ for OS/2, and project files have been provided for both compilers.

Finally, the companion disk includes pre-built libraries and DLLs which can be used with the VisualAge C++ compiler. Executables for the Editor, news, FTP, and Ping are also included on the disk.

To install the companion disk, insert the disk and from an OS/2 command line type: "D:<Enter>", where "D:" is the drive letter of your disk drive. Then type "INSTALL<Enter>" to begin the installation process.

Special Thanks

There are a number of people I would like to thank for assisting with the creation of this book. Most of you have no knowledge of the contributions you have made, but you have been helpful in ways which cannot be imagined.

To my wife, Nancy, a mother and a business woman, who still managed to tolerate all of my demands and annoyances while I was creating this book.

To David Reich, thank you for the OS/2 T-shirt, and for introducing me to "the new IBM." Our candid discussions of OS/2 were instrumental in filling in a great deal of background information.

To David Moskowitz, I am grateful for our candid conversations at the Borland Developer's Conferences and in e-mail over the past few years. Thanks also for your input and suggestions as a beta tester for the NeoLogic Network Suite.

To Len Dorfman, thanks for asking the simple question, "Would you like to write a book?" Thanks also for proofreading my incomplete draft copies.

To Tim McGinn, thanks for looking after some of the software development at NeoLogic while I was distracted writing this book.

To all OS/2 users—without you, there would be no reason for this book. OS/2 is a nice place to set up business and you are all great neighbors.

In this chapter

- ✓ Software requirements
- ✓ Compiler precautions
- ✓ Additional information sources

1

Preparing for Application Development

Software Requirements

Software is really where the interests of most of us lie; before you can develop TCP/IP applications you may need to invest a small fortune to acquire the correct tools. This is not meant to scare you away from software development, but these tools can get expensive, especially if you opt for the so-called "professional" packages, which usually include advanced debugging and analysis tools.

Of course, you need to have OS/2 installed on your system. All of the source code in this book was developed on systems with OS/2 Warp 3.0 installed. Warp ships with a Bonus Pack disk containing the Internet Access Kit (IAK). This is usually enough to run Internet programs; however, in order to develop these TCP/IP applications, you will need additional software.

IBM's current product push is directed toward a product called Warp Connect. This version of the operating system will likely replace the current, more limited Warp package and will be the only offering available for the upcoming Power PC system. Warp Connect offers an integrated TCP/IP interface consisting of two layers of software. The Multi-Protocol Transfer Services (MPTS) contains all the low-level services to interface to a network interface adapter or to a serial modem using a SLIP or PPP layer. The second half of the TCP/IP interface is essentially identical to what the IAK provides, including some basic client applications like WebExplorer.

If you are building new network applications, you would be wise to recommend Warp Connect for your end users since it simplifies the TCP/IP installation and use; however, as a developer you will still need to purchase the IBM TCP/IP

Programmer's Toolkit because the libraries and C header files are not included with Warp Connect.

You will also need a C/C++ compiler. The GNU C/C++ compiler for OS/2 is free; however, it was not used to develop any of the code in this book, so you may experience some unexpected problems. The IBM CSet++ compiler for OS/2 is adequate, as is the C++ for OS/2 offering from Borland International, and you may also want to take a look at the Watcom C++ compiler if you are concerned with portability or executable size.

You will also need a TCP/IP base kit and a Programmer's Toolkit. All the examples in this book were created using the IBM TCP/IP base pack and Programmer's Toolkit. FTP Software also offers a complete TCP/IP development system, so price may be the deciding factor when selecting your development environment.

You can save hundreds of dollars by ordering IBM's Developer Connection for OS/2 CDs. This is not intended to offer a free plug for IBM; the Developer Connection CDs include practically everything you will need to build the applications in this book, as well as lots of additional reference information such as the IBM OS/2 Redbooks, and a number of abbreviated books related to OS/2 programming. The Developer Connection CDs represent the best software value you will find for OS/2 development tools.

The following is a list of software required to create the libraries and applications in this book. These are personal recommendations and do not necessarily represent the best value or most functional products.

Tool	Purpose	Manufacturer(s)
Compiler	Used to convert sources to object format.	IBM CSet++ Borland C++ for OS/2
TCP/IP Base	Basic TCP/IP communications suite.	IBM TCP/IP
TCP/IP Programmer's Toolkit	Used to create TCP/IP applications.	IBM
TCP/IP utilities	Used to gain access to the Internet in order to make inquiries and retrieve information.	NeoLogic Network Suite for OS/2
Miscellaneous development tools	Freeware or shareware applications offering a wealth of capabilities.	Pulse, WatchCat, OS20Memu, SIO

Visual Development Tools

IBM has recently announced VisualAge C++ for OS/2 , which is a new product to replace CSet++. VisualAge C++ is a development package that contains the compiler and debugger tools with which you may already be familiar; however, it also includes an innovative new tool called VisualBuilder, which is a highly graphical development system. VisualBuilder can be used to create applications graphically by dropping "parts" onto a work canvas and connecting them together. Application construction with VisualBuilder actually involves very little programming at all, at least in the traditional sense.

This sounds like the ideal environment, but there is one very large drawback known as a run-time library. The run-time library (which is actually several dynamic link libraries or DLLs) used by VisualBuilder, is the same one that any program built with the IBM ICLUI classes uses, and must accompany any application you develop with VisualBuilder. Including an additional set of DLLs with your application is not a terrible set-back, except that the combined size of the ICLUI DLLs typically hovers at around 1 Mbyte. You can pare this down by remanufacturing the library, but this solution is not an easy one. Alternately, you can statically link to the ICLUI library, but this does not solve the size problem either, since the equivalent ICLUI code then gets buried in your executable, bloating it substantially.

An aphorism that I have sworn by for many years is: You can develop applications fast or you can develop them well. VisualAge and most other graphical development tools live up to this realization. When used as prototyping tools, applications like VisualBuilder work very well. However, this type of tool typically lacks the luster required for production code and subsequent maintenance support. You cannot comment a graphical image, so revisiting an application as part of the maintenance phase of a project can become a serious problem.

Although you could likely develop all of the applications in this book with VisualAge C++ for OS/2, we will deliberately avoid it. This book is an exercise in understanding how to build classes for a user interface and networking, and though I have not specifically touched on the subject, the applications I will build throughout this book are, for the most part, portable to other operating systems. You will of course need to rewrite or modify the PMCLASS, NVCLASS, and NETCLASS classes, but everything else in the applications should recompile on other platforms with minimal modifications, provided you take care to minimize or eliminate calls to the OS/2 specific API.

Please do not infer that I dislike VisualBuilder specifically or visual tools in general. Indeed, VisualBuilder is an excellent tool for prototyping applications quickly, but realize that you cannot get something for nothing—the convenience of the VisualBuilder and ICLUI class library comes with an associated cost.

Additional Tools

There are a number of other tools that you will find invaluable while developing for OS/2. These are summarized in the table below:

Pulse	This CPU performance-monitoring tool ships with the operating system; it can be very useful for detecting CPU-stressing conditions. We will discuss the 1/10 second rule later in the book, but inevitably you will break this rule, and Pulse will assist you in identifying when you have done so.
Pstat	This is another tool that ships with the operating system. Pstat displays lots of information about the state of the system. It can show operating data for running process, dynamic link libraries that are loaded, and semaphore use, to name a few.
WatchCat	This is probably the best shareware tool for monitoring system status. It performs essentially the same job as Pstat, but offers a much improved user interface and the power to selectively terminate processes—including the Workplace Shell. The shareware version of WatchCat is on the companion disk.
Ray Gwinn's SIO serial driver	If you are using a SLIP or PPP connection as your gateway to the Internet, then you absolutely must have Ray Gwinn's SIO asynchronous port driver for OS/2. This driver improves the performance of the serial interface substantially and will noticeably increase your TCP/IP throughput. You will find the shareware version of the SIO driver on the companion disk.
Theseus/2	Although it is quite expensive, this IBM tool does help detect memory problems, etc., and offers a level of detail not found in any other tool.
OS20Memu	This is a freeware tool provided by IBM as part of the Employee Written Software (EWS) initiative. This tool is useful for detecting and correcting memory leaks in your code.
NETSTAT	This utility is supplied with TCP/IP and is useful for tracking the use of TCP/IP sockets in the system.

Compiler Precautions

If you have tried to compile any of the IBM TCP/IP sample applications that ship with the TCP/IP Programmer's Toolkit using the Borland compiler, you already know that you run into some annoying inconsistencies between the compiler and the libraries. The TCP/IP libraries and headers provided by IBM are decidedly slanted toward their own CSet++ compiler, and will generate compile errors using most other compilers.

Although you can use the Borland C++ for OS/2 package to develop TCP/IP applications for OS/2, you will need to make changes to some of Borland's header files. These changes are required to use the IBM TCP/IP Programmer's Toolkit, since it references some keywords which are specific to the CSet++ compiler. These patches may also work for other compilers, such as Watcom C++ or the GNU compiler.

You will need to insert a few additional defines into one of the headers files. Where you do this is not important, as long as you ensure the header file, where the changes are made, is loaded before any of the TCP/IP headers. For the Borland compiler the logical place to add these definitions is the OS2DEF.H header.

Using a text editor (the Borland IDE will do nicely), edit the OS2DEF.H file located in the \INCLUDE subdirectory of the Borland C++ installation. You will see a section of code as follows:

```
#if     defined(__BORLANDC__)
   #define APIENTRY          __syscall
   #define EXPENTRY          __syscall
   #define APIENTRY16        __far16 __pascal
   #define PASCAL16          __far16 __pascal
   #define CDECL16           __far16 __cdecl
   #define FAR16PTR          __far16 *
#else
```

Listing 1-1 Part of original Borland OS2DEF.H

In this section, before the #else, add the following:

```
// Changes to use IBM TCP/IP
#define     _Optlink     __stdcall
#define     _Packed
#define     _System      __syscall
#define     _Export      __export
```

Listing 1-2 Additions to Borland OS2DEF.H

The BASE.MAK file makes reference to some files which you may not immediately appreciate. The .DEF, .RC, and .RES files are unique to OS/2 PM (and Windows) so if you have never programmed for OS/2 they will appear alien. Almost all the applications in Part III will use these files; we'll discuss them in greater detail at that time.

Dynamic Link Libraries

Chances are good that if you have done any serious programming in the past, you are already familiar the concept of object libraries. Libraries are used whenever you have code that you use frequently and choose not to recompile every time you build your application code. Libraries offer the advantage of convenience, but also the distinct disadvantage of bloating your application code. Depending on how the library is constructed, the linker may actually link code from the library that is not used by the application, thus causing unnecessary code bloat. There is a better way, however, and it is known as a dynamic link library.

Dynamic link libraries do not really differ from static object libraries very much. Like static libraries, they can contain all of the common code for applications; however, there are several distinct differences. DLL code is not linked directly into an application. The linker simply links in a set of pointers to DLL functions. The results are smaller on-disk applications.

When an application linked to a DLL is loaded, the operating system verifies that the DLL is loaded into memory for the program to use. If OS/2 does not find the DLL in memory, it loads the DLL into memory automatically. Other than code size, there doesn't appear to be any other significant benefits realized through DLL use. So where are the advantages of dynamic link libraries?

Well, since the operating system controls the loading of the DLL code, it can detect when a copy of the DLL is already in memory. If a second copy of the application is executed, or a second application is developed to use the same DLL, the operating system ensures that only a single copy of the DLL is in memory to serve both programs. This means that, no matter how many programs are executing, there will only ever be *one* copy of the DLL loaded by the operating system, maximizing the efficiency of available system memory.

DLLs offer a second significant advantage for software maintenance. Because a DLL is basically a separate program, problems in the field can often be corrected without having to recompile the application. As long as the function interfaces in a DLL remain unchanged, they can be rebuilt to add new or corrected code without needing to recompile any of the applications that use the library.

If you are still not convinced of the advantages of DLLs, remember that Presentation Manager is essentially a collection of DLLs containing hundreds of kilobytes of code for the graphics engine, window manager, communications, etc. Every PM program will use some portion of this code, so if your basic "Hello World" program did not have the support of the system DLLs it could be as large as 100K or more!

All classes developed in this book will be placed in three DLLs, as follows:

NVCLASS.DLL — This library contains all classes for non-visual components. This includes classes for threading, semaphores, etc.

PMCLASS.DLL — This library contains all classes associated with the components of an application. Windows, buttons, toolbars, and dialogs are all part of this library.

NETCLASS.DLL — The NETCLASS.DLL implements all network-specific code. This contains a basic network class, as well as more specific classes for communicating using the News, FTP, and Gopher protocols. You will likely want to extend this class library to accommodate new network objects for other protocols you may implement.

These DLLs will be developed in the next part of this book, and will be used by all of the applications that we will create in Part III.

Project Directory Structure

The companion disk uses a particular directory structure to separate and organize the source code. Either use this project structure or develop your own architecture, but do take some appropriate action to keep your documentation and source code in order. Many projects have gone awry due to poor organization of source code and electronic documentation. The following diagram illustrates the directory structure used on the companion disk.

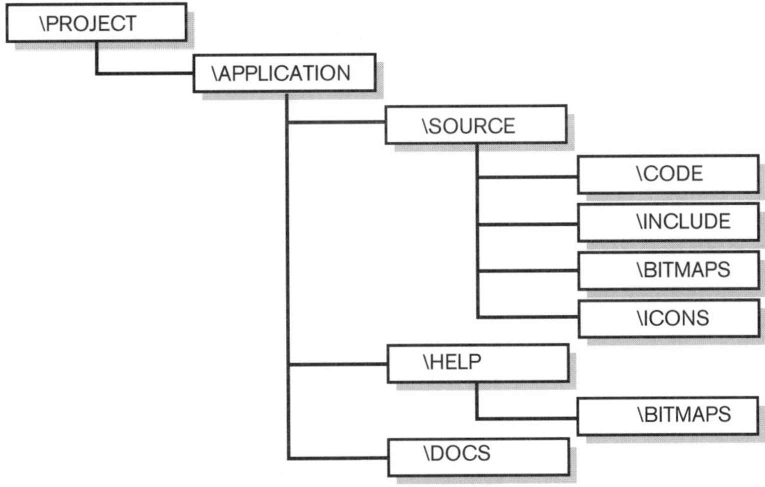

Figure 1-1 Project directory structure

In the structure shown in Figure 1-1 you should rename \APPLICATION to something that is appropriate for your own needs. The \SOURCE directory contains all of the source code related to your application, excluding the source for any help file you may be planning. Depending on the formality required for your project, you may have a number of documents you can store in the \DOCS directory. At the very least you will have some sort of bug list and/or wish list file that you can store in this subdirectory.

Where to Find Additional Tools and Information

There are a number of sites on the Internet where you can locate additional assistance and information. The first place to find an answer to just about any question is the Usenet news service. Newsgroups represent the largest bulletin board on the planet; here you will find several groups and thousands of people waiting to answer your questions (or to have questions answered). I have certainly quizzed many participants in the OS/2 newsgroups to find information for this book, and you would be wise to do the same when you begin writing your own applications. I have summarized some of the Usenet newsgroups catering to OS/2 below, but don't forget that you may also find answers in several of the 13,000 or more common newsgroups—many questions are independent of the operating system, so you may want to ask in groups outside the OS/2 domain.

comp.os.os2.announce	A moderated group covering news of OS/2 events, new books or products, and availability of new OS/2 technical information. A good place to find out about new OS/2 paraphernalia.
comp.os.os2.advocacy	An unmoderated group where you can find out about OS/2's strengths and weaknesses as OS/2 advocates meet advocates of other operating systems head on. This group can be humorous reading at times.
comp.os.os2.apps	If you have questions regarding any current OS/2 applications, this group is usually the place to go.
comp.os.os2.misc	This group deals with miscellaneous OS/2 information.
comp.os.os2.beta	This group contains a discussion of beta releases of OS/2 and other products.
comp.os.os2.bugs	If you find what you think is an OS/2 bug, you can post a request for assistance in this group. Many of OS/2's developers and IBM technical people frequent this group, so it's a good place to get help straight from the source.
comp.os.os2.multimedia	This group discusses the multimedia capabilities of OS/2. This includes setup and use, as well as some programming issues.

comp.os.os2.networking.misc	This group provides information about miscellaneous networking issues, including discussions of LanServer and NetWare, as well as setup for Ethernet cards, etc.
comp.os.os2.networking.mail-news	A relatively recent newsgroup specifically designed to support questions and information related to news and mail programs.
comp.os.os2.networking.tcp-ip	This group focuses on TCP/IP networking; you will want to spend some time here in order to familiarize yourself with the many protocols involved in successful networking. Contributors are generally helpful, and should be able to resolve any problems you may have with TCP/IP services or applications.
comp.os.os2.programmer.misc	This group focuses on miscellaneous programming issues related to OS/2. This is the group where you will ask most of your programming questions.
comp.os.os2.programmer.porting	This groups discusses issues related to porting programs from other platforms into OS/2.
comp.os.os2.programmer.oop	If you are interested in object-oriented programming, then start reading this group. The activity in this group is often minimal, but it does offer a great deal of insight into tools and techniques of OOP as they relate to OS/2.
comp.os.os2.programmer.tools	This group discusses the many OS/2 program development tools available.
comp.os.os2.setup	If you are having any problems related to setting up your OS/2 system, send your questions to this group.
comp.os.os2.games	This is becoming a very popular group as the use of OS/2 for game-playing and game development increases.

There are also a number of useful FTP and Gopher sites available on the Internet. Some sites are dedicated to OS/2, while others are good places to reference TCP/IP-related material. I have summarized a few of them below.

ftp://ftp.cdrom.com/pub/os2	This server is one of two main watering holes for those who thirst for OS/2 software. You will find many megabytes of OS/2 software, ranging from mainstream compilers and applications to obscure graphing applications, etc.
ftp://hobbes.nmsu.edu/pub/os2	This is a mirror of ftp.cdrom.com, useful because the previous site is often quite busy.
ftp://software.watson.ibm.com/pub/os2	This site is IBM's main point for software patches and Employee Written Software. This includes not only OS/2 patches, but also updates for IBM's networking products and software development tools.

ftp://ftp01.ny.us.ibm.net	Another IBM server, dealing specifically with Warp and Internet Access Kit developments and patches. You will also find demos for some of the latest games for OS/2 here.
ftp://ftp.uu.net	This is one of many sites containing copies of the RFCs for TCP/IP. You will also find many other useful programs on this server, but you will have to hunt a bit.
gopher://os2info.gopher.ibm.com	This gopher server contains the entire IBM Employee Written Software library, as well as patches and newsletters for OS/2.
gopher://gopher.micro.umn.edu	The original gopher server at the University of Minnesota, containing a great deal of useful information regarding the Gopher protocol and other data that you may find interesting.

The World Wide Web is exploding into a viable information service and, naturally, there are web pages dedicated to OS/2 as well. You will find dozens of invaluable TCP/IP and Internet related pages out there too. In order to give you a head start on the Web, I have included the following table of relevant home pages.

http://info.cern.ch/	This is the original World Wide Web server. Here you will find a vast array of information regarding WWW and specifications for HTML. If you dig around a bit on this server, you will also find pointers to all of the RFCs for the Internet protocols.
http://webster.ibmlink.ibm.com/	This server is supported by IBM and provides press releases and a list of product specification sheets published by IBM, as well as customer testimonials for these products.
http://www.ibm.net	The main entry point for IBM's OS/2 information services, where you will find a great deal of OS/2 data, including lists of current applications, games, and other programs.
http://www.austin.ibm.com	This page is provided by IBM for OS/2 developers, more specifically for members of the Developer Assistance Program (DAP) or the Software Developer Operations (SDO) program. Here you will find information about special offers, beta programs, and product announcements from IBM.
http://www.teamos2.org	This page has been provided for TeamOS/2 use and offers lots of useful information. It includes a list of recommended shareware applications for OS/2. All program categories are covered, including graphics, communications, networking, etc.
http://www.os2bbs.com	This page is loaded with interesting OS/2 information including David Barnes's page of favorite software.

The information outlined above by no means represents a complete list of on-line sources for TCP/IP or OS/2. In fact, between the time I wrote these words and the time you read them, the number of relevant information sources will likely have doubled or even tripled. If you need some starting points, use a news client to send a query to an appropriate Usenet group.

Chapter Summary

This chapter has discussed necessary preparation for building TCP/IP applications for OS/2. You should now have a better feeling for the compiler and system requirements involved, as well as some background on other debugging and development aids that you may find useful. You should also have a better understanding of where you can find answers to your questions and additional information, using the various Internet sources. Finally, you should now have some appreciation of the methods by which you can organize and manage software projects.

In this chapter

- ✓ OS/2 and PM message queues
- ✓ Minimal C program for Presentation Manager
- ✓ Common User Access specifications

2

OS/2 and Presentation Manager Basics

What is OS/2?

OS/2 was originally developed jointly by IBM and Microsoft at three sites: Microsoft Corp. in Redmond, Washington and IBM at Boca Raton, Florida, and Hursley in the United Kingdom. Version 1.0 arrived in late 1987 and offered users a character-based alternative to DOS. Presentation Manager appeared in 1988 as part of the V1.1 release; it offered a similar look and feel to Microsoft Windows 2.0. In the next two years, OS/2's updates seemed to be mired down, but a Windows 3.0 look was added, as well as more printer drivers and a new print spooler.

It was not until early 1992 that OS/2 finally became viable for many users. By this time, IBM and Microsoft had parted company and IBM was determined to maintain OS/2 by itself. In the absence of Microsoft, IBM enhanced OS/2 with the Workplace Shell, seamless Windows support, and true 32-bit code. What emerged from this work was OS/2 2.0, and the operating system finally started gaining the recognition it deserved. In 1994 IBM further improved this product and released it as OS/2 Warp 3.0. In 1995, IBM released "Warp Connect," an enhanced version of OS/2 which will likely supersede all other versions of OS/2. Connect is definitely the operating system of the 90's since it includes the basic Warp plus requesters for many types of network servers, including our main interest, TCP/IP.

Of course, while IBM was building OS/2, Microsoft too was busy: in 1993 Microsoft introduced Windows NT, partly to address the weaknesses in its own Windows 3.1 product and partly to address the superior platform that OS/2 provided. For the most part, OS/2 compares favorably to NT, with a few notable exceptions that I will go over now before we get into the general features of OS/2.

Even with the release of Warp version 3.0, OS/2 Presentation Manager, like Windows 3.1, still suffers from the restrictions of a single system message queue, which complicates application design somewhat. The issues and problems associated with the single message queue will be discussed in detail in Chapter 4, but this is an excellent time to mention them, since they are part of what makes up OS/2. In the following two diagrams, you may observe the implications of the single message queue versus the multiple asynchronous system message queues supported by Windows NT.

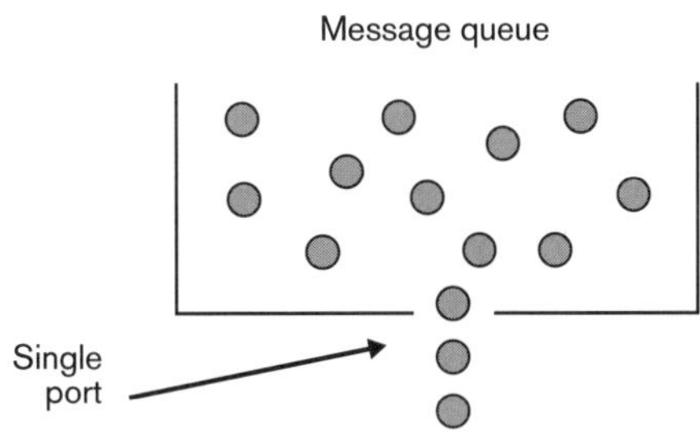

Figure 2-1 OS/2 message model

The OS/2 PM message passing model offers only a single path for messages to fall out of the system queue. No additional messages can be retrieved until the current one is completely processed. The result of this is that processing for the entire PM subsystem can be temporarily halted if the processing for a given message is lengthy and tedious, or worse, involves some form of infinite loop. The immediate solution is, of course, to spin off a new thread to handle processing for the message, but the single message queue is a very serious deficiency in OS/2; it is to be hoped that IBM is seeking a solution. Incidentally, message queues are used only in the PM subsystem, so none of these problems apply to a text mode application running under OS/2.

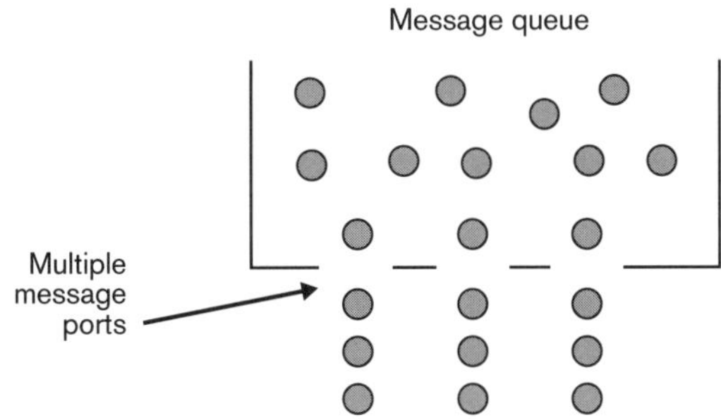

Figure 2-2 Windows NT message model

Contrast the OS/2 model with the Windows NT model in Figure 2-2 and you will quickly note the performance problems associated with the OS/2 queue. NT imposes no limitations on its system message queue. Since messages can be pulled out of the queue asynchronously, no system delays are incurred by lengthy message processing. This does not necessarily equate to faster applications, but can alleviate some of the burden of designing a multithreaded program.

However, enough highlighting of OS/2's problems, since OS/2's strengths far outweigh its weaknesses. The intent of this discussion is to make you aware of one of the key weaknesses of OS/2 PM before we get into the details of how to use the operating system effectively. Since you now know about this queue deficiency, you can more easily work around it. Actually, it is my belief that the single system message queue helps produce better applications. I have seen some really poor code written for NT, primarily because developers no longer need to concern themselves with queue usage. The result can be code that features a flurry of messages clogging operating system queues in a very uncontrolled manner.

Let's move ahead to point out some of OS/2's strengths. The best way to start this journey into OS/2 is by briefly describing the substance of the operating system. Unlike its predecessor, DOS, OS/2 functions as much more than just a simple program loader and interrupt handler. OS/2 was the first viable 32-bit operating system for the 80x86 Intel CPU architecture, offering most of the advantages of operating systems for minicomputers but running completely stand-alone on a desktop system. This isolates the user from the problems and expenses common to larger computers.

One of OS/2's most impressive features is its ability to multitask preemptively (run several programs at once). Each program is protected from the others so that a crash in one application will rarely result in corrupting data from other processes or, worse, hanging the entire system. This is because OS/2 allocates a separate memory region, mouse, keyboard, and display for each application. This contrasts with the operation of Microsoft Windows 3.1, where all applications are designed to share common resources; too often this results in two or more applications colliding, typically forcing the user to reboot the computer.

Multitasking in OS/2 is further extended with *threading,* which is essentially a higher resolution of multitasking. I alluded to threading when comparing OS/2 to Windows NT, both of which support multithreading. UNIX and a number of other operating systems can run more than one application simultaneously, but what sets OS/2 apart is its ability to multitask easily within a program, using threads. UNIX supports "forking" a process, but this is typically a very costly exercise, since, in most implementations of UNIX, it involves loading another copy of the program into memory. Threads, by contrast, are very cheap to produce, and incur relatively little overhead on CPU or system memory.

Why use threads? The answer is simple—to improve user responsiveness. Users like to see things happen immediately, but this is not always possible. In Windows 3.1, the solution is to display an hourglass to indicate that the system is busy. In OS/2 an application can start another thread for a long task and let the user continue working without delay. For example, if you are writing a program that prints a long file to the printer, use a thread. This task typically does not depend on other things a user might choose to do, so give program control back to the user and print the document in the background. In Part III of this book you will find many real-world examples of multithreaded applications.

Deciding where to use threading in an application can be tricky at first, but with a little common sense and experimentation, you will soon develop a threading instinct. Planning for multithreading is the key. You cannot "stick" the threading in an application after it is written, which explains why so many ports of Windows applications are abysmal. Threading must be designed into a program before coding can be started—you cannot effectively plug threads in after an application is written.

Another key feature of OS/2 is its use of the 32-bit flat memory model, also referred to as the "0:32 model." Unlike DOS or DOS/Windows, OS/2 does not use 64K segmented memory, which has long been the bane of many DOS developers. In OS/2 applications each run in their own single 32-bit segment, alleviating the memory-related problems found in DOS. Memory management is further enhanced with virtual memory—you don't have to be concerned with memory constraints as you would in a DOS application when writing OS/2 programs.

Virtual memory, as the name implies, means that your target system can appear to have more application memory than the system physically contains. If your system has 6 Mbytes of memory and you want to write an application that performs data collection of an 8-Mbyte data stream, OS/2 will automatically store the least recently used data from memory to the system swap file and remap the physical memory to new addresses as required. The key word in the last sentence is "automatically"—as a developer, you really do not have to understand how data actually gets swapped in and out of memory. This entire virtual memory operation is transparent to you and your program.

OS/2 adds to its memory capabilities with sparse memory management; if you create a 512-Kbyte buffer and store only a few kilobytes of data, the whole 512K of memory is not allocated. OS/2 allocates memory in 4K blocks, and typically commits memory only when required, but this is user-configurable.

With each new version of OS/2, IBM has improved the system requirements and performance of the operating system; on most hardware its stability now rivals many implementations of UNIX. With the 1994 announcement of OS/2 Warp 3.0, IBM's operating system has finally blossomed into a complete tool, and is attracting Windows users who have been looking for more power and stability. OS/2 users now have almost everything they need to work effectively, including a "works" package with a word processor, database, and spreadsheet, a terminal communications program, and most importantly, integrated one-button access to the Internet. This last feature alone is responsible for introducing many new users to the world of global networking.

How OS/2 is Structured

OS/2 is built using a layered software approach, each layer further isolating the user from the hardware. IBM has taken care to avoid most of the bottlenecks associated with excessive software layering. To improve usability and performance, IBM's operating system developers have taken some shortcuts, so there are circumstances where layers might be skipped. The PM subsystem, for instance, will perform calls directly to the video hardware under certain conditions, eliminating time-consuming interactions with the kernel or video drivers. You need not be concerned with the details of these inner workings of OS/2, which are beyond the scope of this book. It is sufficient to understand the layered approach, as illustrated in the following diagram.

When TCP/IP or any other networking module is added to an OS/2 system, it simply becomes another subsystem in the OS/2 architecture. These subsystems tend to be very specific, and consequently will usually avoid interaction with the kernel or other subsystems. The TCP/IP subsystem interfaces directly with the device driver for the network hardware, and usually has little interaction with the kernel while performing its intended duties.

The following diagram illustrates, in block form, the layers of software in a typical OS/2 system. The arrows indicate communication between the layers. The dash line indicates a possible situation where a layer of software may be skipped to improve efficiency.

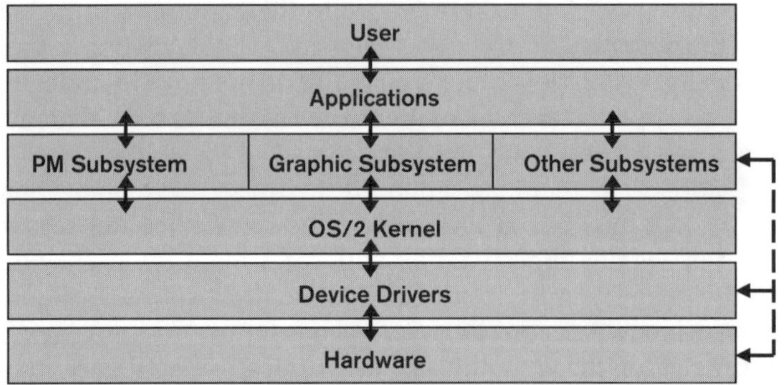

Figure 2-3 OS/2 architecture block diagram

Unlike DOS, OS/2 provides no low-level *INT21* interface to access operating system services. OS/2 does provide something called an IOCTL *Application Program Interface* (API) to perform lower-level operations such as serial communications, but even this interface is at a much higher level than anything provided in DOS. Each OS/2 subsystem provides its own set of API calls, which both enhances and complicates the development of software. OS/2 provides approximately 250

DOS calls, 300 PM calls, and hundreds of other miscellaneous API calls. Fortunately, IBM adopted a consistent and intuitive approach for naming these calls. For example, to create a window you would use the WinCreateWindow() call. It sounds simple, but of course things are not always what they seem to be. Building OS/2 applications can still be a tedious task at times—the real secret is to get a solid design in place before you even start thinking about API interfaces and source code.

A key point to understand is that although OS/2 provides this rich array of subsystems, you do not need to write an application that interfaces to all of them. I discussed message queues in the previous section, and as I noted there, the limitations imposed by the single message queue apply only to PM applications. As shown in Figure 2-3, PM is just one of the many subsystems in OS/2, and it is not necessary to use it at all in an application. As with DOS, you can write text-based applications that do not use a message queue at all. If you are writing a heavy-duty data acquisition program that really has no requirement for a fancy user interface, then you would be better off to avoid PM altogether. This isn't a big problem for the operating system, since it has been designed to let graphical and text-mode applications coexist.

What is Presentation Manager?

Presentation Manager, as the name implies, is a layer of software in OS/2 that manages all aspects of the presentation of any graphical information on the video display and other output devices, such as printers and plotters. PM is not itself a Graphical User Interface (GUI), rather it is an application programming interface providing a set of tools for programmers to use when writing applications for a GUI. The real GUI for OS/2 is the Workplace Shell.

In reality, PM is simply a group of dynamic link libraries (DLLs) containing the hundreds of API calls needed to control and manipulate the graphical display. Its purpose is to isolate you, the programmer, from the low-level parts of the computer system, such as the keyboard, mouse, or screen. Because the PM subsystem is in place on top of the OS/2 kernel, you do not have to provide dozens of drivers for varying display resolutions or potentially hundreds of printer drivers for the myriad of output devices on the market. PM manages all of this for you, permitting you to concentrate solely on designing and building your applications.

All Presentation Manager API calls begin with the letters "Win" to distinguish them from APIs for other subsystems in OS/2, and as mentioned previously, there are about 300 different PM API calls provided by the operating system. You should not be discouraged by this number, however, because the format of these calls is reasonably consistent and, with a little work, you will become familiar with them. The on-line documentation for the PM Toolkit describes each of these 300 calls in great detail, and often includes examples of the use of an API, so answers to your questions are never very far away.

Presentation Manager, like Microsoft Windows, is event driven. This means that program control typically lies within the operating system rather than your application. If you have ever written a DOS program, you know that there is really very little response from the OS unless, of course, your application asks for some information. When you elect to print something, for example, you can simply grab control of the printer to write out your data. In OS/2, however, all interaction with the hardware must be "approved" by the operating system.

The DOS mentality fails in an event-driven system, due in part to the fact that the whole user interface is layered on top of a multitasking operating system. In OS/2 you cannot arbitrarily grab control of anything because some other process may be running concurrently and may be accessing the hardware you are attempting to use. The solution is to drive everything by passing event messages around the system. If your application and OS/2 were people, they would actually be carrying on conversations by passing messages like the following:

OS/2: Hey application, the user told me that you have to print something on the laser printer.

Application: I want to print "Hello World" in 10-point Courier font.

OS/2: OK, it's been printed.

or:

OS/2: The user has done something to cause your window to get messed up, so repaint yourself.

Application: I want to repaint now.

OS/2: OK, here is a paintbrush you can borrow.

Application: I'm done painting, here's your paintbrush back.

OS/2: Thanks.

In both of these conversations it is the operating system that initiates the dialog based on some user interaction. If the user presses a mouse button, the operating system looks to see where the mouse pointer is located, and then informs the correct application that the user did something that requires attention.

This is a pretty simplistic view of what occurs inside the operating system because, while OS/2 is talking to your application, it can also be carrying on other conversations with dozens of other programs, device drivers, and even itself. But the real beauty of OS/2 and PM is that this conversational model is really all you have to understand to write effective applications.

The event-driven world is based primarily on the principle "Don't call us, we'll call you." If you have previously programmed only in DOS, where the reverse is true, this may seem confusing, but by studying some programming examples you should quickly get up to speed. Later in this chapter you will find a few examples of absolute minimums for a PM program; these will be used as the basic framework for all applications presented in this book. As you will see, when we add functionality to the user interface, we need only add a new message handler to support it. It's like playing with building blocks—everything just connects together!

How Does PM Work?

The best way to describe how PM works is to show you a minimal example program for Presentation Manager. This application does nothing but display an empty window, which you can resize, move, or close. But before we do this we need to understand a few of the basic concepts involved with PM programming.

PM programs usually start with the creation of a standard application window much like the one shown in Figure 2-4. This window is really a collection of child windows, typically consisting of a title bar, some system buttons, perhaps a menu, and a sizable border. The central blank area of this window is called the client area and is the location where any child windows will be created. In order for an application to create and display a standard application window, the Presentation Manager API provides a WinCreateStdWindow() API, which must be invoked as part of the program initialization procedure.

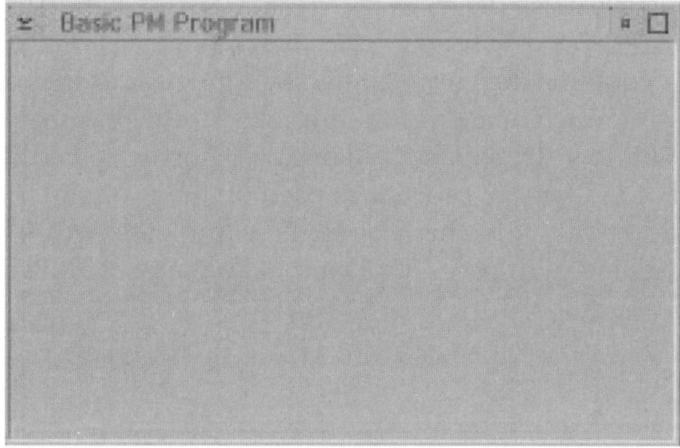

Figure 2-4 Minimal example program output

Child windows are responsible for displaying output or collecting input from the user. These windows, which can take many forms, are said to be owned by the application window. This typically means that they will be enclosed or clipped to the application window, but this is not a hard and fast rule. Dialog boxes are also considered to be child windows, and they can extend beyond the boundaries of the client window. A standard client window is a simple borderless canvas, scaled to the dimensions of the client area, on which any child windows will be displayed. It is a relatively simple process, however, to create child windows that are not bound to the client area.

A final window type you will hear mentioned in OS/2 programming is a control window. Control windows comprise the "gadgets" of the PM interface. Although they include simple buttons, check boxes, etc., more advanced types like notebooks and containers are also considered control windows. PM predefines a Common User Access (CUA) compatible series of child windows that can be added to a client window using the WinCreateWindow() call. A client window may create one or more of these child windows in order to process user input or display output.

Let's look at the minimal PM program code in C. First the header file:

```
//----------------------
// Internal Definitions \
//------------------------------------------------------------------------
#define        D_APPNAME        "Minimal PM App"
#define        D_ID_WINDOW          1

//---------------------
// Function Prototypes \
//------------------------------------------------------------------------
MRESULT EXPENTRY WndProc( HWND, ULONG, MPARAM, MPARAM );
```

Listing 2-1 Minimal C example: H file

Listing 2-1 contains the entire contents of the header file for our minimal C program. There isn't much here—just definitions for the program name, "Minimal PM App" and a window ID, which I will explain shortly. You will also note a function prototype for the window procedure used by the program. For such a simple example we could have avoid the header file completely, but it has been implemented for consistency with other applications in the book. Now let's take a look at the C source.

```
//-------------
// Definitions \
//------------------------------------------------------------------------
#define INCL_WIN

//---------------
// Include Files \
//------------------------------------------------------------------------
#include <os2.h>
#include "hello.h"

//---------
// WndProc \
//------------------------------------------------------------------------
// Window Procedure
// All messages sent to the main window are processed by this function.
```

```
// This function is called by the operating system.
MRESULT EXPENTRY WndProc( HWND hWnd, ULONG msg, MPARAM mp1, MPARAM mp2 )
{
   HPS      hps;
   RECTL    rc;

   switch( msg )
   {
       case WM_PAINT:// Process paint messages

            // Get a handle to our presentation space
            hps = WinBeginPaint( hWnd, 0L, &rc );

            // Fill our client rectangle with some neutral color
            WinFillRect( hps, &rc, SYSCLR_APPWORKSPACE );
            GpiSetColor( hps, CLR_NEUTRAL );

            // Tell PM that we are finished painting
            WinEndPaint( hps );
            break;

       default:         // Let PM process anything that we don't do here
            return WinDefWindowProc( hWnd, msg, mp1, mp2 );
   }

   // Tell PM that we took care of the message we care about
   return (MRESULT)FALSE;
}

int main( void )
{
   HAB      hAB;
   HMQ      hmq;
   HWND     hWnd;
   HWND     hWndFrame;
   QMSG     qmsg;
   ULONG    flCreate;

   // Initialize the PM interface for our application
   hAB = WinInitialize(0);

   // Create a message queue for this app.
   hmq = WinCreateMsgQueue( hAB, 0 );

   // Register our window class with the operating system
   WinRegisterClass( hAB, (PSZ)D_APPNAME, (PFNWP)WndProc, CS_SIZEREDRAW, 0 );

   // Create an instance of our application window on the desktop
```

```
    flCreate = FCF_TITLEBAR | FCF_SYSMENU | FCF_SIZEBORDER | FCF_BORDER
             | FCF_MINBUTTON | FCF_MAXBUTTON | FCF_TASKLIST | FCF_SHELLPOSITION;
    hWndFrame = WinCreateStdWindow( HWND_DESKTOP, WS_VISIBLE, &flCreate,
                    (PSZ)D_APPNAME, (PSZ)"Basic PM Program", 0,
                                        NULLHANDLE, D_ID_WINDOW, &hWnd );

    // Start the message loop to monitor the system queue for any messages
    // That belong to this app.
    while( WinGetMsg( hAB, &qmsg, 0L, 0, 0 ) )
    {
        // Found a message belonging to us, so dispatch it to our window
        // procedure
        WinDispatchMsg( hAB, &qmsg );
    }

    // The user closed our app window, so destroy the window
    WinDestroyWindow( hWndFrame );

    // Disconnect from the system message queue
    WinDestroyMsgQueue( hmq );

    // Deinitialize the PM interface
    WinTerminate( hAB );

    // Return to the operating system
    return 0;
}
```

Listing 2-2 Minimal C example: C file

The C file in Listing 2-2 has a little more code, in fact it seems to have quite a lot of code for a program that does absolutely nothing. I think we had better parse through it to find out why it takes about 40 lines of code to display a simple window on the screen.

Let's start with the first few lines, which are really quite simple. The header file OS2.H is the "include all" header for compiling OS/2 programs and is generally required for every program you will compile for the OS/2 environment. The INCL_WIN definition, placed before the OS2/H include, tells the compiler to build in all of the PM subsystem headers. The header files define other INCL_XXX definitions to reduce the number of items which get included from OS/2 and PM headers, but for the examples in the book I have elected to include everything supplied in the headers for the development toolkit.

Let's now skip to the second function, main(), since that is where the program execution really begins. From your previous C or C++ experience you know that every program needs a main() routine, since this is what the operating system calls when you run a program. A PM application is no different, since it too must have a main(); however, there are a few peculiar things happening in the sample main() that you likely haven't seen if you have never used PM. If you look at the main code, you see first:

```
hAB = WinInitialize(0);
```

The program calls WinInitialize(), which initializes the Presentation Manager engine for the program and returns something called a handle to an anchor block. The first PM call made by any program must be to WinInitialize(), since it sets up the application environment in a particular way that provides access to the graphical interface. The anchor block terminology is derived from IBM's mainframe background, and really is meaningless on an OS/2 platform, so I will leave it at that. Many API calls require the anchor block value to be passed, and although it is not used by the current version of OS/2, you should pass it correctly to ensure upward compatibility with future versions of the operating system.

Near the end of the main() function, you will see a line:

```
WinTerminate( hAB );
```

This is the opposite of WinInitialize(), which frees the anchor block and shuts down the PM graphics engine for the application. You should call this in all PM programs, just before they terminate.

Immediately after the call to WinInitialize(), a call is made to create a message queue:

```
hmq = WinCreateMsgQueue( hAB, 0 );
```

I briefly mentioned message queues in a previous section in this chapter and pointed out that all communication between the operating system and a Presentation Manager program is done by passing event messages. When the operating system has a message in the system queue that it needs to send our application, it needs a place to store it in, a place where our sample application can find it when it needs to process the message—an application message queue. So we need to call WinCreateMsgQueue() to say to PM: "Here's my mail box. If you have something to tell me you can drop it in here."

Now that we have created a queue, our application is ready to start negotiating with OS/2 to create an application window. The first step is to inform OS/2 where the window procedure for our window is located. To do this we need to register our new window class with PM, so we make a call:

```
WinRegisterClass( hAB, (PSZ)D_APPNAME, (PFNWP)WndProc, CS_SIZEREDRAW, 0 );
```

This call tells PM the name of the window class we are registering (D_APPNAME) and the address of the window procedure we have created for this class. All window classes must be registered with the operating system before they can be used by a program. As you will see later, there are a number of predefined window classes already registered with Presentation Manager that we can use. For these classes, PM provides its own window procedure, so there is no need to register new window classes for them.

Now that we have informed PM about our new window class, we can create an instance of it. To do this we write code as follows:

```
flCreate = FCF_TITLEBAR | FCF_SYSMENU | FCF_SIZEBORDER | FCF_BORDER
        | FCF_MINBUTTON | FCF_MAXBUTTON | FCF_TASKLIST | FCF_SHELLPOSITION;
hWndFrame = WinCreateStdWindow( HWND_DESKTOP, WS_VISIBLE, &flCreate,
                        (PSZ)D_APPNAME, (PSZ)"Basic PM Program", 0,
                                NULLHANDLE, D_ID_WINDOW, &hWnd );
```

The first line defines the style of window we want. In this example, we say create a window with a title bar, a system menu, sizable borders, etc. The WinCreateStdWindow() line looks confusing, but is really quite simple. We pass it a handle to the owner window, the desktop in this case, and decide that the new window will initially be visible. Then we pass in the creation flags defined on the previous line. Next we tell PM what class of window this is—note that we use the same name we used for the call to WinRegisterClass. Finally, we pass in an initial window title and an ID (1). Every window requires a unique window ID, which PM uses to deliver control event notifications.

WinCreateWindow() then attempts to create an instance of the new window. If the window creation was successful, PM will insert a message (WM_CREATE) to the message queue to indicate that the window has been created. When we process this message we can perform any start-up initialization required to put our window in the correct state.

The final step in getting our minimal PM application running is to start a message loop, to look in our application message queue, and dispatch any messages found there to the window procedure, WndProc, which was defined by the WinRegisterClass() call.

```
while( WinGetMsg( hAB, &qmsg, OL, 0, 0 ) )
{
    // Found a message belonging to us, so dispatch it to our window
    // procedure
    WinDispatchMsg( hAB, &qmsg );
}
```

Notice that the message loop does not actually call WndProc, rather it calls WinDispatchMsg(). So how does the message get to our WndProc message processor? WinDispatchMsg() looks to see which application queue the message is directed to and sorts out which of its known window classes should get the message. It calls the correct window procedure with the message and any additional information attached to the message.

The next logical piece of this puzzle is the window procedure contained in WndProc() routine.

```
  switch( msg )
  {
      case WM_PAINT:                  // Process paint messages

          // Get a handle to our presentation space
          hps = WinBeginPaint( hWnd, OL, &rc );

          // Fill our client rectangle with some neutral color
          WinFillRect( hps, &rc, SYSCLR_APPWORKSPACE );
          GpiSetColor( hps, CLR_NEUTRAL );

          // Tell PM that we are finished painting
          WinEndPaint( hps );
          break;

      default:          // Let PM process anything that we don't do here
          return WinDefWindowProc( hWnd, msg, mp1, mp2 );
  }

  // Tell PM that we took care of the message we care about
  return (MRESULT)FALSE;
}
```

It looks simple enough—just one big conditional switch statement in which we have coded only a single case, WM_PAINT, and a default case. We know that when an instance of the application window gets created, PM sends a WM_CREATE message to the window procedure, but we have elected to ignore that message, so what happens to it?

WinDefWindowProc() in the default case grabs all messages for which our sample program has no use. This is a handy function provided by Presentation Manager, which takes any message is that not processed by the window procedure and handles it in a default way. We didn't really need to intercept WM_PAINT messages in this minimal example, either, since WinDefWindowProc() can perform default processing on any message. The WM_PAINT message processing is provided only to demonstrate what an actual message processor looks like. Our paint message handler simply paints the client rectangle gray and sets the foreground (text) color to CLR_NEUTRAL, which would turn out to be black if we had displayed some text.

This is all the minimal example in C entails. The full source code for this example is on the companion disk, and you can compile and run it if you wish to play around. However, having described how a C program works, let's forget about it, since, as you will see a little later in this book, we will use a different approach with C++ and avoid a lot of the headaches associated with PM programming, cleaning up the programmer interface at the same time.

In Listing 2-3, you can see what we are heading for as far as ease of design and understanding are concerned. This listing demonstrates the same programming example, using the PMCLASS library that will be developed in the next part of this book.

```
#define    INCL_DOS
#define    INCL_WIN

#include <os2.h>
#include <app.hpp>
#include <window.hpp>
#include <winstd.hpp>

DECLARE_MSG_TABLE( xcMsg )
   DECLARE_MSG( WM_PAINT, C_WINDOW_STD::MsgPaint )
END_MSG_TABLE

void main( void )
{
   C_APPLICATION    xcApp;
   C_WINDOW_STD     xcWindow( xcMsg );

   // Register and create a new program window
   xcWindow.Register( xcApp.AnchorBlock(), "TestClass" );

   // Set the window characteristics
   xcWindow.WCF_SizingBorder();
   xcWindow.WCF_SysMenu();
   xcWindow.WCF_TaskList();
   xcWindow.WCF_ShellPosition();
   xcWindow.WCF_MinButton();
   xcWindow.WCF_MaxButton();
   xcWindow.WCF_TitleBar();

   xcWindow.Create( 1, "Minimal PMCLASS Program" );
   xcWindow.Show();

   // Start the message loop
   xcApp.Run();
}
```

Listing 2-3 Minimal PM example using PMCLASS

I will not describe the example in detail here, since I would be getting too far ahead of myself, but notice that we have reduced the number of lines of code from about 40 down to around 20. Further, the 20 lines we generate are easier to understand (if you know C++). Even knowing nothing about PMCLASS, you should be able to grasp some understanding of the program in Listing 2-3. Notice that there is no message window procedure. This way we can avoid the large and awkward switch() statement found in the previous example. This makes code debugging and maintenance much easier.

Instead of the window procedure, the C++ example uses something called a message table, as shown below:

```
DECLARE_MSG_TABLE( xcMsg )
   DECLARE_MSG( WM_PAINT, C_WINDOW_STD::MsgPaint )
END_MSG_TABLE
```

Message tables are not magical in any way, but they do reduce the complexity of the Presentation Manager code somewhat. The message table from the example has one entry, which states that a WM_PAINT message gets intercepted by a method called MsgPaint() defined in the C_WINDOW_STD class. This method is not coded in any of the sample program source code; rather, it is buried inside the parent object code. This saves us a few lines of code that would otherwise be duplicated in almost every frame window we create.

The message table scheme used in PMCLASS is similar to the technique Borland uses in their Object Windows Library (OWL) class library. Naturally, Borland's library is much more complete than the one presented in this book, but if you are determined, you can make PMCLASS every bit as comprehensive. IBM adopted a similar approach with their competing product ICLUI, but their design is complicated by much multiple inheritance of objects. I have avoided multiple inheritance in the classes developed in this book, since it confounds the code substantially and tends to increase the size of finished applications significantly.

Goals for PM Applications

Before you can really start writing programs, you need to be aware of some of the goals that you should aim for when writing Presentation Manager applications. This is not as obvious as you may think because there is much more involved than simply getting the job done. Indeed, the most important goal is to make it easier for the user to perform his/her job, but this is really a very general statement. How do you accomplish this feat with your software?

If you remember nothing else in this book, remember this: The primary responsibility of any OS/2 application is to provide remarkable response to the end user—not just adequate response, but *remarkable*. If you ever have the opportunity to attend one of David Moskowitz's talks on OS/2 application development, you will quickly realize that he harps on this point endlessly, and rightly so. What this statement means is that when the user presses a key, he expects something to occur and it is your purpose as a developer to ensure that it does. The user will neither expect nor accept unnecessary delays or system stoppages, and building programs that avoid these pitfalls is really not difficult if you correctly apply a few rules to your OS/2 program development.

I hate to point fingers, since my own code is far from perfect, but I once had occasion to use Ami Pro for OS/2, and one startling effect I noticed was that it was slower than the Windows version! I couldn't believe this. The reason, of course, is largely attributable to the fact that Lotus tried to build their OS/2 applications as Windows programs would be built, and of course this doesn't work. In Windows, it is acceptable to chew up lots of CPU cycles to process messages—the system is not a truly multitasking operating system, so the user really cannot do anything else anyway. However, in OS/2, users quickly grow accustomed to performing several tasks simultaneously, so when they find a program that hogs the entire system, they protest (an experience I have had the misfortune to deal with firsthand). In all fairness to Lotus, they have recently updated their OS/2 offering and now promise better performance.

Lotus does not stand alone with this problem, either. Many, if not most, ex-Windows developers also suffer from this. The early versions of my news reader possessed some really ugly characteristics directly attributable to my Windows past. Fortunately, I absorbed the concepts of OS/2 and Presentation Manager so that applications I write now are much better, though I dare not say perfect.

This inability of Windows-driven software companies to write good OS/2 applications also has some devastating effects for the OS/2 platform. Users try a company's OS/2 applications and decide that they are terrible; after finding a few bad applications (and there are many), users begin to doubt the capabilities of OS/2 and the whole promise of 32-bit software. The vicious circle becomes complete, as companies complain that the OS/2 market is nonexistent because no one is buying their products, and in the end everyone sticks with Windows.

This problem is not unique to OS/2, either; Windows NT is also suffering from the same disease. Companies are refusing to write NT applications because, although their current Windows programs run somewhat slower under NT, they do run. The result is that, with the exception of Microsoft, very few companies are willing to risk their bottom lines on NT. It remains to be seen whether software houses will be willing to invest large chucks of development money on Windows'95 for exactly the same reasons.

Your goal for writing OS/2 applications, then, should primarily be to satisfy the end user. The only way to do this is to forget what you know about any other operating system and learn how to write programs specifically for OS/2. Other goals include CUA compliance, program stability, and good old fashioned performance, but all of these really combine to meet the primary goal.

Common User Access

Common User Access, or CUA, is one of four parts of System Application Architecture (SAA), which is a standard developed by IBM and used to implement all of their software. IBM has published this standard and it is freely available for everyone to learn and utilize. The collective goal of SAA is to provide a framework that programmers can use to develop consistent applications for IBM's system platforms, including OS/2 and OS/2 for the Power PC.

The CUA quarter of the SAA standard deals specifically with the user interface portion of an application, and defines the display and operation of all visual controls within a program. The primary goals of Common User Access are:

- Improved consistency and usability within an application.
- Consistency across all applications.
- User- rather than computer-controlled dialog.
- Application-transparent interface (object-oriented desktop).

This really means that all CUA-compliant applications will have the same look and feel so that users can "expect" programs to operate in a certain way.

You should make every attempt to ensure that your own applications are compliant with the CUA standard. If you develop a new program that has a nonstandard feel, users may mistakenly develop the opinion that your program is cumbersome. If you make your living by writing software, a nonstandard interface could hurt your bottom line.

The programs developed in this book are, for the most part, CUA-compliant, though no attempt has been made to ensure this compliance. Much of the CUA standard is unavoidable, since Presentation Manager controls the display of most graphical elements. Controls such as list boxes, containers, and even buttons are all CUA-compliant and unless you subclass them and radically change their presentation, you will have little difficulty producing solid CUA applications.

However, there are occasions when Presentation Manager does provide you with the option of deviating from the CUA standard. Menus are a good example. CUA states that all applications should have a main menu at the top of the main window. (IBM calls these action bars). Though you cannot easily move an action bar, you can elect to disregard the standard and not display one at all. Your users will be completely lost without the action bar, however, so do not do this as a general rule. A typical action bar is shown in Figure 2-5.

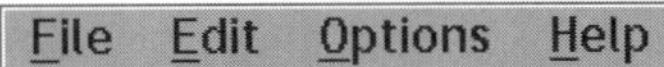

Figure 2-5 Typical action bar

If the application you are writing needs to open, save, or print user files, the CUA standard states that the program should provide a File option as the first available selection on the action bar. CUA further suggests a standard layout for the File submenu, as shown in Figure 2-6.

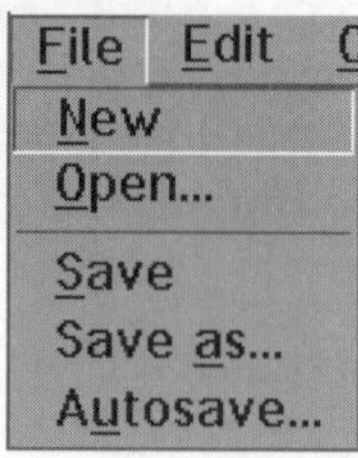

Figure 2-6 Standard File submenu

If the application interacts with the clipboard to copy, cut, or paste data, then an Edit option should follow the File selection on the action bar. Likewise, the Edit submenu has a recommended predefined format, and also makes provision for accelerator keys (key combinations that provide the same functionality as the submenu selection). Figure 2-7 illustrates a typical Edit submenu.

Edit Options Help	
Undo	Alt+Backspace
Cut	Shift+Delete
Copy	Ctrl+Insert
Paste	Shift+Insert
Clear	Delete
Find...	Ctrl+F
Select all	

Figure 2-7 Standard Edit submenu

Finally, all applications should provide some form of on-line help so that your user does not need to keep referencing the printed manual. CUA also defines a standard Help submenu, which should appear as the last option on the action bar. Figure 2-8 shows a sample Help submenu.

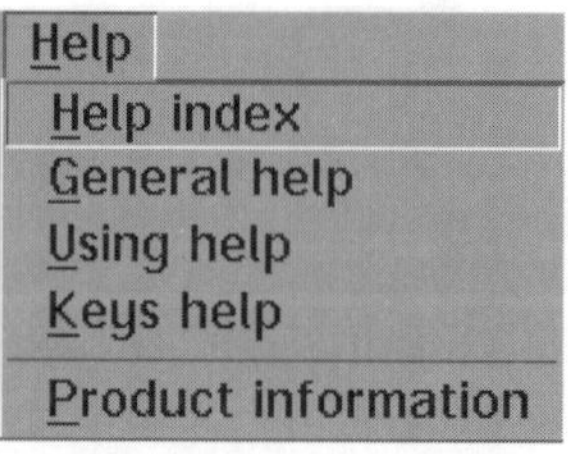

Figure 2-8 Standard Help submenu

The final option on the Help submenu is Product Information. If a user selects this option, your application will display a dialog box containing information about itself (e.g., copyright data, version information, etc.) All PM applications in this book will provide a product information dialog; you can see examples in Part III.

Figure 2-9 shows the product information box used in the NeoLogic News program. This dialog is a good place for you to tell your users who you are, what the program does, the version, etc. Usually the only control you will present to the user is an "OK" button to cancel the dialog and return to the normal program.

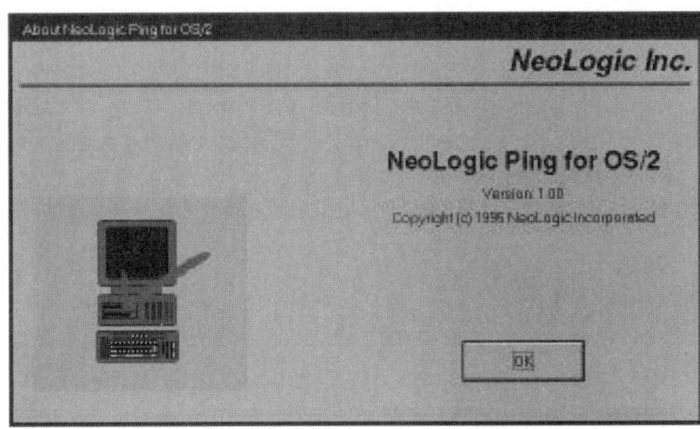

Figure 2-9 Typical product information box

CUA also specifies keyboard accelerators for many operations, as mentioned earlier in this section. Accelerators are the key combinations that a user can select as an alternative to using the mouse to perform menu selections. They are commonly referred to as "shortcut keys." For example, every user knows that pressing the F1 key will invoke help. The following table includes a list of common operations and their equivalent CUA standard accelerator key combinations. This is by no means a complete list of CUA accelerator keys, but does describe the most common operations that you are likely to perform in an application.

Action	Accelerator	Description
Undo	Alt+Backspace	Reverses the user's most recent editing action.
Cut	Shift+Del	Removes the currently selected item or text and copies it to the system clipboard.
Copy	Ctrl+Ins	Duplicates the currently selected item or text on the system clipboard without removing it from its original location.
Paste	Shift+Ins	Copies the contents of the system clipboard into an object at its current insertion point.

Action	Accelerator	Description
Clear	Del	Removes the currently selected item or text from an object.
Help	F1	Displays context-sensitive help for a control for field within an application.
Help for Help	Shift-F10	Describes how to use the help system provided by the operating system.
Extended Help	F2	Optionally provides the user with help by describing the tasks and contents of the application window. Extended help can additionally include operating procedures and processes.
Help Index	F11	Displays an alphabetically sorted index of all help topics for the application.

We need not dwell on Common User Access any further. It is enough for you to know that this standard exists and that it controls virtually every physical aspect of an application. Unless you have a real desire to have your own copy of the CUA standard, the easiest place to find most information about it is by looking at other programs, particularly those from IBM, which are all CUA-compliant.

Other Reference Works

There are many reference materials for OS/2 and TCP/IP. I have listed a few below, but this is just a skeleton for a complete library.

Programming the OS/2 Presentation Manager—Charles Petzold

Petzold is one of the best authors in the industry, and although some of the material in this book is becoming dated, it is still a favorite reference for many OS/2 programmers. If you are just beginning to develop OS/2 applications, this book is a necessity. Petzold assumes you know almost nothing about OS/2 or Presentation Manager and gradually introduces many aspects of the operating system and user interface. ISBN 1-55615-170-5.

Designing OS/2 Applications—David Reich

This book does not contain much example code; however, it is a detailed study of the methodologies one should use for developing OS/2 applications. Before you begin to develop OS/2 applications, you should read and understand this book. ISBN 0-471-58889-X.

Client Server Programming with OS/2—Robert Orfali and Dan Harkey

This book has become the standard by which all other OS/2 programming books are gauged. It is an excellent reference for developing networking applications, and also describes Presentation Manager and Workplace Shell programming in some detail. ISBN 0-442-01219-5.

Internetworking with TCP/IP, Vols. I to III—Douglas Comer and David Stevens

This is good set of books to get you up to speed on the protocols and architecture of TCP/IP and the Internet. ISBN 0-134-7422-2.

TCP/IP Illustrated, Volume I—W. Richard Stevens

This book is another excellent reference, which accurately describes what TCP/IP and the Internet are all about. ISBN 0-201-63354-X.

The Internet Yellow Pages—Harley Hahn and Rick Stout

The Yellow Pages is not a programming book at all, nor is it specific to OS/2. This book is probably the most comprehensive compilation of the resources available on the Internet. It is organized much like the yellow pages of a telephone directory, and includes Internet addresses for almost every subject one could possibly think of. In short, if the information you seek is available on the Internet, then you will likely find a listing for it in this book. ISBN 0-07-882098-7.

Common User Access—Advanced Interface Design Guide—IBM

This specification describes IBM's methodology for Common User Access (CUA). It represents years of study in the science of Human Factors—how people interface with machines. In this guide you will find information concerning almost every aspect of interface development. How should a list box act? What format should a help file have? CUA can answer these questions and many more. IBM Doc # SY0328-300-R00-1089.

On-line Documentation

There is an endless list of on-line documentation for OS/2 and PM programming as well. A few of the more common places to look for answers are shown below. After installing your compiler tools, the PM Toolkit, and the TCP/IP Programmer's Toolkit, you should have most of these.

CSet++ C Library Reference
CSet++ Programming Guide
PM Toolkit Control Program Guide and Reference
PM Toolkit Presentation Manager Reference
TCP/IP Programmer's Reference
IBM OS/2 Redbooks, Volumes 1 though 4

Internet RFCs (Requests for Comment)

The RFCs contain detailed specifications of most network protocols used on the Internet. They also contain a wealth of other information describing the history and development of the network. To read and understand all of the RFCs would be a feat in itself, since there are well over 500 documents, but there are a few you will want to reference. Available via anonymous FTP to ftp.uu.net and many other locations on the Internet.

Chapter Summary

This chapter has covered the basics of OS/2 and Presentation Manager. Since this book is not meant to discuss the inner workings of either OS/2 or PM, an attempt has been made to keep this chapter short and direct. I began with the assumption that you know something about OS/2 and PM, or you have previously worked in Windows, so not much of this chapter should be surprising to you. Nevertheless, I hope that, although you may already be writing OS/2 applications, this chapter has given you insight into concepts that you may not have been familiar with.

In this chapter

- ✓ Basic TCP/IP structure
- ✓ Common TCP/IP protocols
- ✓ Minimal TCP/IP socket application

3

TCP/IP Basics

What is TCP/IP?

Transmission Control Protocol/Internet Protocol is, without question, the single most popular networking protocol in the computer industry. It is supported on virtually every platform from the largest mainframe to the smallest notebook. Recently Personal Digital Assistants (PDAs), such as the Apple Newton, have also gained the capacity to use TCP/IP in a limited form. It is the basic platform on which the entire Internet is based.

Using TCP/IP as a development platform is, of course, your main purpose for reading this book, so it is important to understand the basic background and concepts before you can build an application. The model for TCP/IP is remarkably simple, especially considering the power that it offers computer users.

TCP/IP is the product of evolution rather than revolution. In the late 1960s, the Advanced Research Project Agency began work on a project called ARPANET which was funded by the U.S. government. The goal of ARPANET was to develop a distributed network to permit the U.S. Department of Defense and its contractors to exchange information more rapidly.

In the 1970s, TCP/IP became the standard protocol defined by ARPANET and quickly gained acceptance from most industry researchers. By the mid-1980s, virtually every major research computer site in North America was connected to the Internet via TCP/IP, including defense contractors, government agencies, and most universities. When first recognized as a network in 1983, the Internet had 213 registered hosts; just three years later there were over 2000. Today there are several million hosts connected world wide; considering its current popularity, it is difficult to believe that the Internet did not exist at all less than 15 years ago.

Since its inception, TCP/IP has been expanded to support many network services, such as e-mail, FTP, news, interactive communications—the list is virtually endless. New services are usually specified through the creation of a Request For Comment (RFC), which is a networking protocol specification that can be written and submitted freely by anyone with a need to communicate with others.

How is TCP/IP Structured?

TCP/IP was developed using a standard created by the International Standards Organization known as Open Systems Interconnection or ISO/OSI. This seven-layer architecture has become the basis for virtually all networks, including those based on TCP/IP. The diagram below illustrates the seven-layer OSI model.

For the purposes of this book, it is not imperative that you understand the various middle layers of this model. It is enough that you know that at the lowest level is your network hardware (Ethernet, ISDN, modem, etc.) and that the topmost layer is where your applications are built.

During the course of developing the programs in this book, you will also interface with the Presentation layer; this will be discussed, as required, in later chapters. Your interaction with this layer will be accomplished through the TCP/IP socket *Application Programmer's Interface* (API). Like most APIs, there are dozens of special-purpose calls; however, we will use a very limited set of them. The socket API is relatively standard across most platforms, and you should have little difficulty finding information on API calls not discussed in this book.

7	**Application Layer** Telnet, FTP, Gopher, etc.
6	**Presentation Layer** Application Programming Interface
5	**Session Layer**
4	**Transport Layer** TCP, UDP
3	**Network Layer** IP, ICMP, ARP, RARP
2	**Data Link Layer** Link-level interface, Medium Access Control (MAC) drivers
1	**Physical Layer** Ethernet, Token Ring, FDDI, serial modem

Figure 3-1 ISO/OSI model for TCP/IP

All communications in TCP/IP occur between a client and a server using *datagrams*. Datagrams are the basic unit of information throughout TCP/IP. They consist of one or more data packets that are transferred across the Internet using the code in the TCP/IP Transport Layer. The data packets that make up a datagram can be of virtually any size, and typically include header and trailer data to control delivery and accuracy of the data.

Packets travel between clients and servers using assigned data ports. A port is an end point for communication between applications, which typically refers to a logical connection and typically provides the capability to queue data being transmitted or received. When the port number is combined with an Internet address, the resultant address is referred to as a socket address. Specific port numbers have been reserved for most of the common protocols. News, for instance, uses port 119, but as long as the client and server are using the same port, any one will do.

Socket addresses are another very commonly used terminology in TCP/IP programming. A socket address is simply a unique address created by combining a data port and an Internet address. TCP/IP programs usually communicate at the socket level. Once the network classes are developed in Chapter 6, you will really require little knowledge of ports and sockets, unless you are planning to write a new protocol class; even then the knowledge required will be minimal.

TCP/IP supports two levels of communications—one at a low level called User Datagram Protocol (UDP), and a higher level technique called Transmission Control Protocol (TCP). With UDP packet transmission, packets are sent and received in an unreliable fashion, with only header and data checksums provided, but no retransmission is performed for lost or erroneous data packets. TCP protocols, such as NNTP News or Gopher, operate at a higher level than UDP. These protocols can perform retransmission in the event of packet loss and are generally much more reliable than UDP.

There are number of methods by which a computer can implement TCP/IP at the physical layer. Most schemes typically involve a fast hardware solution, like Ethernet or Token Ring. This usually means that a special hardware board has been inserted into the computer to provide communications at rates of 10 Mbits per second or faster. However, many users of OS/2 Warp have adopted much cheaper but slower implementations of TCP/IP, referred to as Serial Line Internet Protocol (SLIP) or Point-to-Point Protocol (PPP). These implementations typically involve a modem connection via telephone to a local Internet provider. Once a connection is established, the computer is issued either a static IP address or a dynamically defined one (different with each connection). If you want to find more detailed information about SLIP, refer to RFC 1055.

Internet Addressing

All computers on the Internet can be identified by a unique 32-bit address called an Internet Protocol (IP) address, usually specified as 132.223.34.18, for example. However, each computer may also have a domain name specification string as well (e.g., computer.interlink.net). To use the domain name string, you need to have access to a domain name server (or DNS) which converts the string into the appropriate IP. Most Internet service providers provide a name server for their customers, so users generally do not have to surf around the Internet to find one.

A standard Internet address uses a two-part, 32-bit address field consisting of the network address and the local address. Internet addresses can be identified as one of four types, classified as A, B, C or D, depending on the bit allocation. These formats are shown in the following diagrams.

Class A addresses have a 7-bit network number and a 24-bit local address. The highest order bit is set to 0:

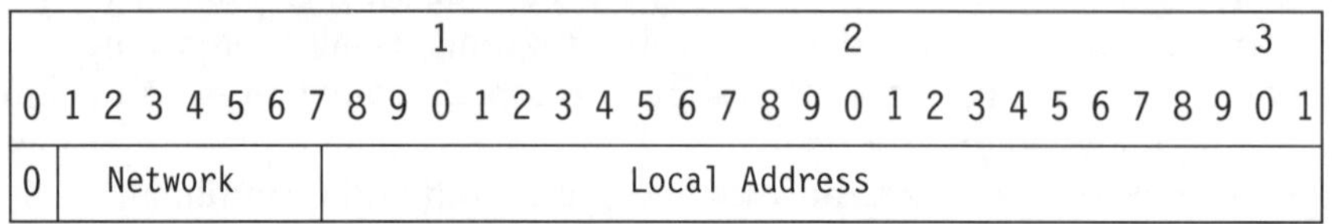

Figure 3-2 Class A Internet addressing

Class B addresses have a 14-bit network number and a 16-bit local address, with the highest order bits set to 01:

```
                     1                   2                   3
 0 1 2 3 4 5 6 7 8 9 0 1 2 3 4 5 6 7 8 9 0 1 2 3 4 5 6 7 8 9 0 1
|1 0|          Network              |        Local Address        |
```

Figure 3-3 Class B Internet addressing

Class C addresses have a 21-bit network number and an 8-bit local address, with the three highest order bits set to 110:

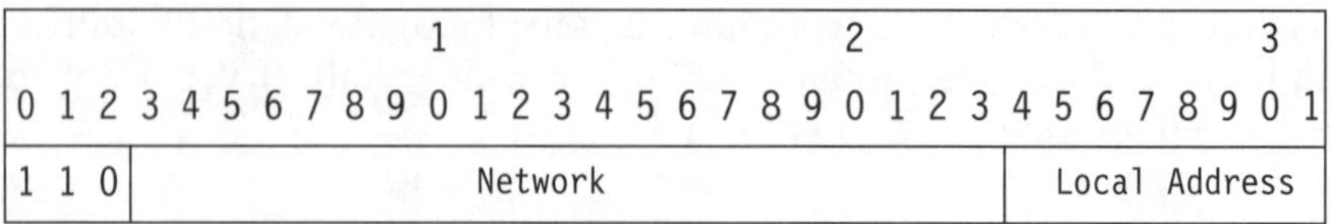

Figure 3-4 Class C Internet addressing

Class D networks are multicast addresses that are sent to selected hosts on the network. The four highest order bits are set to 1110. Note that some implementations of TCP/IP do not support class D network addressing.

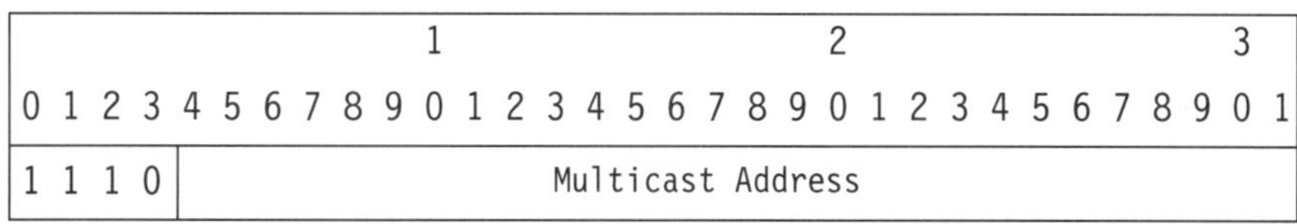

Figure 3-5 Class D Internet addressing

As mentioned previously, a commonly used notation for Internet host addresses is the dotted decimal, which divides the 32-bit address into four 8-bit fields. The value of each field is specified as a decimal number, and the fields are separated by periods to create an address string like 128.234.23.12.

Common Internet Protocols

A number of common protocols are currently used with the Internet and TCP/IP, and we should quickly review the most common of them before we proceed with coding any applications. These protocols range from a very low level, such as IP, to higher level protocols, such as FTP and News.

Internet Protocol (IP)

The Internet Protocol (IP) provides the code to create an interface from the TCP/IP transport layer protocols to the physical-layer protocols. IP is the basic transport mechanism for routing IP packets from one Internet gateway to another. IP provides the capability to transfer data blocks from a source host to a destination host, identified by fixed-length addresses. The IP address header is automatically prefixed to all outgoing data packets and removed from incoming packets.

IP makes no attempt to ensure reliable data transfer between hosts, and does not provide error control for the data within the packets. It does checksum data headers, however. IP does not assume or interpret any relationship between individual packets—each is treated as a separate entity, unrelated to any other packet. Reliability checking is assumed to be performed by higher level protocols using IP for data transfer. For more information about the IP interface, see RFC 79.

Internet Control Message Protocol (ICMP)

Internet Control Message Protocol (ICMP) transfers control messages among hosts, gateways, and routers in the network. ICMP messages can be issued in the following typical situations:

- When a host needs to check to see if another host is available (PING).
- When a host is unable to transmit a packet to its intended destination.
- When a gateway or router can direct a host to send traffic on a shorter route.
- When a host requests a data time stamp.
- When a gateway or router does not have the buffering capacity to forward a packet.

ICMP has the capability to provide dynamic feedback concerning possible problems in the communication environment. The use of ICMP does not in any way guarantee that an IP packet will be delivered reliably or that an ICMP message will be returned to the originating host when an IP packet is not delivered correctly. You can find out more about ICMP by referencing RFC 795.

Address Resolution Protocol (ARP)

Address Resolution Protocol (ARP) is a low-level protocol that maps Internet addresses to network hardware addresses. TCP/IP uses ARP as a means through which collection and distribution of information for mapping tables can be achieved. The ARP protocol is typically unavailable for use by developers or applications, but runs behind the scenes to provide ARP broadcast packets for addresses that do not relate to the mapping table. For a complete description of mapping tables, see *TCP/IP Illustrated*. For more information about the ARP protocol, refer to RFC 826.

Transmission Control Protocol (TCP)

Transmission Control Protocol (TCP) provides a reliable mechanism for transferring packets from one Internet host to another and is by far the preferred method of data transfer. The protocol accepts streams of data that it converts to datagrams and then individually transmits using IP. The destination end of the TCP connection reassembles the datagrams and creates a new data stream. During the transmission and reception, TCP detects corrupted or missing datagrams and requests retransmission as required. For more information about TCP, see RFC 793.

User Datagram Protocol (UDP)

User Datagram Protocol (UDP) provides an unreliable communication mechanism to move data from an Internet source to a desired destination. UDP is a datagram-level protocol lying directly above the IP layer, and is used for application to application data transmission between TCP/IP host programs. UDP is similar to IP, in that it provides no guarantee that a given datagram will be correctly transferred or duplicated. However, it does offer checksums for both the header and data portions of datagrams. Since it offers no delivery protection, the UDP protocol should be avoided in applications requiring even a moderately reliable delivery system. You will find complete details of UDP in RFC 768.

File Transfer Protocol (FTP)

The File Transfer Protocol (FTP) is an application layer protocol providing the capability to transfer data, files, and programs between hosts. Because FTP is built on top of the TCP protocol, it offers reliable transfer.

Later in this book I will develop a simple application implementing the FTP protocol. The application will have the capacity to transfer text or binary files from remote systems onto your local drive. The program will also be able to issue commands to list remote directories, create new directories, and delete old files and directories. RFC 959 details the FTP protocol and its various commands. I will describe this protocol in some detail in Part III of this book.

Network News Transfer Protocol (NNTP)

The Network News Transfer protocol (NNTP) is another application protocol specifically developed for reading Usenet news articles. Like FTP, it supports a number of commands that can be issued to the news server to retrieve newsgroup and article information. NNTP is starting to show its age, however. It offers no mechanism to monitor or abort data transfers, and does not provide support for any form of data compression. News is a very popular protocol that daily moves several hundred megabytes of data across the Internet.

In Part III of this book, I will present a working but limited news application to demonstrate NNTP. The RFC describing NNTP is RFC 977.

Gopher Protocol

The Gopher protocol is also an application protocol that was developed at the University of Minnesota. Gopher is actually the precursor to the World Wide Web, and offers most of the capabilities of WWW without the flashy interface. Though WWW has quickly eaten up much of the Gopher market, many power users still prefer it, since it is incredibly fast by comparison with WWW and simple to use. In the next part of this book, I will also implement a working Gopher client. You can find out more detailed information about the Gopher protocol in RFC 1436.

TCP/IP Sockets

Now that we have briefly discussed TCP/IP sockets, it is a good time to see what a simple C socket program looks like. When we develop the NETCLASS library in Part II of this book, we will be able to simplify this example greatly by eliminating most of the socket code. But the C example is a good stepping stone.

This simple example does not really constitute a complete program by any means, but will serve to make a point. The program creates an FTP connection to ftp.cdrom.com and, once the connection is established, the program sends an FTP "SYST" command. This command causes the server to return a string indicating which type of FTP server it is running. Finally, the program sends an FTP "QUIT" command to end communications with the server. After each of the FTP commands, the program prints the string returned from the server.

```
#define    INCL_DOS

#include <os2.h>
#include <stdio.h>

#include <types.h>
#include <sys\socket.h>
#include <netinet\in.h>
#include <netdb.h>

int main( void )
{
   int      iResult;
   int      iSocket;
   int      iPort = 21;                         // FTP Port
   char     *szServer = "ftp.cdrom.com";        // Example server
   char     szBuffer[512];
   struct   hostent         *pxtHost;
   struct   sockaddr_in     xtSocket;

   // Initialize the socket for communications
   sock_init();
   iSocket = 0;

   // Resolve the host
   xtSocket.sin_addr.s_addr = inet_addr( szServer );
   if( (LONG)xtSocket.sin_addr.s_addr == -1 )
   {
      pxtHost = gethostbyname( szServer );
      if( pxtHost == NULL )
      {
         // Error getting host so terminate
         printf( "Error:Could not get host information\n" );
         return -1;
      }

      bcopy( pxtHost->h_addr, &xtSocket.sin_addr, pxtHost->h_length );
   }

   // Open a socket for this connection
   iSocket = socket( AF_INET, SOCK_STREAM, 0 );
   if( iSocket == -1 )
   {
      // Error getting socket so terminate
      iSocket = 0;
      printf( "Error:Could not create socket\n" );
      return -1;
   }
```

```
    // Connect to the correct port
    xtSocket.sin_family = AF_INET;
    xtSocket.sin_port = htons( iPort );

    if( connect( iSocket, &xtSocket, sizeof( xtSocket ) ) < 0 )
    {
        // Error connecting so terminate
        iSocket = 0;
        printf( "Error:Could not connect\n" );
        return -1;
    }

    //
    // At this point we are connected and ready to go.
    //
    printf( "Connection successful!!\n" );

    // Send a command and get a response
    send( iSocket, "SYST\r\n", (short)6, 0 );
    iResult = recv( iSocket, szBuffer, (short)512, 0 );
    if( iResult > 0 )
    {
        printf( "SYST Response String = %s", szBuffer );
    }

    // See ya!
    send( iSocket, "QUIT\r\n", (short)6, 0 );
    iResult = recv( iSocket, szBuffer, (short)512, 0 );
    if( iResult > 0 )
    {
        printf( "QUIT Response String = %s", szBuffer );
    }

    // Close the connection
    shutdown( iSocket, 2 );
    soclose( iSocket );

    return 0;
}
```

Listing 3-1 Minimal socket example

Let's analyze this simple network program. The first task performed is to include the various required header definition files as such:

```
#define    INCL_DOS

#include <os2.h>
```

```
#include <stdio.h>

#include <types.h>
#include <sys\socket.h>
#include <netinet\in.h>
#include <netdb.h>
```

This includes OS2.H, as in previous examples, but it also includes some of the TCP/IP headers you can find in the \INCLUDE directory of your TCP/IP Programmer's Toolkit installation.

Among the variable definitions you find:

```
int     iPort = 21;                       // FTP Port
char    *szServer = "ftp.cdrom.com";      // Example server
```

This configures the test program to connect to FTP.CDROM.COM, an FTP server, using the FTP port, which is universally defined as port 21.

Then the TCP/IP environment is initialized for the program using:

```
// Initialize the socket for communications
sock_init();
```

This API must be called before any other TCP/IP call, and is usually located near the beginning of a program.

After the socket interface is initialized, the program needs to determine where it is connecting:

```
// Resolve the host
xtSocket.sin_addr.s_addr = inet_addr( szServer );
if( (LONG)xtSocket.sin_addr.s_addr == -1 )
{
    pxtHost = gethostbyname( szServer );
    if( pxtHost == NULL )
    {
        // Error getting host so terminate
        printf( "Error:Could not get host information\n" );
        return -1;
    }

    bcopy( pxtHost->h_addr, &xtSocket.sin_addr, pxtHost->h_length );
}
```

First it attempts to use the contents of szServer as an IP address. This fails, of course, because we have provided a domain string instead. The program then tries to determine the destination by calling gethostbyname(), which should work correctly if you are currently connected to the Internet.

Next, the program needs to open a socket to establish communications between the client and the selected host:

```
// Open a socket for this connection
iSocket = socket( AF_INET, SOCK_STREAM, 0 );
if( iSocket == -1 )
{
    // Error getting socket so terminate
    iSocket = 0;
    printf( "Error:Could not create socket\n" );
    return -1;
}
```

Finally, the program connects to the socket to establish the communications link.

```
// Connect to the correct port
xtSocket.sin_family = AF_INET;
xtSocket.sin_port = htons( iPort );

if( connect( iSocket, &xtSocket, sizeof( xtSocket ) ) < 0 )
{
    // Error connecting so terminate
    iSocket = 0;
    printf( "Error:Could not connect\n" );
    return -1;
}
```

At this point the program can begin sending commands and receiving responses. The TCP/IP API offers several calls to perform these tasks; I have selected the more common send() and recv() functions. Note that each time a command is issued (e.g., SYST), a response string is collected. Almost every Internet protocol works this way, but if you neglect to retrieve the return string, the input buffers will eventually fill up, which will definitely not produce correct results. Synchronization of command transmission and return results is crucial. The example prints the result strings returned from the server so you can see live examples of typical resultant messages.

Once the program has completed its "chat" with the server, it needs to close and destroy the socket. This is accomplished with the API calls:

```
// Close the connection
shutdown( iSocket, 2 );
soclose( iSocket );
```

You can use the NETSTAT program provided in the TCP/IP base package to examine network port activity while this program is operating. Simply open a second OS/2 command window on your desktop and run "NETSTAT -s" concurrently with your network program.

When we discussed the C language Presentation Manager example in the previous chapter, I suggested that a C++ class library would simplify the use of PM. Similarly C++ can ease TCP/IP programming just as well. The following example duplicates the functionality of the C example in Listing 3-2.

```
#define    INCL_DOS
#define    INCL_PM

#include <os2.h>
#include <stdio.h>

//-----------------
// PMCLASS Headers \
//----------------------------------------------------------------------------
#include <app.hpp>
#include <window.hpp>
#include <winstd.hpp>
#include <winchild.hpp>
#include <dialog.hpp>
#include <edit.hpp>
#include <pushbtn.hpp>
#include <menu.hpp>
#include <status.hpp>
#include <button.hpp>
#include <tbar.hpp>
#include <mle.hpp>
#include <contain.hpp>
#include <log.hpp>

#include <net.hpp>
#include <netftp.hpp>

int main( void )
{
   int      iPort = 21;                        // FTP Port
   int      iResult;
   char     *szServer = "ftp.cdrom.com";       // Example server

   // Create an FTP network object
   C_CONNECT_FTP        xcFTPClass( "ftp.cdrom.com", iPort, NULL );

   // Open a connection to the FTP server
   if( xcFTPClass.Open() )
   {
       //
       // At this point we are connected and ready to go.
```

```
      printf( "Connection successful!!\n" );

      iResult = xcFTPClass.SYST();
      printf( "SYST Response = %d", iResult );

      iResult = xcFTPClass.QUIT();
      printf( "Quit Response = %d", iResult );

      // Close the connection
      xcFTPClass.Close();
   }

   return 0;
}
```

Listing 3-2 Minimal socket example using a network class

You will find out more about the FTP class later, but for now notice that the example is far less complicated than the C example. What you do not see, of course, is the underlying code buried in the NETCLASS library, but that is really the way you would like to develop an FTP program. Notice in the C++ example that all mention of sockets has been eliminated—once you have created a base network class, and perhaps an application protocol class, you can isolate your program completely from the TCP/IP API.

The C++ example is very straightforward. The program creates an instance of an FTP connection class, opens it, issues the SYST and QUIT commands, and finally closes the connection. Even if you know nothing about FTP or TCP/IP, you should at least be able to read this code and acquire some appreciation for what it does. The same cannot be said of the C example shown previously.

Chapter Summary

In this chapter, we have examined some of the basic principles that make TCP/IP work, including the typical topology of the Internet and, more importantly, how the Internet arrives at your desktop. There is a lot of work going on behind the scenes in TCP/IP, much of which is beyond the scope of this book; if you want to delve deeper I encourage you to consult other, more detailed, resources.

I have also demonstrated a typical TCP/IP program written in C and a much higher level program that uses the NETCLASS C++ class library, which will be developed later in this book. As you will find out later, the goal of NETCLASS is to hide as much of TCP/IP from you as possible so you can do what interests you most—writing network applications.

In this chapter

- ✓ Understanding the 1/10 second rule
- ✓ Multithread programming in OS/2
- ✓ Object windows in multithreaded programs

4

Considerations for System Performance

The 1/10 Second Rule

In Chapter 1, we discussed OS/2's inability to process more than one message from the system queue at any given time. This has the obvious effect of degrading overall system performance if one message processor grabs the CPU's attention for an extended period of time.

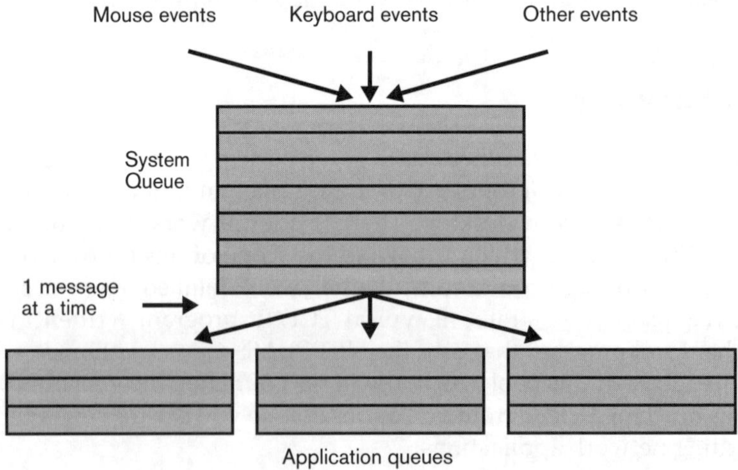

Figure 4-1 Presentation Manager queue flow

Since only one message can be pulled out of the system queue at a time, all of PM waits until that message is completely processed before PM retrieves the next one. The designers of Presentation Manager have decided, with thorough testing, that in order to maintain satisfactory system flow, the processing for any individual message should not use more than 0.1 seconds. This rule of thumb is known as the 1⁄10 second rule.

Note that the 1⁄10 second rule is a general guideline; there are times when you may need to break this rule, but at all times you should be aware of the implications and try to avoid doing this. So how do you know when the rule gets broken? I will show you later, when we develop a class to perform some debugging for us. Briefly, you can print a time stamp at the beginning of a message processor and again at the end and compare them. With the debugging class I will present later, you will not get a totally accurate measurement because the debug code also requires some CPU time; however, you will get a clear indication of how much CPU time you are expending to handle a given message.

There are a number of methods to avoid bogging the CPU down during message processing. The obvious solution is to use additional threads, since threads do not rely on the application's message queue. The message processor need only spin off a new thread with the appropriate data and terminate, resulting in almost no CPU usage for the message. Avoid going over-board on thread use, however, since too many threads can be almost as bad as too few.

A second method to prevent breaking of the 1⁄10 second rule is to create an *object window,* which is a window that has no visual existence. I will talk about object windows shortly; for the present, let's conduct a more detailed investigation of threading.

Multithreading

OS/2 was one the first microcomputer operating systems to provide multiple threads of execution. Multithreading offers a solution for improving the usage of the CPU resources of a system. If you realize that most of the time your CPU is sitting idle while other hardware items in your computer try to catch up (disk drives are particularly slow), you will have better appreciation for what threads do.

What is a thread? IBM defines a thread as the dispatchable unit of OS/2—a rather vague definition. Every program has at least one thread of execution, which starts at main() (in C or C++) and lives until the program is terminated. OS/2, however, can manage many threads per application.

For instance, if you were writing a word processor which provided a spelling checker, you could have two threads of execution—the main word processor thread and a second spell-checker thread. This would permit the user to start checking spelling while continuing to edit the document text. The spell-checker thread could continue in the background until the check was complete, without requiring further user intervention unless a spelling error was detected.

A more practical example, as you will see later, is a thread in your program to perform a time-intensive task like loading a list of news articles into a container control. Containers are notoriously lazy, and if you need to load more than 20 or more items into one, you will definitely need a separate thread. Similarly, you will want to use a thread to read the data from the container and save it to a disk file in order to preserve any changes to the data.

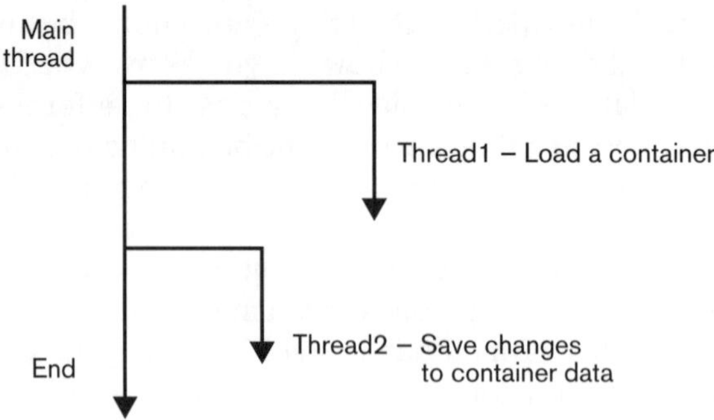

Figure 4-2 Multiple thread flow in an application

Let's look at a simple multithreaded program (see Listing 4-1). This program does not do very much, but it does demonstrate the power of multithreading. The main() routine of the program first creates two threads and waits for them to complete. If you've never seen a multithreaded program before, this could look a little strange.

```
#define INCL_DOS

#include <os2.h>
#include <stdio.h>
#include <process.h>

void _Optlink Thread1( void *pvData )
{
   int     iCtr;

   // Loop 5 times printing the count
   for( iCtr = 0; iCtr < 10; iCtr++)
   {
      printf( "Thread1:%d\n", iCtr );

      // Sleep for 10 msec
      DosSleep( 10 );
   }
}
```

```
void _Optlink Thread2( void *pvData )
{
   int      iCtr;

   // Loop 5 times printing the count
   for( iCtr = 0; iCtr < 10; iCtr++)
   {
      printf( "Thread2:%d\n", iCtr );

      // Sleep for 5 msec
      DosSleep( 5 );
   }
}

void main( void )
{
   PID      Thread1Pid;
   PID      Thread2Pid;

   printf( "Thread demo started\n" );

   // Start a couple of threads
#ifdef __BORLANDC__
   Thread1Pid = _beginthread( Thread1, 10000, 0 );
   Thread2Pid = _beginthread( Thread2, 10000, 0 );
#else
   Thread1Pid = _beginthread( Thread1, 0, 10000, 0 );
   Thread2Pid = _beginthread( Thread2, 0, 10000, 0 );
#endif

   // Don't exit until the threads have completed
   printf( "Waiting for threads to complete\n" );
   DosWaitThread( &Thread1Pid, DCWW_WAIT );
   DosWaitThread( &Thread2Pid, DCWW_WAIT );

   // See ya!
   printf( "Thread demo completed\n" );
}
```

Listing 4-1 Simple multithreading example

The main() function calls _beginthread() twice, specifying a different thread function in each case. The thread functions (Thread1 and Thread2) are essentially separate programs buried within the same EXE, and run completely independently of each other.

Once the main routine starts these threads, it calls the DosWaitThread() API which says, "Wait until the specified thread is done before continuing." What this

```
//--------------
// Include Files \
//-----------------------------------------------------------------------
#include <os2.h>

#include <stdio.h>
#include <stdlib.h>
#include <process.h>

#include "objwin.h"

void _Optlink ThreadObject( void *pvData )
{
   HAB          hABThread;
   HMQ          hMQThread;
   QMSG         qmsg;
   T_SHARE      *pxtWnd;

   // Create a PM process for this thread
   hABThread = WinInitialize( 0 );
   hMQThread = WinCreateMsgQueue( hABThread, 0 );

   pxtWnd = (T_SHARE *)pvData;

   // Register our object window class with the operating system
   WinRegisterClass( hABThread, "TestObjWindow", (PFNWP)ObjWndProc,
                                              0, sizeof( T_SHARE *) );

   // Create an instance of the object window
   pxtWnd->hWndObj = WinCreateWindow( HWND_OBJECT, "TestObjWindow", "",
       0, 0, 0, 0, 0, HWND_OBJECT, HWND_BOTTOM, 0, pxtWnd, NULL );

   // Start the message loop to monitor the system queue for any messages
   // that belong to this app.
   while( WinGetMsg( hABThread, &qmsg, 0L, 0, 0 ) )
   {
       // Found a message belonging to us, so dispatch it to our window
       // procedure
       WinDispatchMsg( hABThread, &qmsg );
   }

   // Tell the client window to quit
   WinPostMsg( pxtWnd->hWnd, WM_QUIT, 0, 0 );

   WinDestroyWindow( pxtWnd->hWndObj );

   WinDestroyMsgQueue( hMQThread );
}
```

```
MRESULT EXPENTRY ObjWndProc( HWND hWnd, ULONG msg, MPARAM mp1, MPARAM mp2 )
{
   HPS         hps;
   RECTL       rc;
   T_SHARE     *pxtWnd;

   switch( msg )
   {
      case WM_CREATE:
         // Save a point to the global data in the object window data
         // area
         WinSetWindowULong( hWnd, QWL_USER, (ULONG)mp1 );
         break;

      case WM_SLEEP:
         DosSleep( 1000 );
         DosBeep( 100, 100 );
         DosSleep( 1000 );
         DosBeep( 300, 100 );
         DosBeep( 50, 100 );
         break;

      case WM_CLOSE:
         WinPostMsg( hWnd, WM_QUIT, 0, 0 );
         break;

      default:
         return WinDefWindowProc( hWnd, msg, mp1, mp2 );
   }
   return (MRESULT)FALSE;
}

//---------
// WndProc \
//-----------------------------------------------------------------------
MRESULT EXPENTRY WndProc( HWND hWnd, ULONG msg, MPARAM mp1, MPARAM mp2 )
{
   HPS         hps;
   RECTL       rc;
   T_SHARE     *pxtWnd;

   switch( msg )
   {
      case WM_CREATE:
         pxtWnd = (T_SHARE *)malloc( sizeof( T_SHARE ) );
         WinSetWindowULong( hWnd, QWL_USER, (ULONG)pxtWnd );
         pxtWnd->hWndFrame = WinQueryWindow( QW_PARENT, hWnd );
         pxtWnd->hWnd = hWnd;
```

```
            pxtWnd->hWndObj = NULLHANDLE;

#ifdef __BORLANDC__
            _beginthread( ThreadObject, 40000, pxtWnd );
#else
            _beginthread( ThreadObject, 0, 40000, pxtWnd );
#endif
            break;

        case WM_COMMAND:
            pxtWnd = (T_SHARE *)WinQueryWindowULong( hWnd, QWL_USER );
            switch( COMMANDMSG( &msg )->cmd )
            {
                case DM_DO_SLEEP:
                    WinPostMsg( pxtWnd->hWndObj, WM_SLEEP, 0, 0 );
                    break;
            }
            break;

        case WM_PAINT:// Process paint messages
            // Get a handle to our presentation space
            hps = WinBeginPaint( hWnd, 0L, &rc );

            // Fill our client rectangle with some neutral color
            WinFillRect( hps, &rc, SYSCLR_APPWORKSPACE );
            GpiSetColor( hps, CLR_NEUTRAL );

            // Tell PM that we are finished painting
            WinEndPaint( hps );
            break;

        default:        // Let PM process anything that we don't do here
            return WinDefWindowProc( hWnd, msg, mp1, mp2 );
    }

    // Tell PM that we took care of the message we care about
    return (MRESULT)FALSE;
}

int main( void )
{
    HAB     hAB;
    HMQ     hmq;
    HWND    hWnd;
    HWND    hWndFrame;
    QMSG    qmsg;
    ULONG   flCreate;

    // Initialize the PM interface for our application
```

```
    hAB = WinInitialize(0);

    // Create a message queue for this app.
    hmq = WinCreateMsgQueue( hAB, 0 );

    // Register our window class with the operating system
    WinRegisterClass( hAB, (PSZ)D_APPNAME, (PFNWP)WndProc,
                                CS_SIZEREDRAW, sizeof( T_SHARE * ) );

    // Create an instance of our application window on the desktop
    flCreate = FCF_STANDARD;
    hWndFrame = WinCreateStdWindow( HWND_DESKTOP, WS_VISIBLE,
            &flCreate, (PSZ)D_APPNAME, (PSZ)"ObjectWindow PM Program",
                                0, NULLHANDLE, D_ID_WINDOW, &hWnd );

    // Start the message loop to monitor the system queue for any messages
    // that belong to this app.
    while( WinGetMsg( hAB, &qmsg, 0L, 0, 0 ) )
    {
        // Found a message belonging to us, so dispatch it to our window
        // procedure
        WinDispatchMsg( hAB, &qmsg );
    }

    // The user closed our app window, so destroy the window
    WinDestroyWindow( hWndFrame );

    // Disconnect from the system message queue
    WinDestroyMsgQueue( hmq );

    // Deinitialize the PM interface
    WinTerminate( hAB );

    // Return to the operating system
    return 0;
}
```

Listing 4-2 PM example using object windows

The main() procedure is almost identical to the minimal PM application presented earlier. It registers a window class and creates an instance of the new window. The application window procedure WndProc() is a little different.

```
        case WM_CREATE:
            pxtWnd = (T_SHARE *)malloc( sizeof( T_SHARE ) );
            WinSetWindowULong( hWnd, QWL_USER, (ULONG)pxtWnd );
            pxtWnd->hWndFrame = WinQueryWindow( QW_PARENT, hWnd );
            pxtWnd->hWnd = hWnd;
```

```
            pxtWnd->hWndObj = NULLHANDLE;

#ifdef __BORLANDC__
            _beginthread( ThreadObject, 40000, pxtWnd );
#else
            _beginthread( ThreadObject, 0, 40000, pxtWnd );
#endif
            break;
```

This code allocates some global memory space for the data to be shared between the application window and the object window. Then it starts a second thread to create and control the object window.

The ThreadObject() code appears similar to the main() routine. It initializes the required parts of PM, creates an object window, then starts a message loop.

```
// Register our object window class with the operating system
WinRegisterClass( hABThread, "TestObjWindow", (PFNWP)ObjWndProc,
                                          0, sizeof( T_SHARE *) );

// Create an instance of the object window
pxtWnd->hWndObj = WinCreateWindow( HWND_OBJECT, "TestObjWindow", "",
    0, 0, 0, 0, 0, HWND_OBJECT, HWND_BOTTOM, 0, pxtWnd, NULL );
```

The creation of the object window differs only slightly from a normal display window. Instead of telling PM that the window belongs to the desktop (HWND_DESKTOP), we create it as a child of HWD_OBJECT. This informs PM that the new window gets managed as an object window.

That is the only difference between an object window and a visible application window. Both types have a window procedure, and because the program allocates some shared memory and stores the handles to each window, the two window types can communicate with each other by sending messages.

In the situation in the example, where the user invokes the SLEEP menu option, the main window procedure sends a message to the object window telling it do its processing for the WM_SLEEP message.

```
        case DM_DO_SLEEP:
            WinPostMsg( pxtWnd->hWndObj, WM_SLEEP, 0, 0 );
            break;
```

In the object window code WM_SLEEP does the following:

```
case WM_SLEEP:
    DosSleep( 1000 );
    DosBeep( 100, 100 );
    DosSleep( 1000 );
    DosBeep( 300, 100 );
    DosBeep( 50, 100 );
    break;
```

The process sleeps for one second, beeps, then sleeps for another second and beeps again. If you were to implement this same message in your application window (try it), you would see that it ties up the whole PM interface for every running process, including the desktop. However, because the long delay is implemented in an object window where the 1⁄10 second rule does not apply, no system degradation occurs.

This is a pretty simple example. In a real application, the main window would possibly be performing other processing while the long process is running. Once complete, the long process would typically send a message back to the application window to notify it, at which point some additional processing might be triggered.

Chapter Summary

In this chapter we have discussed the features and pitfalls of working in a multithreaded operating system like OS/2. Though I did not mention all the problems that multithreading can cause, you did see some restrictions imposed by the 1⁄10 second rule. We looked at two different methods by which you can write multithreaded PM applications. These were a simple thread creation and the powerful object window support in PM. We will make use of multithreading in the applications we will build in Part III of this book in order to improve the performance of our applications.

This concludes Part I of the book. By now you should have a better understanding of TCP/IP, OS/2, and Presentation Manager. We will start applying this knowledge in the next part as we begin to create the user interface and networking class libraries that will be used as a foundation for the applications later in the book.

In this chapter

- ✓ Using classes to build better applications
- ✓ Importance of code portability
- ✓ Non-visual programming in PM

5

Developing a Class Library for Nonvisual Objects

Why Build a Class Library?

If you have not had much experience in C++ or other object-oriented programming language, the first question you are probably asking yourself is, "What is a class library?" A class library is a group of classes that have a hierarchical dependency on one another. For instance, in C++, you could define a "window" class as a general object type. You might then determine that there are several types of window objects (e.g., application windows, child windows, dialog boxes, and even buttons). If you were to build these classes with C code, you would likely recode large portions of the basic window functionality for each type of window. Developing a C++ class library offers the following advantages.

Code Reuse

Code reuse is one of the key advantages of C++ over non object-oriented languages like C. In our object-oriented user interface class library, we will code as much of the common window characteristics in the "window" class as we possibly can. We can then inherit these attributes and methods in all of the derived classes of this parent. Since an application window will be derived from the basic window class, it will already know how to act like a window because it will reuse all the intelligence previously coded in the parent. All that remains is to recreate some additional code to distinguish an application window from any other type. This extra code will include functionality like how to attach a menu or a title bar.

Ease of Use

I alluded to this in the previous point, but as a side effect of code reuse you will also realize a significant increase in productivity. Because each newly derived class adds an increasing amount of knowledge, coding with higher-level objects actually increases the number of lines of code you can write. We have all heard about the proverbial three lines-per-day programming metric—well, this applies whether you are writing three lines of assembly language or three lines of code using some very high-level language. Ease of use will also become apparent as you begin to debug the programs you write. If, for instance, you find a bug in the Window base class, you can fix the error and, almost magically, every class derived from this base class will be corrected as well.

Portability

I have been skirting the whole issue of portability, only briefly mentioning it in a previous chapter, but portability is becoming increasingly important to developers who want to offer their wares on several platforms. Properly designed C++ classes can render a porting exercise trivial, and the class libraries in this book have been designed with portability in mind. I have devoted the next section in this chapter to this concept of writing portable code, since it has become such a hot topic in recent years.

The Question of Portability

The most obvious reason for making programs portable is to permit creation of similar applications on more than one platform with a minimum of effort. However, there are a few more subtle but equally important reasons to write portable code.

The first benefit you will realize is saved time—not because you have no need to recode, but rather because you can eliminate the often significant learning curve associated with a new API and operating system. If you create a standard portable class library and learn it well, you have already cleared the largest hurdle in your porting exercise.

The second advantage portability offers is simplified configuration management. This means that you need to manage only a single set of documents and source code. If you change the code for one platform, a quick recompile adds the change to any other platform to which your code is portable.

With Windows, OS/2, and UNIX X proliferating in the marketplace, it makes economic sense to invest a little extra time to build solid, portable class libraries. This is not as big a challenge as you might first think.

How is portable code created? The simplest method is to use an object-oriented programming language like C++ and create a set of class libraries. If you are successful at creating a complete set of classes and use these classes throughout your code, the application itself will be portable. The class libraries, which would typically represent a smaller portion of your application code, would need to be rewritten, however, once this coding is complete; any applications you develop can be transferred to the new platform simply by recompiling. All it takes is a little common sense when building your classes.

Although porting classes is beyond the scope of this book, I have gone to great lengths to ensure that the classes should be easily transferable to the Window 95 or NT platform. My efforts disintegrate somewhat in the CUA 91 controls, such as containers, because there is no direct mapping to any window classes on the Windows platform. Windows provides a child window class called a *view*—actually, Microsoft created several different types of view windows that are similar to the views of a PM container control. With a little additional persistence, you can create a suitable class on the Windows platform to mimic the PMCLASS C_CONTAINER object that will be defined in the next chapter.

All of the programs in Part III of this book are written using the class libraries developed in the next few chapters. You will discover that there is little, if any, specific code for OS/2 or PM. Although I will not be creating a Windows version of the class libraries, you are welcome to, and you can rest assured that the applications should recompile under Windows with minimal effort on your part.

One final point to note about portability: Do not make objects so tight that you prevent the use of native API calls. There are times when portability takes a back seat to getting the job done, so you want to avoid locking yourself out of the native operating system. Occasionally, a few lines of native API calls can save hours of work attempting to create portable classes to perform similar tasks. This points out a definite problem with many commercial class libraries. If you have ever written a program with Borland's Object Windows Library (OWL) or IBM's ICLUI class library, then you already know that embedding native API calls can be tedious or impossible. Regardless of how portable you want to make your classes, do not fall into this trap or you will discover that your library is not very functional on any platform.

The NVCLASS Class Library

The NVCLASS library is a collection of classes required for some nonvisual operations. These classes do not display output in windows or text screens; rather, they act as the essential glue to assist in connecting the DOS-level API into your programs in a portable way.

The classes are, for the most part, wrappers around existing nonportable operating system functionality for which OS/2 currently provides a non-object-oriented interface. In order to make these non-visual portions of the operating system mesh with the visual classes we will build in the next chapter, I have created a class library for them.

The following diagram illustrates the object hierarchy for the NVCLASS class library:

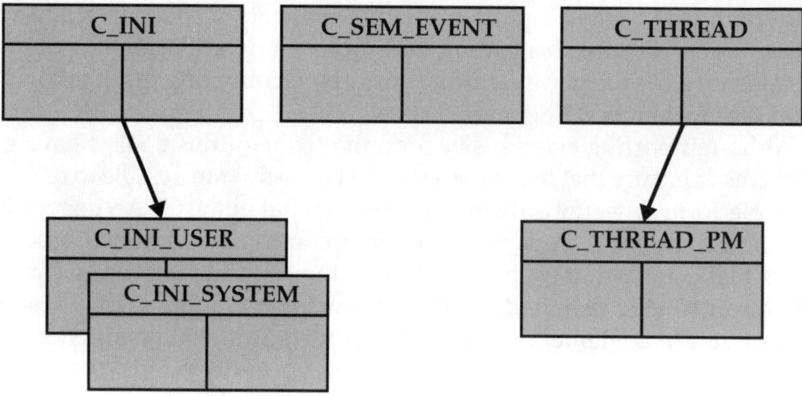

Figure 5-1 NVCLASS class hierarchy

The nonvisual class library is small—only six objects. As you develop code of your own, you may want to expand on this. Now let's make a more detailed investigation of these objects.

The C_INI Class

There will be times when you need to store data from a program in a persistent area of the operating system. OS/2 provides an interface to create INI files, which you may have noticed in your OS/2 system directory. The operating system makes extensive use of OS2.INI and OS2SYS.INI to store and maintain virtually every configuration setting for itself and its support programs. You can create your own INI files, if you wish, you may use OS2.INI. The C_INI class is the simplest class created in this book, so it is a good place to start looking at class libraries.

The following figure illustrates the C_INI class:

C_INI			
char	szIniFile[256]	C_INI()	
char	szAppName[256]	void	Open( )
HINI	hIni	void	Close()
		void	Read()
		void	Write()

Figure 5-2 C_INI class

The header file for C_INI is shown in Listing 5-1:

```
class C_INI
{
  protected:
      char    szIniFile[256];      // Filename of INI file
      char    szAppName[256];      // Application name of program
      HINI    hIni;                // INI handle

  public:
      _Export C_INI( char *szFile, char *szAppName );
      void _Export    Open( void );
      void _Export    Close( void );
      void _Export    Read(char *szField, char *szData,
                                char *szDefault, int iLength);
      void _Export    Write( char *szField, char *szData );
};
```

Listing 5-1 INI.HPP - Class definition for C_INI

The C_INI class implements just one constructor. The constructor for the class is very straightforward, consisting of two calls—one to copy the input strings for the INI filename and another to copy the identifying string, which is usually the program name.

```
//-------------
// Constructor \
//---------------------------------------------------------------------------
//
// Parameters:
//     szFile          - Full path name of INI file
//     szName          - Name of application
//
// Returns:
//             none
//
C_INI::C_INI( char *szFile, char *szName )
{
  // Save the supplied data within the class attributes
  strcpy( szIniFile, szFile );
  strcpy( szAppName, szName );
}
```

Once an instance of C_INI has been created, the INI file needs to be opened. The class provides an Open() method to accomplish this. The method calls the OS/2 API PrfOpenProfile() to open the INI file and saves the INI file handle within the hIni class attribute.

```
//------
// Open \
//--------------------------------------------------------------------------
// Description:
//     This method will open the INI File associated with this instance.
//
// Parameters:
//     none
//
// Returns:
//     none
//
void C_INI::Open( void )
{
   // Open the INI file saving the handle to the file
   hIni = PrfOpenProfile( 0, (PSZ)szIniFile );
}
```

The Close() method complements Open(), and should be called once INI reading and writing is complete. The method calls the OS/2 API PrfCloseProfile().

```
//-------
// Close \
//--------------------------------------------------------------------------
// Description:
//     This method will close the INI File associated with this instance.
//
// Parameters:
//     none
//
void C_INI::Close( void )
{
   if( strlen( szIniFile ) )
   {
      // Close the INI file
      PrfCloseProfile( hIni );
   }
}
```

Once the INI file has been open, data can be read or written. Although OS/2 supports a complete set of reading and writing capabilities for strings, integers, and decimal values, the NVCLASS implements only string support. If you have a requirement to store numbers, you have the option of adding your own method to support this capability or, alternately, you may convert the number into string using the provisions of C/C++ string support.

In order to read a value from the INI file, we need to know a number of specific bits of information. Each item in the INI file is stored by referencing a key value, and this key must be supplied to Read() in order to retrieve the information successfully. Additionally, the Read() method requires a buffer area, where the data read from the INI file will be deposited, and also a default value for the buffer in the event that no data is stored for the supplied key. Finally, Read() needs to know the size of the buffer area.

```
//------
// Read \
//---------------------------------------------------------------------------
// Description:
//     This method will read a string from the INI file as specified by
//     the supplied keyword. If the value is not extracted from the INI
//     file, then the supplied default will be returned.
//
// Parameters:
//     szField      - Keyword to be fetched
//     szData       - Pointer to buffer where data from INI will be written
//     szDefault    - Pointer to the default string
//     iLength      - Maximum size of the output buffer
//
// Returns:
//     none
//
void C_INI::Read( char *szField, char *szData, char *szDefault, int iLength )
{
   // Query the INI file for a string
   PrfQueryProfileString(hIni, (PSZ)szAppName, (PSZ)szField,
                                    (PSZ)szDefault, (PSZ)szData, iLength );
}
```

The Write() method is a little simpler, requiring only the necessary key and the data that will be written.

```
//-------
// Write \
//---------------------------------------------------------------------------
// Description:
//     This method will write a string to the INI file as specified by
//     the supplied parameters.
//
// Parameters:
//     szField      - Keyword to be fetched
//     szData       - Pointer to buffer where data from INI will be written
//
// Returns:
//     none
//
```

```
void C_INI::Write(char *szField, char *szData )
{
  // Write the supplied string to the INI file
  PrfWriteProfileString( hIni, (PSZ)szAppName, (PSZ)szField, (PSZ)szData );
}
```

This short programming example illustrates the use of the C_INI class:

```
void LoadIniData( void )
{
  char    szString[256];

  // Create an instance of the class
  C_INI   xcIni( "TEST.INI", "TestProgram" );

  // Open the INI file
  xcIni.Open();

  // Write a test string
  xcIni.Write( "TestKey", "This is a test" );

  // Now read it back
  xcIni.Read( "TestKey", szString, "Invalid", 256 );
  printf( "Read:%s\n", szString );

  // All done
  xcIni.Close();
}
```

Listing 5-2 Sample use of C_INI

The C_INI_USER Class

OS/2 provides two specific INI files designed to maintain the operating system itself as well as any other application that needs to track persistent information. The first of these is OS2.INI; NVCLASS provides a C_INI class to support it.

This class is shown in Figure 5-3.

C_INI_USER	
	C_INI_USER() void Open( )

Figure 5-3 C_INI_USER class

C_INI_USER builds on the previous C_INI class by predefining the INI file handle. Under normal OS/2 API code the OS2.INI file can be accessed by referencing the HINI_USERPROFILE handle. Since this handle is never supposed to be opened or closed, this creates a big inconsistency in the way OS/2 manages these files when compared to other INI files. NVCLASS alleviates these problems by providing an Open/Close scenario, as it does for any other C_INI instance.

The header file for C_INI_USER is shown in Listing 5-3:

```
class C_INI_USER : public C_INI
{
   public:
        _Export C_INI_USER( char *szAppName );
        void _Export     Open( void );
#ifdef __BORLANDC__
        virtual void _Export    Close( void ) {};
#else
        virtual void     Close( void ) {};
#endif
};
```

Listing 5-3 INIUSER.HPP - Class definition for C_INI_USER

The C_INI_USER class has no attributes and just two methods. The constructor simply calls its parent but does not provide an INI filename; instead, it supplies a null string.

```
//-------------
// Constructor \
//----------------------------------------------------------------------
//
// Parameters:
//      szFile       - Full path name of INI file
//      szName       - Name of application
//
// Returns:
//      none
//
C_INI_USER::C_INI_USER( char *szName ) : C_INI( "", szName )
{
}
```

The OS2.INI file should never be acted on by an API PrfOpenProfile() call. For this reason C_INI_USER needs to implement a special Open() method that overrides the previous definition created by the C_INI parent. The new Open() simply defaults the hIni attribute of the parent to HINI_USERPROFILE.

```
//------
// Open \
//------------------------------------------------------------------------
// Description:
//     This method will open the OS2USER.INI File associated with this
//     instance.
//
// Parameters:
//     none
//
// Returns:
//     none
//
void C_INI_USER::Open( void )
{
   // We don't need to open the OS2USER.INI file, we can just use it
   hIni = HINI_USERPROFILE;
}
```

The C_INI_SYSTEM Class

The other special INI file is OS2SYS.INI. Generally this file will never be written to, since is supposed to be reserved for use by the operating system. However, you may need to write to, or, more likely, read information from this file, so NVCLASS provides a C_INI_SYSTEM class.

This class is virtually identical to the previous C_INI_USER class, except that it manipulates a different file. For this reason we need not go into great detail here. Figure 5-4 shows the class graphically.

C_INI_SYSTEM	
	C_INI_SYSTEM() void Open( )

Figure 5-4 C_INI_SYSTEM class

The header file for C_INI_SYSTEM is shown in Listing 5-4:

```
class C_INI_SYSTEM : public C_INI
{
   public:
       _Export C_INI_SYSTEM( char *szAppName );
       void _Export    Open( void );
#ifdef __BORLANDC__
       virtual void _Export     Close( void ) {};
```

```
#else
       virtual void     Close( void ) {};
#endif
};
```

Listing 5-4 INISYS.HPP - Class definition for C_INI_SYSTEM

The basic difference in this class is the replacement of the HINI_USER-PROFILE handle with HINI_SYSTEMPROFILE. This occurs in the Open() method as shown below.

```
//------
// Open \
//-----------------------------------------------------------------------------
// Description:
//      This method will open the OS2.INI File associated with this instance.
//
// Parameters:
//      none
//
// Returns:
//      none
//
void C_INI_SYSTEM::Open( void )
{
   // We don't need to open the OS2.INI file, we can just use it
   hIni = HINI_SYSTEMPROFILE;
}
```

The C_THREAD Class

We discussed multithreading and OS/2 several times in the previous chapter. Like other APIs in OS/2, the calls for threading are C-based rather than C++ -based, so we need to create an object to wrap this functionality to make it easier to use in our own applications.

The C_THREAD class implements a simple class wrapper to support this, by providing a limited interface to create and monitor threads; like every other class I will create in this book, there is room for expansion. For instance, I have defined only a single monitoring function, WaitIndefinite(). OS/2 also supports checking a thread's status based on a timed wait or no wait at all. If this functionality is important to you, you can add two more methods to create this interface.

The following object diagram illustrates the methods and attributes that combine to form the thread class:

C_THREAD	
void *pvThreadData TID hThreadID	C_THREAD() void Create() void Kill() void WaitIndefinite() void * ThreadData()

Figure 5-5 C_THREAD class

The header file for C_THREAD is shown in Listing 5-5:

```
class C_THREAD
{
  private:
      void    *pvThreadData;
      TID     hThreadID;

  public:
      _Export     C_THREAD( void );
      _Export     C_THREAD( void (*ThreadFunction)(void *),
                            unsigned int iStackSize, void *pvData );

      // Inline methods
#ifdef __BORLANDC__
      void *  _Export     ThreadData( void )       { return pvThreadData; };
#else
      void *  ThreadData( void )                   { return pvThreadData; };
#endif

      // Regular methods
      void    _Export     Create( void *ThreadFunction,
                            unsigned int iStackSize, void *pvData );
      void    _Export     Kill( void );
      void    _Export     WaitIndefinite( void );
};
```

Listing 5-5 THREAD.HPP - Class definition for C_THREAD

The C_THREAD class implements two constructor interfaces. The first is a simple void constructor that does not create a thread, but rather notes only that the C_THREAD object has been created. The second constructor can be thought of as the "on the fly" version; it creates an instance of the C_THREAD class but also creates the actual thread itself by calling the create method.

Threads are essentially separate programs running from the operating system, and, as such, they require a specified amount of stack space in order to execute without error. You could calculate this value, but is isn't really necessary. In most of the thread examples in this book I have arbitrarily selected a stack size that works—there's no real penalty for assigning a larger stack than required, since OS/2's memory management will ensure that no memory space is wasted.

```
//-------------
// Constructor \
//------------------------------------------------------------------------------
C_THREAD::C_THREAD( void )
{
   hThreadID = 0;
}

//-------------
// Constructor \
//------------------------------------------------------------------------------
//
// Parameters:
//     ThreadFunction  - Pointer to the desired thread function
//     StackSize       - Default stack size for the thread
//     pvData          - Pointer to any data passed to the thread function
//
C_THREAD::C_THREAD( void *ThreadFunction), unsigned int iStackSize,
                                                       void *pvData )
{
   // Call the create method to create a thread upon instantiation
   Create( ThreadFunction, iStackSize, pvData );
}
```

The Create() method wraps the operating system call that starts a new thread. It requires a pointer to a thread function, an initial stack size for the thread, and a pointer to any data that might be supplied to the thread from the caller. In addition to this data, a thread has access to any global memory and system resources that have been allocated by the host application.

```
//--------
// Create \
//------------------------------------------------------------------------------
// Description:
//     This method wraps the operating system dependent call to create a
//     new thread of execution.
//
// Parameters:
//     ThreadFunction      - Pointer to the desired thread function
//     StackSize           - Default stack size for the thread
//     pvData              - Pointer to any data passed to the thread function
//
```

```
// Returns:
//      none
//
void C_THREAD::Create( void *ThreadFunction, unsigned int iStackSize,
                                                            void *pvData )
{
   // Save a pointer to the supplied data
   pvThreadData = pvData;

   // Create a new thread of execution
#ifdef __BORLANDC__
   hThreadID = _beginthread( (void (*)(void *))ThreadFunction, iStackSize, this );
#else
   hThreadID = _beginthread( (void (* _LNK_CONV)( void * ))ThreadFunction,
                                                  0, iStackSize, this );
#endif
}
```

Once a thread has been created, we also need a way to kill it in some circumstances. The Kill() method wraps the operating system specific call DosKillThread() to accomplish this.

Like DosKillThread(), use of the C_THREAD::Kill() method is not recommended, since it can cause improper memory deallocation in a thread.

```
//------
// Kill \
//-------------------------------------------------------------------------
// Description:
//      This method wraps the operating system dependent call to terminate
//      a thread.
//
// Parameters:
//      none
//
// Returns:
//      none
//
void C_THREAD::Kill( void )
{
   // If the thread has previously been started
   if( hThreadID )
   {
      // Kill the thread
      DosKillThread( hThreadID );
   }
}
```

The C_THREAD class implements one more method to monitor thread status. WaitIndefinite() polls for the status of the thread until the thread completes; it consists of simple wrapper code to hide the operating-system-specific call.

```
//----------------
// WaitIndefinite \
//--------------------------------------------------------------------------
// Description:
//     This method wraps the operating-system-dependent call to wait for
//     the thread to complete its execution.
//
// Parameters:
//     none
//
// Returns:
//     none
//
void C_THREAD::WaitIndefinite( void )
{
   // If the thread has previously been started
   if( hThreadID )
   {
       // Wait for the thread to complete
       DosWaitThread( &hThreadID, DCWW_WAIT );
   }
}
```

I won't provide a threading example at this point because we will use threading extensively in the applications in Part III of this book; use of the C_THREAD class will be highlighted at that time. However, I will point out that thread functions used by the C_THREAD class differ slightly from those of stock OS/2. With C_THREAD thread functions, the data pointer passed into the function always contains a pointer to the thread object, not the buffer point specified when the thread is created. You can access this data area using an inline method ThreadData(), provided by C_THREAD.

C_THREAD should be used for all threading in text-mode applications and may also be used in PM applications in circumstances where no PM messages need to be sent from within the thread. In these situations you need to use the C_THREAD_PM class described next.

The C_THREAD_PM Class

As alluded to in the last section, threading from within Presentation Manager applications poses some additional problems that can once again be attributed to the single message queue problems of PM. If you want to create a thread to do something that requires PM windows message sending, then you need to perform a few more calls at the beginning and end of your thread function. Rather than replicate this code for each thread, it is much easier and more efficient to create a new class. We can thus implement the code once and reuse it.

The C_THREAD_PM class builds on the knowledge of its parent C_THREAD by implementing two additional methods that need to be called from within the thread function. These calls create and destroy a message queue the thread needs in order to be able to send messages to PM. Without this queue, the messages sent will be queued until the thread terminates.

Figure 5-6 illustrates the extensions added by the C_THREAD_PM object.

C_THREAD_PM	
HAB hABThread HMQ hMQThread	C_THREAD_PM() void InitializeThread() void TerminateThread()

Figure 5-6 C_THREAD_PM class

The header file for C_THREAD_PM is shown in Listing 5-6:

```
class C_THREAD_PM : public C_THREAD
{
   private:
       HAB      hABThread;
       HMQ      hMQThread;

   public:
       _Export      C_THREAD_PM( void );
       _Export      C_THREAD_PM( void (*ThreadFunction)(void *),
                                 unsigned int iStackSize, void *pvData );
       void         _Export     InitializeThread( void );
       void         _Export     TerminateThread( void );
};
```

Listing 5-6 THREADPM.HPP - Class definition for C_THREAD_PM

Like its parent, C_THREAD_PM implements two constructors, both of which add no additional functionality to the construction process. The second of these two constructors is shown below.

```
//------------
// Constructor \
//---------------------------------------------------------------------
// Description:
//    This method wraps the operating system dependent call to create a
```

```
//      new thread of execution for a Presentation Manager. To be able to
//      send PM messages, a thread in PM must create its own message
//      queue. This constructor does this.
//
// Parameters:
//      ThreadFunction  - Pointer to the desired thread function
//      StackSize       - Default stack size for the thread
//      pvData          - Pointer to any data passed to the thread function
//
// Returns:
//      none
//
C_THREAD_PM::C_THREAD_PM( void (*ThreadFunction)(void *),
                    unsigned int iStackSize, void *pvData )
                    : C_THREAD( ThreadFunction, iStackSize, pvData )
{
}
```

The InitializeThread() method should be placed near the beginning of a PM thread function to set up the required message queue. As you can see, it initializes the PM interface for the method and then creates a new message queue.

```
//------------------
// InitializeThread \
//--------------------------------------------------------------------------
// Description:
//      This method wraps the operating system dependent calls to create
//      a new message queue. This should be called at the beginning of
//      the thread function.
//
// Parameters:
//      none
//
// Returns:
//      none
//
void C_THREAD_PM::InitializeThread( void )
{
   // Create a PM process for this thread
   hABThread = WinInitialize( 0 );
   hMQThread = WinCreateMsgQueue( hABThread, 0 );
}
```

The complement to InitializeThread() is the TerminateThread() method. It is used to destroy the thread's message queue resources and return them to the system pool. TerminateThread() should be called immediately before the thread ends.

```
//-----------------
// TerminateThread \
//----------------------------------------------------------------------------
// Description:
//     This method wraps the operating system dependent calls to destroy
//     a thread's message queue. This should be called at the end of the
//     thread function.
//
// Parameters:
//     none
//
// Returns:
//     none
//
void C_THREAD_PM::TerminateThread( void )
{
   // Terminate the thread
   WinDestroyMsgQueue( hMQThread );
   WinTerminate( hABThread );
}
```

At this point I should note something critical to using threads within a PM program that may save you hours of debugging. As you probably know, the automatic variables defined within a window message handler method are not preserved when the method terminates. For instance, if you are using the "new" handler to allocate a thread dynamically in one message handler routine, do not assume that you can use the thread pointer in another method since it will undoubtedly be invalid—resulting in a program crash.

If, after creation of the thread, you need to access the thread pointer, you should declare the pointer in the class definition. Alternatively, C_THREAD and C_THREAD_PM have been designed so that a static declaration of these classes can be used rather than dynamic allocation at run time. This simplifies use of the thread classes, since you do not need to be concerned about deallocation.

For more details concerning correct use of the C_THREAD classes, study the sample programs in Part III of this book.

The C_SEM_EVENT Class

The NVCLASS class library contains a final class called C_SEM_EVENT, which implements event semaphores. As I mentioned previously, the term "semaphore" is an just a fancy way of saying flag. We've all used flags in programs in order to control execution of the program, and semaphores are really not much different. However, in a multitasking operating system one needs to take care to avoid race conditions where two threads might want to access a flag at the same time. The effects can be disastrous.

OS/2 and most other multitasking operating systems solve this problem by implementing semaphores that are flags created by an application but managed by the system in order to avoid application conflicts. A number of semaphore types are used for specific purposes, including event management, resource management, and resource management requiring exclusive access. In this book, I will implement a class only for event semaphores; however, this class consists only of API wrapping so that you can implement additional classes for other types of semaphores if you require them. The class structure is as follows:

C_SEM_EVENT	
HEV hSemaphore	C_SEM_EVENT()
char szName[256]	int Create( )
	int Open()
	int Close()
	int Reset()
	int Post()
	int WaitIndefinite()

Figure 5-7 C_SEM_EVENT class

The header file for C_SEM_EVENT is shown in Listing 5-7:

```
class C_SEM_EVENT
{
  private:
      char    szName[256];         // Semaphore name string
      HEV     hSemaphore;          // Handle for an OS/2 semaphore

  public:
      _Export C_SEM_EVENT( char *szSemaphoreName );
      _Export C_SEM_EVENT( void );
      int      _Export     Create( void );
      int      _Export     Open( void );
      int      _Export     Close( void );
      int      _Export     Reset( ULONG *plPostCount );
      int      _Export     Post( void );
      int      _Export     WaitIndefinite( void );
};
```

Listing 5-7 SEMEV.HPP - Class definition for C_SEM_EVENT

C_SEM_EVENT supplies two constructors. The first implements no functionality and is supplied to create an unnamed semaphore. The second requires the specification of a name string parameter used to create a named semaphore.

```
//-------------
// Constructor \
//------------------------------------------------------------------------------
C_SEM_EVENT::C_SEM_EVENT( void )
{
   // Unnamed semaphore
   strcpy( szName, "" );
}

//-------------
// Constructor \
//------------------------------------------------------------------------------
C_SEM_EVENT::C_SEM_EVENT( char *szSemaphoreName )
{
   // Named semaphore
   strcpy( szName, szSemaphoreName );
}
```

The first method is Create() which, like all of the remaining class methods, simply hides the operating system specific call from the class user. In all methods of this class, the return value is passed directly from the operating system and any error values are system specific. This may be a concern if you are planning to port code, since the return values will be system specific.

```
//--------
// Create \
//------------------------------------------------------------------------------
// Description:
//     This method wraps the operating system dependent call to create
//     a new event semaphore.
//
// Parameters:
//     none
//
// Returns:
//     Operating system status of create operation
//
int C_SEM_EVENT::Create( void )
{
   // Create a new event semaphore
   return (int)DosCreateEventSem( szName, &hSemaphore, 0, FALSE );
}
```

The Open() method should be called for a semaphore that has been created previously. This may be done in another program, since semaphores are global to the system.

```
//------
// Open \
//----------------------------------------------------------------------------
// Description:
//     This method wraps the operating system dependent call to open an
//     event semaphore.
//
// Parameters:
//     none
//
// Returns:
//     Operating system status of open operation
//
int C_SEM_EVENT::Open( void )
{
   // Open an event semaphore
   return (int)DosOpenEventSem( szName, &hSemaphore );
}
```

When an application is finished with a semaphore, the Close() method should be called.

```
//-------
// Close \
//----------------------------------------------------------------------------
// Description:
//     This method wraps the operating system dependent call to close an
//     event semaphore.
//
// Parameters:
//     none
//
// Returns:
//     Operating system status of close operation
//
int C_SEM_EVENT::Close( void )
{
   // Close the event semaphore
   return (int)DosCloseEventSem( hSemaphore );
}
```

The semaphore maintains an internal count of the number of times it has been posted. Reset() retrieves this count and resets the internal counter to zero. It would be a wise practice to call Reset() before the semaphore is first used, since there is no guarantee that the post count will be zero.

```
//-------
// Reset \
//--------------------------------------------------------------------------
// Description:
//     This method wraps the operating system dependent call to reset an
//     event semaphore.
//
// Parameters:
//     plPostCount     pointer to the number of times the semaphore
//                     has been posted
//
// Returns:
//     Operating system status of reset operation
//
int C_SEM_EVENT::Reset( ULONG *plPostCount )
{
   // Reset the event semaphore
   return (int)DosResetEventSem( hSemaphore, plPostCount );
}
```

To post to the event semaphore, call the Post() method. Posting is used to indicate the completion of whatever event the semaphore is indicating.

```
//------
// Post \
//--------------------------------------------------------------------------
// Description:
//     This method wraps the operating system dependent call to post an
//     event semaphore.
//
// Parameters:
//     none
//
// Returns:
//     Operating system status of post operation
//
int C_SEM_EVENT::Post( void )
{
   // Post the event semaphore
   return (int)DosPostEventSem( hSemaphore );
}
```

There may be times during the execution of an application when no further processing can occur until a given event takes place. The WaitIndefinite() method manages this. OS/2 and most other operating systems support timed wait and no-wait testing of a semaphore, but I have elected to implement only the indefinite wait. Adding additional methods to support these extensions is not difficult.

```
//----------------
// WaitIndefinite \
//--------------------------------------------------------------------------
// Description:
//     This method wraps the operating system dependent call to wait
//     indefinitely for the semaphore to be posted.
//
// Parameters:
//     none
//
// Returns:
//     Operating system status of wait operation
//
int C_SEM_EVENT::WaitIndefinite( void )
{
   // Post the event semaphore
   return (int)DosWaitEventSem( hSemaphore, SEM_INDEFINITE_WAIT );
}
```

Chapter Summary

In this chapter, we have developed all the nonvisual classes for the NVCLASS class library. We will use most of these classes to create sample applications in Part III. I have also noted some of the advantages of C++ and object-oriented programming and briefly discussed the importance of considering portability when writing applications. Most of the code in this chapter consists of simple wrappers to hide OS/2-specific code from the rest of our applications. In the next chapter we will create the visual portions of our class library, and you will start to see more complex code and some examples of how these classes fit together to save time and effort.

In this chapter

- ✓ Message tables in Presentation Manager
- ✓ Visual control windows using PMCLASS
- ✓ Some CUA'91 visual controls

6

Developing a Simple PM Class Library

The PMCLASS Class Library

One of the advantages of the OS/2 operating system is its integrated Presentation Manager interface; if you hunger to write software, you will undoubtedly want your applications to run on the graphical desktop. The standard C API for PM is much like that of Microsoft Windows in that it does not offer a well-conceived object-oriented interface. Instead, implementing an application using the PM interface involves a confused weaving of massive case statements to process window messages. This solution was adequate before C++; however, today it is an unacceptable answer to a very complex problem. Both IBM and Microsoft have realized the limitations of the C API and are working on proper C++ interfaces.

The solution I propose is PMCLASS, a C++ class library that is far less complex than either the IBM or Microsoft offerings, but does include unique capabilities of its own. This library eliminates many of the inconsistencies of the standard API by providing a consistent interface through sound object-oriented design. Code developed with PMCLASS doesn't require large case statements; instead, separate methods provide control for each message processed by a window.

All PMCLASS window message processing is managed by implementing message tables as shown below:

```
DECLARE_MSG_TABLE( xtMsgMain )
   DECLARE_MSG( PM_CREATE,          C_WINDOW_MAIN::MsgCreate )
   DECLARE_MSG( PM_GROUP_CLOSE,     C_WINDOW_MAIN::MsgGroupClose )
```

```
    DECLARE_MSG( PM_SUB_CLOSE,        C_WINDOW_MAIN::MsgSubscriptionClose )
    DECLARE_MSG( WM_CLOSE,            C_WINDOW_MAIN::MsgClose )
    DECLARE_MSG( WM_SIZE,             C_WINDOW_MAIN::MsgSize )
    DECLARE_MSG( WM_CONTROL,          C_WINDOW_MAIN::MsgControl )
    DECLARE_MSG( WM_PAINT,            C_WINDOW_STD::MsgPaint )
END_MSG_TABLE
```

Each message that the program cares about receives an entry in the message table for the window. These entries contain a window message followed by a class method reference that the window manager calls when the message is received. Since PMCLASS is made up entirely of C++ objects, message tables can also contain message handlers from parent classes. For example, notice in the previous table that the entry for WM_PAINT references C_WINDOW_STD::MsgPaint, which is implemented in the parent class.

The use of message tables forces developers to implement an individual method for each message. This rigor imposes better design habits, since it mandates that each member function performs only one task. Debugging becomes a trivial exercise. This technique also offers some coding advantages. It is very easy to create a prototype of an application and then gradually add full functionality. The examples that will be presented in Part III are skeletal, but with a little work you could turn these into full feature applications simply by adding more methods to the various classes. If you want to add a new toolbar button, just create the bitmap, add it to the toolbar object for the desired window, then add a new command processor method to handle the button's message.

PMCLASS also manages other types of tables. When a user selects a menu option or presses a button, PM generates a WM_COMMAND message that sparks another large case statement to process each of the various command messages. Since PMCLASS manages the WM_CO1MMAND window message, it is not recommended that you implement your own handler for this message unless you are absolutely certain of the effects. A typical command table follows.

```
DECLARE_COMMAND_TABLE( xtCommandMain )
    DECLARE_COMMAND( DM_GROUPS,            C_WINDOW_MAIN::CmdGroups )
    DECLARE_COMMAND( DM_SUBSCRIPTIONS,     C_WINDOW_MAIN::CmdSubscriptions )
    DECLARE_COMMAND( DM_EXIT,              C_WINDOW_MAIN::CmdExit )
    DECLARE_COMMAND( DM_CONNECT,           C_WINDOW_MAIN::CmdConnect )
    DECLARE_COMMAND( DM_INFO,              C_WINDOW_MAIN::CmdHelpInfo )
END_MSG_TABLE
```

Figure 6-1 illustrates the classes and inheritance in the PMCLASS library. Each class in this library will be described in detail in this chapter.

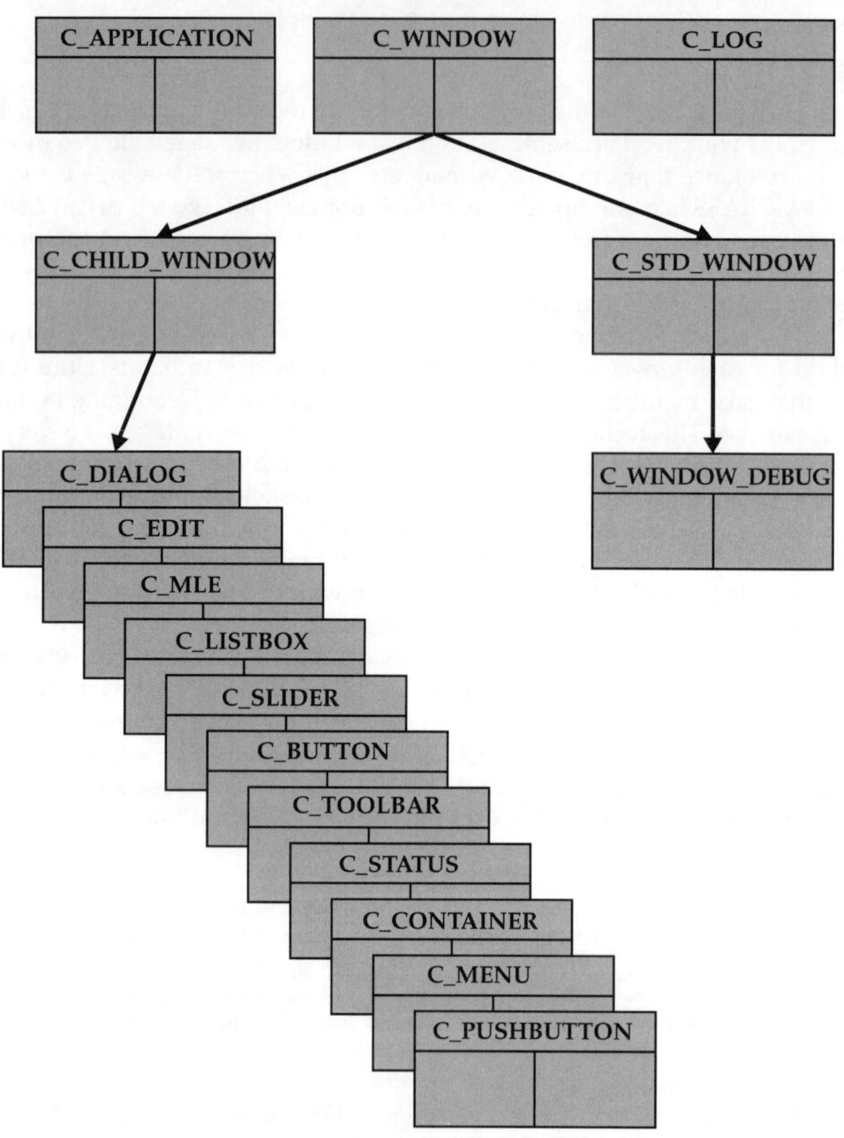

Figure 6-1 **PMCLASS** class hierarchy

Application Class

The most obvious problem with building Presentation Manager applications is the arduous task of starting up even the simplest of programs. In Chapter 2, we looked at the simplest possible application, and the startup involved initializing the windowing engine, creating a message queue and starting a message loop. After the window was closed, we had to reverse the process by destroying the message queue and shutting down the window manager. What makes this process even worse is the fact that you will have to recode this startup in virtually every PM application you write.

PMCLASS provides a cleaner solution to this problem. There is very little startup code to write and nothing to recode. PM applications can be created simply by creating an instance of C_APPLICATION. This class controls all the procedures required to initialize and then destroy an application, as well as returning constant system metric values such as the height of a title bar in pixels.

C_APPLICATION is relatively simple, containing only a few basic methods. The class is shown in Figure 6-2.

C_APPLICATION	
HAB hAB HMQ hMQ	C_APPLICATION() ~C_APPLICATION() void Run() HAB AnchorBlock() int DesktopHeight() int DesktopWidth() int MenuHeight() int TitleBarHeight() int DialogBorderHeight()

Figure 6-2 C_APPLICATION class

The header file for C_APPLICATION is shown below:

```
//-------------------------------
// C_APPLICATION class definition \
//---------------------------------------------------------------------
class C_APPLICATION
{
  private:
      HAB     hAB;            // Handle to application's anchor block
      HMQ     hMQ;            // Handle to application's message queue
```

```
public:
     _Export          C_APPLICATION( void );
     _Export         ~C_APPLICATION( void );
     void     _Export          Run( void );
     HAB      _Export          AnchorBlock( void );

     // System Metrics
     int      _Export          DesktopHeight( void );
     int      _Export          DesktopWidth( void );
     int      _Export          MenuHeight( void );
     int      _Export          TitleBarHeight( void );
     int      _Export          DialogBorderHeight( void );
};
```

Listing 6-1 APP.HPP – Class definition for C_APPLICATION

C_APPLICATION implements a single constructor which performs the initialization for a PMCLASS application. It calls WinInitialize() to initialize the window manager and return a handle to the application's anchor block (HAB). As discussed in Chapter 2, the HAB is a throwback to IBM mainframe days and is of little use, but C_APPLICATION implements support for anchor blocks in case it becomes important in future versions of OS/2.

The constructor also creates a basic application message by calling the WinCreateMsgQueue(). This queue collects messages from the system and stores them for the application's use. This queue gets loaded by the message loop in the Run() method.

```
//-------------
// Constructor \
//-------------------------------------------------------------------------
//
// Description:
//     This constructor initializes the window manager and create a
//     message queue for the application.
//
// Parameters:
//     none
//
C_APPLICATION::C_APPLICATION( void )
{
   // Initialize the window manager
   hAB = WinInitialize(0);

   // Create a message queue for this application
   hMQ = WinCreateMsgQueue( hAB, 0 );
}
```

The destructor for C_APPLICATION essentially reverses the work performed by the constructor. It calls WinDestroyMsgQueue() to dispose of the applications queue, then calls WinTerminate() to shut down the window manager. The destructor is the last piece of code executed before the application terminates.

```
//------------
// Destructor \
//---------------------------------------------------------------------------
//
// Description:
//     This destructor tears down the application. It destroys the
//     application's message queue and deinitializes the window manager.
//
// Parameters:
//     none
//
C_APPLICATION::~C_APPLICATION( void )
{
   // Get rid of the application's queue
   WinDestroyMsgQueue( hMQ );

   // Terminate the window manager function
   WinTerminate( hAB );
}
```

Since PMCLASS supports the use of the anchor block handle, C_APPLICATION provides a method called AnchorBlock() that returns the HAB. If you are writing "safe" code, use AnchorBlock() to supply the HAB for any code that requires it.

```
//-------------
// AnchorBlock \
//---------------------------------------------------------------------------
//
// Description:
//     This method returns a value for the application's anchor block.
//
// Parameters:
//     none
//
// Returns:
//     HAB              - Handle of the app's anchor block
//
HAB C_APPLICATION::AnchorBlock( void )
{
   return hAB;
}
```

The final part needed to start a PMCLASS application is the message loop. The Run() method implements this code, which extracts messages out of the system message queue and dispatches them to the application.

```
//-----
// Run \
//------------------------------------------------------------------------
//
// Description:
//     This method is called to start the message loop for the application.
//     It retrieves messages from the system queue and dispatches them to
//     the application's message queue.
//
// Parameters:
//     void
//
// Returns:
//     void
//
void C_APPLICATION::Run( void )
{
   QMSG     qmsg;

   // Start the message loop
   while( WinGetMsg( hAB, &qmsg, 0L, 0, 0 ) )
   {
       // Dispatch the message to the application queue
       WinDispatchMsg( hAB, &qmsg );
   }
}
```

The remainder of the methods in the C_APPLICATION class return system metric values, which are constants for various system parameters. When I say "constant," I do not use the term in the traditional sense. The system metrics are the same for every running application; however, some of them can be changed, either through basic system setup or through device reconfiguration. For example, the user can change the thickness of the dialog borders and, by rebooting, the user can alter the display resolution. The important thing to note is that these metrics are the same for every running application.

The first of these system metric methods is DesktopHeight(), which returns the height of the desktop window in pixels. This is useful information if you are writing an application that must scale to the desktop regardless of the resolution. There are several standard display resolutions ranging from 640 x 480 to 1280 x 1024 or higher; however, there is nothing preventing someone from writing a new video driver capable of 1063 x 796 (or some other odd resolution); if your program depends on the resolution of the display, then it should detect this properly.

```
//---------------
// DesktopHeight \
//-------------------------------------------------------------------------
//
// Description:
//     This method returns a value for the height of the desktop window in
//     pixels.
//
// Parameters:
//     none
//
// Returns:
//     int     - Height of the desktop in pixels
//
int C_APPLICATION::DesktopHeight( void )
{
   RECTL   rc;

   WinQueryWindowRect( HWND_DESKTOP, &rc );
   return rc.yTop;
}
```

Similarly, the width of the desktop window in pixels can be returned using the DesktopWidth() method in C_APPLICATION.

```
//--------------
// DesktopWidth \
//-------------------------------------------------------------------------
//
// Description:
//     This method returns a value for the width of the desktop window in
//     pixels.
//
// Parameters:
//     none
//
// Returns:
//     int     - Width of the desktop in pixels
//
int C_APPLICATION::DesktopWidth( void )
{
   RECTL   rc;

   WinQueryWindowRect( HWND_DESKTOP, &rc );
   return rc.xRight;
}
```

The height of the menu bar for an application menu can be returned by placing a call to the MenuHeight() method.

```
//------------
// MenuHeight \
//---------------------------------------------------------------------------
//
// Description:
//     This method returns a value for the height of a menu in pixels.
//
// Parameters:
//     none
//
// Returns:
//     int      - Height of a menu bar in pixels
//
int C_APPLICATION::MenuHeight( void )
{
   return WinQuerySysValue( HWND_DESKTOP, SV_CYMENU );
}
```

The pixel height of the caption (title bar) can be returned using the TitleBar-Height() method.

```
//----------------
// TitleBarHeight \
//---------------------------------------------------------------------------
//
// Description:
//     This method returns a value for the height of a title bar in pixels.
//
// Parameters:
//     none
//
// Returns:
//     int      - Height of a title bar in pixels
//
int C_APPLICATION::TitleBarHeight( void )
{
   return WinQuerySysValue( HWND_DESKTOP, SV_CYTITLEBAR );
}
```

Finally, the thickness or height of a dialog border can be returned by the DialogBorderHeight().

```
//--------------------
// DialogBorderHeight \
//----------------------------------------------------------------------
//
// Description:
//   This method returns a value for the height of a dialog border in pixels.
//
// Parameters:
//     none
//
// Returns:
//     int     - Height (thickness) of a dialog border in pixels
//
int C_APPLICATION::DialogBorderHeight( void )
{
   return WinQuerySysValue( HWND_DESKTOP, SV_CYDLGFRAME );
}
```

Notice that I have implemented only enough of the system metric code required. Undoubtedly you will want to implement some additional system metric code to support the applications you will be writing with PMCLASS. Add your additional member function to the C_APPLICATION class.

Basic Window Class

The basic building block for any graphical user interface is, of course, the window. Windows can take many forms—in fact, almost every visual effect on an OS/2 screen is a type of window. Applications are obviously windows, but less obvious window types include list boxes, push buttons, and check boxes; even the title bar of a frame window is a type of window that can be manipulated like any other.

The base class for all windows in the PMCLASS library is C_WINDOW, which provides the generic functionality for all derived windows. This includes such characteristics as the foreground and background colors, the font, the current text contents, the visibility of the window, etc. C_WINDOW is the largest class in this book, consisting of more than 30 methods, and is about as large as you will ever want to make a class. However, so much of the functionality for all windows is common that the base class tends to be much bigger than any of its children. Don't be too concerned about the size of C_WINDOW, though, as most of the methods are simple wrappers around OS/2 specific API functions. The C_WINDOW class is illustrated in Figure 6-3.

C_WINDOW	
HWND hFrameWnd HWND hWnd char *szClassName ULONG lFrameFlags T_MSG_TABLE *pxtMsgTable T_MSG_TABLE *pxtCommandTable	C_WINDOW() ~C_WINDOW() HWND ParentWindow() HWND Window() void Window() void ParentWindow() void * SendMsg() void PostMsg() void SetText() void GetText() void Enable() void Show() void Hide() void Update() char * ClassName() void ClassName() void GetSizePosition() void GetSize() void GetPosition() void SetForegroundColor() void SetBackgroundColor() void SetFont() void GetForegroundColor() void GetBackgroundColor() void GetFont() void Focus() void Invalidate() BOOL Register() void Create() void Destroy() void MessageTable() void CommandTable() virtual void * WindowProc()

Figure 6-3 C_WINDOW class

The header file for C_WINDOW is shown in Listing 6-2:

```
class C_WINDOW;             // Predefine the class so we can use it in the
                            // following definitions
```

```
//----------------
// T_MSG_FUNCTION \
//--------------------------------------------------------------------------
// Definition, used by class to reference message methods
typedef void *(C_WINDOW::*T_MSG_FUNCTION)( void *, void * );

//-------------
// T_MSG_TABLE \
//--------------------------------------------------------------------------
// Definition used to define message table elements
typedef struct
{
   ULONG                lMsg;
   T_MSG_FUNCTION       Function;
} T_MSG_TABLE;

//----------------------
// DECLARE_MESSAGE_TABLE \
//--------------------------------------------------------------------------
// macro used to define the start of a message table
#define                 DECLARE_MSG_TABLE( msg_table )\
   T_MSG_TABLE          msg_table[] =\
   {\

//-------------------
// END_MESSAGE_TABLE \
//--------------------------------------------------------------------------
// macro used to define the end of a message table
#define                 END_MSG_TABLE\
   { 0, 0 }\
};\

//-------------
// DECLARE_MSG \
//--------------------------------------------------------------------------
// macro used to define a message table element
#define                 DECLARE_MSG( msg, function )\
                        { (msg), ((T_MSG_FUNCTION)(function)) },

//----------------
// Command Macros \
//--------------------------------------------------------------------------
// The following macros are used to define command table constructors
// Since these are the format as the MESSAGE macros we can simply redefine
// the message macros.
#define     DECLARE_COMMAND_TABLE        DECLARE_MSG_TABLE
#define     DECLARE_COMMAND              DECLARE_MSG
#define     END_COMMAND_TABLE            END_MSG_TABLE
```

```
//---------------------
// PMCLASS Message ID's \
//---------------------------------------------------------------------------
// PM_CREATE is the first message that a window receives after it has been
// created.
// PM_USER is the first message that can be user defined
//
#define    PM_CREATE   WM_USER        // Sent when window is created
#define    PM_USER     WM_USER + 1    // First available user defined message

//-------------------------
// C_WINDOW class definition \
//---------------------------------------------------------------------------
class      C_WINDOW
{
  private:
      HWND    hFrameWnd;            // Frame window handle
      HWND    hWnd;                 // Handle to this window
      char    *szClassName;         // Class name string
      ULONG   lFrameFlags;          // Frame creation flags

  public:
      T_MSG_TABLE    *pxtMsgTable;        // Table of Window messages
      T_MSG_TABLE    *pxtCommandTable;    // Table of Window command handlers

      _Export     C_WINDOW( void );
      _Export     C_WINDOW( T_MSG_TABLE *pxtMsg );
      _Export     ~C_WINDOW( void );

      HWND     _Export     ParentWindow( void );
      HWND     _Export     Window( void );
      void     _Export     Window( HWND hNewWindow );
      void     _Export     ParentWindow( HWND hNewWindow );
      void *   _Export     SendMsg( ULONG lMsg, void *mp1, void *mp2 );
      void     _Export     PostMsg( ULONG lMsg, void *mp1, void *mp2 );
      void     _Export     SetText( char *szString );
      void     _Export     GetText( char *szString, int iBufferLength );
      void     _Export     Enable( BOOL bState );
      void     _Export     Show( void );
      void     _Export     Hide( void );
      void     _Export     Update( void );
      char *   _Export     ClassName( void );
      void     _Export     ClassName( char *szClass );
      void     _Export     GetSizePosition( int *piX, int *piY,
                                     int *piCX, int *piCY );
      void     _Export     GetSize( int *piCX, int *piCY );
      void     _Export     GetPosition( int *piX, int *piY );
      void     _Export     SetForegroundColor( BYTE byRed,
                                   BYTE byGreen, BYTE byBlue );
```

```
    void    _Export    SetBackgroundColor( BYTE byRed,
                                           BYTE byGreen, BYTE byBlue );
    void    _Export    SetFont( char *szFont, int iSize );
    void    _Export    GetForegroundColor( BYTE *pbyRed,
                                           BYTE *pbyGreen, BYTE *pbyBlue );
    void    _Export    GetBackgroundColor( BYTE *pbyRed,
                                           BYTE *pbyGreen, BYTE *pbyBlue );
    void    _Export    GetFont( char *szFont );
    void    _Export    Focus( void );
    void    _Export    Invalidate( void );
    BOOL    _Export    Register( char *szClassName );
    void    _Export    Create( HWND hFrameWnd, HWND hWnd );
    void    _Export    Destroy( void );
    void    _Export    MessageTable( T_MSG_TABLE *pxtMsg );
    void    _Export    CommandTable( T_MSG_TABLE *pxtCommands );

    virtual void * _ExportWindowProc( ULONG lMsg, void *mp1, void *mp2 );
};

// OS/2 PM window procedure
MRESULT EXPENTRY StdWndProc( HWND hWnd, ULONG lMsg, MPARAM mp1, MPARAM mp2 );
```

Listing 6-2 WINDOW.HPP – Class definition for C_WINDOW

C_WINDOW provides two constructors; which one a derived classes calls depends on the presence of a window message table. This first of these is the void constructor; this simply initializes the important attributes in the base class.

```
//-------------
// Constructor \
//-------------------------------------------------------------------------
//
// Description:
//     This is the void constructor for the C_WINDOW class. It simply
//     defaults the created window parameters.
//
// Parameters:
//     none
//
C_WINDOW::C_WINDOW( void )
{
   // Initialize the window handles
   hFrameWnd = NULLHANDLE;
   hWnd = NULLHANDLE;
   pxtMsgTable = 0;
   pxtCommandTable = 0;
   szClassName = 0;
}
```

The complementary operation to returning the current window handle is to set it. The Window() method is overloaded and can also accept a window handle that it uses to set the window attribute within C_WINDOW. This method is typically called by a constructor from a derived class and would not normally be called by application code.

```
//--------
// Window \
//---------------------------------------------------------------------------
//
// Description:
//     This method assigns a handle to the PM window parameter within
//     the class.
//
// Parameters:
//     hNewWnd      - Window handle of the window
//
// Returns:
//     void
//
void C_WINDOW::Window( HWND hNewWnd )
{
   hWnd = hNewWnd;
}
```

The ParentWindow() method is also overloaded like Window(). With this method, a derived class constructor can set the owner window attribute.

```
//--------------
// ParentWindow \
//---------------------------------------------------------------------------
//
// Description:
//     This method assigns a handle to the parent window parameter within
//     the class.
//
// Parameters:
//     hNewWnd      - Window handle of the parent/owner window
//
// Returns:
//     void
//
void C_WINDOW::ParentWindow( HWND hNewWnd )
{
   hFrameWnd = hNewWnd;
}
```

The Presentation Manager API supplies a WinSendMsg() function that is used to send a message to a specified window. What this really does is drop the new message into the system queue and wait for the message to be fully processed by the target window before returning.

```
//---------
// SendMsg \
//-------------------------------------------------------------------------
//
// Description:
//     This method wraps the API call to send a message and its parameters
//     to the window message handler.
//
// Parameters:
//     lMsg        - Window message to send
//     mp1,mp2     - message parameters send with the message
//
// Returns:
//     void *      - result of the send operation
//
void *C_WINDOW::SendMsg( ULONG lMsg, void *mp1, void *mp2 )
{
   // Send a message to this window
   return (void *)WinSendMsg( hWnd, lMsg, mp1, mp2 );
}
```

WinSendMsg() does not work on objects; however, we can wrap the function within our class. SendMsg() provides this functionality for the C_WINDOW class. The WinSendMsg() function can still be called as follows:

```
   WinSendMsg( xcObject.Window(), WM_CLOSE, 0, 0 );
```

Though this line is valid, it detracts from the object-oriented goal we are striving for. A better way would be:

```
xcObject.SendMsg( WM_CLOSE, 0, 0 );
```

The PostMsg() method is similar to SendMsg(), except it wraps the WinPostMsg() API function instead. Posting a message in OS/2 places the message in the system queue and returns immediately; this method should be used when possible to provide smoother program execution. You need to be cautious about posting messages that reference temporary data, however, because the data pointers may be lost before the message actually reaches its target window; a program crash (access violation) will be the probable result.

```
//---------
// PostMsg \
//--------------------------------------------------------------------------
//
// Description:
//     This method wraps the API call to post a message and its parameters
//     to the window message handler.
//
// Parameters:
//     lMsg         - Window message to post
//     mp1,mp2      - Message parameters send with the message
//
// Returns:
//     void
//
void C_WINDOW::PostMsg( ULONG lMsg, void *mp1, void *mp2 )
{
   // Post a message to this window
   WinPostMsg( hWnd, lMsg, mp1, mp2 );
}
```

The text within a window can be set using the C_WINDOW::SetText() method. This sets the text in the client area of the window, which means the window must be some type of control window like an edit control, for example. This method does not set the title of an application window.

```
//---------
// SetText \
//--------------------------------------------------------------------------
//
// Description:
//     This method wraps the API call to set the text contents of a window
//     to a specific string.
//
// Parameters:
//     szString     - Pointer to new text string
//
// Returns:
//     void
//
void C_WINDOW::SetText( char *szString )
{
   // Set the window text (title)
   WinSetWindowText( hWnd, szString );
}
```

The text can be retrieved from the window by using the GetText() method. This method wraps the WinQueryWindowText() API function, and has the same requirements as SetText(). It will not return the title of an application window.

```
//---------
// GetText \
//-------------------------------------------------------------------------
//
// Description:
//     This method wraps the API call to retrieve the text contents of a
//     window and write this string to an output buffer.
//
// Parameters:
//     szString      - Pointer to a location where text string will be written
//     iBufferSize   - Size of the output buffer
//
// Returns:
//     void
//
void C_WINDOW::GetText( char *szString, int iBufferSize )
{
   // Set the window text (title)
   WinQueryWindowText( hWnd, iBufferSize, szString );
}
```

Presentation Manager provides the capability to enable or disable windows. C_WINDOW wraps this feature into the Enable() member function. This method accepts a Boolean value that will either enable the window if TRUE or disable the window is FALSE.

For a child window, such as a push button, this has the effect of graying the button and preventing the user from pressing it—a useful capability for preventing the activation of an operation that is temporarily invalid. The FTP application in Chapter 11 uses this feature to prevent the entry of FTP commands while a command is being processed.

```
//--------
// Enable \
//-------------------------------------------------------------------------
//
// Description:
//     This method wraps the API call to enable or disable the window,
//     which allows or prevents the user from invoking any action. This
//     is particularly useful for enabling of disabling child controls.
//
// Parameters:
//     bState      - TRUE or FALSE to enable or disable the window
//
```

```
// Returns:
//     void
//
void C_WINDOW::Enable( BOOL bState )
{
   // Enable or disable the window
   WinEnableWindow( hWnd, bState );
}
```

The visibility of a window is controlled by the Show() and Hide() methods in the C_WINDOW class. The Show() method makes a call to the standard PM API WinSetWindowPos(). Show() specifies the SWP_SHOW and SWP_RESTORE options to this function, which forces the window to become visible and restores it to its normal size and position.

```
//------
// Show \
//-------------------------------------------------------------------------
//
// Description:
//     This method wraps the API call to display a window at the top of the
//     window stack. If the window is currently hidden or minimized it is
//     restored.
//
// Parameters:
//     void
//
// Returns:
//     void
//
void C_WINDOW::Show( void )
{
   WinSetWindowPos( hFrameWnd, HWND_TOP, 0, 0, 0, 0,
                    SWP_SHOW | SWP_ZORDER | SWP_ACTIVATE | SWP_RESTORE );
}
```

The Hide() method is the functional opposite of Show(). It uses the WinShowWindow() function to remove the window from the screen.

```
//------
// Hide \
//-------------------------------------------------------------------------
//
// Description:
//     This method wraps the API call to hide a window. The window is
//     removed from the screen but is not destroyed.
//
```

```
// Parameters:
//     void
//
// Returns:
//     void
//
void C_WINDOW::Hide( void )
{
   WinShowWindow( hFrameWnd, FALSE );
}
```

Windows derived from the C_WINDOW class can be updated by calling the Update() method. This is a simple wrapper for the PM API that calls the WinUpdateWindow() function.

```
//--------
// Update \
//---------------------------------------------------------------------------
//
// Description:
//     This method wraps the API call to update a window display.
//
// Parameters:
//     void
//
// Returns:
//     void
//
void C_WINDOW::Update( void )
{
   // Update the window to show any changes
   WinUpdateWindow( hFrameWnd );
}
```

C_WINDOW implements a ClassName() method to set the name of the PM window class. This must be called before the window is registered and is called only by the C_WINDOW::Register() method. You should not call this under normal circumstances for an application window derived from C_WINDOW_STD.

Control windows, such as the list box, are already registered by PM as part of its startup process. PMCLASS, however, still requires some knowledge of the class name for its own internal purposes during window creation. As you will see when the C_LISTBOX class is described later in this chapter, its constructor explicitly calls ClassName().

```
//-----------
// ClassName \
//-----------------------------------------------------------------------------
//
// Description:
//     This method sets the internal class name attribute within C_WINDOW.
//     This attribute is used to register the class with the operating system.
//
// Parameters:
//     szClass     - Pointer to name for this window class
//
// Returns:
//     void
//
void C_WINDOW::ClassName( char *szClass )
{
   szClassName = szClass;
}
```

ClassName() is an overloaded C++ member function. In this second method, the class name string is returned to the caller.

```
//-----------
// ClassName \
//-----------------------------------------------------------------------------
//
// Description:
//     This method returns the internal class name attribute within C_WINDOW.
//     This attribute is used to register the class with the operating system.
//
// Parameters:
//     void
//
// Returns:
//     char *      - Pointer to the name of this window class
//
char *C_WINDOW::ClassName( void )
{
   return szClassName;
}
```

As I mentioned previously, all objects derived from the C_WINDOW class have a size and position on the screen. To retrieve this information, C_WINDOW provides a GetSizePosition() method, which returns the coordinates of the lower left corner of the window, as well as its width and height.

GetSizePosition() wraps the PM function WinQueryWindowPos(), which returns an SWP structure. The actual dimensions and position of the window are broken out of this structure and returned to the caller.

```
//-------------------
// GetSizePosition() \
//-------------------------------------------------------------------------
//
// Description:
//      This method retrieves the current window size and position relative
//      to its owner.
//
// Parameters:
//      *piX, *piY    - Pointers to a data area to get the X,Y coordinates
//      *piCX,*piCY   - Pointers to a data area to get the window dimensions
//
// Returns:
//      void
//
void C_WINDOW::GetSizePosition( int *piX, int *piY, int *piCX, int *piCY )
{
   SWP      swp;

   WinQueryWindowPos( hWnd, &swp );

   *piX = swp.x;
   *piY = swp.y;
   *piCX = swp.cx;
   *piCY = swp.cy;
}
```

GetSize() executes similar code to GetSizePosition() except that only the dimensions of the window are returned to the caller.

```
//-----------
// GetSize() \
//-------------------------------------------------------------------------
//
// Description:
//      This method retrieves the current window size.
//
// Parameters:
//      *piW,*piL     - Pointers to a data area to get the window dimensions
//
// Returns:
//      void
//
void C_WINDOW::GetSize( int *piCX, int *piCY )
{
   SWP      swp;

   WinQueryWindowPos( hWnd, &swp );
```

```
   *piCX = swp.cx;
   *piCY = swp.cy;
}
```

The position of the window can also be returned by itself. Placing a call to the GetPosition() method returns the coordinates of the window origin.

```
//---------------
// GetPosition() \
//---------------------------------------------------------------------
//
// Description:
//     This method retrieves the current window position relative
//     to its owner.
//
// Parameters:
//     *piX, *piY     - Pointers to a data area to get the X,Y coordinates
//     *piW,*piL      - Pointers to a data area to get the window dimensions
//
// Returns:
//     void
//
void C_WINDOW::GetPosition( int *piX, int *piY )
{
   SWP      swp;

   WinQueryWindowPos( hWnd, &swp );

   *piX = swp.x;
   *piY = swp.y;
}
```

C_WINDOW provides full capability of setting window colors. The text color can be set by calling the SetForegroundColor() method. This method accepts three parameters representing the red, green, and blue color levels of the color being set. This RGB value ranges from 0,0,0 to 255,255,255 to produce around 65,000 distinct colors. Note that, due to limitations in the video drive or hardware, some of these color values may be rendered using a dithering process.

After the color is set using the WinSetPresParam() API function, the window is redrawn by calling the Invalidate() and Update() methods.

```
//----------------------
// SetForegroundColor() \
//---------------------------------------------------------------------
//
// Description:
//     This method sets the foreground (text) color of the window using
//     the specified RGB color parameters.
```

```
//
// Parameters:
//     byRed        - Red level for the window
//     byGreen      - Green level for the window
//     byBlue       - Blue level for the window
//
// Returns:
//     void
//
void C_WINDOW::SetForegroundColor( BYTE byRed, BYTE byGreen, BYTE byBlue )
{
   RGB2    rgb;

   // Create an RGB value
   rgb.bRed = byRed;
   rgb.bGreen = byGreen;
   rgb.bBlue = byBlue;
   rgb.fcOptions = 0;

   // Set the foreground color
   WinSetPresParam( Window(), PP_FOREGROUNDCOLOR, sizeof(RGB2), &rgb );

   // Force the window to update
   Invalidate();
   Update();
}
```

The background color of a window can be set with the SetBackgroundColor() method. The operation of the method is essentially identical to the SetForegroundColor() method shown previously, so we need not repeat it here.

```
//----------------------
// SetBackgroundColor() \
//------------------------------------------------------------------------
//
// Description:
//     This method sets the background color of the window using
//     the specified RGB color parameters.
//
// Parameters:
//     byRed        - Red level for the window
//     byGreen      - Green level for the window
//     byBlue       - Blue level for the window
//
// Returns:
//     void
//
void C_WINDOW::SetBackgroundColor( BYTE byRed, BYTE byGreen, BYTE byBlue )
```

```
{
   RGB2     rgb;

   // Create an RGB value
   rgb.bRed = byRed;
   rgb.bGreen = byGreen;
   rgb.bBlue = byBlue;
   rgb.fcOptions = 0;

   // Change the background color
   WinSetPresParam( Window(), PP_BACKGROUNDCOLOR, sizeof(RGB2), &rgb );

   // Force the window to update
   Invalidate();
   Update();
}
```

The text font used to display information within a window can be changed using the SetFont() method. This member function accepts a font name and a size, and formats an OS/2 compatible font string, issuing it to the window using the WinSetPresParam() API function.

```
//-----------
// SetFont() \
//------------------------------------------------------------------------
//
// Description:
//     This method sets the font of the window to the value specified.
//
// Parameters:
//     szFont       - New font
//     iSize        - Font size
//
// Returns:
//     void
//
void C_WINDOW::SetFont( char *szFont, int iSize )
{
   char    szString[256];

   // Create an OS/2 compatible font string
   sprintf( szString, "%d.%s", szFont, iSize );

   // Set the new font string
   WinSetPresParam( Window(), PP_FONTNAMESIZE, 256, szFont );
}
```

C_WINDOW supplies complementary methods to retrieve the colors and font specified for a current window. The GetForegroundColor(), GetBackground-Color(), and GetFont() methods are very similar; all three call the PM API function WinQueryPresParam() to request the specified color or font from the window.

```
//----------------------
// GetForegroundColor() \
//-----------------------------------------------------------------------------
//
// Description:
//     This method gets the foreground (text) color of the window returning
//     it as separated RGB values.
//
// Parameters:
//     pbyRed       - Pointer to output location for Red level for the window
//     pbyGreen     - Pointer to output location for Green level for the window
//     pbyBlue      - Pointer to output location for Blue level for the window
//
// Returns:
//     void
//
void C_WINDOW::GetForegroundColor( BYTE *pbyRed, BYTE *pbyGreen, BYTE *pbyBlue )
{
   RGB2    rgb;

   // Get the foreground color
   WinQueryPresParam( Window(), PP_FOREGROUNDCOLOR, 0, NULL, sizeof(RGB2),
                                              &rgb, QPF_NOINHERIT );

   // Separate the RGB values
   *pbyRed = rgb.bRed;
   *pbyGreen = rgb.bGreen;
   *pbyBlue = rgb.bBlue;
}

//----------------------
// GetBackgroundColor() \
//-----------------------------------------------------------------------------
//
// Description:
//     This method gets the background color of the window, returning
//     it as separated RGB values.
//
// Parameters:
//     pbyRed       - Pointer to output location for Red level for the window
//     pbyGreen     - Pointer to output location for Green level for the window
//     pbyBlue      - Pointer to output location for Blue level for the window
//
```

```
// Returns:
//     void
//
void C_WINDOW::GetBackgroundColor( BYTE *pbyRed, BYTE *pbyGreen, BYTE *pbyBlue )
{
   RGB2    rgb;

   // Get the background color
   WinQueryPresParam( Window(), PP_BACKGROUNDCOLOR, 0, NULL, sizeof(RGB2),
                                              &rgb, QPF_NOINHERIT );

   // Separate the RGB value
   *pbyRed = rgb.bRed;
   *pbyGreen = rgb.bGreen;
   *pbyBlue = rgb.bBlue;
}

//-----------
// GetFont() \
//------------------------------------------------------------------------
//
// Description:
//     This method gets the current font of the window, returning as a
//     string in the format size.font.
//
// Parameters:
//     szFont      - Pointer to current window font
//
// Returns:
//     void
//
void C_WINDOW::GetFont( char *szFont )
{
   char    szString[256];

   WinQueryPresParam( Window(), PP_FONTNAMESIZE, 0, NULL, 256, szString,
                                              QPF_NOINHERIT );
   strcpy( szFont, szString );
}
```

The PM API function call WinInvalidateRect() is used to force a window to repaint itself. In PMCLASS the C_WINDOW method also provides this functionality. In fact, the Invalidate() member function simply wraps the WinInvalidate-Rect() function to isolate this operating system specific code from the application.

```
//--------------
// Invalidate() \
//---------------------------------------------------------------------------
//
// Description:
//     This method wraps the WinInvalidateRect() API function used to
//     force a redraw of the window.
//
// Parameters:
//     void
//
// Returns:
//     void
//
void C_WINDOW::Invalidate( void )
{
   // Force the window to be redrawn
   WinInvalidateRect( hWnd, NULL, TRUE );
}
```

Another simple code wrapper is the Focus() method. It forces PM to assign control of the mouse and keyboard to the window associated with this instance.

If you are using Focus() in a window creation method, you should have the function return a TRUE value rather than the typical FALSE. Failing to do this can result in a focus setting failure. If you are setting the focus and it is failing, this is the first thing you should check.

```
//---------
// Focus() \
//---------------------------------------------------------------------------
//
// Description:
//     This method wraps the WinSetFocus() API function and is used to
//     give control of the mouse and keyboard to the window.
//
// Parameters:
//     void
//
// Returns:
//     void
//
void C_WINDOW::Focus( void )
{
   WinSetFocus( HWND_DESKTOP, hWnd );
}
```

As I mentioned earlier, before we can create any window, it needs to be registered with Presentation Manager. Using the standard API, this operation involves several tedious steps complicated by multiple parameters. Using the interface provided in the PMCLASS library, new window objects typically manage all of this automatically, using just two calls to C_WINDOW methods.

The first of these methods is Register(). Like WinRegisterWindow(), Register() tells the operating system about a new window, but it does this simply by specifying a class name string. All window message procedure handling is performed for a window class by virtue of being derived from C_WINDOW.

```
//------------
// Register() \
//---------------------------------------------------------------------------
//
// Description:
//     This method registers a window class of the specified name. This
//     must be performed before the window can be created.
//
// Parameters:
//     szClass      - Name of the class being registered
//
// Returns:
//     BOOL         - Error result of the registration
//
BOOL C_WINDOW::Register( char *szClass )
{
   ClassName( szClass );

   return WinRegisterClass( 0, szClassName, (PFNWP)StdWndProc,
                                    CS_SIZEREDRAW, sizeof(C_WINDOW *) );
}
```

The second method required to initiate a new window instance with PMCLASS is, of course, Create(). If you look at the source code for C_WINDOW::Create(), you will notice that nothing actually gets created. The handles for the window and its owner are stored in the class, and the method sends a PM_CREATE to the window. No windows get created—so where are the windows? As you will see when we examine the C_WINDOW_CHILD and C_WINDOW_STD classes, the real windows get created there. The reason for this is that there are several types of windows created in distinct ways.

Control windows that originate within dialog resources are automatically created when the dialogs are loaded. All PMCLASS objects need to do is "connect" to an existing window.

The C_WINDOW::Create() method manages all the window creation code common to all types of windows. For example, look at C_LISTBOX; you will see that C_LISTBOX::Create() performs some list box specific creation and finishes by calling the C_WINDOW::Create() method.

```
//----------
// Create() \
//-----------------------------------------------------------------------
//
// Description:
//     This method accepts a parent/owner window and a window handle and
//     creates an association between the two. If a message table was
//     specified when the instance was created, a PM_CREATE message
//     is generated.
//
// Parameters:
//     hFrameWnd   - Owner window handle
//     hWnd        - Window handle of this instance
//
// Returns:
//     void
//
void C_WINDOW::Create( HWND hFrameWnd, HWND hWnd )
{
   // Make sure our parent knows about the new window handle
   ParentWindow( hFrameWnd );
   Window( hWnd );

   // Tell the Window procedure about the this pointer
   if( pxtMsgTable )
       SendMsg( PM_CREATE, MPFROMP( this ), 0 );
}
```

After a window has reached the end of its useful life, it should be destroyed. The PM way to accomplish this is by placing a call to WinDestroyWindow() function. PMCLASS wraps this operating system specific code into an equivalent method Destroy().

```
//-----------
// Destroy() \
//-----------------------------------------------------------------------
//
// Description:
//     This method can be called to destroy a window. It wraps the
//     WinDestroyWindow() API to accomplish this.
//
// Parameters:
//     void
//
// Returns:
//     void
//
void C_WINDOW::Destroy( void )
```

```
{
   // Destroy the frame window for this instance
   WinDestroyWindow( WinQueryWindow( hWnd, QW_PARENT ) );
}
```

To associate the message table with the window object, C_WINDOW implements the MessageTable() method. This routine is used internally by the class and should never be invoked from user code.

```
//----------------
// MessageTable() \
//-------------------------------------------------------------------------
//
// Description:
//     This method assigns a value to the message table class attribute.
//
// Parameters:
//     void
//
// Returns:
//     void
//
void C_WINDOW::MessageTable( T_MSG_TABLE *pxtMsg )
{
   pxtMsgTable = pxtMsg;
}
```

Each window in the system has the option of processing command messages that are generated using the WM_COMMAND window message. To assign a command table to begin processing WM_COMMAND messages, use the CommandTable() method. Once this table is attached, processing of commands begins automatically.

```
//----------------
// CommandTable() \
//-------------------------------------------------------------------------
//
// Description:
//     This method assigns a value to the command table class attribute.
//
// Parameters:
//     void
//
// Returns:
//     void
//
void C_WINDOW::CommandTable( T_MSG_TABLE *pxtCommands )
```

```
{
   pxtCommandTable = pxtCommands;
}
```

The key feature of PMCLASS that distinguishes it from ordinary Presentation Manager code is the use of message and command tables. These tables eliminate the need for those unwieldy case statements familiar to OS/2 C programmers. No application written with PMCLASS needs to have these huge case statements. Instead, the mother of all PMCLASS windows, C_WINDOW, provides a WindowProc() method that controls the flow of window messages.

WindowProc() examines messages as they arrive in the window's message loop. For each message, the message table is scanned for a match and, if found, the associated message handler is called. If the message arriving into WindowProc() is a WM_COMMAND, WindowProc() scans any assigned command table owned by the instance.

The result of the table implementation supported by WindowProc() is a very clean, compact design that can be used for both rapid prototyping and finished applications. The important distinction between PMCLASS and other commercial class libraries is that is does not prevent or complicate interfacing to the standard PM API. API calls can be embedded transparently.

```
//------------
// WindowProc \
//------------------------------------------------------------------------
//
// Description:
//     This method is the message manager for the window. It accepts a
//     message and two optional parameters and compares the supplied
//     message to those stored in the window's message table. If a
//     message match is found the appropriate message handler is invoked.
//
// Parameters:
//     lMsg         - Message passed to the dialog window
//     mp1          - Pointer to first optional parameter
//     mp2          - Pointer to second optional parameter
//
// Returns:
//     Result of command or default handler result.
//
void *C_WINDOW::WindowProc( ULONG lMsg, void *mp1, void *mp2 )
{
   int      iCtr;
   int      iCmdCtr;
   void *(C_WINDOW::*Function)( void *, void * );

   iCtr = 0;
   while( (pxtMsgTable+iCtr)->lMsg )
```

```
    {
        // If this is a WM_COMMAND message, see if the window has defined
        // a command table
        if( lMsg == WM_COMMAND && pxtCommandTable )
        {
            // Scan the window's command table for the command
            iCmdCtr = 0;
            while( (pxtCommandTable+iCmdCtr)->lMsg )
            {
                // Did we find a command match
                if( (pxtCommandTable+iCmdCtr)->lMsg == COMMANDMSG(&lMsg)->cmd )
                {
                    // Process the window command by calling the correct
                    // processor
                    Function = (pxtCommandTable+iCmdCtr)->Function;
                    return (this->*Function)( mp1, mp2 );
                }

                iCmdCtr++;
            }
        }

        if( (pxtMsgTable+iCtr)->lMsg == lMsg )
        {
            Function = (pxtMsgTable+iCtr)->Function;
            return (this->*Function)( mp1, mp2 );
        }

        iCtr++;
    }

    return WinDefWindowProc( Window(), lMsg, mp1, mp2 );
}
```

The final function in the WINDOW.CPP source file is a C function called StdWndProc(). This function acts as the link between the unwieldy world of C API and the control and comfort of PMCLASS. StdWndProc() is a standard Presentation Manager window procedure referenced by the Register() method.

All PMCLASS windows (except dialogs) are managed by the same window function, forcing developers to write a separate window manager procedure for each window. StdWndProc() first monitors incoming window messages looking for a WM_CREATE message. When this message arrives, a pointer to the window instance is stored in the user data area for this window. This helps to eliminate global memory use and allows StdWndProc() to determine which window the message needs to be sent to. Once the instance information is stored in the user area of the window, all further message processing is managed by C_WINDOW::WindowProc().

StdWndProc() also looks for WM_DESTROY messages. This is the last message that a window will see—it is the notification that StdWndProc() uses to remove the object data pointer from its user data area, thus preventing the PMCLASS window handler, WindowProc(), from trying to process anything else.

```
//-------------
// StdWndProc \
//---------------------------------------------------------------------------
//
// Description:
//     Function acts as the interface between the PM C API interface
//     and the C++ class interface used by the PMCLASS library. Once
//     the instance has been created, all message processing passes
//     to the handler methodwithin the object. If the window instance has
//     not yet been created, the PM default interface manages the message.
//
// Parameters:
//     lMsg          - Message passed to the window
//     mp1           - Pointer to first optional parameter
//     mp2           - Pointer to second optional parameter
//
// Returns:
//     Result of command or default handler result.
//
MRESULT EXPENTRY StdWndProc( HWND hWnd, ULONG lMsg, MPARAM mp1, MPARAM mp2 )
{
   C_WINDOW    *pxcThis;

   // Look for PM_CREATE messages
   if( lMsg == PM_CREATE )
   {
       // Set the user window word to an instance of this
       WinSetWindowULong( hWnd, 0, (ULONG)mp1 );
   }

   // Look for WM_DESTROY
   if( lMsg == WM_DESTROY )
   {
       // Remove the pointer to this from the window word
       WinSetWindowULong( hWnd, 0, (ULONG)0 );
   }

   // Get a pointer to the current window instance
   pxcThis = (C_WINDOW *)WinQueryWindowULong( hWnd, 0 );

   // If the instance is defined and it has a window, pass the message
   // to the objects window message handler
   if( pxcThis && pxcThis->Window() )
```

```
    {
        return pxcThis->WindowProc( lMsg, mp1, mp2 );
    }

    // No instance so default the message
    return WinDefWindowProc( hWnd, lMsg, mp1, mp2 );
}
```

As you can appreciate, C_WINDOW is a huge class, but for the most part it contains mundane function wrappers used to hide the PM API in a truly object-oriented shell. The key features of C_WINDOW are the use of window message and command tables, and I hope I have provided sufficiently detailed information. These features will be crucial in Part III of this book, but we will begin to see tables used in the classes in this chapter. For example, look at C_TBAR_BUTTON or C_TOOLBAR class code.

Standard Window Class

At least one window in any application you write for Presentation Manager will probably be a standard window. A standard window typically has a sizable border, a title bar, and a menu, and acts as the primary interface between your application and your users.

PMCLASS implements a C_WINDOW_STD class to account for the features required to create standard application windows. You will be using most of the methods in this class, though the class itself will generally be abstract. Most of the standard windows you create will have their own specific features, so you will typically derive new classes from C_WINDOW_STD.

C_WINDOW_STD is shown graphically in Figure 6-4.

C_WINDOW_STD			
char *	szClassName	C_WINDOW_STD()	
ULONG	lFrameFlags	void	Create()
		void	GetSizePosition()
		void	SetSizePosition()
		void	SetPosition()
		void	SetSize()
		void	SetTitle()
		void	GetTitle()
		void	WCF_Standard()
		void	WCF_Icon()
		void	WCF_SysMenu()

C_WINDOW_STD *(Continued)*		
	void	WCF_Menu()
	void	WCF_MinButton()
	void	WCF_MaxButton()
	void	WCF_TitleBar()
	void	WCF_Border()
	void	WCF_DialogBorder()
	void	WCF_SizingBorder()
	void	WCF_TaskList()
	void	WCF_ShellPosition()
	virtual void *	MsgPaint()

Figure 6-4 C_WINDOW_STD class

The header file for C_WINDOW_STD is shown in Listing 6-3:

```
class C_WINDOW_STD : public C_WINDOW
{
  private:
      char    *szClassName;
      ULONG   lFrameFlags;

  public:
      _Export      C_WINDOW_STD( void );
      _Export      C_WINDOW_STD( T_MSG_TABLE *pxtMsg );
      void    _Export     Create( int iID, char *szTitle );
      void    _Export     GetSizePosition( int *piX, int *piY,
                                           int *piW, int *piL );
      void    _Export     GetSize( int *piX, int *piY );
      void    _Export     GetPosition( int *piW, int *piL );
      void    _Export     SetSizePosition( int iX, int iY, int iCX, int iCY );
      void    _Export     SetPosition( int iX, int iY );
      void    _Export     SetSize( int iCX, int iCY );
      void    _Export     SetTitle( char *szTitle );
      void    _Export     GetTitle( char *szTitle, int iLength );

      void    _Export WCF_Standard( void );
      void    _Export WCF_Icon( void );
      void    _Export WCF_SysMenu( void );
      void    _Export WCF_Menu( void );
      void    _Export WCF_MinButton( void );
      void    _Export WCF_MaxButton( void );
      void    _Export WCF_TitleBar( void );
      void    _Export WCF_Border( void );
      void    _Export WCF_DialogBorder( void );
```

```
        void    _Export WCF_SizingBorder( void );
        void    _Export WCF_TaskList( void );
        void    _Export WCF_ShellPosition( void );

        // Window Message Handlers
        virtual void *  _Export     MsgPaint( void *mp1, void *mp2 );
};
```

Listing 6-3 WINSTD.HPP – Class definition for C_WINDOW_STD

C_WINDOW_STD implements two constructors. Like many of the classes in the PMCLASS library, its first constructor is the void constructor code, which actually does very little; however, it is included to simplify debugging later.

The first constructor defaults the window style word to FCF_SHELLPOSITION, which prompts the Presentation Manager to size and position the window automatically when it is created.

```
//-------------
// Constructor \
//---------------------------------------------------------------------------
//
// Description:
//      This is the void constructor for the C_WINDOW_STD class. It defaults
//      the created window style word to FCF_SHELLPOSITION.
//
// Parameters:
//      none
//
C_WINDOW_STD::C_WINDOW_STD( void ) : C_WINDOW()
{
   lFrameFlags = FCF_SHELLPOSITION;
}
```

The second constructor is the one that you will use most often when interfacing to your own code. This constructor accepts a pointer to a PMCLASS message table, which it relays to the C_WINDOW base class. This constructor initializes the window style word to zero, since it requires one or more of the WCF_ methods to be called before the window is displayed.

```
//-------------
// Constructor \
//---------------------------------------------------------------------------
//
// Description:
//      This constructor for the C_WINDOW_STD class accepts a pointer to a
//      message table and sets up the message handler for the instance.
//      It defaults the created window style word to 0.
```

```
//
// Parameters:
//     pxtMsg      - Pointer to window message table
//
C_WINDOW_STD::C_WINDOW_STD( T_MSG_TABLE *pxtMsg ) : C_WINDOW( pxtMsg )
{
   lFrameFlags = 0;
}
```

The C_WINDOW_STD class references something referred to previously as the "window style word." This attribute is passed into the style parameter of the PM API WinCreateStdWindow() function in order to attach certain characteristics to a window. For example, a window may have a title or a system menu, or you may want to display a window of a fixed size and prevent the user from resizing or moving it.

PMCLASS implements several WCF_ methods to select the various window embellishments individually. The first of these methods is WFC_Standard(). This method creates a standard default window with a title bar, minimize and maximize buttons, a system menu and an application menu, and implements a sizable border.

For most purposes, this is the method you will want to invoke when creating an application window.

```
//----------------
// WCF_Standard() \
//-------------------------------------------------------------------------
//
// Description:
//     This method adds the standard window style to the style word.
//
// Parameters:
//     void
//
// Returns:
//     void
//
void C_WINDOW_STD::WCF_Standard( void )
{
   lFrameFlags |= FCF_STANDARD;
}
```

If you are not using the WFC_Standard() method, then you can choose the window characteristics individually. WFC_SysMenu() enables the system menu button in the upper left corner of the window.

```
//---------------
// WCF_SysMenu() \
//---------------------------------------------------------------------------
//
// Description:
//     This method adds the system menu window style to the style word.
//
// Parameters:
//     void
//
// Returns:
//     void
//
void C_WINDOW_STD::WCF_SysMenu( void )
{
   lFrameFlags |= FCF_SYSMENU;
}
```

To implement a program icon for your window, call the WCF_Icon() method. This replaces the system menu button with a micro-representation of the program icon in the program's resource file and also displays a normal-sized icon when the program is minimized.

The resource file must have an icon defined with the same resource identifier as the window, or the creation of the window will fail.

```
//------------
// WCF_Icon() \
//---------------------------------------------------------------------------
//
// Description:
//     This method adds the program icon style to the style word.
//     PM assumes that there will be an icon resource with the same
//     id number as the window or window creation will fail.
//
// Parameters:
//     void
//
// Returns:
//     void
//
void C_WINDOW_STD::WCF_Icon( void )
{
   lFrameFlags |= FCF_ICON;
}
```

To implement an application menu, call the WCF_Menu() method. This assumes that a menu with the same resource identifier as the window exists in the resource file. If the menu does not exist, window creation will fail.

This method also adds FCF_ACCELTABLE to the window style word. This indicates the menu has an associated keyboard accelerator table. This table must also have the same resource identifier as the application window that owns it.

```
//------------
// WCF_Menu() \
//-------------------------------------------------------------------------
//
// Description:
//     This method adds the program menu style to the style word. The PM window
//     handler assumes that there will be menu and accelerator resources with
//     the same id number as the window or the window creation will fail.
//
// Parameters:
//     void
//
// Returns:
//     void
//
void C_WINDOW_STD::WCF_Menu( void )
{
   lFrameFlags |= (FCF_MENU | FCF_ACCELTABLE);
}
```

To add a minimize button to the upper right corner of the window, call the WCF_MinButton().

```
//-----------------
// WCF_MinButton() \
//-------------------------------------------------------------------------
//
// Description:
//     This method adds a minimize button to the window.
//
// Parameters:
//     void
//
// Returns:
//     void
//
void C_WINDOW_STD::WCF_MinButton( void )
{
   lFrameFlags |= FCF_MINBUTTON;
}
```

Calling the WCF_MaxButton() method adds a maximize button to the upper right corner of the application window, beside the minimize button.

```
//-----------------
// WCF_MaxButton() \
//-------------------------------------------------------------------------
//
// Description:
//     This method adds a maximize button to the window.
//
// Parameters:
//     void
//
// Returns:
//     void
//
void C_WINDOW_STD::WCF_MaxButton( void )
{
   lFrameFlags |= FCF_MAXBUTTON;
}
```

Most applications need a title bar so users can distinguish one application from another. The WCF_TitleBar() method causes the title bar to be shown when the application window is displayed. Note that use of the system menu button, icon, or minimize/maximize buttons necessitates the use of a title bar, so you may be required to call WCF_TitleBar() as part of the window setup.

```
//----------------
// WCF_TitleBar() \
//-------------------------------------------------------------------------
//
// Description:
//     This method adds a title bar to the window.
//
// Parameters:
//     void
//
// Returns:
//     void
//
void C_WINDOW_STD::WCF_TitleBar( void )
{
   lFrameFlags |= FCF_TITLEBAR;
}
```

Three types of borders can be assigned to an application window. The first border type is a simple thin border that cannot be resized. This border is of limited use for applications windows; nevertheless, it has been implemented because it is supported by Presentation Manager. To add this type of border to an application window, call the WCF_Border method.

```
//--------------
// WCF_Border() \
//-----------------------------------------------------------------------------
//
// Description:
//     This method adds a thin-line border to the window.
//
// Parameters:
//     void
//
// Returns:
//     void
//
void C_WINDOW_STD::WCF_Border( void )
{
   lFrameFlags |= FCF_BORDER;
}
```

The second border type is a thicker border that is also not resizable. This border is most often observed in dialog window displays, but for some applications this border style may be desirable. To create this style, call the WCF_DialogBorder() method.

```
//--------------------
// WCF_DialogBorder() \
//-----------------------------------------------------------------------------
//
// Description:
//     This method adds a dialog border to the window.
//
// Parameters:
//     void
//
// Returns:
//     void
//
void C_WINDOW_STD::WCF_DialogBorder( void )
{
   lFrameFlags |= FCF_DLGBORDER;
}
```

The final border type is one that you will most often see implemented for applications. This is a thicker border that can be resized as desired. A call to WCF_SizingBorder() adds this border style to an application window.

Note that the three border types are mutually exclusive. No attempt should be made to specify more than one of these borders for a window, or results will be unpredictable.

```
//--------------------
// WCF_SizingBorder() \
//-------------------------------------------------------------------------------
//
// Description:
//     This method adds a sizable border to the window.
//
// Parameters:
//     void
//
// Returns:
//     void
//
void C_WINDOW_STD::WCF_SizingBorder( void )
{
   lFrameFlags |= FCF_SIZEBORDER;
}
```

The OS/2 WorkPlace Shell interface offers a useful feature called the task list. This is a list of all open windows known to WPS, and offers users the ability to show or hide windows or to close them completely. You can optionally prevent your application from showing up in this list, although such action is not recommended. A call to WCF_TaskList() causes Presentation Manager to add the title of the window to the WPS task list.

```
//----------------
// WCF_TaskList() \
//-------------------------------------------------------------------------------
//
// Description:
//     This method adds the window to the WPS task list.
//
// Parameters:
//     void
//
// Returns:
//     void
//
void C_WINDOW_STD::WCF_TaskList( void )
{
```

```
   lFrameFlags |= FCF_TASKLIST;
}
```

The window can be configured such that, when it is displayed for the first time, Presentation Manager will place it on the WPS desktop automatically. Both the initial size and position of the application window are under PM control. If this is what you wish, then call WCF_ShellPosition() when setting up the window.

Enabling automatic window placement may be undesirable in some situations. If the application preserves its window size and position between sessions, then the WCF_ShellPosition() method should not be called, otherwise an annoying flicker will result because PM will display the window, and then the application code will resize and/or move the window.

```
//---------------------
// WCF_ShellPosition() \
//-------------------------------------------------------------------------
//
// Description:
//     This method tells PM to size the window automatically when it is
//     created.
//
// Parameters:
//     void
//
// Returns:
//     void
//
void C_WINDOW_STD::WCF_ShellPosition( void )
{
   lFrameFlags |= FCF_SHELLPOSITION;
}
```

With the WCF_ methods behind us, let's move on to some of the other capabilities of the C_WINDOW_STD class. The remainder of the methods in the class deal with setting or detecting window size and position.

The first of these methods is GetSizePosition(). This method returns the location and dimensions of the application window. Note that the location for an application window is always relative to the OS/2 desktop with coordinate (0,0) representing the lower left corner of the window.

```
//-------------------
// GetSizePosition() \
//-------------------------------------------------------------------------
//
// Description:
//     This method retrieves the current window size and position relative
//     to the WPS desktop.
```

```
//
// Parameters:
//     *piX, *piY   - Pointers to a data area to get the X,Y coordinates
//     *piW,*piL    - Pointers to a data area to get the window dimensions
//
// Returns:
//     void
//
void C_WINDOW_STD::GetSizePosition( int *piX, int *piY, int *piW, int *piL )
{
   SWP      swp;

   // Query PM to get the size and position of the window
   WinQueryWindowPos( WinQueryWindow( Window(), QW_PARENT ), &swp );

   // Format the size and position into a form we can use
   *piX = swp.x;
   *piY = swp.y;
   *piW = swp.cx;
   *piL = swp.cy;
}
```

The GetPosition() method returns only positional information for the application window. This data is returned in pixels and is relative to the OS/2 desktop.

```
//---------------
// GetPosition() \
//--------------------------------------------------------------------------
//
// Description:
//     This method retrieves the current window position relative to the
//     WPS desktop.
//
// Parameters:
//     *piX, *piY   - Pointers to a data area to get the X,Y coordinates
//
// Returns:
//     void
//
void C_WINDOW_STD::GetPosition( int *piX, int *piY )
{
   SWP      swp;

   // Query PM to get the size and position of the window
   WinQueryWindowPos( WinQueryWindow( Window(), QW_PARENT ), &swp );

   // Format the position into a form we can use
   *piX = swp.x;
   *piY = swp.y;
}
```

The GetSize() method returns a frame window's size in pixels. Note that the C_WINDOW class implements methods with the same names, but because there is a distinction between the frame window and the client area window, C_WINDOW_STD requires additional methods to interact specifically on the frame. Rather than create methods with new names, the C_WINDOW methods are overloaded. This avoids the confusion of having multiple methods performing the same function for different types of windows.

If you are planning to port PMCLASS to Windows, or some other graphical environment, there may be no difference between the client and the frame, so these extra methods can likely be omitted.

```
//-----------
// GetSize() \
//--------------------------------------------------------------------------
//
// Description:
//     This method retrieves the current window size.
//
// Parameters:
//     *piW,*piL    - Pointers to a data area to get the window dimensions
//
// Returns:
//     void
//
void C_WINDOW_STD::GetSize( int *piW, int *piL )
{
   SWP     swp;

   // Query PM to get the size and position of the window
   WinQueryWindowPos( WinQueryWindow( Window(), QW_PARENT ), &swp );

   // Format the size into a form we can use
   *piW = swp.cx;
   *piL = swp.cy;
}
```

Both the size and position of an application window can be set with a call to the SetSizePosition() method. This method accepts an X and Y coordinate for the lower left corner of the window and a width and height for the window.

```
//-------------------
// SetSizePosition() \
//-----------------------------------------------------------------------------
//
// Description:
//     This method sets the current window size and position relative
//     to the WPS desktop.
//
// Parameters:
//     iX, iY       -  The new X,Y coordinates of the window
//     iCX,iCY      -  The new dimensions of the window
//
// Returns:
//     void
//
void C_WINDOW_STD::SetSizePosition( int iX, int iY, int iCX, int iCY )
{
   // Set the window size and position
   WinSetWindowPos( WinQueryWindow( Window(), QW_PARENT ), HWND_TOP,
       iX, iY, iCX, iCY, SWP_MOVE | SWP_SIZE | SWP_ZORDER | SWP_SHOW );
}
```

The position may be set independently by calling the SetPosition() method in the C_WINDOW_STD class. This position is measured in pixels and is relative to the OS/2 desktop.

```
//---------------
// SetPosition() \
//-----------------------------------------------------------------------------
//
// Description:
//     This method sets the current window position relative to the WPS
//     desktop.
//
// Parameters:
//     iX, iY       - The new X,Y coordinates of the window
//
// Returns:
//     void
//
void C_WINDOW_STD::SetPosition( int iX, int iY )
{
   // Set the window position
   WinSetWindowPos( WinQueryWindow( Window(), QW_PARENT ),
                               HWND_TOP, iX, iY, 0, 0, SWP_MOVE );}
}
```

Setting the size of a window can be achieved with a call to the SetSize() method. This window size is adjusted according to parameters passed to the method, leaving the position unchanged.

```
//-----------
// SetSize() \
//-----------------------------------------------------------------------
//
// Description:
//     This method sets the current size of the window in pixels.
//
// Parameters:
//     iCX,iCY     -  The new dimensions of the window
//
// Returns:
//     void
//
void C_WINDOW_STD::SetSize( int iCX, int iCY )
{
   // Set the window size
   WinSetWindowPos( WinQueryWindow( Window(), QW_PARENT ),
                                   HWND_TOP, 0, 0, iCX, iCY, SWP_SIZE );
}
```

The title shown in the title bar of the application can be set by calling the SetTitle(). Though the Presentation Manager window does not specify limits for the title, I have found empirically that the title is limited to 56 characters.

```
//------------
// SetTitle() \
//-----------------------------------------------------------------------
//
// Description:
//     This method sets the current window title shown in the title bar.
//
// Parameters:
//     szTitle     - Pointer to new title string
//
// Returns:
//     void
//
void C_WINDOW_STD::SetTitle( char *szTitle )
{
   // Show the new window title
   WinSetWindowText( ParentWindow(), szTitle );
}
```

The window title can be retrieved by calling the C_WINDOW_STD method GetText(). GetText() accepts a pointer to a target character string and a length of the buffer where the title string will be stored.

```
//------------
// GetTitle() \
//---------------------------------------------------------------------------
//
// Description:
//     This method retrieves the current window title shown in the title bar.
//
// Parameters:
//     szTitle     - Pointer to a data area to get the current title string
//     iLength     - Size of the out buffer in bytes
//
// Returns:
//     void
//
void C_WINDOW_STD::GetTitle( char *szTitle, int iLength )
{
   // Get the title from the title bar
   WinQueryWindowText( ParentWindow(), iLength, szTitle );
}
```

So far we have looked at many methods for the C_WINDOW_STD class, but as yet none of the methods described actually creates the window. The Create() method does this by calling the WinCreateStdWindow() function, which is part of the Presentation Manager API.

Create() accepts a window resource identifier and a pointer to a null terminated title string. As I mentioned previously, the window identifier is also used to control the display of a window icon, system menus, and keyboard accelerator table, and can be an integer of any size.

```
//----------
// Create() \
//---------------------------------------------------------------------------
//
// Description:
//     This method performs the actual window creation by calling the PM API
//     WinCreateStdWindow(). It creates a window using the parameters
//     specified by the caller.
//
// Parameters:
//     iID         - Window ID for the new window
//     szTitle     - Title string for the window
//
```

```
// Returns:
//     void
//
void C_WINDOW_STD::Create( int iID, char *szTitle )
{
   HWND        hFrameWnd;
   HWND        hWnd;

   // Create a new standard window
   hFrameWnd = WinCreateStdWindow( HWND_DESKTOP, 0, &lFrameFlags,
               ClassName(), szTitle, 0, (HMODULE)NULL, iID, &hWnd );

   // Associate the client window with the frame
   C_WINDOW::Create( hFrameWnd, hWnd );
}
```

Virtually every standard application window that you will ever create will need to perform some sort of default painting operation to paint its client area. When I started building OS/2 applications, I noticed that the code to process the WM_PAINT message was the same for every application window. When I made the shift to C++, I decided that the plan for PMCLASS should include a default paint handler so I didn't have to keep reproducing the same code.

The MsgPaint() method in C_WINDOW_STD is a virtual method that accomplishes this. In the rare event that a new paint handler is required, this one can be overridden using the capabilities of the compiler. To invoke this method to handle WM_PAINT messages in child windows, add the following line to any message tables.

```
   DECLARE_MSG( WM_PAINT,       C_WINDOW_STD::MsgPaint )
```

MsgPaint() calls the WinBeginPaint() and WinEndPaint() APIs as required by PM, and in between these calls, acquires the dimensions of the client area rectangle and paints it a neutral color (typically button gray).

```
//----------
// MsgPaint \
//-----------------------------------------------------------------------
// Event:        WM_PAINT
// Cause:        Issued by the OS when the window needs to be redrawn
// Description: This method is so commonly used that it has been provided
//               at this level in the code to avoid having to recode it for
//               each application window.
//
void *C_WINDOW_STD::MsgPaint( void *mp1, void *mp2 )
{
   HPS     hps;
   RECTL   rc;
```

```
    hps = WinBeginPaint( Window(), 0L, &rc );

    WinFillRect( hps, &rc, SYSCLR_APPWORKSPACE );
    GpiSetColor( hps, CLR_NEUTRAL );

    WinEndPaint( hps );

    return FALSE;
}
```

Child Window Class

Child windows include all the embellishments used in GUI programming, including toolbars, buttons, list boxes, etc., all modified forms of basic windows. Most of the remaining classes in this chapter are derived from the C_WINDOW_CHILD class.

The abstract C_WINDOW_CHILD class is actually fairly small, primarily consisting of overridden methods defined in the C_WINDOW parent class. Under normal circumstances you will not be much interested in the contents of this class, but you may derive your own child objects, so for that reason I will describe it.

C_WINDOW_CHILD		
C_WINDOW *pxcParent	C_WINDOW_CHILD()	
	void	ParentObject()
	C_WINDOW	*ParentObject()
	void	Create()
	void	SetSizePosition()
	void	SetPosition()
	void	SetSize()

Figure 6-5 C_WINDOW_CHILD class

The header file for C_WINDOW_CHILD is shown in Listing 6-4:

```
class C_WINDOW_CHILD : public C_WINDOW
{
   private:
      C_WINDOW     *pxcParent;      // Pointer to parent window

   public:
     _Export   C_WINDOW_CHILD( void );
     _Export   C_WINDOW_CHILD( T_MSG_TABLE *pxtMsg );
     _Export   C_WINDOW_CHILD( C_WINDOW *pxcParentObj, T_MSG_TABLE *pxtMsg );
```

```
    void  _Export     ParentObject( C_WINDOW *pxcParentObj );
    void  _Export     Create( int iID, int iMode, char *szTitle,
                                    int iX, int iY, int iCX, int iCY );
    void  _Export    SetSizePosition( int iX, int iY, int iCX, int iCY );
    void  _Export    SetPosition( int iX, int iY );
    void  _Export    SetSize( int iCX, int iCY );

    C_WINDOW * _Export    ParentObject( void );
};
```

Listing 6-4 WINCHILD.HPP – Class definition for C_WINDOW_CHILD

There are three constructors for the C_WINDOW_CHILD class. The first of these is the default constructor, which will be of marginal use unless you are debugging and want to embed debugging statements here.

```
//-------------
// Constructor \
//---------------------------------------------------------------------------
//
// Description:
//    This is the void constructor for the C_WINDOW_CHILD class. It does
//    nothing, but has been placed here for debugging purposes.
//
// Parameters:
//    none
//
C_WINDOW_CHILD::C_WINDOW_CHILD( void ) : C_WINDOW()
{
}
```

The second constructor accepts a pointer to a message table, which it relays to the C_WINDOW parent. Like the previous constructor, you can embed debugging statements into the body if you wish.

```
//-------------
// Constructor \
//---------------------------------------------------------------------------
//
// Description:
//    This is the void constructor for the C_WINDOW_CHILD class. It
//    accepts a pointer to a message table and passes this to the
//    C_WINDOW constructor which is its parent.
//
// Parameters:
//    pxtMsg      - Pointer to window message table
//
```

```
C_WINDOW_CHILD::C_WINDOW_CHILD( T_MSG_TABLE *pxtMsg ) : C_WINDOW( pxtMsg )
{
}
```

The final constructor is the one that will be used most often. It accepts a pointer to an owner object as well as a pointer to a message table for the object. It sets the parent object attribute in the class equal to the owner window, so any of the class methods can access this information.

```
//-------------
// Constructor \
//------------------------------------------------------------------------
//
// Description:
//     This is the void constructor for the C_WINDOW_CHILD class. It
//     accepts a pointer to a message table and passes this to the
//     C_WINDOW constructor which is its parent. The constructor also
//     accepts a pointer to a parent/owner object window.
//
// Parameters:
//     pxcParentObj     - Pointer to parent window object
//     pxtMsg           - Pointer to window message table
//
C_WINDOW_CHILD::C_WINDOW_CHILD( C_WINDOW *pxcParentObj, T_MSG_TABLE *pxtMsg )
                                                : C_WINDOW( pxtMsg )
{
   ParentObject( pxcParentObj );
}
```

The child window needs to keep track of who created it. The ParentObject() method accepts a pointer to a window and sets the internal class attribute for the owner window accordingly.

```
//----------------
// ParentObject() \
//------------------------------------------------------------------------
//
// Description:
//     This method sets the parent object attribute within the class. This
//     attribute is referenced by many of the other methods within the class.
//
// Parameters:
//     pxcParentObj     - Pointer to parent window object
//
// Returns:
//     void
//
```

```
void C_WINDOW_CHILD::ParentObject( C_WINDOW *pxcParentObj )
{
   pxcParent = pxcParentObj;
}
```

Methods in C_WINDOW_CHILD or its derivative classes may need to access the owner window data. The second ParentObject() method accepts no parameters and returns a pointer to the owner window.

```
//----------------
// ParentObject() \
//---------------------------------------------------------------------
//
// Description:
//     This method queries the class attribute area and returns a pointer
//     to the parent object of this instance's window.
//
// Parameters:
//     void
//
// Returns:
//     C_WINDOW *          - Returns pointer to parent window object
//
C_WINDOW *C_WINDOW_CHILD::ParentObject( void )
{
   return pxcParent;
}
```

Although an instance of C_WINDOW_CHILD may be created, the actual visual window has not yet been made. The Create() method places a call to the standard WinCreateWindow() API function to create the window, and then calls the Create() method from the C_WINDOW parent class to associate the parent widow with this instance.

```
//----------
// Create() \
//---------------------------------------------------------------------
//
// Description:
//     This method performs the actual window creation by calling the PM API
//     WinCreateWindow(). It creates a window using the parameters specified
//     by the caller.
//
// Parameters:
//     iID         - Window ID for the new window
//     iMode       - OS specific parameters for the window creation
//     szTitle     - Title string for the window
```

```
//      iX,iY          - X,Y coordinates for the new window relative to owner
//      iCX,iCY        - Width and height of the window in pels
//
// Returns:
//      void
//
void C_WINDOW_CHILD::Create( int iID, int iMode, char *szTitle,
                                int iX, int iY, int iCX, int iCY )
{
   HWND    hWnd;

   // Create a new child window using the parameters specified
   hWnd = WinCreateWindow( ParentObject()->Window(), ClassName(), szTitle,
          iMode, iX, iY, iCX, iCY, ParentObject()->Window(),
                                          HWND_TOP, iID, 0, 0 );

   // Call the parent create to associate the new window with the parent
   C_WINDOW::Create( ParentObject()->Window(), hWnd );
}
```

Child windows created dynamically (i.e., not within a dialog resource) may need to be resized or repositioned within the owner window's client area. The SetSizePosition() method accepts an X,Y coordinate and a width and height from the caller and performs both of these tasks. It places a call to the standard PM API function WinSetWindowPos(), but hides this operating system specific functionality from PMCLASS-based programs.

```
//-------------------
// SetSizePosition() \
//--------------------------------------------------------------------------
//
// Description:
//      This method accepts new X,Y and width, height and sets the size and
//      position of the window accordingly.
//
// Parameters:
//      iX,iY          - X,Y coordinates for the window relative to owner
//      iCX,iCY        - Width and height of the window in pels
//
// Returns:
//      void
//
void C_WINDOW_CHILD::SetSizePosition( int iX, int iY, int iCX, int iCY )
{
   WinSetWindowPos( Window(), HWND_TOP,
          iX, iY, iCX, iCY, SWP_MOVE | SWP_SIZE | SWP_ZORDER | SWP_SHOW );
}
```

The SetPosition() method is almost identical in nature to the previous method; however, only the position of the child window is changed.

```
//---------------
// SetPosition() \
//------------------------------------------------------------------------
//
// Description:
//     This method accepts new X,Y and sets the position of the window
//     accordingly.
//
// Parameters:
//     iX,iY       - X,Y coordinates for the window relative to owner
//
// Returns:
//     void
//
void C_WINDOW_CHILD::SetPosition( int iX, int iY )
{
   WinSetWindowPos( Window(), HWND_TOP, iX, iY, 0, 0, SWP_MOVE );
}
```

The SetSize() method changes only the size and leaves the position intact. It should be noted that all dimensions for SetSizePosition(), SetPosition(), and SetSize() are in pixels and are relative to the owner window. For example, an X,Y coordinate of (0,0) positions the child window in the bottom left corner of the owner window's client area.

```
//-----------
// SetSize() \
//------------------------------------------------------------------------
//
// Description:
//     This method accepts a new width, height and sets the size of the
//     window accordingly.
//
// Parameters:
//     iCX,iCY         - Width and height of the window in pels
//
// Returns:
//     void
//
void C_WINDOW_CHILD::SetSize( int iCX, int iCY )
{
   WinSetWindowPos( Window(), HWND_TOP, 0, 0, iCX, iCY, SWP_SIZE );
}
```

Dialog Class

Dialog boxes are a fundamental part of every graphical user interface. These windows are normally created using a resource editor to create the entire dialog window as it will appear in the finished application, including the creation of various embellishments such as text strings, edit fields, and list boxes.

Since dialogs play such a key role, PMCLASS needs to address the issue of attaching an object to a dialog. The C_DIALOG class implements this capability of attaching C++ classes directly to dialog resources. The diagram shown in Figure 6-6 illustrates the class definition for C_DIALOG.

C_DIALOG	
	C_DIALOG() void Create() ULONG Process() void Close() void *DialogProc()

Figure 6-6 C_DIALOG class

The header file for C_DIALOG is shown in Listing 6-5:

```
class C_DIALOG : public C_WINDOW_CHILD
{
   public:
       _Export     C_DIALOG( C_WINDOW *pxcParentObj, T_MSG_TABLE *pxtMsg );
       void         _Export     Create( int iID );
       ULONG        _Export     Process( void );
       void         _Export     Close( int iFlag );
       void *       _Export     DialogProc( ULONG lMsg, void *mp1, void *mp2 );
};
```

Listing 6-5 DIALOG.HPP – Class definition for C_DIALOG

C_DIALOG provides a single constructor, which is used to supply pointers to the parent/owner object and a pointer to the message table used to process window messages for the dialog.

```
//-------------
// Constructor \
//---------------------------------------------------------------------------
//
// Description:
//     This constructor creates an instance of the C_DIALOG class. It
```

```
//     accepts a pointer to a parent window object and a pointer to a
//     message table and passes both of these to its parent constructor.
//
// Parameters:
//     pxcParentObj    - Pointer to owner object window
//     pxtMsg          - Pointer to message table for this class
//
C_DIALOG::C_DIALOG( C_WINDOW *pxcParentObj, T_MSG_TABLE *pxtMsg ) :
                              C_WINDOW_CHILD( pxcParentObj, pxtMsg )
{
}
```

The constructor does not actually associate a dialog resource with the object. To accomplish this, the Create method must be called. Create() accepts a resource identifier that determines which dialog will be loaded from the resource section of the EXE file.

Once the dialog is loaded into memory, the owner window attribute is set within the object. This is the object that was specified in the constructor.

```
//--------
// Create \
//---------------------------------------------------------------------------
//
// Description:
//     This method is used to create the window associated with this
//     instance. It first loads the dialog resource from the resource
//     section of the EXE, then calls the C_WINDOW::Create() method to
//     associate the object with its parent window. The owner of the
//     dialog window is set to the WPS desktop.
// Parameters:
//     iID                 - Resource identifier of the dialog
//
// Returns:
//     void
//
void C_DIALOG::Create( int iID )
{
   HWND        hWnd;

   // Load the dialog box into memory
   hWnd = WinLoadDlg( HWND_DESKTOP, ParentObject()->Window(),
                                    StdDlgProc, 0, iID, this );

   // Tell the C_WINDOW portion of the code about the dialog
   C_WINDOW::Create( ParentObject()->Window(), hWnd );
}
```

The C_DIALOG class provides a second, more specific way to create a dialog. The CreateWithParent() method does not default the window owner to HWND_DESKTOP, as Create() does. Instead, the parent window is specified with the same parameter as the owner, ParentObject()->Window().

This method is particularly useful in certain situations. For example, if you are creating a notebook control and inserting pages, each page (a dialog resource) must be owned by the notebook window rather than the desktop, or operation of the notebook will be unpredictable at best.

```
//------------------
// CreateWithParent \
//------------------------------------------------------------------------
//
// Description:
//     This method is used to create the window associated with this
//     instance. It first loads the dialog resource from the resource
//     section of the EXE, then calls the C_WINDOW::Create() method to
//     associate the object with its owner window. Both the parent and
//     owner of this dialog window are set to the parent window.
//
//     This creation technique is used when the dialog requires an owner
//     window that is not the WPS desktop. For example, a notebook dialog
//     page must be owned by the notebook control.
//
// Parameters:
//     iID                  - Resource identifier of the dialog
//
// Returns:
//     void
//
void C_DIALOG::CreateWithParent( int iID )
{
   HWND        hWnd;

   // Load the dialog box into memory
   hWnd = WinLoadDlg( ParentObject()->Window(), ParentObject()->Window(),
                                      StdDlgProc, 0, iID, this );

   // Tell the C_WINDOW portion of the code about the dialog
   C_WINDOW::Create( ParentObject()->Window(), hWnd );
}
```

To execute the dialog code the Process() method needs to be executed. This method is a simple code wrapper to isolate the application code from the native OS/2 API. Once this method is called, execution in the current thread shifts to the dialog code and will not return until the dialog is dismissed.

```
//---------
// Process \
//----------------------------------------------------------------------------
//
// Description:
//     This method is a simple wrapper that calls the standard API
//     function to process the dialog box.
//
// Parameters:
//     none
//
// Returns:
//     void
//
ULONG C_DIALOG::Process( void )
{
   // Process the dialog box
   return WinProcessDlg( Window() );
}
```

Dialog windows can be closed and their resources reallocated by calling the Close() method. This method will typically be called in the application code responsible for the "Cancel" or "OK" buttons within dialogs. Any message handler intercepting the WM_CLOSE message should call this method as part of its processing.

```
//-------
// Close \
//----------------------------------------------------------------------------
//
// Description:
//     This method is called to close the window and dispose of any system
//     resources it is using.
//
// Parameters:
//     flag    - Set TRUE or FALSE to pass to the Dismiss API function.
//
// Returns:
//     void
//
void C_DIALOG::Close( int iFlag )
{
   // Prevent class from processing further messages
   WinSetWindowULong( Window(), 0, (ULONG)0 );

   // Get rid of the dialog
   WinDismissDlg( Window(), iFlag );
}
```

We discussed the message handler code for the C_WINDOW class earlier. C_DIALOG also provides a method to manage processing window messages; however, where C_DIALOG differs is in how it deals with messages that the handler does not process. In the standard OS/2 API, dialog messages that are not processed are sent to the WinDefDlgProc() routine instead of WinDefWindowProc().

PMCLASS invokes the DialogProc() method anytime a message is sent to the dialog window. DialogProc() scans the message list supplied when the instance was created and, using a simple look-up table mechanism, invokes the correct class method to process the message. Any messages that are not processed are automatically sent to the default message handler in the PM API.

Like the message handler for C_WINDOW, DialogProc() detects WM_COMMAND messages and calls a class method for any command messages that have been specified during the object construction process.

```
//------------
// DialogProc \
//--------------------------------------------------------------------------
//
// Description:
//     This method is the main window message manager for the window.
//     It accepts a message and two optional parameters and compares the
//     supplied message to those stored in the dialogs message table. If a
//     message match is found the appropriate message handler is invoked.
//
// Parameters:
//     lMsg        - Message passed to the dialog window
//     mp1         - Pointer to first optional parameter
//     mp2         - Pointer to second optional parameter
//
// Returns:
//     Result of command or default handler result.
//
void *C_DIALOG::DialogProc( ULONG lMsg, void *mp1, void *mp2 )
{
   int      iCtr;
   int      iCmdCtr;
   void *(C_WINDOW::*Function)( void *, void * );

   iCtr = 0;
   while( (pxtMsgTable+iCtr)->lMsg )
   {
       // If this is a WM_COMMAND message, see if the window has defined
       // a command table
       if( lMsg == WM_COMMAND && pxtCommandTable )
       {
           // Scan the window's command table for the command
           iCmdCtr = 0;
```

```
            while( (pxtCommandTable+iCmdCtr)->lMsg )
            {
                // Did we find a command match
                if( (pxtCommandTable+iCmdCtr)->lMsg == COMMANDMSG(&lMsg)->cmd )
                {
                    // Process the window command by calling the correct
                    // processor
                    Function = (pxtCommandTable+iCmdCtr)->Function;
                    return (this->*Function)( mp1, mp2 );
                }

                iCmdCtr++;
            }
        }

        if( (pxtMsgTable+iCtr)->lMsg == lMsg )
        {
            Function = (pxtMsgTable+iCtr)->Function;
            return (this->*Function)( mp1, mp2 );
        }

        iCtr++;
    }

    return WinDefDlgProc( Window(), lMsg , mp1, mp2 );
}
```

The StdDlgProc() procedure is not a member of the C_DIALOG class, yet the class depends heavily on this function to implement an interface between the C world of the PM API and the C++ world of PMCLASS.

StdDlgProc is responsible for processing window messages for a dialog until its C_DIALOG object has been instantiated and initialized. It also has the responsibility of detecting the WM_INITDLG message sent by Presentation Manager when it creates a dialog window. When this occurs, StdDlgProc() stores a pointer to the object instance in the first window word in the window's user area, in order to permit access to the instance data while processing messages.

Once the object has been completely constructed, StdDlgProc passes all messages to the DialogProc method described previously. Before this, all messages are passed to the default window handler in the PM API.

```
//------------
// StdDlgProc \
//-----------------------------------------------------------------------
//
// Description:
//     Function acts as the interface between the PM C API interface
//     and the C++ class interface used by the PMCLASS library. Once the
```

```
//    instance has been created, all message processing passes to the
//    handler method within the object. If the window instance has not
//    yet been created the PM default interface manages the message.
//
// Parameters:
//    iID              - Resource identifier of the dialog
//
// Returns:
//    void
//
MRESULT EXPENTRY StdDlgProc( HWND hWnd, ULONG lMsg, MPARAM mp1, MPARAM mp2 )
{
   C_DIALOG    *pxcThis;

   // If we are initializing the window
   if( lMsg == WM_INITDLG )
   {
       // Get a pointer to the instance
       pxcThis = (C_DIALOG *)mp2;

       // Save the instance pointer so the class methods can access it
       WinSetWindowULong( hWnd, 0, (ULONG)pxcThis );
   }

   // Get a pointer to this instance
   pxcThis = (C_DIALOG *)WinQueryWindowULong( hWnd, 0 );

   // if this instance has be constructed, then let its handler method
   // look after message processing
   if( pxcThis && pxcThis->Window() )
       return pxcThis->DialogProc( lMsg, mp1, mp2 );

   // The object hasn't been created yet so we have to let PM handle
   // all the messages
   return WinDefDlgProc( hWnd, lMsg , mp1, mp2 );
}
```

Push Button Class

Most graphical user interfaces support controls that mimic push buttons. These controls are typically fairly simple in design—in the case of Presentation Manager, a button control clicked by the user generates a WM_COMMAND message.

The PMCLASS library supports buttons as part of its wrap of the PM API. The C_PUSHBUTTON control shown in Figure 6-7 illustrates a class containing only a constructor with no other methods and no attribute data, a testament to the simplicity of this class.

C_PUSHBUTTON	
	C_PUSHBUTTON()

Figure 6-7 C_PUSHBUTTON class

The header file for C_PUSH_BUTTON is shown in Listing 6-6:

```
class C_PUSHBUTTON : public C_WINDOW_CHILD
{
   public:
      _Export     C_PUSHBUTTON( C_WINDOW *pxcParentObj, int iID,
                                   int iMode, char *szText );
      _Export     C_PUSHBUTTON( C_DIALOG *pxcParentObj, int iID );
};
```

Listing 6-6 PUSHBTN.HPP – Class definition for C_PUSHBUTTON

The C_PUSHBUTTON class contains two constructors. The first accepts a pointer to an owner window and a window, which is fairly typical of PMCLASS classes. It also accepts a mode parameter to add any additional operating system specific configuration for the button control. The final parameter accepted by this constructor is the text that will be displayed on the button face when it is created.

```
//-------------
// Constructor \
//------------------------------------------------------------------------
//
// Description:
//
// Parameters:
//      pxcParentObj     - Pointer to owner object window
//      iID              - Button window identifier
//      iMode            - Additional OS specific parameters
//      szText           - Text used for the button face
//
C_PUSHBUTTON::C_PUSHBUTTON( C_WINDOW *pxcParentObj, int iID, int iMode,
                            char *szText ) : C_WINDOW_CHILD( pxcParentObj, 0 )
{
   ClassName( WC_BUTTON );
   Create( iID, WS_VISIBLE | BS_PUSHBUTTON | iMode, szText, 0, 0, 90, 30 );
}
```

The second C_PUSHBUTTON constructor is used for referencing buttons defined within dialog boxes. This code does not accept the text or mode parameters, since all configuration for the button is determined by the dialog.

```
//-------------
// Constructor \
//----------------------------------------------------------------------------
//
// Description:
//
// Parameters:
//      pxcParentObj         - Pointer to owner object window
//      iID                  - Push button window identifier
//
C_PUSHBUTTON::C_PUSHBUTTON( C_DIALOG *pxcParentObj, int iID )
                          : C_WINDOW_CHILD( (C_WINDOW *)pxcParentObj, 0 )
{
   ClassName( WC_BUTTON );

   // The window was created by the dialog system, so all we need to
   // do is call our parent Create().
   C_WINDOW::Create( ParentObject()->Window(),
                 WinWindowFromID( ParentObject()->Window(), iID ) );
}
```

List Box Class

Almost every program written with a graphical user interface needs to display information in a list form, permitting users to select one or more data items. These list boxes are supported by virtually every graphical user interface, and are typically one of the easier controls for a developer to use. The basic functions required for a list box are adding and removing items, and perhaps a search capability.

The PMCLASS library implements a C_LISTBOX class, which wraps the functionality found in the OS/2 API, as well as Windows. The basic class definition for the C_LISTBOX class is shown in Figure 6-8, as follows.

C_LISTBOX	
	C_LISTBOX() void Insert() void Delete() void DeleteAll() void Select() int Selection() int ItemCount() void ItemText()

Figure 6-8 C_LISTBOX class

The header file for C_LISTBOX is shown in Listing 6-7:

```
class C_LISTBOX : public C_WINDOW_CHILD
{
   public:
        _Export     C_LISTBOX( C_WINDOW *pxcParentObj, int iID, int iMode );
        _Export     C_LISTBOX( C_WINDOW *pxcParentObj, int iID );
        _Export     C_LISTBOX( C_DIALOG *pxcParentObj, int iID );
        void  _Export  Insert( char *szText, int iHow );
        void  _Export  Delete( int iItem );
        void  _Export  DeleteAll( void );
        void  _Export  Select( int iItem, BOOL bBoolean );
        int   _Export  Selection( int iFrom );
        int   _Export  ItemCount( void );
        void  _Export  ItemText( int iIndex, char *szString, int iBufferSize );
};

//----------------------------------
// ListBox Insert() iHow parameters \
//---------------------------------------------------------------------------
#define    LB_INSERT_END     LIT_END            // Insert at end of list
#define    LB_INSERT_SORTA   LIT_SORTASCENDING  // Insert in ascending order
#define    LB_INSERT_SORTD   LIT_SORTDESCENDING // Insert in descending order

//--------------------------------------
// ListBox Selection() iFrom parameters \
//---------------------------------------------------------------------------
#define    LB_SELECT_FIRST   LIT_FIRST          // Start at first item
```

Listing 6-7 LISTBOX.HPP – Class definition for C_LISTBOX

C_LISTBOX implements three constructors; the first two are used for dynamic creation during the execution of a program. The first constructor accepts a pointer to a parent/owner window, and a list box control window identifier.

There is also a third parameter in this constructor, which can be used to specify any additional operating system specific configuration parameters for the list box control. These parameters can include such things as the sort order, the selection method (single or multiple items), etc.

The following table summarizes some of the more common list box modes supported by Presentation Manager.

LS_HORZSCROLL	The list box control enables the user to scroll the list box horizontally with the attached scrollbar.
LS_MULTIPLESEL	The list box control enables the operator to select more than one item at any one time.

LS_EXTENDEDSEL — This style is specified to permit extended selection from the user. It is a variant of multiple selection.

LS_NOADJUSTPOS — This style causes the list box control to be drawn at the size specified. Without this parameter, list boxes will be automatically sized so that no items will be clipped at the top or bottom of the list box.

```
//-------------
// Constructor \
//---------------------------------------------------------------------------
//
// Description:
//     This constructor creates an instance of the C_STATUS class. It is
//     used for dynamic list box creation, and accepts a pointer to a parent
//     window object, and a list box window identifier. The third iMode
//     parameter is used to supply any additional operating system specific
//     parameters for the list box control.
//
// Parameters:
//     pxcParentObj     - Pointer to owner object window
//     iID              - List box window identifier
//     iMode            - Additional OS specific list box parameters
//
C_LISTBOX::C_LISTBOX( C_WINDOW *pxcParentObj, int iID, int iMode )
                                : C_WINDOW_CHILD( pxcParentObj, 0 )
{
   ClassName( WC_LISTBOX );
   Create( iID, iMode, " ", 0, 0, 90, 30 );
}
```

The second constructor is similar to the first, except that it configures the list box control so that a mode parameter is not needed. Using this constructor, the list box is created in a visible state by default.

```
//-------------
// Constructor \
//---------------------------------------------------------------------------
//
// Description:
//     This constructor creates an instance of the C_STATUS class. It is
//     used for dynamic list box creation, and accepts a pointer to a parent
//     window object, and a list box window identifier. This construct
//     defaults the control to be visible and doesn't allow it to adjust
//     its position automatically.
//
```

```
// Parameters:
//      pxcParentObj     - Pointer to owner object window
//      iID              - List box window identifier
//
C_LISTBOX::C_LISTBOX( C_WINDOW *pxcParentObj, int iID )
                            : C_WINDOW_CHILD( pxcParentObj, 0 )
{
   ClassName( WC_LISTBOX );
   Create( iID, WS_VISIBLE | LS_NOADJUSTPOS, " ", 0, 0, 90, 30 );
}
```

The final constructor for the C_LISTBOX class is used when the list box is part of a dialog box resource. The caller specifies an owner window that is a C_DIALOG object and an identifier for the list box control within the dialog. All configuration of the list box is specified at compile time using a resource editor.

```
//-------------
// Constructor \
//---------------------------------------------------------------------------
//
// Description:
//      This constructor creates an instance of the C_STATUS class. It is
//      used for creation of a list box that is already part of a dialog
//      resource. Any modes for the list box are supplied by the dialog
//      resource when it is loaded.
//
//
// Parameters:
//      pxcParentObj          - Pointer to owner object window
//      iID                   - List box window identifier
//
C_LISTBOX::C_LISTBOX( C_DIALOG *pxcParentObj, int iID )
                        : C_WINDOW_CHILD( (C_WINDOW *)pxcParentObj, 0 )
{
   ClassName( WC_LISTBOX );

   // The window was created by the dialog system, so all we need to
   //  do is call our parent Create().
   C_WINDOW::Create( ParentObject()->Window(),
                WinWindowFromID( ParentObject()->Window(), iID ) );
}
```

To add items to a list box object, C_LISTBOX provides an Insert() class. This accepts an operating system specific parameter used to determine how the item will be inserted. For example, an item can be added to the beginning of the list or the end, or can be placed at an absolute location within the list. The second parameter required for the Insert() method is the list text itself. This is specified exactly as it will appear when the list box is displayed.

```
//--------
// Insert \
//------------------------------------------------------------------------
//
// Description:
//     This method is a wrapper to hide the system specific code to insert
//     an item into the list box.
//
// Parameters:
//     szText          - Pointer to text string to insert
//     iHow            - System specific parameter to indicate how the
//                       item will be inserted
// Returns:
//     void
//
void C_LISTBOX::Insert( char *szText, int iHow )
{
   SendMsg( LM_INSERTITEM, MPFROMSHORT( iHow ), MPFROMP( szText ) );
}
```

List items can be removed from a list dynamically. C_LISTBOX provides a Delete() method to accomplish this. The Delete() method must be supplied with an item number to remove, which in OS/2 is a number between zero (for the first item) and the total number of items in the list.

```
//--------
// Delete \
//------------------------------------------------------------------------
//
// Description:
//     This method is a wrapper to hide the system specific code to delete
//     an item from the list box.
//
// Parameters:
//     iItem           - Item to remove from the list (0-n)
//
// Returns:
//     void
//
void C_LISTBOX::Delete( int iItem )
{
   SendMsg( LM_DELETEITEM, MPFROMSHORT( iItem ), 0 );
}
```

All items can be removed from the list box control by calling the DeleteAll() method. Like most other methods in C_LISTBOX, this is a simple code wrapper used to hide the specifics of OS/2 from applications written using the PMCLASS library.

```
//-----------
// DeleteAll \
//------------------------------------------------------------------------
//
// Description:
//     This method is a wrapper to hide the system specific code to delete
//     all items from the list box.
//
// Parameters:
//     none
//
// Returns:
//     void
//
void C_LISTBOX::DeleteAll( void )
{
   SendMsg( LM_DELETEALL, 0, 0 );
}
```

Although the user can select items in a list box manually, there may be times when you wish to force the selection of an item or items. For example, once a list has been populated you will probably want to select the first item so the user has a starting point.

C_LISTBOX provides a Select() method; this accepts an item number to select or deselect and a TRUE or FALSE state for the selection. Items are numbered zero through "n" in OS/2.

```
//--------
// Select \
//------------------------------------------------------------------------
//
// Description:
//     This method is a wrapper to hide the system specific code to select
//     an item from the list box.
//
// Parameters:
//     iItem           - Item to select from the list (0-n)
//     bBoolean        - TRUE to select, FALSE to deselect
//
// Returns:
//     void
//
void C_LISTBOX::Select( int iItem, BOOL bBoolean )
{
   SendMsg( LM_SELECTITEM, MPFROMSHORT( iItem ), MPFROMSHORT( bBoolean ) );
}
```

The currently selected item(s) in the list box can be determined using the Selection() method. This routine accepts an item number representing the starting item for the search. For list boxes where multiple selections are permitted, the iFrom parameter will be set to the current list item each time a selection is found.

```
//-----------
// Selection \
//------------------------------------------------------------------------
//
// Description:
//     This method is a wrapper to hide the system specific code to query
//     the current list selection.
//
// Parameters:
//     iFrom            - Item number to start searching from (0-n)
//
// Returns:
//     int              - Item number select. <0 = no selection
//
int C_LISTBOX::Selection( int iFrom )
{
   return (int)SendMsg( LM_QUERYSELECTION, MPFROMSHORT( iFrom ), 0 );
}
```

To determine the number of items in a list box, C_LISTBOX implements an ItemCount() method. It returns an integer value indicating how many items are currently in the list box.

```
//-----------
// ItemCount \
//------------------------------------------------------------------------
//
// Description:
//     This method is a wrapper to hide the system specific code to query
//     the number of items in the list box.
//
// Parameters:
//     none
//
// Returns:
//     int      - Number of items in the list box.
//
int C_LISTBOX::ItemCount( void )
{
   return (int)SendMsg( LM_QUERYITEMCOUNT, 0, 0 );
}
```

To return the text string for a given item in the list box, use the ItemText() method. This accepts an item number whose text will be returned and a pointer to an output buffer area and its size. After the call to this method, the text from the list will be written to the output buffer.

```
//----------
// ItemText \
//-------------------------------------------------------------------------
//
// Description:
//     This method is a wrapper to hide the system specific code to query
//     the text string for a specified item.
//
// Parameters:
//     iItem           - Item to query from the list (0-n)
//     szString        - Pointer to buffer where text will be written
//     iBufferSize     - Size of the output buffer in bytes.
//
// Returns:
//     void
//
void C_LISTBOX::ItemText( int iItem, char *szString, int iBufferSize )
{
   SendMsg( LM_QUERYITEMTEXT, MPFROM2SHORT( iItem, iBufferSize ),
                                          MPFROMP( szString ) );
}
```

Status Line Class

In many applications there may be a requirement to display information for the user without actually creating a dialog box and interrupting the user's activities. PMCLASS toolbars, for example, can implement fly-over help text to inform the user of the exact purpose of each button. The user has no desire to be interrupted with a dialog box for this, and he or she would become really annoyed if you wrote an application that did. Hints, however, are often welcome; to accomplish this you can create a C_STATUS instance.

The C_STATUS window object is actually very simple, containing only a constructor and a single method to set the status line text; there are no attributes at all. The C_STATUS is shown in the following object diagram:

C_STATUS	
	C_STATUS() void Text()

Figure 6-9 C_STATUS class

The header file for C_STATUS is shown in Listing 6-8:

```
class C_STATUS : public C_WINDOW_CHILD
{
   public:
       _Export      C_STATUS( C_WINDOW *pxcParentObj );
       void _Export    Text( char *szFormat, ... );
};

#define        D_ID_STATUS          110
```

Listing 6-8 STATUS.HPP – Class definition for C_STATUS

The constructor creates the instance of a basic single line text editor window. The edit line is marked as read-only so the user cannot modify it, and it is formatted to look like a status line. The colors are set to a gray background with black text, the same color scheme used for buttons in Presentation Manager.

```
//-------------
// Constructor \
//-------------------------------------------------------------------------
//
// Description:
//    This constructor creates an instance of the C_STATUS class. It sets
//    the initial font and color for the window and configures the test
//    limit at 256 characters.
//
// Parameters:
//    pxcParentObj    - Pointer to owner object window
//
C_STATUS::C_STATUS( C_WINDOW *pxcParentObj ) : C_WINDOW_CHILD( pxcParentObj, 0 )
{
   // Create the status window
   ClassName( WC_ENTRYFIELD );
   Create( D_ID_STATUS, WS_VISIBLE|ES_READONLY, "", 0, 20, 90, 30 );

   // Limit the line to 265 characters
   PostMsg( EM_SETTEXTLIMIT, MPFROMSHORT( 256 ), 0 );

   // Set the default font and colors for the status line
   SetFont( "10.Helv" );
   SetBackgroundColor( 204, 204, 204 );
   SetForegroundColor( 0, 0, 0 );
}
```

The Text() method in C_STATUS accepts a "printf"-style string and parameter list. The variable argument code in Text() formats an output string and writes it to the status line window.

```
//------
// Text \
//--------------------------------------------------------------------------
//
// Description:
//     This method accepts a variable argument printf-style string and after
//     formatting, it will display the string within the status line window.
//
// Parameters:
//     szFormat    - Pointer to printf-style string
//
// Returns:
//     void
//
void C_STATUS::Text( char *szFormat, ... )
{
   char        szString[1024];
   va_list     xtArgs;

   // Format the text
   va_start( xtArgs, szFormat );
   vsprintf( szString, szFormat, xtArgs );
   va_end( xtArgs );

   // Set the text in the status window
   SetText( szString );
}
```

My goal was to keep the C_STATUS object very simple; however, there are a number of possible enhancements that could be implemented in the C_STATUS class. A chiseled border could be added around the perimeter of the status window. Study the WM_PAINT handler in C_TOOLBAR to get some hints on how to accomplish this. Also, users may want to have larger or smaller text appear in the status line. You could add code to determine the current font and dynamically size the status line accordingly.

Menu Class

Almost every application window will offer the user some form of action menu; Presentation Manager provides a full suite of operations to manipulate the menu and its operations. For example, under program control, a menu can have options added or removed, depending on the current operating mode of the program. An existing menu option can also be modified, which is useful for operations that toggle each time they are selected.

PMCLASS implements a C_MENU class having a limited set of menu operations. I added support for only those features I required; you may find that you need to add methods to support other functions. For instance, the C_MENU class has no provision for adding bitmaps to menus, which may be important in some situations. The goal for C_MENU, as well as the whole PMCLASS library, was to write a set of classes as small as possible, so I avoided adding code for which I had no immediate need. The C_MENU class is illustrated in Figure 6-10.

C_MENU	
	C_MENU() void EnableItem() void DisableItem() void SetItemText() void GetItemText()

Figure 6-10 C_MENU class

The header file for C_MENU is shown in Listing 6-9:

```
class C_MENU : public C_WINDOW_CHILD
{
  public:
      _Export     C_MENU( C_WINDOW *pxcParentObj );
      void     _Export     EnableItem( int iIDItem );
      void     _Export     DisableItem( int iIDItem );
      void     _Export     SetItemText( int iIDItem, char *szText );
      void     _Export     GetItemText( int iIDItem, char *szText, int iSize );
};
```

Listing 6-9 MENU.HPP – Class definition for C_MENU

C_MENU implements a single constructor. Unlike other control window classes in this chapter, you cannot create a menu dynamically, or load one from a dialog. This class assumes that the menu already exists as part of a window, so there is no need to provide constructors to support these capabilities. You could add this capability, since it is supported by OS/2; I saw no immediate need, so I omitted it.

The C_MENU constructor associates the current menu for the owner window with its instance. It acquires the menu handle using the WinWindowFromID() API function, referencing the FID_MENU identifier defined by Presentation Manager. It then invokes the C_WINDOW::Create() method to link the parent window and the menu.

```
//-------------
// Constructor \
//--------------------------------------------------------------------------
//
// Description:
//     This constructor retrieves a window handle for the owner window's menu.
//
// Parameters:
//     pxcParentObj    - Pointer to owner of the menu.
//
C_MENU::C_MENU( C_WINDOW *pxcParentObj ) : C_WINDOW_CHILD( pxcParentObj, 0 )
{
   HWND    hWnd;

   // This window is of the menu class
   ClassName( WC_MENU );

   // The window was created by the parent window, so all we need to
   // do is find out where it is
   hWnd = WinWindowFromID( ParentObject()->ParentWindow(), FID_MENU );
   C_WINDOW::Create( ParentObject()->ParentWindow(), hWnd );
}
```

Every option in an action menu should be specified by a unique identifier; every action performed for a menu option must reference this identifier.

The first method implemented in C_MENU is EnableItem(). This method wraps a call to the WinEnableMenuItem() API function, which isolates this operating system specific call from the application. EnableItem() accepts a menu option identifier and enables that option.

```
//------------
// EnableItem \
//-----------------------------------------------------------------------
//
// Description:
//     This method enables the menu item with the specified identifier.
//
// Parameters:
//     iIDItem     - ID of the menu item to enable
//
// Returns:
```

The C_SLIDER from the PMCLASS library is quite simple, consisting of only three methods and a single attribute. It is illustrated in Figure 6-11.

C_SLIDER	
SLDCDATA slData	C_SLIDER() void Scale() void Value()

Figure 6-11 C_SLIDER class

The header file for C_SLIDER is shown in Listing 6-10:

```
class C_SLIDER : public C_WINDOW_CHILD
{
   private:
       SLDCDATA        slData;               // Slider data area

   public:
       _Export         C_SLIDER( C_WINDOW *pxcParentObj, int iID, int iMode,
                                  int iIncrements, int iScale );
       _Export         C_SLIDER( C_DIALOG *pxcParentObj, int iID );
       void _Export    Scale( int iIncrements, int iSpacing );
       void _Export    Value( int iValue );
};
```

Listing 6-10 SLIDER.HPP – Class definition for C_SLIDER

C_SLIDER implements two constructors. The first of these is used to create a slider at run time as a child of a specified parent/owner window. Like other control class windows, the constructor also requires a window identifier used when monitoring events sent to the owner of the slider window.

The final parameter sent to this constructor is the mode. The mode value consists of various OS/2 specific slider configuration parameters, as shown in the following table:

SLS_VERTICAL	Specifies that the slider has a vertical orientation
SLS_HORIZONTAL	Specifies that the slider has a horizontal orientation
SLS_CENTER	The slider is centered within its window
SLS_BOTTOM	The slider is positioned at the bottom of its window rectangle

SLS_TOP	The slider is positioned at the top of its window rectangle
SLS_HOMELEFT	For horizontal sliders, the home position is at the left
SLS_HOMERIGHT	For horizontal sliders, the home position is at the right
SLS_HOMETOP	For vertical sliders, the home position is at the top
SLS_HOMEBOTTOM	For vertical sliders, the home position is at the bottom
SLS_BUTTONSLEFT	For horizontal sliders, the value adjusting buttons are at the left
SLS_BUTTONSRIGHT	For horizontal sliders, the value adjusting buttons are at the right
SLS_BUTTONSTOP	For vertical sliders, the value adjusting buttons are at the top
SLS_BUTTONSBOTTOM	For vertical sliders, the value adjusting buttons are at the bottom
SLS_READONLY	The slider is not changeable by the user
SLS_SNAPTOINCREMENT	The slider arm value moves only between exact increment values
SLS_RIBBONSTRIP	As the slider arm moves, the slider is filled from the home position to the current value

This table represents only a quick overview of the styles acceptable to the control. For more details on the control styles valid for a slider control, refer to Presentation Manager on-line documentation.

The final parameters to the constructor are the increment and scale. These values are used by the Scale() method, which is called by the constructor code and will be discussed later in this section. Refer to the C_SLIDER::Scale() method for more details.

```
//-------------
// Constructor \
//---------------------------------------------------------------------------
//
// Description:
//     This constructor creates a slider control which has a C_WINDOW parent.
//
// Parameters:
//     pxcParentObj     - Pointer to owner of the slider.
//     iID              - Window ID for the slider
```

```
//      iMode           - Any additional OS/2 specific scale modifiers
//      iIncrements     - The number of increments on the slider
//      iSpacing        - The spacing between increments
//
C_SLIDER::C_SLIDER( C_WINDOW *pxcParentObj, int iID, int iMode,
           int iIncrements, int iScale ) : C_WINDOW_CHILD( pxcParentObj, 0 )
{
   HWNDhWnd;

   // Set some default scale increments
   Scale( iIncrements, iScale );

   ClassName( WC_SLIDER );
   hWnd = WinCreateWindow( ParentObject()->Window(), WC_SLIDER, NULL,
       SLS_PRIMARYSCALE1 | WS_VISIBLE | iMode,
       0,0,22,16, ParentObject()->Window(), HWND_TOP, iID, &slData, 0 );

   // Tell the main Window interface about the window
   C_WINDOW::Create( ParentObject()->Window(), hWnd );
}
```

The second constructor is used to interface to slider controls that reside within dialog resources. There is no need to specify a mode parameter for this constructor, since the slider characterization is performed within the resource editor.

```
//-------------
// Constructor \
//-----------------------------------------------------------------------
//
// Description:
//      This constructor connects to a slider control which originates
//      inside a dialog resource.
//
// Parameters:
//      pxcParentObj    - Pointer to dialog owner of the slider
//      iID             - Window ID for the slider
//
C_SLIDER::C_SLIDER( C_DIALOG *pxcParentObj, int iID )
                        : C_WINDOW_CHILD( (C_WINDOW *)pxcParentObj, 0 )
{
   ClassName( WC_SLIDER );

   // The window was created by the dialog system, so all we need to
   //  do is call our parent Create()
   C_WINDOW::Create( ParentObject()->Window(),
                WinWindowFromID( ParentObject()->Window(), iID ) );
}
```

C_SLIDER provides the Scale() function to set the number of increments within the slider as well as the pixel spacing between slider increments. If the spacing value is set to zero, then PM spaces the increments automatically.

Scale() must be called before the window is created. For this reason it is called in the constructor.

```
//-------
// Scale \
//--------------------------------------------------------------------------
//
// Description:
//     This method defines the number of increments and the spacing of
//     the slider scale.
//
// Parameters:
//     iIncrements     - The number of increments on the slider
//     iSpacing        - The spacing between increments
//
// Returns:
//     void
//
void C_SLIDER::Scale( int iIncrements, int iSpacing )
{
   slData.cbSize = sizeof( SLDCDATA );
   slData.usScale1Increments = iIncrements;
   slData.usScale1Spacing = iSpacing;
}
```

To set the value of the slider, C_SLIDER provides a Value() function that accepts an integer representing the new slider value. The value must be within the range of the slider—C_SLIDER performs no range checking on the value supplied.

```
//-------
// Value \
//--------------------------------------------------------------------------
//
// Description:
//     This method sets the value contained in the slider to that specified.
//     The iValue parameter should be less than the number of increments
//     on the slider.
//
// Parameters:
//     iValue      - New value for the slider position
//
// Returns:
//     void
//
```

```
void C_SLIDER::Value( int iValue )
{
   WinSendMsg( Window(), SLM_SETSLIDERINFO, MPFROM2SHORT(
            SMA_SLIDERARMPOSITION, SMA_INCREMENTVALUE ),
                                          MPFROMSHORT( (SHORT)iValue ) );
}
```

Of all the classes in this book, this one offers the most potential for expansion. Many of the capabilities of the native PM slider control are untapped, and if you use sliders at all, you will want to make some alterations.

Toolbar Button Class

We need not delve too deeply into the code dealing with toolbar buttons since this code is mostly internal to PMCLASS. However, there may be occasions when you want to create a button with a graphic, rather than the ordinary text button supplied by Presentation Manager, so I will present the code and describe how PMCLASS's buttons function at a high level.

All toolbar buttons that you will notice in the applications in Part III are actually instances of the C_BUTTON_TBAR class in the PMCLASS library. C_BUTTON_TBAR offers the ability to create buttons with graphical faces rather than ordinary text, and also features the capability of presenting different graphics in each of the three possible button states (Up, Down, and Disabled).

To simplify creation of button graphics, the C_BUTTON_TBAR class uses graphics in PM ICON or POINTER format and that can be constructed using OS/2's ICONEDIT program. The icons are stored in the resource file associated with an application and are linked into the executable program when it is built.

The C_BUTTON_TBAR class can be shown as follows:

C_BUTTON_TBAR			
int	iID;	C_BUTTON_TBAR()	
int	iX;	void	Initialize()
int	iY;	void *	MsgMouseMove()
int	iState;	void *	MsgPaint()
int	iIdUp;	void *	MsgButton1Down()
int	iIdDn;	void *	MsgButton1Up()
int	iIdDisable;	void	State()
char	*szButtonText;	void	Toggle()
		int	State()
		int	ID()
		char *	Text()
		int	X()

C_BUTTON_TBAR *(Continued)*	
	int Y()
	int Up()
	int Down()
	int Disable()

Figure 6-12 C_BUTTON_TBAR class

C_BUTTON_TBAR is a window object like any other in PMCLASS. As such, it must process certain window messages, and so must provide a message table to reference methods within the class and equate them with the messages it needs to process.

```
DECLARE_MSG_TABLE( xtButtonMsg )
   DECLARE_MSG( WM_MOUSEMOVE,          C_BUTTON_TBAR::MsgMouseMove )
   DECLARE_MSG( WM_PAINT,              C_BUTTON_TBAR::MsgPaint )
   DECLARE_MSG( WM_BUTTON1DOWN,        C_BUTTON_TBAR::MsgButton1Down )
   DECLARE_MSG( WM_BUTTON1UP,          C_BUTTON_TBAR::MsgButton1Up )
END_MSG_TABLE
```

The header file for C_BUTTON_TBAR is shown in Listing 6-11:

```
class C_BUTTON_TBAR : public C_WINDOW_CHILD
{
   private:
        int         iID;
        int         iX;
        int         iY;
        int         iState;

        int         iIdUp;
        int         iIdDn;
        int         iIdDisable;
        char        *szButtonText;

   public:
        _Export     C_BUTTON_TBAR( void );
        _Export     C_BUTTON_TBAR( C_WINDOW *pxcParentObj );

        void    _Export     Initialize( int iButtonID, int iXPos, int iYPos,
                                int iUp, int iDn, int iDis, char *szText );

        void *  _Export     MsgMouseMove( void *mp1, void *mp2 );
        void *  _Export     MsgPaint( void *mp1, void *mp2 );
        void *  _Export     MsgButton1Down( void *mp1, void *mp2 );
        void *  _Export     MsgButton1Up( void *mp1, void *mp2 );
```

```
        void    _Export     State( int iNewState );
        void    _Export     Toggle( void );

#ifdef __BORLANDC__
        int     _Export     State( void ) { return iState; };
        int     _Export     ID( void ) { return iID; };
        char *  _Export     Text( void ) { return szButtonText; };
        int     _Export     X( void ) { return iX; };
        int     _Export     Y( void ) { return iY; };
        int     _Export     Up( void ) { return iIdUp; };
        int     _Export     Down( void ) { return iIdDn; };
        int     _Export     Disable( void ) { return iIdDisable; };
#else
        int     State( void ) { return iState; };
        int     ID( void ) { return iID; };
        char *  Text( void ) { return szButtonText; };
        int     X( void ) { return iX; };
        int     Y( void ) { return iY; };
        int     Up( void ) { return iIdUp; };
        int     Down( void ) { return iIdDn; };
        int     Disable( void ) { return iIdDisable; };
#endif
};

//-----------------
// Button messages \
//------------------------------------------------------------------------
#define         BM_CREATE    PM_USER
#define         BM_BUTTON    PM_USER+1
#define         BM_TEXT      PM_USER+2
#define         BM_BUTTON1DOWNPM_USER+3

//---------------
// Button states \
//------------------------------------------------------------------------
#define         D_BUTTON_UP1
#define         D_BUTTON_DN2
#define         D_BUTTON_DIS-1
```

Listing 6-11 BUTTON.HPP – Class definition for C_BUTTON_TBAR

C_BUTTON_TBAR offers two constructors. The first is the basic void constructor that simply presents the message table to the C_WINDOW_CHILD parent class. The second constructor additionally associates this button object with a specific parent or owner object.

```
//-------------
// Constructor \
//-----------------------------------------------------------------------
//
// Description:
//     This constructor creates an instance of the C_BUTTON_TBAR class.
//
// Parameters:
//     none
//
C_BUTTON_TBAR::C_BUTTON_TBAR( void ) : C_WINDOW_CHILD( xtButtonMsg )
{
}

//-------------
// Constructor \
//-----------------------------------------------------------------------
//
// Description:
//     This constructor creates an instance of the C_BUTTON_TBAR class.
//
// Parameters:
//     pxcParentObj    - Pointer to owner object
//
C_BUTTON_TBAR::C_BUTTON_TBAR( C_WINDOW *pxcParentObj )
                            : C_WINDOW_CHILD( pxcParentObj, xtButtonMsg )
{
}
```

The initialize method sets up the default characteristics for the button. All buttons possess an X,Y location relative to their parent, as well as a button ID. The iUp, iDn and iDis parameter should contain the resource identifiers of the icons used to paint the button in the up, down, and disabled states, respectively. If the button does not feature one of these states, the disable state for example, the resource ID can be set to a value of zero.

The final parameter for a button is the fly-over text. This text is sent to the button owner window as part of a BM_TEXT message that tells the owner what help text it should display in its status line. This text is completely optional; the parameter may be supplied as NULL if necessary.

```
//--------------
// Initialize() \
//-----------------------------------------------------------------------
//
// Description:
//     This method sets up the initial default values for the button instance.
//     Then it registers and creates a window for the button object, setting
//     its initial state to the UP position.
```

```
//
// Parameters:
//     iButtonID        - Button ID for the button
//     iXPos,iYPos      - The initial X,Y position relative to the owner
//     iUp              - Resource ID of the Up position ICON
//     iDn              - Resource ID of the Down position ICON
//     iDis             - Resource ID of the Disable position ICON
//     szText           - Pointer to the fly over help text string
//
// Returns:
//     void
//
void C_BUTTON_TBAR::Initialize( int iButtonID,
           int iXPos, int iYPos, int iUp, int iDn, int iDis, char *szText )
{
   // Save the important things
   iID = iButtonID;
   iX = iXPos;
   iY = iYPos;
   iIdUp = iUp;
   iIdDn = iDn;
   iIdDisable = iDis;
   iState = D_BUTTON_UP;
   szButtonText = NULL;
   if( strlen( szText ) )
       szButtonText = szText;

   // Make sure the toolbar class has been registered
   Register( "TBarButton" );

   Create( iID, WS_VISIBLE, "TBarButton", iX,  iY, 32, 32 );

   // Set the initial button state
   State( D_BUTTON_UP );
}
```

The MsgMouseMove() method is called whenever the mouse pointer is moved over the button. Its only function is to inform the owner window of fly-over help text if it exists.

```
//--------------
// MsgMouseMove \
//-----------------------------------------------------------------------
// Event:       WM_MOUSEMOVE
// Cause:       Issued by the OS if the mouse is moved over the button
// Description:This method gets called when the user moves the mouse over
//              the button region. This forces the fly-over text to be set
//              for the button by issuing a BM_TEXT message to the owner.
```

```
void *C_BUTTON_TBAR::MsgMouseMove( void *mp1, void *mp2 )
{
   if( strlen( Text() ) > 2 )
   {
      // If the mouse is moving over the button, tell the parent to
      // display this buttons helper text in the status window
      ParentObject()->SendMsg( BM_TEXT, (void *)ID(), (void *)Text() );
   }

   return FALSE;
}
```

The MsgPaint() method controls the visual aspects of the button object. This method is invoked whenever the button needs to process the WM_PAINT message. When this occurs, the code determines which state the button is in and loads the correct icon from the resource pool of the EXE.

```
//----------
// MsgPaint \
//---------------------------------------------------------------------------
// Event:       WM_PAINT
// Cause:       Issued by the OS when the button needs to be redrawn
// Description:This method gets called when the button needs to be redrawn
//              for any reason.
void *C_BUTTON_TBAR::MsgPaint( void *mp1, void *mp2 )
{
   HPS            hps;
   RECTL          rc;
   HPOINTER       hPointer;

   hps = WinBeginPaint( Window(), 0L, &rc );

   // Draw the correct button face
   switch( State() )
   {
      case D_BUTTON_UP:
         hPointer = WinLoadPointer( HWND_DESKTOP, 0, Up() );
         break;
      case D_BUTTON_DN:
         hPointer = WinLoadPointer( HWND_DESKTOP, 0, Down() );
         break;
      default:
         hPointer = WinLoadPointer( HWND_DESKTOP, 0, Disable());
         break;
   }

   WinDrawPointer( hps, 0, 0, hPointer, DP_NORMAL );
   WinDestroyPointer( hPointer );
```

```
   WinEndPaint( hps );

   return FALSE;
}
```

The MsgButton1Down() and MsgButton1Up() methods are controlled by the user operation of the left mouse button while the mouse pointer is positioned over the button. These methods simply notify the button owner that some activity has occurred. The button will be forced to repaint in the new state to provide visual feedback to the user.

```
//------------------
// MsgBMButton1Down \
//--------------------------------------------------------------------------
// Event:       WM_BUTTON1DOWN
// Cause:       Issued by the OS when user presses the first mouse button
// Description:This method gets called when the user presses mouse button 1
//              while over button. It toggles the state of the button and
//              sends a BM_BUTTON1DOWN message to the owner.
void *C_BUTTON_TBAR::MsgButton1Down( void *mp1, void *mp2 )
{
   // Set the correct state for the button
   if( State() == D_BUTTON_UP && strlen( Text() ) > 2 )
   {
      Toggle();

      ParentObject()->PostMsg( BM_BUTTON1DOWN, 0, 0 );
   }

   return FALSE;
}

//----------------
// MsgBMButton1Up \
//--------------------------------------------------------------------------
// Event:       WM_BUTTON1DOWN
// Cause:       Issued by the OS when user presses the first mouse button
// Description:This method gets called when the user presses mouse button 1
//              while over button. It toggles the state of the button and
//              sends a BM_BUTTON1DOWN message to the owner.
void *C_BUTTON_TBAR::MsgButton1Up( void *mp1, void *mp2 )
{
   if( State() == D_BUTTON_DN  && strlen( Text() ) > 2 )
   {
      Toggle();

      // Tell the parent that this button has changed states
```

```
        ParentObject()->PostMsg( BM_BUTTON, (void *)ID(),0);

        // Force the button to be repainted
        MsgPaint( 0, 0 );
    }

    return FALSE;
}
```

The final two methods in the C_BUTTON_TBAR class are essentially state controllers. The State() method can be used to set the state of a button to a predetermined position. Valid values passed to State() are D_BUTTON_UP, D_BUTTON_DN, or D_BUTTON_DIS.

```
//-------
// State \
//---------------------------------------------------------------------
// Description:
//     This method sets the state of the button to one of D_BUTTON_UP,
//     D_BUTTON_DN, or D_BUTTON_DIS.
//
// Parameters:
//         iNewState    - The new state of the button
//
// Returns:
//             none
//
void C_BUTTON_TBAR::State( int iNewState )
{
    // Change the state and force a redraw
    iState = iNewState;
    Invalidate();
}
```

The Toggle() method is similar, except that state is simply toggled between the unpressed position and the depressed position. These methods permit much more flexibility to the C_BUTTON_TBAR object than one can achieve with the standard PM button control. With C_BUTTON_TBAR, you can create buttons capable of being "latched" in a given position, something that is more difficult with stock PM buttons.

Toggling is useful for creating buttons to control modes of operation. If you have seen the FTP client in the NeoLogic Network Suite, then I will point out that this application uses the Toggle() method to switch between ASCII and binary file transfer modes. The icon graphic for each of the states is such that the user can scan the toolbar to determine exactly which mode is currently set.

```
//--------
// Toggle \
//---------------------------------------------------------------------------
// Description:
//    This method toggles the state of the button from up to down or
//    vice versa.
//
// Parameters:
//            none
//
// Returns:
//            none
//
void C_BUTTON_TBAR::Toggle( void )
{
   // If the button is up
   if( State() == D_BUTTON_UP )
   {
      // Set the button in the down position
      State( D_BUTTON_DN );
   }
   else
   {
      // Otherwise, if the button is down
      if( State() == D_BUTTON_DN )
      {
         // Set the button in the up position
         State( D_BUTTON_UP );
      }
   }
}
```

Toggle() could have been simplified greatly using the "?:" conditional operator in C/C++; however, this would come at the expense of more convoluted code. For example:

```
void C_BUTTON_TBAR::Toggle( void )
{
   // Toggle the state of the button
   State( State() == D_BUTTON_UP ? D_BUTTON_UP : D_BUTTON_UP );
}
```

As you can see, the meaning of this single line of code is not nearly as clear. Realize that a good optimizing compiler like Borland's or IBM's will reduce the Toggle() code to this equivalent abbreviated form anyway; it would be a wise move to leave the code in its current form for simple readability.

Toolbar Class

One of the simplest ways to improve the appearance and usability of an application is to implement a toolbar, a popular feature so simple to implement that one wonders why so many programs still do not offer them. A toolbar is nothing but a simple window that contains or "owns" a set of buttons. The buttons can provide feedback to the toolbar control, which in turn can relay this information to its owner, usually the client window of an application frame window.

PMCLASS implements a rudimentary toolbar system in the C_TOOLBAR class. Although this class is marked by simplicity, it is surprisingly capable, and with a little experience, you should be dropping toolbars into every application you create. The C_TOOLBAR class is typically used as an abstract class from which specific toolbars are derived. The child class code, however, usually consists only of a set of tables to define the buttons to be inserted into the toolbar and to create a reference between a button and a WM_COMMAND message that will be sent to the owner window when a button is pressed. Very little real code is required to create powerful and appealing toolbars.

The C_TOOLBAR class is illustrated as follows:

C_TOOLBAR			
C_STATUS	*pxcStatus	C_TOOLBAR()	
int	iID	~C_TOOLBAR()	
int	iHeight	void *	MsgCreate()
C_BUTTON_TBAR	Button[20]	void *	MsgBMButton()
int	iButtonCount	void *	MsgBMText()
int	iLastID	void *	MsgBMButton1Down()
char	szOldText[256]	void *	MsgMouseMove()
int	iText	void *	MsgPaint()
int	iMouseButton	char *	OldText()
		int	ButtonCount()
		int	LastID()
		void	LastID()
		void	Status()
		void	Control()
		void	CreateButtons()
		void	ButtonToggle()
		void	ButtonState()
		void	ButtonEnable()
		C_BUTTON_TBAR *	Buttons()
		C_STATUS *	Status()
		C_BUTTON_TBAR *	ButtonData()

Figure 6-13 C_TOOLBAR class

```
#else
      char *            OldText( void ) { return szOldText; };
      C_BUTTON_TBAR *  Buttons( void ) { return xcButton; };
      int               ButtonCount( void ) { return iButtonCount; };
      int               LastID( void ) { return iLastID; };
      void              LastID( int iValue ) { iLastID = iValue; };
      C_STATUS *        Status( void ) { return pxcStatus; };
#endif

      void        _Export     Status( C_STATUS *pxcStatusWindow );
      void        _Export     Control( ULONG mp1,
                                          T_BUTTON_CMD_TABLE *xtLookup );

      void        _Export     CreateButtons(
                                      T_BUTTON_TABLE *pxtButtonTable );
      C_BUTTON_TBAR * _Export  ButtonData( int );
      void        _Export     ButtonToggle( int );
      void        _Export     ButtonState( int iButtonId, int iState );
      void        _Export     ButtonEnable( int iButtonId, int iValue );
};
```

Listing 6-12 TBAR.HPP – Class definition for C_TOOLBAR

C_TOOLBAR implements a single constructor. Unlike most of the other classes in the PMCLASS library, you cannot implement a toolbar in a dialog window, so we have no need of a second dialog-based constructor. The constructor method accepts a pointer to a parent window and an identifier like most other class constructors; however, it also accepts a window height.

In the previous discussion of toolbar buttons we saw that the graphics for these controls are derived from standard 32x32 pixel icons or pointers. The height of the window therefore needs to be slightly larger, and is normally set at 40 pixels in order to produce a toolbar that is one continuous line across the owner window. The height can be changed if you decide you want a toolbar with smaller graphics or more than one row of buttons.

```
//-------------
// Constructor \
//---------------------------------------------------------------------
//
// Description:
//    This constructor creates an instance of the C_TOOLBAR class. This
//    class will typically be abstract so this constructor will generally
//    not be called directly.
//
// Parameters:
//    pxcParentObj      - Pointer to owner object window
//    iTBarID           - Resource ID of the toolbar window
```

```
//      iTBarHeight      - Height of the toolbar in pixels
//
C_TOOLBAR::C_TOOLBAR( C_WINDOW *pxcParentObj, int iTBarID, int iTBarHeight )
                        : C_WINDOW_CHILD( pxcParentObj, xtToolBarMsg )
{
    // Save the important things
    pxcStatus = NULLHANDLE;
    iHeight = iTBarHeight;
    iButtonCount = 0;
    iLastID = 0;
    iID = iTBarID;

    ParentObject( pxcParentObj );

    // Make sure the toolbar class has been registered
    Register( "ToolBar" );

    Create( iTBarID, 0, "ToolBar", 0, 0, 0, iHeight );
}
```

C_TOOLBAR implements a destructor as well. Its only purpose is to reset the button count, which prevents the toolbar from sending messages to buttons that no longer exist.

```
//------------
// Destructor \
//---------------------------------------------------------------------------
// Description:
//      This destructor resets the button count to zero.
//
// Parameters:
//      none
//
C_TOOLBAR::~C_TOOLBAR( void )
{
    // Reset the button count because all of them are now invalid
    iButtonCount = 0;
}
```

Since C_TOOLBAR is a window class, it processes some specific messages from Presentation Manager. The first of these is the WM_CREATE message handled by the MsgCreate() method.

MsgCreate() sets the mouse pointer to a normal arrow. You normally would not need this line, but I have implemented it in case you want to change the pointer to something else. The remainder of the code in MsgCreate() is used to reset the fly-over help text feature of the toolbar.

```
//-----------
// MsgCreate \
//---------------------------------------------------------------------------
// Event:       PM_CREATE
// Cause:       Issued by OS when window is created
// Description:This method gets called when the window is initially created.
//              It initializes all the visual aspects of the class.
void *C_TOOLBAR::MsgCreate( void *mp1, void *mp2 )
{
   WinSetPointer( HWND_DESKTOP,
              WinQuerySysPointer( HWND_DESKTOP, SPTR_ARROW, FALSE ) );

   LastID( 0 );
   strcpy( OldText(), "" );
   iText = 0;
   iMouseButton = 0;

   return FALSE;
}
```

MsgBMButton() is invoked whenever the user presses a toolbar button. The first message parameter, mp1, contains the window identifier of the button that was pressed. The method records this button press and relays a WM_CONTROL message to the toolbar owner window notifying it of the user action.

```
//-------------
// MsgBMButton \
//---------------------------------------------------------------------------
// Event:       BM_BUTTON
// Cause:       Issued by a button when it is pressed by the user
// Description:This method gets called when the user presses a toolbar
//              button. mp1 holds the ID of button pressed.
void *C_TOOLBAR::MsgBMButton( void *mp1, void *mp2 )
{
   int      iButtonID;

   // Get the ID of the button that was pressed
   iButtonID = (int)mp1;
   iMouseButton = 0;

   // Send message to parent to say a button was pressed
   ParentObject()->PostMsg( WM_CONTROL, MPFROM2SHORT( iID, iButtonID ), 0 );

   return FALSE;
}
```

The MsgBMText() method is executed whenever the user moves the mouse pointer over a button or moves it off a button. This causes the fly-over text in the status line to change or be restored to the previous contents.

```
//-----------
// MsgBMText \
//--------------------------------------------------------------------------
// Event:      BM_TEXT
// Cause:      Issued by a button when the fly-over text changes
// Description:This method gets called when the user moves the mouse
//             over a toolbar button causing the fly-over text to change.
void *C_TOOLBAR::MsgBMText( void *mp1, void *mp2 )
{
   // Display the button help text in the status window if the
   // button has changed
   if( LastID() != (int)mp1 )
   {
      if( !iText )
      {
         Status()->GetText( OldText(), 256 );
         iText = 1;
      }
      LastID( (int)mp1 );
      Status()->Text( (char *)mp2 );
   }
   return FALSE;
}
```

MsgBMButtonDown() is invoked when the user presses one of the buttons on the toolbar. The method simply acknowledges that the event has occurred by setting the iMouseButton attribute. When the MsgMouseMove() method determines that the mouse has been moved off a button that is currently depressed, it needs to restore the button to its normal state.

```
//------------------
// MsgBMButton1Down \
//--------------------------------------------------------------------------
// Event:      BM_BUTTON1DOWN
// Cause:      Issued by a button when user presses a toolbar button
// Description:This method gets called when the user presses mouse button 1
//             while over a toolbar button.
void *C_TOOLBAR::MsgBMButton1Down( void *mp1, void *mp2 )
{
   iMouseButton = 1;
   return FALSE;
}
```

The MsgMouseMove() method is called by Presentation Manager when the mouse is moved in the toolbar window. If the mouse was moved off a toolbar button, the code determines if the button was depressed at the time. If so, the button is restored to its normally unpressed state. The status line text in existence before the mouse was moved over the buttons is restored.

```
//--------------
// MsgMouseMove \
//---------------------------------------------------------------------------
// Event:       WM_MOUSEMOVE
// Cause:       Issued by the OS if the mouse is moved over the toolbar
// Description:This method gets called when the user moves the mouse over
//              the toolbar window. This forces the fly-over text for the last
//              button to be trashed, restoring to the status line what was
//              there previously.
void *C_TOOLBAR::MsgMouseMove( void *mp1, void *mp2 )
{
   WinSetPointer( HWND_DESKTOP,
                  WinQuerySysPointer( HWND_DESKTOP, SPTR_ARROW, FALSE ) );
   if( LastID() )
   {
      // If the mouse button is depressed, make sure we toggle
      // the state of the last button pressed
      if( iMouseButton )
      {
         ButtonState( LastID(), D_BUTTON_UP );
      }

      iMouseButton = 0;
      LastID( 0 );
      Status()->Text( OldText() );
      iText = 0;
   }

   return FALSE;
}
```

Although you are never likely to change the appearance of a toolbar object, I'll describe the MsgPaint() method. Toolbar windows have a chiseled appearance that is controlled by this method. MsgPaint() uses GPI line drawing to accomplish this by displaying a basic rectangle with drawn lines of dark gray and white forming the shaded highlight.

After completing the basic look of the toolbar, MsgPaint() then invalidates each button to ensure that they get repainted correctly.

```
//----------
// MsgPaint \
//-----------------------------------------------------------------------
// Event:       WM_PAINT
// Cause:       Issued by the OS when the window needs to be redrawn
// Description:This method gets called when the toolbar needs to be redrawn
//              for any reason. This causes the chiseled look to be drawn around
//              the toolbar window and forces each button to be repainted.
void *C_TOOLBAR::MsgPaint( void *mp1, void *mp2 )
{
   HPS          hps;
   POINTL       pt;
   RECTL        rc;
   SWP          swp;
   int          iCtr;

   hps = WinBeginPaint( Window(), 0L, &rc );

   // Fill the basic client area with the menu color first
   WinFillRect( hps, &rc, SYSCLR_MENU );
   GpiSetColor( hps, CLR_NEUTRAL );

   // Draw the chiseled window highlights (bottom and right first)
   WinQueryWindowPos( Window(), &swp );
   pt.x = 0;
   pt.y = 0;
   GpiMove( hps, &pt );
   GpiSetColor( hps, SYSCLR_BUTTONDARK );
   pt.x = swp.cx;
   GpiLine( hps, &pt );
   pt.y = swp.cy;
   GpiLine( hps, &pt );
   GpiSetColor( hps, SYSCLR_BUTTONLIGHT );
   pt.x = 0;
   GpiLine( hps, &pt );
   pt.y = 0;
   GpiLine( hps, &pt );

   // Now draw the left and top edges
   pt.x = 1;
   pt.y = 1;
   GpiMove( hps, &pt );
   GpiSetColor( hps, SYSCLR_BUTTONDARK );
   pt.x = swp.cx - 2;
   GpiLine( hps, &pt );
```

```
    pt.y = swp.cy - 2;
    GpiLine( hps, &pt );
    GpiSetColor( hps, SYSCLR_BUTTONLIGHT );
    pt.x = 1;
    GpiLine( hps, &pt );
    pt.y = 1;
    GpiLine( hps, &pt );

    WinEndPaint( hps );

    // Invalidate all the buttons to force them to repaint
    for( iCtr = 0; iCtr < ButtonCount() - 1; iCtr++ )
    {
        if( (xcButton + iCtr) )
            (xcButton + iCtr)->Invalidate();
    }
    return FALSE;
}
```

The Status() routine is very simple indeed. It accepts a pointer to a status line object and stores this pointer internally within the object so it can be referenced by the class methods.

```
//----------
// Status() \
//------------------------------------------------------------------------
//
// Description:
//     This method sets the reference status line associated with the toolbar.
//     This status line is used to display fly-over help.
//
// Parameters:
//     pxcStatusWindow      - Pointer to status object to use for fly-over help
//
// Returns:
//     void
//
void C_TOOLBAR::Status( C_STATUS *pxcStatusWindow )
{
    pxcStatus = pxcStatusWindow;
}
```

All toolbar buttons generate WM_COMMAND messages to the owner of the toolbar window. The Control() method is called when a toolbar button press operation has been completed. Control() translates these activities into the appropriate WM_COMMAND message for the owner window.

```
//-----------
// Control() \
//----------------------------------------------------------------------
//
// Description:
//     This method manages control messages for the toolbar. It determines
//     which button invoked the control message, then passes this as a new
//     WM_COMMAND message back to the owner of the toolbar object.
//
// Parameters:
//     mp1                    - Control parameter containing button ID
//     pxtCommandLookup       - Pointer to button command table
//
// Returns:
//     void
//
void C_TOOLBAR::Control( ULONG mp1, T_BUTTON_CMD_TABLE *pxtCommandLookup )
{
   int     iCtr;

   // Test for a parent window
   if( ParentObject()->Window() )
   {
       // Look at each button in the button table
       iCtr = 0;
       while( (pxtCommandLookup+iCtr)->iButtonId != 0 )
       {
           // If we found a match, send the associated WM_COMMAND message
           if( SHORT2FROMMP( mp1 ) == (pxtCommandLookup+iCtr)->iButtonId )
           {
               // Send the associated command ID to the owner window
               ParentObject()->SendMsg( WM_COMMAND,
                       (void *)(pxtCommandLookup+iCtr)->iCommandId, 0);
           }
           iCtr++;
       }
   }
}
```

The CreateButtons() method in C_TOOLBAR accepts an array of button definitions and creates a graphical button for each entry in the table.

C_TOOLBAR currently limits the maximum number of buttons to 15. This is due to an apparent problem in the Borland C++ compiler associated with dynamic memory allocation. When I originally designed the toolbar class, I used IBM CSet++ and the button objects were allocated dynamically. Later, when compiling the same code with the Borland compiler, I discovered that the toolbar code was crashing due to a severe memory leak. The quick-and-dirty solution was to allocate a fixed number of buttons statically.

```
//---------------
// CreateButtons \
//------------------------------------------------------------------------
//
// Description:
//     This function accepts an array of button descriptions and will
//     allocate an instance of a button for each item in the array.
//
// Parameters:
//     pxtButtonTable          - Pointer to the button table
//
// Returns:
//     void
//
void C_TOOLBAR::CreateButtons( T_BUTTON_TABLE *pxtButtonTable )
{
   int            iCtr;
   C_BUTTON_TBAR*pxcTemp;

   // Determine the number of buttons in the button table
   iButtonCount = 0;
   while( (pxtButtonTable+iButtonCount)->iID != 0 )
       iButtonCount++;

   // Create an instance of each button in the button table
   for( iCtr = 0; iCtr < iButtonCount; iCtr++ )
   {
       pxcTemp = (C_BUTTON_TBAR *)(xcButton + iCtr);

       // Populate the new button
       pxcTemp->ParentObject( this );
       pxcTemp->Initialize( (pxtButtonTable+iCtr)->iID,
               (pxtButtonTable+iCtr)->iX, (pxtButtonTable+iCtr)->iY,
               (pxtButtonTable+iCtr)->iIdUp, (pxtButtonTable+iCtr)->iIdDown,
                       (pxtButtonTable+iCtr)->iIdDisable,
                                           (pxtButtonTable+iCtr)->szText);
   }
}
```

The ButtonData() method returns a pointer to a specific button object. The caller supplies the identifier of the button whose object is to be returned, and ButtonData() scans the button array to find the requested button. If the identifier is not located, a NULL value is returned.

```
//------------
// ButtonData \
//---------------------------------------------------------------------
//
// Description:
//     This function returns a pointer to a button structure for the
//     specified button id in the specified toolbar window.
//
// Parameters:
//     iId         - Id of button to return
//
// Returns:
//     void
//
C_BUTTON_TBAR *C_TOOLBAR::ButtonData( int iId )
{
   int         iCtr;

   // Search each button in the table for the specified ID
   for( iCtr = 0; iCtr < iButtonCount; iCtr++ )
   {
      // If we found our ID
      if( (xcButton + iCtr)->ID() == iId )
      {
         // Return a pointer to the button's object
         return (xcButton + iCtr);
      }
   }
}
```

Toolbar buttons can also be toggled. This is useful for creating buttons that are used to switch operating modes in a program. We will use a toggled button in the FTP program later in the book in order to switch between binary and ASCII file transfer modes.

ButtonToggle() accepts an identifier for the button that will be toggled. The button array is scanned and when the button is located, its state is toggled. For example, if the button is currently in its unpressed state, toggling will force the button to switch to a depressed and locked state.

```
//--------------
// ButtonToggle \
//---------------------------------------------------------------------
//
// Description:
//     This routine will toggle the specified button. This basically
//     involves swapping the up and down graphics and repainting.
//
```

```
// Parameters:
//      iId         - Id of button to toggle
//
// Returns:
//      void
//
void C_TOOLBAR::ButtonToggle( int iButtonId )
{
   int          iCtr;

   // Search each button in the table for the specified ID
   for( iCtr = 0; iCtr < iButtonCount; iCtr++ )
   {
      // If we found the correct button
      if( (xcButton + iCtr)->ID() == iButtonId )
      {
         // Toggle it.
         (xcButton + iCtr)->Toggle();
         return;
      }
   }
}
```

The state of a button can also be set to a specific state. ButtonState() accepts a button identifier and a button state. The valid button states are D_BUTTON_UP, D_BUTTON_DOWN, and D_BUTTON_DIS for the up, down, and disabled states, respectively.

```
//-------------
// ButtonState \
//-----------------------------------------------------------------------
//
// Description:
//      This routine will set the state of the specified button.
//
// Parameters:
//      iButtonId   - Id of button whose state will be changed
//      iState      - New button state
//
// Returns:
//      void
//
void C_TOOLBAR::ButtonState( int iButtonId, int iState )
{
   int          iCtr;

   // Search each button in the table for the specified ID
   for( iCtr = 0; iCtr < iButtonCount; iCtr++ )
```

```
    {
        // If we found the button ID
        if( (xcButton + iCtr)->ID() == iButtonId )
        {
            // Set the buttons' state as specified
            (xcButton + iCtr)->State( iState );
            return;
        }
    }
}
```

The final method in the C_TOOLBAR class allows button windows to be enabled or disabled. Like many other toolbar methods, ButtonEnable() requires a button identifier; it also accepts a Boolean value to enable or disable the button.

```
//--------------
// ButtonEnable \
//------------------------------------------------------------------
//
// Description:
//     This routine will enable/disable the specified button.
//
// Parameters:
//     iButtonId    - Id of button to enable/disable
//     iValue       - TRUE or FALSE to indicate new state
//
// Returns:
//     void
//
void C_TOOLBAR::ButtonEnable( int iButtonId, int iValue )
{
    int         iCtr;

    // Search each button in the table for the specified ID
    for( iCtr = 0; iCtr < iButtonCount; iCtr++ )
    {
        // If we found the correct button ID
        if( (xcButton + iCtr)->ID() == iButtonId )
        {
            // Enable the button
            if( !iValue )
                (xcButton + iCtr)->State( D_BUTTON_DIS );
            else
                (xcButton + iCtr)->State( iValue );
            return;
        }
    }
}
```

The following code is actually that used in the news program in Part III to create a main toolbar. Notice that there is really no code associated with this—the file contains mostly lookup tables for buttons and command references.

When the main toolbar is constructed, it creates a group of items known as a button table. Button tables are descriptors that define the ID for the button followed by the icon image resource identifiers used to draw the three possible states for the button. The next item in the button descriptor is the string used to provide fly-over help when the user moves the mouse over the button. Finally the X,Y location relative to the toolbar itself must be provided.

I misled you a little by saying there wasn't any code involved in creating toolbars. The mechanism controlling fly-over help requires some knowledge of where the text will be displayed. One of the C_TOOLBAR class methods manages this. If fly-over help is used, the constructor must make a call to Status():

```
// Set the status bar object used by the toolbar
Status( pxcStatus );
```

The final step in the construction procedure is to create instances of all the buttons defined in the button table. The constructor does this by passing a pointer to the table into the C_TOOLBAR::CreateButtons() method.

```
//------------
// Constructor \
//---------------------------------------------------------------------------
C_TOOLBAR_TOP::C_TOOLBAR_TOP( C_WINDOW *pxcParentObj, C_STATUS *pxcStatus )
                            : C_TOOLBAR( pxcParentObj, D_TOP_TBAR, 40 )
{
   DECLARE_BUTTON_TABLE( xtButtons )
      DECLARE_BUTTON( DB_CONFIG, DB_CONFIG_UP, DB_CONFIG_DN, 0,
                      "Configure the program", 8, 4 )
      DECLARE_BUTTON( DB_WND_GRP, DB_GRP_UP, DB_GRP_DN, DB_GRP_DIS,
                      "Toggle the list of available groups", 48, 4 )
      DECLARE_BUTTON( DB_WND_SUB, DB_SUB_UP, DB_SUB_DN, DB_SUB_DIS,
                  "Toggle the list of current subscriptions", 80, 4 )
   END_BUTTON_TABLE

   // Set the status bar object used by the toolbar
   Status( pxcStatus );

   // Add some toolbar buttons
   CreateButtons( xtButtons );
}
```

One other method is required to completely implement a toolbar. The Control() method defines a Button-Command table that translates button presses into equivalent WM_COMMAND messages, as you will see when news is implemented later. The window object that owns the toolbar must intercept the

WM_CONTROL message (since a toolbar is a control) to watch for activity from the toolbar. If the WM_CONTROL message handler determines that a message is originating from the toolbar, it calls the toolbar's Control() methods to deal with the situation.

Again, we have to write a line of code to call the C_TOOLBAR::Control() method, passing it the Button-Command table for this toolbar.

```
//---------
// Control \
//-------------------------------------------------------------------------
void C_TOOLBAR_TOP::Control( ULONG mp1 )
{
   // Button-Command cross reference
   DECLARE_BUTTON_CMD_TABLE( xtCommandLookup )
       DECLARE_BUTTON_CMD( DB_CONFIG, DM_CONFIGURE )
       DECLARE_BUTTON_CMD( DB_WND_GRP, DM_GROUPS )
       DECLARE_BUTTON_CMD( DB_WND_SUB, DM_SUBSCRIPTIONS )
   END_BUTTON_CMD_TABLE

   // Call the parent controller to process the items
   C_TOOLBAR::Control( mp1, xtCommandLookup );
}
```

As you can see, this code builds a complete toolbar with three lines of code and a couple of simple tables. How much easier could it be? This code will remain unchanged for most of the toolbars you will ever write.

The source of almost every toolbar developed in Part III is the same. Once you create the first one, you can make new toolbar objects in a matter of minutes.

Edit Class

Most applications built for Presentation Manager need to display lines of data or collect responses from the user. There are many methods in place to accomplish these tasks, but the most common of these is an edit control. Edit controls are windows capable of editing or displaying single lines of information. The control provided by Presentation Manager fully supports cut and paste operations, so no additional code is required to manipulate the clipboard.

PMCLASS wraps the PM API for edit controls and provides a very simple C_EDIT class. Though this class contains only three constructors, it is derived from the C_WINDOW_CHILD and C_WINDOW classes, which means that it has surprising capabilities. For example, an editor control can be moved, or resized, or the colors or font can be changed using methods from the parent classes.

The C_EDIT class is shown in the following diagram.

```
//-------------
// TextLimit() \
//----------------------------------------------------------------------------
//
// Description:
//     This method set the text limit of the edit control to a specified number
//     of characters. It simply wraps the PM API that performs the same operation.
//
// Parameters:
//     iLimit          -  Character limit to set for the control
//
// Returns:
//     void
//
void C_EDIT::TextLimit( int iLimit )
{
   // Call the API to set the character limit
   SendMsg( EM_SETTEXTLIMIT, MPFROMSHORT( iLimit ), 0 );
}
```

Multiline Editor Class

There will be many occasions when you write applications for which you will want to display an editor window to permit the user to examine and possibly modify multiple lines of information. Several of the applications that ship with OS/2 can do this—E, the OS/2 system editor, for example, uses a multiline editor or MLE control to load a selected file for the user to edit. At the completion of the edit process, the user can save the contents of the MLE back to the disk.

The PMCLASS library offers extensive support for MLE controls; if you wanted, you could duplicate the functionality of E with less than 300 lines of application code. The reason for this simple implementation is that the C_MLE class in the PMCLASS library implements much of the functionality you need. C_MLE also adds some additional functionality that is not provided by the Presentation Manager control: the ability to save and load files, for example.

The news and FTP programs use this class as part of the file/article viewer window code. As you will see later, the viewer creates the C_MLE object, then loads a file to it with a single line of code. If you have had experience with the OS/2 MLE control, you will appreciate the magnitude of this accomplishment.

The C_MLE class is illustrated in Figure 6-15:

C_MLE	
MLE_SEARCHDATA xtSearch;	C_MLE() void ReadOnlyStatus() void WordWrap()

C_MLE *(Continued)*		
	void	ResetDirtyBufferFlag()
	int	IsBufferDirty()
	void	Undo()
	void	Copy()
	void	Cut()
	void	Paste()
	void	Clear()
	LONG	BufferLength()
	void	DisableRefresh()
	void	EnableRefresh()
	void	Insert()
	void	Delete()
	void	Select()
	void	QuerySelection()
	void	TransferBuffer()
	void	ExportBuffer()
	void	FindFirst()
	void	FindNext()
	LONG	Line()
	LONG	Column()
	LONG	NumberOfLines()
	void	Load()
	void	Save()

Figure 6-15 C_MLE class

The header file for C_MLE is shown in Listing 6-14:

```
class C_MLE : public C_WINDOW_CHILD
{
   private:
       MLE_SEARCHDATAxtSearch;

   public:
       _Export     C_MLE( C_WINDOW *pxcParentObj, int iMLEID, int iMode );
       _Export     C_MLE( C_WINDOW *pxcParentObj, int iMLEID );
       _Export     C_MLE( C_DIALOG *pxcParentObj, int iMLEID );
       void _Export    ReadOnlyStatus( short iBool );
       void _Export    WordWrap( short iBool );
       void _Export    ResetDirtyBufferFlag( void );
       int  _Export    IsBufferDirty( void );
       void _Export    Undo( void );
       void _Export    Copy( void );
```

```
        void _Export    Cut( void );
        void _Export    Paste( void );
        void _Export    Clear( void );
        LONG _Export    BufferLength( void );
        void _Export    DisableRefresh( void );
        void _Export    EnableRefresh( void );
        void _Export    Insert( char *szString );
        void _Export    Delete( LONG lStart, LONG lCount );
        void _Export    Select( LONG lStart, LONG lEnd );
        void _Export    QuerySelection( LONG *pAnchor, LONG *pCursor );
        void _Export    TransferBuffer( char *szString, LONG lSize );
        void _Export    ExportBuffer( LONG *ipStart, LONG *ipEnd );
        int  _Export    FindFirst( char *szString, int iCase );
        int  _Export    FindNext( int iCase );
        int  _Export    FindFromCursor( char *szString, int iCase );
        int  _Export    ChangeAll( char *szFind, char *szReplace, int iCase );
        LONG _Export    Line( LONG lCursor );
        LONG _Export    Column( LONG lLine );
        LONG _Export    NumberOfLines( void );
        void _Export    Load( C_STATUS *pxcStatus, char *szFilename );
        void _Export    Save( C_STATUS *pxcStatus, char *szFilename );
};
```

Listing 6-14 MLE.HPP – Class definition for C_MLE

C_MLE implements three constructors; which one you choose to call depends on your specific needs. The first constructor is the most generic and is shown below. This constructor accepts a pointer to a parent/owner window object and an integer ID used by PM. The third parameter can include any PM-specific attributes for a multiline edit control window. This includes attributes that can be "ORed" together, such as MLS_VSCROLL | MLS_HSCROLL | MLS_BORDER, which will enable scrollbars on the MLE and force it to draw a border. These attributes are summarized below.

MLS_BORDER	Draws a thin border around the MLE window.
MLS_READONLY	Prevents the user from altering the contents of the MLE window.
MLS_WORDWRAP	Enables text word-wrapping in the MLE window.
MLS_HSCROLL	Provides a horizontal scroll bar in the MLE window.
MLS_VSCROLL	Provides a vertical scroll bar in the MLE window.
MLS_IGNORETAB	Tab characters are ignored by the MLE window.
MLS_DISABLEUNDO	Undo actions are not permitted by the MLE.

The code makes two calls. The first sets the class name to WC_MLE, the OS/2 standard name for a multiline edit control. The second call invokes the C_WINDOW_CHILD::Create() method to create a run-time instance of an MLE.

Use this constructor only if you do not want the C_MLE default operation, which includes the MLS_ parameters shown in the previous paragraph.

```
//-------------
// Constructor \
//-----------------------------------------------------------------------
//
// Parameters:
//     pxcParentObj     - Pointer to parent window object which owns this
//     iMLEID           - ID of the control
//     iMode            - OS specific parameters to configure the MLE
C_MLE::C_MLE( C_WINDOW *pxcParentObj, int iMLEID, int iMode )
                                 : C_WINDOW_CHILD( pxcParentObj, 0 )
{
   // Set the class to the default OS/2 control name
   ClassName( WC_MLE );

   // Create the MLE control
   Create( iMLEID, iMode, " ", 0, 0, 90, 30 );
}
```

The second constructor performs a similar operation to the one just described, except that it does not accept the additional mode parameters. Instead, it defaults the MLE to include both horizontal and vertical scrollbars and a thin border and initially makes the MLE visible.

```
//-------------
// Constructor \
//-----------------------------------------------------------------------
//
// Parameters:
//     pxcParentObj     - Pointer to parent window object which owns this
//     iMLEID           - ID of the control
C_MLE::C_MLE( C_WINDOW *pxcParentObj, int iMLEID )
                                 : C_WINDOW_CHILD( pxcParentObj, 0 )
{
   // Set the class to the default OS/2 control name
   ClassName( WC_MLE );

   // Create the MLE control with some default characteristics
   Create( iMLEID, WS_VISIBLE | MLS_VSCROLL | MLS_HSCROLL | MLS_BORDER,
                                          "", 0, 0, 90, 30 );
}
```

The final C_MLE constructor is a special case constructor that manages MLE controls embedded in dialog windows stored in resource files. Previous constructors are used to create an MLE control at run time, while this one assumes that the MLE already exists, as it would after the creation of a dialog box. No mode parameters can be specified for this version of the constructor because all the MLE characteristics are defined in the resource file.

```
//-------------
// Constructor \
//------------------------------------------------------------------------
//
// Parameters:
//     pxcParentObj     - Pointer to parent dialog object which owns this
//     iMLEID           - ID of the control
//     iMode            - OS specific parameters to configure the MLE
C_MLE::C_MLE( C_DIALOG *pxcParentObj, int iMLEID )
                            : C_WINDOW_CHILD( (C_WINDOW *)pxcParentObj, 0 )
{
   // Set the class to the default OS/2 control name
   ClassName( WC_MLE );

   // The window was created by the dialog system, so all we need to
   // do is associate the instance with a resource from the RES file
   C_WINDOW::Create( ParentObject()->Window(),
                  WinWindowFromID( ParentObject()->Window(), iMLEID ) );
}
```

If you are creating an MLE viewer in which you want the user to make no modifications, you can invoke the ReadOnlyStatus() method. This routine wraps a PM window message call to MLM_SETREADONLY, supplying it with the appropriate enable/disable flag.

```
//----------------
// ReadOnlyStatus \
//------------------------------------------------------------------------
//
// Parameters:
//     iBool       - Set the read-only status of the MLE on or off
//
// Returns:
//     none
//
void C_MLE::ReadOnlyStatus( short iBool )
{
   // Toggle the editor's read-only status
   SendMsg( MLM_SETREADONLY, MPFROMSHORT( iBool ), 0 );
}
```

The WordWrap() method in C_MLE has been provided to toggle the presence of word wrapping within the editor control. This method accepts a Boolean value that enables or disables wrapping.

```
//----------
// WordWrap \
//--------------------------------------------------------------------------
//
// Parameters:
//     iBool       - Set the word-wrap state of the MLE on or off
//
// Returns:
//     none
//
void C_MLE::WordWrap( short iBool )
{
   // Set the word-wrap state
   SendMsg( MLM_SETWRAP, MPFROMSHORT( iBool ), 0 );
}
```

After modifications have been made to the text buffer, exiting from most editing programs usually involves stepping through a dialog warning you that changes will be lost. The dialog then permits you to save your changes to a file.

The C_MLE class provides two methods that combine to implement this capability. ResetDirtyBufferFlag() can be called to reset the state of the "dirty" flag, which OS/2 sets automatically for the MLE when the user modifies the buffer. This method is called by the C_MLE::Load() and Save() methods.

```
//----------------------
// ResetDirtyBufferFlag \
//--------------------------------------------------------------------------
//
// Description:
//     This method resets the detection mechanism used to determine
//     if the MLE buffer has changed.
//
// Parameters:
//     none
//
// Returns:
//     none
//
void C_MLE::ResetDirtyBufferFlag( void )
{
   // Clear the dirty buffer indicator
   SendMsg( MLM_SETCHANGED, 0, 0 );
}
```

A program using the C_MLE control can query the IsBufferDirty() method to determine the buffer has changed since the last Save() or Load() operation. IsBufferDirty() returns a Boolean value representing the state of the editor buffer.

```
//---------------
// IsBufferDirty \
//-----------------------------------------------------------------------
//
// Description:
//     This method returns the states of the "dirty buffer" flag which a
//     program can use to determine if the user has made any changes
//     to the MLE contents.
//
// Parameters:
//     none
//
// Returns:
//     TRUE or FALSE indicating the dirtiness of the MLE
//
int C_MLE::IsBufferDirty( void )
{
   // Toggle the editor's read-only status
   return (int)SendMsg( MLM_QUERYCHANGED, 0, 0 );
}
```

The next several methods manage clipboard interaction with the MLE control. These operations are so common when implementing MLE-equipped applications that they have become part of the basic functionality for the C_MLE class. For the most part, operations on the CUA standard "Edit" menu will equate directly to calls to these methods.

The first of these clipboard methods is Copy(), which determines the range of MLE text that is selected and copies that text to the OS/2 clipboard.

```
//------
// Copy \
//-----------------------------------------------------------------------
//
// Returns:
//     none
//
void C_MLE::Copy( void )
{
   // Copy selected text to the clipboard
   SendMsg( MLM_COPY, 0, 0 );
}
```

Cut() is similar to Copy() except that it removes the selected text from the MLE window. The text that is removed is placed on the system clipboard.

```
//-----
// Cut \
//------------------------------------------------------------------------
//
// Returns:
//     none
//
void C_MLE::Cut( void )
{
   // Cut selected text to the clipboard
   SendMsg( MLM_CUT, 0, 0 );
}
```

The Paste() method copies whatever text is currently sitting on the OS/2 system clipboard and writes it into the MLE window at the current insertion point (i.e. the location of the cursor). Any information that was on the clipboard remains there for subsequent pasting.

```
//-------
// Paste \
//------------------------------------------------------------------------
//
// Returns:
//     none
//
void C_MLE::Paste( void )
{
   // Paste clipboard contents into editor
   SendMsg( MLM_PASTE, 0, 0 );
}
```

Users of your applications are bound to make mistakes and, realizing this, you should provide the capability to reverse out of editing operations. C_MLE implemented an Undo() method that will undo the user's last edit operation.

```
//------
// UnDo \
//------------------------------------------------------------------------
//
// Returns:
//     none
//
void C_MLE::Undo( void )
{
```

```
   // Undo the last edit operation
   SendMsg( MLM_UNDO, 0, 0 );
}
```

The final text manipulation method is Clear(), which does not interact with the clipboard. Instead, Clear() finds the selected region of text in the MLE window and simply deletes it.

```
//-------
// Clear \
//------------------------------------------------------------------------
//
// Returns:
//     none
//
void C_MLE::Clear( void )
{
   // Clear the current text selection
   SendMsg( MLM_CLEAR, 0, 0 );
}
```

The BufferLength() method returns the number of characters (including any line breaks, tab characters, etc.) to the caller. BufferLength() is used internally in the C_MLE class, but has been made public because it may be useful in some applications. For example, you may be writing an editor in which you would like to have the buffer size in characters displayed in the status line. Most programmer's editors will perform this operation.

```
//--------------
// BufferLength \
//------------------------------------------------------------------------
//
// Returns:
//     Number of bytes currently stored in the MLE
//
LONG C_MLE::BufferLength( void )
{
   // Return the number of bytes in the editor control
   return (LONG)SendMsg( MLM_QUERYTEXTLENGTH, 0, 0 );
}
```

The next two methods are described together. The EnableRefresh() and DisableRefresh() methods permit you to enable or disable updates to the MLE window. This allows you to add several lines of text without causing the MLE to repaint (and possibly flicker). These operations are used typically when loading or unloading the MLE window text, and are called by the Load() and Save() methods shown later.

```
//----------------
// DisableRefresh \
//--------------------------------------------------------------------------
//
// Returns:
//     none
void C_MLE::DisableRefresh( void )
{
   // Disable MLE refreshing
   SendMsg( MLM_DISABLEREFRESH, 0, 0 );
}

//---------------
// EnableRefresh \
//--------------------------------------------------------------------------
//
// Returns:
//     none
void C_MLE::EnableRefresh( void )
{
   // Enable editor refreshing
   SendMsg( MLM_ENABLEREFRESH, 0, 0 );
}
```

When you need to insert a buffer of text into an MLE, you can use the Insert() method. The string pointer that Insert() accepts as a parameter can point to a single character or a buffer containing a large block of text. The only restriction is that the buffer must be NULL terminated.

If you take a quick peek at the Load() method code, you will see that it uses this method to load text files into the window. Instead of inserting a line at a time, notice that Load() inserts a block of up to 2 Kbytes. This is done to improve the performance of loading.

Something to bear in mind when loading an MLE control with Insert()—depending on the size of your insertion buffer, you may want to consider a separate thread for loading the MLE window. This can be a time-intensive task and will hold up system operation if the 1/10 second rule is violated.

```
//--------
// Insert \
//--------------------------------------------------------------------------
// Parameters:
//     szString    - Pointer to string data to be inserted into the MLE
//
// Returns:
//     none
void C_MLE::Insert( char *szString )
{
```

```
   // Insert the supplied text into the MLE at the current insertion point
   SendMsg( MLM_INSERT, (void *)szString, 0 );
}
```

Since the MLE is a completely interactive editor, the user has been provided with the capability of inserting or deleting text on demand. However, as a programmer you may find it useful to delete blocks of text from within code as well. A good example of this in an editor would be a situation in which the user wanted to load a different file into the window. The code must first remove the current editor contents before loading the new text.

The Delete() method accepts a byte offset within the MLE window and a character count. It invokes the MLM_DELETE message in the MLE manager to start from the specified offset to delete the specified number of characters. Text repositioning and reformatting is managed automatically by the MLE control code.

```
//--------
// Delete \
//-------------------------------------------------------------------------
// Parameters:
//     lStart      - Starting byte offset in MLE buffer for the delete
//     lCount      - Number of bytes to delete from the MLE
//
// Returns:
//     none
void C_MLE::Delete( LONG lStart, LONG lCount )
{
   // Delete a range of text from the editor starting at byte lStart for
   // lCount bytes.
   SendMsg( MLM_DELETE, lStart, lCount );
}
```

Under programmer control, an MLE control can also mimic the selection mechanism that is typically invoked by the user to select blocks of text. The Select() method accomplishes this by accepting a starting and ending byte offset in the MLE buffer and issuing the MLM_SETSEL message in the PM control code.

```
//--------
// Select \
//-------------------------------------------------------------------------
// Parameters:
//     lStart      - Starting byte offset in MLE buffer for the selection
//     lEnd        - Ending byte offset in MLE buffer for the selection
//
// Returns:
//     none
void C_MLE::Select( LONG lStart, LONG lEnd )
```

```
{
   // Select the specified range of text
   SendMsg( MLM_SETSEL, lStart, lEnd );
}
```

The opposite of setting the selection is the query operation; the C_MLE method QuerySelection() manages this functionality. This method makes two calls to the PM MLE control code to return the current anchor point and cursor position representing the start and end offsets of the current selection.

```
//----------------
// QuerySelection \
//-----------------------------------------------------------------------
// Parameters:
//      pAnchor      - Pointer to location where selection anchor point
//                     byte offset will be stored
//      pCursor      - Pointer to location where selection cursor byte
//                     offset will be stored
//
// Returns:
//      none
void C_MLE::QuerySelection( LONG *pAnchor, LONG *pCursor )
{
   // Query the current anchor point
   *pAnchor = (LONG)SendMsg( MLM_QUERYSEL, MPFROMSHORT( MLFQS_ANCHORSEL ),0 );

   // Query the current cursor location
   *pCursor = (LONG)SendMsg( MLM_QUERYSEL, MPFROMSHORT( MLFQS_CURSORSEL ),0 );
}
```

In order to read sections of the MLE text buffer into a C/C++ data area, PM has certain restrictions not typical on other platforms. To transfer any data from an MLE, you must first indicate where the output buffer is located. C_MLE provides a TransferBuffer() method to assign this address. Once this address is set, data importing and exporting operations can be performed.

TransferBuffer() is a simple wrapper for the MLM_SETIMPORTEXPORT message. It accepts a pointer to the transfer buffer and the size of the buffer and passes these to the MLE control code.

```
//----------------
// TransferBuffer \
//-----------------------------------------------------------------------
// Description:
//      This method sets the buffer where MLE transfers will take place.
//      This is primarily used by OS/2 to control the import and export
//      of text from the MLE window.
//
```

```
// Parameters:
//      szString     - Pointer to import/export buffer
//      lSize        - Size of the buffer
//
// Returns:
//      none
//
void C_MLE::TransferBuffer( char *szString, LONG lSize )
{
   // Set the import/export transfer buffer
   SendMsg( MLM_SETIMPORTEXPORT, (void *)szString, lSize );
}
```

Assuming that the transfer buffer has been set correctly, the ExportBuffer() method can be called to extract a block of text from the MLE window into the transfer area. The Save() method uses this method to extract text it writes to a file.

This method accepts pointers to two parameters representing the beginning and end byte offsets of the MLE text block which is being transferred.

```
//--------------
// ExportBuffer \
//---------------------------------------------------------------------------
// Description:
//      This method exports the text in the specified range to the transfer
//      buffer.
//
// Parameters:
//      ipStart      - Byte offset to start of export
//      ipEnd        - Byte offset for end of export
//
// Returns:
//      none
//
void C_MLE::ExportBuffer( LONG *ipStart, LONG *ipEnd )
{
   SendMsg( MLM_EXPORT, (void *)ipStart, (void *)ipEnd );
}
```

The C_MLE class also offers complete support for text searches within the MLE window. The FindFirst() and find Next() methods implement this capability. Both methods use the xtSearch class attribute, which is provided by Presentation Manager to hold search setup parameters.

FindFirst() accepts a pointer to the search string and initializes the xtSearch attributes to perform a search for an exact match, without regard to the text case. If a match is found, the xtSearch attribute will be returned with information that can be used to perform subsequent searches. If no search string is located in the MLE buffer, the method will produce an error tone.

When performing FindNext() operations, an error tone will be produced if the previous search returned no result (xtSearch.cchFind = 0) or there are no further matches. One important thing to note with search operations is that the cursor and MLE text view will be updated so that any matching string will be placed in the viewable portion of the MLE. Window scrolling will be performed, if required, by the control itself.

```
//----------
// FindFirst \
//---------------------------------------------------------------------------
// Description:
//     This method searches for the first instance of the specified string
//     within the editor window.
//
// Parameters:
//     szString    - String to search for
//
// Returns:
//     none
//
void C_MLE::FindFirst( char *szString )
{
   memset( &xtSearch, 0, sizeof( MLE_SEARCHDATA ) );
   xtSearch.cb = sizeof( MLE_SEARCHDATA );
   xtSearch.pchFind = szString;
   xtSearch.cchFind = (short)strlen( szString );
   xtSearch.iptStart = 0;
   xtSearch.iptStop = -1;
   if( !(BOOL)SendMsg( MLM_SEARCH, (void *)MLFSEARCH_SELECTMATCH,
                              (void *)&xtSearch ) )
   {
       DosBeep( 100, 100 );
   }
}


//---------
// FindNext \
//---------------------------------------------------------------------------
// Description:
//     This method searches for the next instance of the previously defined
//     search string.
//
// Parameters:
//     none
//
// Returns:
//     none
//
```

Load() first removes all previously loaded text by calling the Delete() member function, then disables updates to the MLE in order to prevent unnecessary screen flicker while text is being loaded. In order to improve performance, Load() reads lines of text from the specified file into a large static buffer until approximately 2 Kbytes are acquired. At this point the buffer is transferred to the MLE window and reinitialized for the next block of text. This is done to reduce the number of writes required for the MLE, since each one involves a significant overhead in Presentation Manager.

When the file is transferred to the MLE, it is re-enabled and the cursor is repositioned to the first line and column.

```
//------
// Load \
//-----------------------------------------------------------------------
// Description:
//     This method loads the specified file contents into the editor window.
//
// Parameters:
//     pxcStatus           - Pointer to optional status line where load status
//                           will be displayed
//     szFileName          - Filename to load
//
// Returns:
//     none
//
void C_MLE::Load( C_STATUS *pxcStatus, char *szFileName )
{
   char    szBuffer[3000];
   char    szString[512];
   FILE    *hFile;

   // Disable refresh and ensure that the MLE is erased
   Delete( 0, BufferLength() );
   SendMsg( MLM_FORMAT, MPFROMSHORT( MLFIE_CFTEXT ), 0 );
   DisableRefresh();

   if( pxcStatus )
       pxcStatus->Text( "Loading..." );

   hFile = fopen( szFileName, "rt" );
   if( hFile )
   {
       strcpy( szBuffer, "" );
       while( !feof( hFile ) && fgets( szString, 512, hFile ) )
       {
           // Replace EOL with a NULL
```

```
            if( strstr( szString, "\r" ) )
                *strstr( szString, "\r" ) = 0;
            if( strstr( szString, "\n" ) )
                *strstr( szString, "\n" ) = 0;

            strcat( szBuffer, szString );
            strcat( szBuffer, "\r\n" );

            if( strlen( szBuffer ) > 2048 )
            {
                Insert( szBuffer );
                strcpy( szBuffer, "" );
            }
        }

        Insert( szBuffer );

        fclose( hFile );
    }

    // Clear the selection and refresh the window
    Select( 0, 0 );
    EnableRefresh();

    if( pxcStatus )
        pxcStatus->Text( "Loading Complete..." );

    // Reset the "dirty" buffer flag so we can detect any changes
    ResetDirtyBufferFlag();
}
```

The complementary operation to loading a file is saving. The C_MLE class also provides a Save() method, used to transfer text from the MLE window back to a specified filename. This routine consists primarily of a loop to extract every line in the MLE. It first determines byte offset of the start of each line and the length of the line and exports the information to a temporary string. Each line is then written to the output file.

A very important point needs to be made with regard to Load() and Save(). These methods can consume a relatively large amount of CPU time, depending on the size of file. For this reason, these methods should never be called from the main thread of execution. Doing so would most likely violate the 1⁄10 second rule and result in system slowdowns. The proper use of these methods requires a separate thread of execution, of which you will see examples in the news and FTP applications in Part III of this book.

```
//------
// Save \
//--------------------------------------------------------------------------
// Description:
//     This method saves the edit window contents to the specified file.
//
// Parameters:
//     pxcStatus          - Pointer to optional status line where save status
//                          will be displayed
//     szFileName         - Filename to save
//
// Returns:
//     LONG               - Line number containing the specified point
//
void C_MLE::Save( C_STATUS *pxcStatus, char *szFileName )
{
   char    szString[4096];
   FILE    *hFile;
   IPT     iPoint;
   IPT     iEndPoint;
   LONG    lTotal;
   LONG    lCount;

   hFile = fopen( szFileName, "w" );

   lTotal = NumberOfLines();

   SendMsg( MLM_FORMAT, MPFROMSHORT( MLFIE_NOTRANS ), 0 );
   TransferBuffer( szString, 4096 );
   iPoint = 0;

   for( lCount = 0; lCount < lTotal; lCount++ )
   {
       // Get the text parameter for the current line
       iPoint = Column( lCount );
       iEndPoint = (IPT)SendMsg(MLM_QUERYLINELENGTH, (void *)iPoint, 0 );

       // Get the text for the current line
       memset( szString, 0, 4096 );
       ExportBuffer( &iPoint, &iEndPoint );

       if( strlen( szString ) )
       {
           // Replace EOL with a NULL
           if( strstr( szString, "\r" ) )
               *strstr( szString, "\r" ) = 0;
           if( strstr( szString, "\n" ) )
               *strstr( szString, "\n" ) = 0;
```

```
            fprintf( hFile, "%s\r\n", szString );
        }
    }

    fclose( hFile );

    if( pxcStatus )
        pxcStatus->Text( "Saving Complete..." );

    // Reset the "dirty" buffer flag so we can detect any changes
    ResetDirtyBufferFlag();
}
```

CUA Container Class

The container control is a special CUA'91 control supplied by Presentation Manager. A container is simply a very fancy list box, which permits the user to select items or scroll through a list of items. However, this is where the comparison ends.

Container controls support a myriad of enhancements over a normal list box. For example, a container can be configured in one of several views, including a detail view which can display fields for each record item, or an icon view that permits rearrangement of items and caters to the direct manipulation capabilities of OS/2. There are other views as well, but the most unique view is the tree view. Tree view permits container items to have an infinite number of children and grandchildren, and produces a hierarchical list of items.

Each of the views offers its own capabilities and limitations. Detail view supports columns and multiple selection, tree supports a dichotomy display but prevents multiple selection. In all views, however, it is easy to embed icons or bitmaps—something much more difficult to accomplish with a simple list box.

The PMCLASS library implements container control support. However, because this is a CUA'91 control, it has no direct equivalent in Windows; portability was not a prime concern when designing it. In particular, detail view still requires that you write PM API code rather than creating objects for each column. Though I have not devoted much time to a C++ column class, you should be able to implement one in your own designs if you dislike the thought of a hybrid C/C++ application.

The C_CONTAINER class in the PMCLASS library implements the definition for the container class. This class is illustrated in the following figure.

C_CONTAINER	
int iView	C_CONTAINER() ~C_CONTAINER() void Setup()

C_CONTAINER *(Continued)*	
	void Insert()
	void InsertUpdate()
	void Remove()
	void Erase()
	void Redraw()
	void Sort()
	void *Search()
	void *ParentRecord()
	void *FirstRecord()
	void *MemoryFirstRecord()
	void *MemoryNextRecord()
	void *NextRecord()
	void *PreviousRecord()
	void *FirstChild()
	void *LastChild()
	void *FirstSelected()
	void *NextSelected()
	void ExpandTree()
	void CompressTree()
	void SelectRecord()

Figure 6-16 C_CONTAINER class

The header file for C_CONTAINER is shown in Listing 6-15:

```
//-----------------------------------
// View definitions for a container \
//--------------------------------------------------------------------------
#define    D_VIEW_NONE            -1  // Invisible (no view)
#define    D_VIEW_DETAIL_TITLE     0  // Detail view with titles
#define    D_VIEW_DETAIL           1  // Detail view - no titles
#define    D_VIEW_TREE             2  // Tree View
#define    D_VIEW_ICON             3  // Icon View (Currently unsupported)

//-----------------------------
// C_CONTAINER class definition \
//--------------------------------------------------------------------------
class C_CONTAINER : public C_WINDOW_CHILD
{
   private:
     int   iView;      // Display view

   public:
```

```
    _Export   C_CONTAINER( C_WINDOW *pxcParentObj, int iID, int iView,
                                            int iFlags, int iMode );
    _Export   C_CONTAINER( C_WINDOW *pxcParentObj, int iID, int iView,
                                            int iFlags );
    _Export   C_CONTAINER( C_DIALOG *pxcParentObj, int iID, int iView,
                                            int iFlags );
    _Export   ~C_CONTAINER( void );
    void _Export  Setup( int iView, int iFlags );
    void * _Export    Allocate( ULONG iLength, USHORT iCtr );
    void _Export  Insert( void *pParent, void *pRecord,
                                            int iCount, int iUpdate );
    void _Export  Insert( void *pParent, void *pRecord, int iCount );
    void _Export  InsertUpdate( void *pParent, void *pRecord, int iCount );
    void _Export  Remove( void );
    void _Export  Remove( void*pvData, short iCount );
    void _Export  Redraw( void *pRecord );
    void _Export  Sort( void * );
    void * _Export    Search( void *pStart, char *szString,unsigned int iType );
    void * _Export    ParentRecord( void *hCurrent );
    void * _Export    FirstRecord( void );
    void * _Export    MemoryFirstRecord( void );
    void * _Export    MemoryNextRecord( void *hCurrent );
    void * _Export    NextRecord( void *hCurrent );
    void * _Export    PreviousRecord( void *hCurrent );
    void * _Export    FirstChild( void *hParent );
    void * _Export    LastChild( void *hParent );
    void * _Export    FirstSelected( void );
    void * _Export    NextSelected( void *hCurrent );
    void _Export ExpandTree( void *pRecord );
    void _Export CompressTree( void *pRecord );
    void _Export SelectRecord( void *pRecord, short sBool );
};

// Structure used by icon and tree views to hold icon resources
typedef struct
{
   char        szType[2];
   int         iResource;
   HPOINTER    hIcon;
} T_LOOKUP;
```

Listing 6-15 CONTAIN.HPP – Class definition for C_CONTAINER

The C_CONTAINER class implements three constructors. The first two are used if the container is created dynamically at run time. The first of these provides an iMode parameter with which you can provide additional creation parameters for the window. These parameters are operating system dependent, so refer to the PM API documentation to determine the valid parameters for a container window.

Valid container styles supported by Presentation Manager are summarized in the following table.

CCS_AUTOPOSITION	In icon view, icons are automatically positioned according to a grid.
CCS_MINIRECORDCORE	Containers use a smaller record type that uses less memory but is more limited in its capabilities.
CCS_READONLY	Container records are set as read only.
CCS_VERIFYPOINTERS	Records are verified to valid items in the container's linked list before they are used.
CCS_SINGLESEL	Single record selection is supported.
CCS_MULTIPLESEL	Multiple record selection is permitted.
CCS_EXTENDEDSEL	Extended multiple selection is supported.

```
//-------------
// C_CONTAINER \
//---------------------------------------------------------------------------
//
// Description:
//     This constructor creates an instance of the C_CONTAINER class. This
//     class will typically be abstract, so this constructor will generally
//     not be called directly.
//
// Parameters:
//     pxcParentObj    - Pointer to owner object window
//     iID             - Resource ID of the container window
//     iView           - View of the container (see header file)
//     iFlags          - Any additional setup flags
//     iMode           - Any additional container window parameters
//
C_CONTAINER::C_CONTAINER( C_WINDOW *pxcParentObj, int iID, int iView,
                    int iFlags, int iMode ) : C_WINDOW_CHILD( pxcParentObj, 0 )
{
   ClassName( WC_CONTAINER );
   // Create the group list box
   if( iView == D_VIEW_NONE )
       Create( iID, iMode, "", 0, 0, 90, 30 );
   else
       Create( iID, WS_VISIBLE | iMode, "", 0, 0, 90, 30 );
   // Setup the group container
   Setup( iView, iFlags );
}
```

The iView parameter determines which view is to be used when the container is displayed. Below is a code fragment from the CONTAIN.HPP file showing the valid view values.

```
//----------------------------------
// View definitions for a container \
//----------------------------------------------------------------------------
#define    D_VIEW_NONE               -1  // Invisible (no view)
#define    D_VIEW_DETAIL_TITLE       0   // Detail view with titles
#define    D_VIEW_DETAIL             1   // Detail view - no titles
#define    D_VIEW_TREE               2   // Tree View
#define    D_VIEW_ICON               3   // Icon View (Currently unsupported)
```

The second constructor is similar to the first, except that it defaults the container mode parameters to some predetermined values permitting extended item selection and preventing the user from performing editing operations.

```
C_CONTAINER::C_CONTAINER( C_WINDOW *pxcParentObj, int iID, int iView,
                        int iFlags ) : C_WINDOW_CHILD( pxcParentObj, 0 )
{
  ClassName( WC_CONTAINER );

  // Create the group list box
  if( iView == D_VIEW_NONE )
     Create( iID, CCS_READONLY|CCS_EXTENDSEL|
           CCS_VERIFYPOINTERS|CCS_AUTOPOSITION, "", 0, 0, 90, 30 );
  else
     Create( iID, WS_VISIBLE|CCS_READONLY|CCS_EXTENDSEL|
           CCS_VERIFYPOINTERS|CCS_AUTOPOSITION, "", 0, 0, 90, 30 );

  // Setup the group container
  Setup( iView, iFlags );
}
```

The final constructor is used if the container is created as part of a dialog from a resource file. In this situation, the container window already exists, so all the C_CONTAINER code needs to do is connect to it.

```
//--------------
// C_CONTAINER \
//----------------------------------------------------------------------------
//
// Description:
//     This constructor creates an instance of the C_CONTAINER class which
//     originates in a dialog box supplied by the resource file. This
//     class will typically be abstract, so this constructor will generally
//     not be called directly.
```

```
//
// Parameters:
//     pxcParentObj        - Pointer to owner object dialog
//     iID                 - Resource ID of the container window
//     iView               - View of the container (see header file)
//     iFlags              - Any additional setup flags
//     iMode               - Any additional container window parameters
//
C_CONTAINER::C_CONTAINER( C_DIALOG *pxcParentObj, int iID, int iView,
                          int iFlags ) : C_WINDOW_CHILD( pxcParentObj, 0 )
{
   ClassName( WC_CONTAINER );

   // The window was created by the dialog system, so all we need to
   // do is atach the instance to it.
   C_WINDOW::Create( ParentObject()->Window(),
                     WinWindowFromID( ParentObject()->Window(), iID ) );

   // Setup the group container
   Setup( iView, iFlags );
}
```

The C_CONTAINER class implements a destructor which ensures that all container items are removed, freeing any dynamic memory associated with them.

```
//---------------
// ~C_CONTAINER \
//-----------------------------------------------------------------------------
// Description:
//     This destructor removes all items from the container before it is
//     destroyed.
//
// Parameters:
//     none
//
C_CONTAINER::~C_CONTAINER( void )
{
   // Remove all records in the container
   Remove();
}
```

Each of the constructors place a call to the Setup() method. This method is typically internal, so it will likely never be called directly by a program unless you want to implement code to support multiple views. This code sets view for a container object. The iFlags parameter specifies any additional operating system specific container window attributes. See the PM on-line API documentation for details of these additional flags.

```
//--------
// Setup \
//--------------------------------------------------------------------------
// Description:
//     This method sets up the container according to specified view.
//
// Parameters:
//     iView            - D_VIEW_DETAIL_TITLE, D_VIEW_DETAIL, D_VIEW_TREE
//     iFlags           - Any additional PM container flags
//
// Returns:
//     none
//
void C_CONTAINER::Setup( int iView, int iFlags )
{
   CNRINFO     CI;

   // Setup the container format
   CI.cb = sizeof( CNRINFO );

   // Configure the correct container view
   switch( iView )
   {
       case D_VIEW_DETAIL_TITLE:
           CI.flWindowAttr = CV_DETAIL | CA_TITLESEPARATOR |
                                        CA_DETAILSVIEWTITLES | iFlags;
           break;
       case D_VIEW_DETAIL:
           CI.flWindowAttr = CV_DETAIL | iFlags;
           break;
       case D_VIEW_TREE:
           CI.flWindowAttr = CV_TREE | CV_ICON | CA_TREELINE | iFlags;
           break;
   }

   // Set the icon size and spacing for any icons that get shown
   CI.cyLineSpacing = 0;
   CI.slBitmapOrIcon.cx = WinQuerySysValue( HWND_DESKTOP, SV_CYMENU );
   CI.slBitmapOrIcon.cy = CI.slBitmapOrIcon.cx;

   // Perform the container setup
   SendMsg( CM_SETCNRINFO, MPFROMP( &CI ), MPFROMLONG(
                CMA_FLWINDOWATTR | CMA_LINESPACING|CMA_SLBITMAPORICON ) );
}
```

A container is really just a large linked list with display capability. In order to insert new items into this list, space must first be allocated dynamically. The Allocate() method manages this task.

There are two basic techniques for loading a container; depending on the specific situation, you may want to use either. For initial loading of a container, performance is better if the number of items to be inserted is first determined, then enough space allocated for all items. If you are inserting 3,000 records into a container, allocate space for 3,000 first rather than allocating space for each record as you go. This also has implications for memory use—allocating large memory blocks at the outset usually results in more efficient memory use.

For updates or additions to a container, you can allocate space for a single record and insert it. However, if this is an operation regularly performed by your program, then you may want to design a small memory manager that allocates records in groups and assigns them as required.

```
//----------
// Allocate \
//-------------------------------------------------------------------------
// Description:
//     This method allocates dynamic space for the specified number of
//     new container records.
//
// Parameters:
//     iLength          - Size of the record structure for the container
//     iCtr             - Number of records to allocate
//
// Returns:
//     none
//
void *C_CONTAINER::Allocate( ULONG iLength, USHORT iCtr )
{
   ULONG        cbData;

   // Determine the additional data space required
   cbData = iLength - sizeof(RECORDCORE);

   // Allocate a record
   return (void *)SendMsg( CM_ALLOCRECORD,
                            MPFROMLONG( cbData ), MPFROMSHORT(iCtr) );
}
```

C_CONTAINER implements three methods for inserting records into a container; since all three perform the same basic task, I will handle them as a unit. These operations are performed after space has been allocated and really equate to adding new items to the linked list. The distinction is the addition of an update parameter to the calling sequence.

Records can be updated (and possibly redrawn) on a record by record basis by setting the update parameter to a TRUE value. If you are inserting many records, however, you will likely not want to do this because of the significant

CPU overhead incurred by redrawing each item individually. A better method is to perform one large update after the container is completely loaded.

```
//---------
// Insert \
//---------------------------------------------------------------------
// Description:
//     This method inserts a specified number of records into the
//     container. If the pParent attribute points to an existing record,
//     then the inserts will become children of the parent record. This is
//     used primarily for Tree View. The update determines if the container
//     should be repainted after the records have been inserted.
//
// Parameters:
//     pParent          - Optional parent record
//     pRecord          - Pointer to array of records to be inserted
//     iCount           - Number of records to be inserted
//     iUpdate          - Set if repaint is required after insert
//
// Returns:
//     none
//
void C_CONTAINER::Insert( void *pParent, void *pRecord, int iCount, int iUpdate )
{
   RECORDINSERT    RI;

   // Create Insert information
   RI.cb = sizeof(RECORDINSERT);
   RI.pRecordOrder = (RECORDCORE *)CMA_END;
   RI.pRecordParent = (RECORDCORE *)pParent;
   RI.zOrder = (ULONG)CMA_TOP;
   RI.cRecordsInsert = iCount;
   RI.fInvalidateRecord = iUpdate;

   // Insert the record
   SendMsg( CM_INSERTRECORD, MPFROMP( pRecord ), MPFROMP( &RI ) );
}
```

Each of the update methods also accepts a count, and I should note that this means you can (and probably should) insert records in groups. Inserting 100 single records is much more time-consuming than creating the same 100 records and inserting them as a group.

```
//---------
// Insert \
//---------------------------------------------------------------------
// Description:
//     This method inserts a specified number of records into the
```

```
//     container. If the pParent attribute points to an existing record,
//     then the insertswill become children of the parent record. This is
//     used primarily for Tree View.
//
// Parameters:
//     pParent          - Optional parent record
//     pRecord          - Pointer to array of records to be inserted
//     iCount           - Number of records to be inserted
//
// Returns:
//     none
//
void C_CONTAINER::Insert( void *pParent, void *pRecord, int iCount )
{
   Insert( pParent, pRecord, iCount, FALSE );
}
```

The pParent parameter in the Insert method is used only for tree view containers; otherwise it should always have a NULL value. In tree view this parameter contains a pointer to a parent record, which, when displayed, will appear as a secondary branch in the record tree associated with that specified parent.

```
//--------------
// InsertUpdate \
//---------------------------------------------------------------------------
// Description:
//     This method inserts a specified number of records into the
//     container. If the pParent attribute points to an existing record,
//     then the inserts will become children of the parent record. This
//     is used primarily for Tree View.
//
// Parameters:
//     pParent          - Optional parent record
//     pRecord          - Pointer to array of records to be inserted
//     iCount           - Number of records to be inserted
//
// Returns:
//     none
//
void C_CONTAINER::InsertUpdate( void *pParent, void *pRecord, int iCount )
{
   Insert( pParent, pRecord, iCount, TRUE );
}
```

For removing records from a container, C_CONTAINER provides two methods. The first is a simple call to remove all records.

```
//---------
// Remove \
//-----------------------------------------------------------------------
// Description:
//     This method removes all records from the container and frees the
//     memory associated with the items. If records within the container use
//     dynamic memory, this memory is nOT freed by this function.
//
// Parameters:
//     none
//
// Returns:
//     none
//
void C_CONTAINER::Remove( void )
{
   // Remove all records from the container
   SendMsg( CM_REMOVERECORD, 0, MPFROM2SHORT( 0, CMA_FREE ) );
}
```

The second method accepts a pointer to an initial record and a number of records to remove, starting from the initial item. Note that the C_CONTAINER class will not free up any dynamic space allocated by derived classes. It is the responsibility of those individual classes to clean up any dynamic memory space used by each container item's members.

```
//---------
// Remove \
//-----------------------------------------------------------------------
// Description:
//     This method removes a specified number of records from the container
//     and frees the memory associated with the items. If records within the
//     container use dynamic memory, this memory is not freed by this function.
//
// Parameters:
//     pvData      - Pointer to first container record to be removed
//     iCount      - Number of record to remove
//
// Returns:
//     none
//
void C_CONTAINER::Remove( void *pvData, short iCount )
{
   PRECORDCORE     *pRecordArray;

   pRecordArray = (PRECORDCORE *)new PRECORDCORE[iCount];
```

```
    pRecordArray[0] = (PRECORDCORE)pvData;
    SendMsg( CM_REMOVERECORD, pRecordArray, MPFROM2SHORT( iCount, CMA_FREE ) );

    delete pRecordArray;
}
```

When container records change, they may need to be redrawn. C_CONTAINER implements a Redraw() method to manage this operation. It can accept a pointer to an individual record to redraw, or a NULL value to redraw the entire container.

```
//---------
// Redraw \
//-------------------------------------------------------------------------
// Description:
//     This method forces all records in the container to be refreshed,
//     forcing the entire container to redraw.
//
// Parameters:
//     pvData       - Pointer to first container record to be redrawn
//
// Returns:
//     none
//
void C_CONTAINER::Redraw( void *pRecord )
{
    PRECORDCORE     *pRecordArray;

    // Redraw records in the container
    if( pRecord )
    {
        pRecordArray = (PRECORDCORE *)new PRECORDCORE[1];
        pRecordArray[0] = (PRECORDCORE)pRecord;

        SendMsg( CM_INVALIDATERECORD, pRecordArray,
                                    MPFROM2SHORT( 1, CMA_TEXTCHANGED ) );
        delete pRecordArray;
    }
    else
        SendMsg( CM_INVALIDATERECORD, 0, MPFROM2SHORT( 0, CMA_ERASE ) );
}
```

Container records can also be sorted, either at insertion time or as part of a re-sort operation. For the latter operation, C_CONTAINER offers a Sort() method that accepts a pointer to a sorting function.

```
//-------
// Sort \
//--------------------------------------------------------------------------
// Description:
//     This method forces all records in the container to be sorted
//     according to the sort "C" function specified. The sort function
//     must be defined with "C" linkage to prevent compiler errors.
//
// Parameters:
//     SortFunc        - Pointer to the sorting function
//
// Returns:
//     none
//
void C_CONTAINER::Sort( void *SortFunc )
{
   // Remove all records from the container
   SendMsg( CM_SORTRECORD, SortFunc, 0 );
}
```

A sort function has a particular format, but is really a pretty simple function to create. In the code fragment below shows a short method to sort records by their date fields.

```
SHORT APIENTRY SortMsgByDate( T_MSGRECORD *r1, T_MSGRECORD *r2, PVOID pvStorage )
{
   return (SHORT)strcmp( r2->szDate, r1->szDate );
}
```

The first two parameters are pointers to record structures used by the container. You will hear more about these later. Basically the sort function above compares the date fields for the two supplied records and returns a value less than zero, greater than zero, or equal to zero. This return value is used by the sorting mechanism to determine if a swap should occur.

C_CONTAINER also makes provision for string searches in container records. You can specify the starting record for a search, the string for which you are searching, and the view that will be searched. The search method implemented here is limited to full word, case-insensitive searches; however, adding another method or modifying the one supplied will provide these extensions.

```
//---------
// Search \
//--------------------------------------------------------------------------
// Description:
//     This method accepts a starting record and string and searches for
//     the specified string in the container view determined by the iType
//     parameter.
```

```
//
//     iType is one of CV_DETAIL, CV_ICON, or CV_TREE views.
//
// Parameters:
//     pStart      - Search starting record (0 for first record)
//     szString    - Pointer to search string
//     iType       - Container view to search
//
// Returns:
//     none
//
void *C_CONTAINER::Search( void *pStart, char *szString, unsigned int iType )
{
   SEARCHSTRINGxtSearch;

   // Set up general search parameters
   xtSearch.cb = sizeof( SEARCHSTRING );
   xtSearch.pszSearch = (PSZ)szString;
   xtSearch.usView = iType;
   xtSearch.fsPrefix = (ULONG)FALSE;
   xtSearch.fsCaseSensitive = (ULONG)FALSE;

   // Convert NULL start points to a real container start (CMA_FIRST)
   if( pStart == NULL )
       pStart = (void *)CMA_FIRST;

   // Search the container for the selected record
   return SendMsg( CM_SEARCHSTRING, MPFROMP( &xtSearch ), MPFROMP( pStart ) );
}
```

If you are using tree view, there may be times when you need to determine if there is a parent record associated with the record you are working with. Using C_CONTAINER derived classes, you can place a call to the ParentRecord() method, which will either return a pointer to the parent record or a NULL if there is no parent.

```
//---------------
// ParentRecord \
//------------------------------------------------------------------------------
// Description:
//     This method will return a pointer to the parent record of the container
//     record specified. If no parent exists, a NULL value is returned. The
//     function would only be applicable to tree views of containers.
//
// Parameters:
//     hCurrent    - Pointer to child record
//
```

```
// Returns:
//     none
//
void *C_CONTAINER::ParentRecord( void *hCurrent )
{
   // Return the first record
   return SendMsg( CM_QUERYRECORD, hCurrent,
                        MPFROM2SHORT( CMA_PARENT, CMA_ITEMORDER ) );
}
```

There are a number of methods used to traverse records within a container. The simplest are the FirstRecord(), NextRecord(), and PreviousRecord() methods.

```
//-------------
// FirstRecord \
//-------------------------------------------------------------------
// Description:
//     This method will return a pointer to the first record in the container.
//     If the container is empty, this method will return a NULL pointer.
//
// Parameters:
//     none
//
// Returns:
//     none
//
void *C_CONTAINER::FirstRecord( void )
{
   // Return the first record
   return SendMsg( CM_QUERYRECORD, 0,MPFROM2SHORT( CMA_FIRST, CMA_ITEMORDER ) );
}
```

FirstRecord() simply returns a pointer to the first record in the container, respecting the sorting technique currently in place. Note that the first record inserted into the container is not necessarily the first record returned by this method, since sorting may shuffle items around.

NextRecord() steps to the next record after the one supplied as a parameter. Again, sort order is respected by this method. If the end of the list is reached, the returned value will be NULL.

```
//------------
// NextRecord \
//-------------------------------------------------------------------
// Description:
//     This method will return a pointer to the next record from the
//     specified current record. If the current record is the last record,
//     a NULL value is returned.
//
```

```
// Parameters:
//     hCurrent        - Pointer to current record
//
// Returns:
//     none
//
void *C_CONTAINER::NextRecord( void *hCurrent )
{
   // Return the next record
   return SendMsg( CM_QUERYRECORD, hCurrent,
                         MPFROM2SHORT( CMA_NEXT, CMA_ITEMORDER ) );
}
```

PreviousRecord() can be used to step back one record from the record specified. If the beginning of the list is reached, the returned value is NULL.

```
//-----------------
// PreviousRecord \
//--------------------------------------------------------------------------
// Description:
//     This method will return a pointer to the previous record from the
//     specified current record. If the current record is the first record,
//     a NULL value is returned.
//
// Parameters:
//     hCurrent        - Pointer to current record
//
// Returns:
//     none
//
void *C_CONTAINER::PreviousRecord( void *hCurrent )
{
   // Return the next record
   return SendMsg( CM_QUERYRECORD, hCurrent,
                         MPFROM2SHORT( CMA_PREV, CMA_ITEMORDER ) );
}
```

To use these methods effectively to hit every record in the container, use the following code fragment as a template. Traversing records can become a time-consuming task, so use this code in a separate thread to avoid hogging the system message queue.

```
// Get the first record
pRecord = (T_RECORD *)FirstRecord();

// Loop until we reach the end of the list
while( pRecord )
{
```

```
   // Do some processing for the record

   // Go to the next record
   pRecord = (T_RECORD *)NextRecord( pRecord );
}
```

Since the FirstRecord(), NextRecord(), and PreviousRecord() methods respect the current sort order of a container, there is a significant overhead associated with using them. There is a faster but more limited way to perform the same task with C_CONTAINER. The FirstMemoryRecord() and NextMemoryRecord() methods operate in exactly the same manner, except that they operate directly on the linked list of records, thus avoiding a great deal of required processing. The disadvantage to these methods is that they have no respect for the sort order of containers, which may be a problem in applications where order is an issue. However, if you are writing code to change an attribute of every record, the memory methods perform better.

```
//--------------------
// MemoryFirstRecord \
//--------------------------------------------------------------------------
// Description:
//     This method will return a pointer to the first record in the container.
//     If the container is empty, this method will return a NULL pointer.
//
// Parameters:
//     none
//
// Returns:
//     none
//
void *C_CONTAINER::MemoryFirstRecord( void )
{
   // Return the first record
   return SendMsg( CM_QUERYRECORD, 0, MPFROM2SHORT( CMA_FIRST, CMA_ZORDER ) );
}
//------------------
// MemoryNextRecord \
//--------------------------------------------------------------------------
// Description:
//     This method will return a pointer to the next record from the
//     specified current record by using the memory pointer rather than
//     performing an actual query to the container.
//     NOTE:  This method is only useful for performing fast deletes because
//     the order is not guaranteed to be correct.
//     If the current record is the last record, a NULL value is returned.
//
// Parameters:
```

```
//    hCurrent       - Pointer to current record
//
// Returns:
//    none
//
void *C_CONTAINER::MemoryNextRecord( void *hCurrent )
{
   RECORDCORE *pRecord;

   pRecord = (RECORDCORE *)hCurrent;

   // Return the next record
   return (void *)pRecord->preccNextRecord;
}
```

The tree view container complicates things. Each new branch in a tree view essentially represents a new linked list. Consequently, the FindFirst()/FindNext() loop shown previously will not work. Instead, C_CONTAINER provides some additional methods to scan the children of a parent record. FirstChild() and LastChild() return the first and last child records for a specified parent container record respectively.

```
//-------------
// FirstChild \
//--------------------------------------------------------------------------
// Description:
//    This method will return a pointer to the first child record of the
//    specified parent record. If no child exists, this method returns
//    a NULL pointer.
//
// Parameters:
//    hParent        - Pointer to parent record
//
// Returns:
//    none
//
void *C_CONTAINER::FirstChild( void *hParent )
{
   void    *pRecord;

   // Return the first record
   pRecord = SendMsg( CM_QUERYRECORD, hParent,
                          MPFROM2SHORT( CMA_FIRSTCHILD, CMA_ZORDER ) );
   if( (LONG)pRecord == -1 )
      return 0;
   return pRecord;
}
```

```
//-----------
// LastChild \
//---------------------------------------------------------------------------
// Description:
//     This method will return a pointer to the last child record of the
//     specified parent record. If no child exists, this method return
//     a NULL pointer.
//
// Parameters:
//     hParent          - Pointer to parent record
//
// Returns:
//     none
//
void *C_CONTAINER::LastChild( void *hParent )
{
   // Return the next record
   return SendMsg( CM_QUERYRECORD, hParent,
                          MPFROM2SHORT( CMA_LASTCHILD, CMA_ZORDER ) );
}
```

The presence of child records also complicates things if we want to modify an attribute in every record in a list. Previously, I showed a code fragment for a single-level container; now, I will give you an example that accesses every record, including children, in a bi-level tree.

```
// Get the first record
pRecord = (T_RECORD *)FirstRecord();

// Loop until we reach the end of the list
while( pRecord )
{
   // Do some processing on the parent record

   // See if there are any children
   pChild = (T_RECORD *)FirstChild( pRecord );
   while( pChild )
   {
      // Do some stuff to the child record

      // Go to the next child record
      pChild = (T_RECORD *)NextRecord( pChild );
   }

   // Go to the next parent record
   pRecord = (T_RECORD *)NextRecord( pRecord );
}
```

The code required becomes far more complex for a container with several levels of children. In such cases you may need to adopt a recursion algorithm to access every record. Always be aware of the performance of container access, however, or your application will suffer from the effects of CPU loading.

Stepping through every record in a container is not practical if you want to access only those record(s) currently selected by the user. To accomplish this, C_CONTAINER provides the FirstSelected() and NextSelected() methods, which work similarly to the First/Next methods shown previously, but access only those records selected.

```
//----------------
// FirstSelected \
//-----------------------------------------------------------------------------
// Description:
//     This method will return a pointer to the first record that is selected
//     within the container. If no record is selected, this method will
//     return a NULL pointer.
//
// Parameters:
//     none
//
// Returns:
//     none
//
void *C_CONTAINER::FirstSelected( void )
{
   // Get the currently selected record
   return SendMsg( CM_QUERYRECORDEMPHASIS, (void *)CMA_FIRST,
                                 (void *)MPFROMSHORT( CRA_SELECTED ) );
}
```

These methods can be placed in a loop arrangement (similar to the one previously shown) to access every record selected by the user. There are a couple of points to note about these methods, however. First, the container must have the multiple selection or extended selection attribute set, otherwise the NextSelected() method will be of limited use.

```
//---------------
// NextSelected \
//-----------------------------------------------------------------------------
// Description:
//     This method will return a pointer to the next record that is selected
//     within the container. If no record is selected, this method will
//     return a NULL pointer. This is useful only if the container is a
//     detailed view with multiselection enabled.
//
// Parameters:
//     none
```

```
//
// Returns:
//     none
//
void *C_CONTAINER::NextSelected( void *hCurrent )
{
   LONG    lValue;

   // Get the currently selected record
   lValue = (LONG)SendMsg( CM_QUERYRECORDEMPHASIS,
                           hCurrent, MPFROMSHORT( CRA_SELECTED ) );
   if( lValue == -1 )
       lValue = 0;

   return (void *)lValue;
}
```

Second, the view must be set correctly. Tree view containers do not support multiple selection; again, the NextSelected() method is useless in this view.

The tree view container has some special characteristics. For instance, if you create a record that has children, you will notice that to the immediate left of the record in the display a "+" will appear, indicating the presence of child records. If you click the "+" icon, the tree will be expanded and the icon will change to a "-"; clicking the "-" bitmap will again collapse the tree.

Most of this functionality is handled automatically by the PM container code for the user interaction, but there may be times when you want to expand or collapse tree branches in code. C_CONTAINER implements two methods to manage this. The first of these is ExpandTree(), which accepts a parent record to expand.

```
//-------------
// ExpandTree \
//---------------------------------------------------------------------
// Description:
//     This method will expand the children of the specified parent record
//     in tree fashion. This is useful only in tree view containers.
//
// Parameters:
//     pRecord             - Pointer to current record
//
// Returns:
//     none
//
void C_CONTAINER::ExpandTree( void *pRecord )
{
   // Get the currently selected record
   SendMsg( CM_EXPANDTREE, pRecord, 0 );
}
```

The CompressTree() method collapses the specified record. Note that in both methods passing a parameter of NULL will expand or collapse all trees in the container.

```
//---------------
// CompressTree \
//-----------------------------------------------------------------------
// Description:
//     This method will compress the children of the specified parent record
//     in tree fashion. This is useful only in tree view containers.
//
// Parameters:
//     pRecord              - Pointer to current record
//
// Returns:
//     none
//
void C_CONTAINER::CompressTree( void *pRecord )
{
   // Get the currently selected record
   SendMsg( CM_COLLAPSETREE, pRecord, 0 );
}
```

The last method provided in C_CONTAINER is the SelectRecord() routine. This method permits you to select or deselect items in a container as if the user had selected them with a mouse. SelectRecord() requires a pointer to a record and a TRUE/FALSE flag to indicate whether the record is being selected or deselected.

```
//---------------
// SelectRecord \
//-----------------------------------------------------------------------
// Description:
//     This method will select or deselect the specified record as
//     determined by the Boolean state flag passed from the caller.
//
// Parameters:
//     pRecord          - Pointer to current record
//     sBool            - Select or Deselect the record (TRUE or FALSE)
//
// Returns:
//     none
//
void C_CONTAINER::SelectRecord( void *pRecord, short sBool )
{
   // Get the currently selected record
   SendMsg( CM_SETRECORDEMPHASIS, pRecord,
                 MPFROM2SHORT( sBool, CRA_SELECTED ) );
}
```

At the beginning of this section, I mentioned the column support in a detail view container. So far, however, I have not shown any code to implement this. The PMCLASS library does not implement anything like a column class; rather, it relies on the use of PM API code to create the columns in a container.

Creating the column code for a container is not difficult, and to show you just how simple it is I have included the following code fragment. This code is actually cut from the news application in Part III of this book; it derives the C_CONTAINER_MSG from the C_CONTAINER class presented here.

The first task for the Columns() method is to remove any previous columns from the container and allocate new ones—four of them in this case. It then creates a column entry for each item, including a number of parameters, as well as the columns label, which can be optionally displayed at the top of the container output, and a pointer to the record structure attribute displayed in the container.

Although I elected not to create any C++ class to define columns, this can easily be added to the library if you are a real C++ zealot; I saw little need to create another class for such a simple process. However, if you are planning to write code that creates or destroys fields dynamically during program execution, you may want to invest some time to create a class in order to simplify the task further.

```
void C_CONTAINER_MSG::Columns( void )
{
    PFIELDINFO          pfi;
    PFIELDINFO          pfiFirst;
    FIELDINFOINSERT     fii;

    // Remove any previous container column data
    pfi = (PFIELDINFO)SendMsg( CM_QUERYDETAILFIELDINFO,
                                0, MPFROMSHORT( CMA_FIRST ) );
    if( pfi )
        SendMsg( CM_REMOVEDETAILFIELDINFO,
                        MPFROMP( pfi ), MPFROM2SHORT( 0, CMA_FREE ) );

    // Allocate memory for the container column data
    pfi = (PFIELDINFO)SendMsg( CM_ALLOCDETAILFIELDINFO,
                            MPFROMLONG( 4 ), NULL );
    pfiFirst = pfi;

    // Set up information about each container column
    pfi->flData     = CFA_STRING | CFA_HORZSEPARATOR | CFA_LEFT | CFA_SEPARATOR;
    pfi->flTitle    = CFA_LEFT;
    pfi->pTitleData = "Number";
    pfi->offStruct = (ULONG)&(((T_MSGRECORD *)0)->szNumber );

    pfi             = pfi->pNextFieldInfo;
    pfi->flData     = CFA_STRING | CFA_HORZSEPARATOR | CFA_LEFT | CFA_SEPARATOR;
    pfi->flTitle    = CFA_LEFT;
    pfi->pTitleData = "Lines";
```

```
    pfi->offStruct = (ULONG)&(((T_MSGRECORD *)0)->szLines );

    pfi            = pfi->pNextFieldInfo;
    pfi->flData    = CFA_STRING | CFA_HORZSEPARATOR | CFA_LEFT | CFA_SEPARATOR;
    pfi->flTitle   = CFA_LEFT;
    pfi->pTitleData = "Subject";
    pfi->offStruct = (ULONG)&(((T_MSGRECORD *)0)->szSubject );

    pfi            = pfi->pNextFieldInfo;
    pfi->flData    = CFA_STRING | CFA_LEFT | CFA_HORZSEPARATOR;
    pfi->flTitle   = CFA_LEFT;
    pfi->pTitleData = "Author";
    pfi->offStruct = (ULONG)&(((T_MSGRECORD *)0)->szAuthor );

    // Fill in information about the column data we are about to give the
    // container.
    (void) memset( &fii, 0, sizeof( FIELDINFOINSERT ) );
    fii.cb = sizeof( FIELDINFOINSERT );
    fii.pFieldInfoOrder = (PFIELDINFO)CMA_FIRST;
    fii.cFieldInfoInsert = (SHORT)4;
    fii.fInvalidateFieldInfo = TRUE;

    // Give the container the column information
    SendMsg( CM_INSERTDETAILFIELDINFO, MPFROMP( pfiFirst ), &fii );
}
```

The result of this code is a container window, as shown in Figure 6-17.

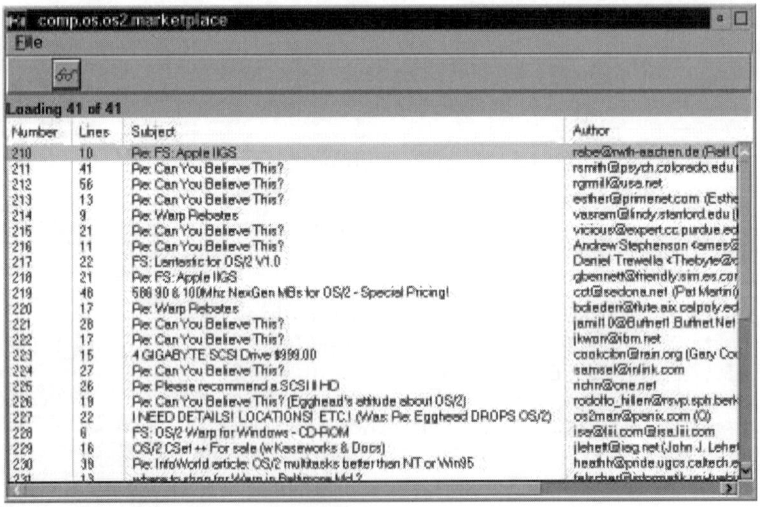

Figure 6-17 Sample container column output

To find out more detail about using the C_CONTAINER object to derive new container views, reference the news and FTP applications in Part III of this book. The use of containers will be described in more detail there.

Debug / Data Logging Class

One of the biggest headaches associated with coding is the debugging process. You need to compile and re-compile until you get a clean run. Often the debuggers most compiler vendors supply are just no use in solving a software problem. This is particularly true if you are involved in any sort of realtime (or near realtime) programming. With this type of application you cannot simply stop in mid-process to examine the state of things. Also, if the bug is related to timing, running the code inside a debugger may actually give correct results.

Debugging can be further complicated in the field once you deliver a product. Inevitably, one of the users of your software will report a bug that you simply cannot reproduce in the sterile conditions of a test lab. This is usually because users follow a different sequence of steps than you in attempting to reproduce the error, or perhaps in explaining the crash procedure to you the user inadvertently omits one or more crucial steps.

There is thus a need for a different kind of debugging. You need to be able to build debugging capability into an application so that, when a bug appears, you can examine the series of events that led to the problem in pseudo realtime. PMCLASS offers a solution to this problem in the form of a C_LOG class that writes pretty much anything you need into a programmer specified log file. By placing calls to C_LOG methods you can write time-stamped printf()-style strings into your log. Later you can analyze the log file for problems.

The C_LOG class offers two modes of operation. The first mode causes the log code simply to write the log information into the specified log file. The second, more advanced mode, makes use of the C_MLE class discussed previously to write any additional log information into a debug window created when the log file is open. This provides some realtime logging that is useful for trekking through multithreaded applications.

The C_LOG class is illustrated as follows:

C_LOG			
char	szFileName[256]	C_LOG()	
FILE	*hLogFile	~C_LOG()	
int	iLogging	void	Open()
C_WINDOW_DEBUG	*pxcDebug	void	Close()
		void	Write()

Figure 6-18 C_LOG class

C_LOG contains a pointer to the C_WINDOW_DEBUG class, which is also defined in the PMCLASS library and is dedicated to the MLE portion of C_LOG. This class should not be constructed outside PMCLASS, but I mention it here in case you want to make some enhancements to this portion of the debugging code.

C_WINDOW_DEBUG		
C_MLE	*pxcDebugMLE	C_WINDOW_DEBUG() ~C_WINDOW_DEBUG() void *MsgCreate() void *MsgAdd() void *MsgSize()

Figure 6-19 Internal C_WINDOW_DEBUG class

Since the C_WINDOW_DEBUG class is necessary for C_LOG, we will look at the code for it first. You should have some understanding of its inner workings before you attempt to determine how C_LOG uses this class.

The header file for C_LOG and C_WINDOW_DEBUG is shown below:

```
//-----------------------------------
// C_WINDOW_DEBUG class definition \
//--------------------------------------------------------------------------
class C_WINDOW_DEBUG : public C_WINDOW_STD
{
   private:
      C_MLE    *pxcDebugMLE;

   public:
      _Export C_WINDOW_DEBUG( void );
      _Export ~C_WINDOW_DEBUG( void );
      void * _Export MsgCreate( void *mp1, void *mp2 );
      void * _Export MsgAdd( void *mp1, void *mp2 );
      void * _Export MsgSize( void *mp1, void *mp2 );
};

//-----------------------
// C_LOG class definition \
//--------------------------------------------------------------------------
class     C_LOG
{
   private:
      char             szFileName[256];        // Name of log file
      FILE             *hLogFile;              // Log file handle
      int              iLogging;               // Logging mode (TRUE or FALSE)
      C_WINDOW_DEBUG   *pxcDebug;              // Debug window class
```

```
    public:
        _Export      C_LOG( char *szLogFile, int iLogMode );
        _Export      ~C_LOG( void );
        void _Export     Open( void );
        void _Export     Close( void );
        void _Export     Write( char *, ... );
};

//-----------------------------------
// C_WINDOW_DEBUG message definition \
//-----------------------------------------------------------------------------
#define         DM_DEBUG_ADD     PM_USER
```

Listing 6-18 LOG.HPP – Class definition for C_LOG

At the beginning of this chapterm I described the use of message tables and how they interrelate with PMCLASS to process window messages. Since it has a complete application window that is sizable, a system, menu, and an instance of C_MLE object to display information to the user, C_WINDOW_DEBUG could almost stand alone as a program. As such, C_WINDOW_DEBUG needs to implement a message table to tell PMCLASS how to react. The class really only cares about four window messages, as shown below. The message methods for these will be described in detail shortly.

```
DECLARE_MSG_TABLE( xtMsgDebug )
    DECLARE_MSG( PM_CREATE,          C_WINDOW_DEBUG::MsgCreate )
    DECLARE_MSG( DM_DEBUG_ADD,       C_WINDOW_DEBUG::MsgAdd )
    DECLARE_MSG( WM_SIZE,            C_WINDOW_DEBUG::MsgSize )
    DECLARE_MSG( WM_PAINT,           C_WINDOW_STD::MsgPaint )
END_MSG_TABLE
```

Like all other C++ classes, C_WINDOW_DEBUG is constructed before it is used. The constructor for this class is incredibly simple (see below). Its only requirement is to call its parent constructor, C_WINDOW_STD, to inform it about the new message table.

```
//--------------
// Constructor \
//-----------------------------------------------------------------------------
//
// Description:
//      This constructor creates an instance of the MLE window.
//
// Parameters:
//      none
//
```

```
    // Determine the size of the client area
    GetSize( &iCX, &iCY );

    // Draw the MLE Window
    pxcDebugMLE->SetSizePosition( 0, 0, iCX, iCY );

    return FALSE;
}
```

That's all there is to the C_WINDOW_DEBUG class. Now let's start looking at how C_LOG uses this class, and how debug output is written to a log file.

The basic design criteria for C_LOG are that it must operate passively, without affecting any other operation of a program, and that it must be easy to use. To meet this goal, C_LOG presents only a single constructor that accepts a log filename and the mode of operation. The mode can have values 0 through 2, determining the level of debugging to use. A zero value indicates no logging. A value of 1 indicates that C_LOG will write debug data to the log file only, and a value of 2 tells the object to write data to both the log file and to the MLE window as well. If the constructor receives a mode of 2, it registers and creates an instance of the C_WINDOW_DEBUG class. The debug window receives a sizable border and system menu, as well as a title and minimize/maximize buttons. For convenience, the window is also placed in the Workplace Shell task list also.

```
//--------------
// Constructor \
//---------------------------------------------------------------------------
//
// Description:
//      This constructor creates an instance of the C_LOG class. If the
//      iLogMode is set to 2, then the MLE display window is also created.
//
// Parameters:
//      szLogFile       - Pointer to debug log filename
//      iLogMode        - Log mode (0=no log, 1=file, 2=file and MLE)
//
C_LOG::C_LOG( char *szLogFile, int iLogMode )
{
    strcpy( szFileName, szLogFile );
    iLogging = iLogMode;
    pxcDebug = NULL;

    // If an MLE output is required, create an instance
    if( iLogging == 2 )
    {
        // Create an instance of a debugging window
        pxcDebug = (C_WINDOW_DEBUG *)new C_WINDOW_DEBUG;
        pxcDebug->Register( "DebugConsole" );
```

```
        // Set the window characteristics
        pxcDebug->WCF_SizingBorder();
        pxcDebug->WCF_SysMenu();
        pxcDebug->WCF_TaskList();
        pxcDebug->WCF_ShellPosition();
        pxcDebug->WCF_MinButton();
        pxcDebug->WCF_MaxButton();
        pxcDebug->WCF_TitleBar();
    }
}
```

C_LOG also provides a destructor method. This code frees up the dynamic data area used to create the instance of C_WINDOW_DEBUG in the constructor.

```
//--------------
// Destructor \
//------------------------------------------------------------------------
//
// Description:
//      This destructor destroys the MLE display window if it was created
//      during the construction process.
//
C_LOG::~C_LOG( void )
{
    if( pxcDebug )
        delete pxcDebug;
}
```

The newly created C_LOG instance cannot yet be written to; it first needs to be opened. The Open() method first deletes any previous log file, then opens a new file handle used to write the debug data. If the MLE window is being used, then the C_WINDOW_DEBUG object is created and displayed as well.

```
//---------
// Open() \
//------------------------------------------------------------------------
//
// Description:
//      This method opens the debug log. It first creates a new log file then,
//      if required, displays the MLE window.
//
// Parameters:
//      none
//
// Returns:
//      void
//
void C_LOG::Open( void )
```

```
{
   // Remove any log file left from a previous run
   DosForceDelete( (PSZ)szFileName );

   if( iLogging )
   {
       hLogFile = fopen( szFileName, "w" );
       if( iLogging == 2 )
       {
           pxcDebug->Create( 99999, "PMCLASS Debugging Window" );
           pxcDebug->Show();
       }
       Write( "Log Open" );
   }
}
```

When debug logging is finished, the log file (and possibly the C_WINDOW_DEBUG instance) needs to be closed, otherwise there is a risk of leaving open file handles floating around the system. The C_LOG::Close() method closes the file handle used for debug logging and, if necessary, hides the MLE window.

```
//----------
// Close() \
//--------------------------------------------------------------------------
//
// Description:
//     This method closes the debug log. If the MLE window is currently
//     visible it will be hidden.
//
// Parameters:
//     none
//
// Returns:
//     void
//
void C_LOG::Close( void )
{
   if( iLogging )
   {
       Write( "Log Closed" );
       fclose( hLogFile );
       if( iLogging == 2 )
           pxcDebug->Hide();
   }
}
```

The final method in C_LOG is the most important. Write() accepts a variable number of arguments since it features a printf() style input; after formatting the output string, it is written to the log file and optionally to the MLE window.

Write() further aids the debugging process by prefixing a time stamp to each line it writes. This time stamp has the format MM:SS:HH, where MM is the time in minutes, SS is the number of seconds, and HH is the number of hundredths of seconds.

If the MLE window is enabled, Write() sends a DM_DEBUG_ADD message to the C_WINDOW_DEBUG object accompanied by a pointer to the output string. This causes the information to be written to the MLE buffer, followed by a carriage return.

C_LOG::Write() has a restriction of which you should be aware. Notice that the szString variable, which is used to hold the formatted output string, is a static buffer of 4K. This prevents you from displaying anything larger than this without risking a memory protection violation. Write() makes no attempt to verify that the output buffer will not exceed a size of 4 Kbytes.

```
//----------
// Write() \
//---------------------------------------------------------------------------
//
// Description:
//     This method accepts a printf-style string and will format and write
//     the string to the log file and optionally to the MLE window. A
//     time stamp will be prefixed to all strings written.
//
// Parameters:
//     szFormat     - A printf-style variable argument list
//
// Returns:
//     void
//
void C_LOG::Write( char *szFormat, ... )
{
   DATETIME     dt;
   va_list      xtArgs;
   char         szString[4096];
   char         szTemp[80];

   if( iLogging )
   {
       va_start( xtArgs, szFormat );
       vsprintf( szString, szFormat, xtArgs );
       va_end( xtArgs );

       DosGetDateTime( &dt );
```

```
        fprintf( hLogFile, "%02d:%02d:%02d->", dt.minutes, dt.seconds,
                                            dt.hundredths );
        fprintf( hLogFile, "%s\n", szString );
        fflush( hLogFile );

        if( iLogging == 2 )
        {
            sprintf( szTemp, "%02d:%02d:%02d->", dt.minutes,
                                        dt.seconds, dt.hundredths );
            pxcDebug->SendMsg( DM_DEBUG_ADD, szTemp, 0 );
            strcat( szString, "\n" );
            pxcDebug->SendMsg( DM_DEBUG_ADD, szString, 0 );
        }
    }
}
```

Chapter Summary

In this chapter, we have developed all the visual classes in the PMCLASS class library. PMCLASS will be used extensively in applications later in the book. It is hoped that you now understand the concepts and source code of these classes.

PMCLASS can be considered a hybrid class library for OS/2. It operates at a higher, more object-oriented level than the standard OS/2 API, but it by no means represents a complete wrap of the API, like the IBM ICLUI classes or Borland Object Windows Library. It does, however, lend itself to easy expansion to further isolate developers from the basic API, and also features a very simple route back to the API if you find that you need a function from the basic PM library. Although not constructed with portability in mind, PMCLASS should be relatively easy to port should you need to create applications spanning several platforms. Windows NT or Windows'95 should be relatively easy ports, since the Windows API is so similar to OS/2's. Other platforms, like UNIX X Motif, will likely be more difficult because (although some would disagree) these APIs are relatively primitive by comparison with OS/2's.

PMCLASS is best viewed as a foundation to build on. I would fully expect you to add new classes to suit your own needs. For example, PMCLASS currently offers no GDI graphing interface other than that accessible from the standard PM API. For many developers, graphics capability is very important; building expansion classes into PMCLASS for this should not be difficult.

In this chapter

- Eliminating TCP/IP socket interfaces
- TCP/IP network protocols with NETCLASS
- Enhanced network throughput with multithreading

7

Developing a Network Interface Class Library

What is NETCLASS?

In this chapter we will finally start to discuss the classes associated with TCP/IP networking, and we will study several different protocols. All the classes developed in this chapter will be placed in a separate class library DLL called NETCLASS.DLL. In the third part of this book we will use the classes in NETCLASS to create working applications.

The object hierarchy for the NETCLASS library can be shown as follows:

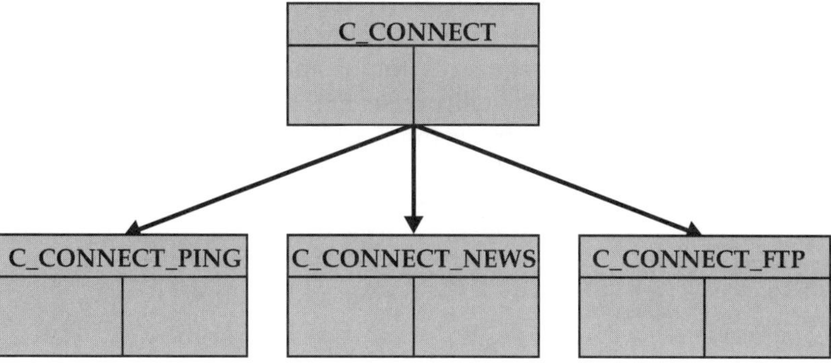

Figure 7-1 NETCLASS class hierarchy

In an earlier chapter I mentioned RFCs (Requests For Comment), which are documents describing changes or additions to the way the Internet communicates. When required, all class code described in this chapter will reference the appropriate RFCs.

The goal in developing a network class library is to isolate the programmer from the perils of normal TCP/IP programming. The TCP/IP API contains many confusing data structures and function calls; for the most part you will use very few of them. The most logical step in developing a C++ class library for TCP/IP, therefore, is to eliminate as much of the complexity as possible by implementing classes that encapsulate the important aspects of TCP/IP, while hiding the rest.

One of the most confusing aspects of TCP/IP programming is the use of network sockets. In the NETCLASS library, the socket code is wrapped in the base class and hidden from the derived children. This makes the design and implementation of the derived classes much less complicated. Once the base network class is in place, adding derived classes to support different network protocols should be a relatively simple exercise.

The NETCLASS library developed in this chapter implements classes to support Ping, NNTP News, and FTP protocols, but more protocol classes can be added as required to support such applications as IRC, Gopher, or Mail.

The C_CONNECT Class

The C_CONNECT class is the basis for all network classes in the class library. In contains all the code needed to wrap the TCP/IP API and hide most of its internals from the programmer. This class creates a complete set of methods needed to implement all the child networking classes used in this book, and you should also be able to use this base class to derive classes for other protocols.

If you decide to create additional applications, you will need to derive a new child class, and may need to expand the capabilities of the C_CONNECT class. Generally, it is best to push as much logic as possible into the base class because you may need the same code in several applications. News and FTP use virtually identical connection sequences, for instance, and it would be counterproductive to implement this functionality in several places in the code.

The following figure illustrates the C_CONNECT class:

C_CONNECT			
char	szServer[256]	C_CONNECT()	
int	iPort	void	Initialize()
int	iSocket	int	FindHost()
int	iBusy	int	Protocol()
char	szNetBuffer[D_NET_BUFFER+1]	int	StreamSocket()
char	*szNetBufferPtr	int	RawSocket()

C_CONNECT *(Continued)*	
struct sockaddr_in xtSocket struct protoent *pxtProtocol	int Open() void Close() int Send() int SendTo() int ReceiveFrom() int ReceiveBuffer() void Receive() void LoadFile() char * Server() int Port() int Socket() void Busy() int Busy()

Figure 7-2 C_CONNECT class

The header file for C_CONNECT is shown in Listing 7-1:

```
//---------------------------------
// IBM TCP/IP header files required \
//-----------------------------------------------------------------------------
#ifndef NET_INCL
#define NET_INCL
extern "C"
{
   #include <types.h>
   #include <sys\socket.h>
   #include <netinet\in.h>
   #include <netinet\in_systm.h>
   #include <netinet\ip.h>
   #include <netinet\ip_icmp.h>
   #include <netdb.h>
}
#endif

//---------------------------
// Network error return codes \
//-----------------------------------------------------------------------------
#define    D_NET_OK         0          // Net operation successful
#define    D_NET_HOST       -1         // Error resolving host
#define    D_NET_SOCKET     -2         // Error while creating socket
#define    D_NET_CONNECT    -3         // Error while connecting
#define    D_NET_RECV       -4         // Error while receiving
#define    D_NET_BUSY       -5         // Error: Connection Busy
```

```
#define    D_NET_PROTOCOL  -6         // Error in protocol

#define    D_NET_BUFFER    4096       // Size of network read buffer

//--------------------------------
// C_CONNECT base class definition \
//--------------------------------------------------------------------------
class C_CONNECT
{
  protected:
      char    szServer[256];                   // Domain Name or IP
      int     iPort;                           // Port number used
      int     iSocket;                         // Socket for connection
      int     iBusy;                           // Set if instance is busy
      char    szNetBuffer[D_NET_BUFFER+1];     // Buffer for network data
      char    *szNetBufferPtr;                 // Current pointer to buffer

      struct  sockaddr_in     xtSocket;        // Socket structure used
      struct  protoent        *pxtProtocol;    // Protocol used

  public:
      _Export C_CONNECT( char *szConnectServer, int iPort );
#ifdef __BORLANDC__
      _Export C_CONNECT( void ) {};
#else
      C_CONNECT( void ) {};
#endif
      void  _Export  Initialize( char *szConnectServer, int iConnectPort );
      int   _Export  FindHost( void );
      int   _Export  Protocol( char *szProtocol );
      int   _Export  StreamSocket( void );
      int   _Export  RawSocket( void );
      int   _Export  Open( void );
      void  _Export  Close( void );
      int   _Export  Send( char *szCommand );
      int   _Export  SendTo( char *pbyBuff, short sLength );
      int   _Export  ReceiveFrom( char *pbyBuffer, short sLength,
                                       struct sockaddr_in *pxsFrom );
      int    _Export  ReceiveBuffer( char *szBuffer, int iSize );
      void   _Export  Receive( char *szBuffer );
      void   _Export  LoadFile( char *szFilename );

      // Inline methods
#ifdef __BORLANDC__
      char *  _Export  Server( void )        { return szServer; };
      int     _Export  Port( void )          { return iPort; };
      int     _Export  Socket( void )        { return iSocket; };
      void    _Export  Busy( int iValue )    { iBusy = iValue; };
```

```
	int	_Export  Busy( void )		{ return iBusy; };
#else
	char *	Server( void )			{ return szServer; };
	int	Port( void )			{ return iPort; };
	int	Socket( void )			{ return iSocket; };
	void	Busy( int iValue )		{ iBusy = iValue; };
	int	Busy( void )			{ return iBusy; };
#endif
};
```

Listing 7-1 NET.HPP - Class definition for C_CONNECT

C_CONNECT implements a single constructor that initializes the socket connection. Since this class will likely never be constructed—it is a base class after all—it will be called only as part of the creation process for the child classes.

The C_CONNECT constructor accepts a pointer to a server string. This string can contain either an IP address or a domain name string because the code that determines the host address can detect which address format it has been passed and process it accordingly. The constructor also requires a port number. Most protocols require a port in order to make a connection. Ping is a notable exception that uses a different technique (ICMP) for establishing a TCP/IP connection operating at a much lower level.

```
//-------------
// Constructor \
//---------------------------------------------------------------------------
//
// Parameters:
//	szConnectServer		- Address of server to connect to
//	iConnectPort		- Port number used for this connection
//
// Returns:
//		none
//
C_CONNECT::C_CONNECT( char *szConnectServer, int iConnectPort )
{
   // Transfer parameter data into class attributes
   Initialize( szConnectServer, iConnectPort );
}
```

As you can see from the constructor code, all it does is invoke the Initialize() method. Initialize() initializes the required class attributes, but it also calls the sock_init() API from the TCP/IP library. As previously described, this call is necessary to start a TCP/IP program correctly. Since every type of TCP/IP protocol requires this call, we have placed it in the lowest class level.

```
//-----------
// Initialize \
//------------------------------------------------------------------------
// Description:
//     This method is called to initialize the required class attributes.
//
// Parameters:
//     szConnectServer        - Pointer to domain name or IP string of server
//     iConnectPort           - TCP/IP port to be used for this connection
//
// Returns:
//             none
//
void C_CONNECT::Initialize( char *szConnectServer, int iConnectPort )
{
   // Transfer parameter data into class attributes
   strcpy( szServer, szConnectServer );
   iPort = iConnectPort;

   // Initialize the network read buffers
   strcpy( szNetBuffer, "" );
   memset( szNetBuffer, 0, D_NET_BUFFER + 1 );
   szNetBufferPtr = szNetBuffer;

   // Initialize the socket for communications
   pxtProtocol = NULL;

   // Initialize the TCP/IP socket interface
   sock_init();

   // Default the socket number
   iSocket = 0;
}
```

As part of the process of connecting to a TCP/IP system, the program needs to be able to create a host structure for the TCP/IP connection to use. The code implemented in FindHost() does this by initializing the socket structures. FindHost() then places a call to inet_addr() from the TCP/IP API library. This tests to see if the address passed into the constructor was an IP address or a domain name string. If the call to inet_addr() fails, FindHost() assumes that the address was a domain name string. Assuming that a valid host address string was passed when the CONNECT object was instantiated, FindHost() populates the socket structure.

```
//---------
// FindHost \
//------------------------------------------------------------------------
// Description:
//     This method attempts to build the host portion of the socket
```

```
//     structure. The server address attribute must previously be set.
//
// Parameters:
//     none
//
// Returns:
//     D_NET_HOST                  - Host definition error
//     D_NET_SOCKET                - Could not get a socket
//     D_NET_CONNECT               - Error during connection
//     D_NET_OK                    - Connection established successfully
//
int C_CONNECT::FindHost( void )
{
   struct hostent          *pxtHost;

   // Initialize the socket structure
   bzero( &xtSocket, sizeof( struct sockaddr ) );
   xtSocket.sin_addr.s_addr = 0;
   xtSocket.sin_family = AF_INET;

   // Try to resolve the INET address
   xtSocket.sin_addr.s_addr = inet_addr( szServer );
   if( (LONG)xtSocket.sin_addr.s_addr == -1 )
   {
      // Try to resolve the server by name
      pxtHost = gethostbyname( szServer );
      if( pxtHost == NULL )
      {
         // Couldn't resolve the server
         return D_NET_HOST;
      }

      // Copy the host data into the socket structure
      bcopy( pxtHost->h_addr, &xtSocket.sin_addr, pxtHost->h_length );
   }

   // Host was initialized correctly
   return D_NET_OK;
}
```

I mentioned earlier the requirement for a port, which applies to virtually every type of TCP/IP communication. However, there are a number of methods by which a port number can be attained. The simplest is, of course, to supply a hard-coded port number, but this procedure is not reliable for protocols where ports are dynamically allocated, so we have to supply an alternative approach.

If you look at the PROTOCOL file in your TCP/IP installation (typically in the \ETC subdirectory), you will find a list of network protocols equated to port numbers. If we can reference a protocol string rather than a hard-coded number we can make the program essentially independent of port numbers. If the user decides to use your program on a different port, all he would be required to do is edit the PROTOCOL file. To accomplish this using the C_CONNECT class, you would call the Protocol() method, supplying it with a string indicating the protocol you wish to use. For example, "ICMP" or "FTP."

Protocol() is a simple wrapper for the TCP/IP API call, getprotobyname(). As shown below, it makes the API call and returns the appropriate error code. As you will see later in this chapter, the C_CONNECT_PING class uses a call to Protocol() to select the "ICMP" protocol.

```
//----------
// Protocol \
//--------------------------------------------------------------------------
// Description:
//     This method permits the caller to specify a protocol for the
//     connection. (i.e. "icmp" )
//
// Parameters:
//     szProtocol               - Protocol definition string
//
// Returns:
//     D_NET_PROTOCOL           - Error setting protocol
//     D_NET_OK                 - Connection established successfully
//
int C_CONNECT::Protocol( char *szProtocol )
{
   // Try to set the selected protocol
   pxtProtocol = getprotobyname( szProtocol );
   if( !pxtProtocol )
   {
      // Could find the specified protocol
      return D_NET_PROTOCOL;
   }

   // Protocol was set correctly
   return D_NET_OK;
}
```

Depending on the network protocol used by an application, it may have to transmit and receive data using different methods. TCP/IP supports several techniques, including streaming sockets, datagram sockets, and a raw sockets. With streaming sockets, data transmission uses the TCP protocol and is connection-oriented and reliable. There are protocols in place to ensure that data is transmitted without errors or duplication and received in the correct order. The news and FTP applications presented in later chapters use streaming sockets.

Datagram sockets are used for connectionless TCP/IP services in the UDP layer. Each datagram is sent as a separate packet, and there are no protocols in place to guarantee the reliability or integrity of the data transfer. Network File System (NFS) is an example of a protocol that makes use of datagram sockets. I have not implemented a datagram application in this book.

Raw sockets permit access to low-level protocols such as IP or ICMP. This socket type is typically used for testing the integrity of the network link or lower-level protocols.

TCP/IP does support extending the socket interface. This means you can define new types of socket interfaces to provide enhanced or application specific capabilities.

The C_CONNECT class provides two member functions for setting the socket interface: StreamSocket() and RawSocket(). The code for these follows:

```
//--------------
// StreamSocket \
//-----------------------------------------------------------------------
// Description:
//     This method set the socket interface to stream.
//
// Parameters:
//     none
//
// Returns:
//     D_NET_SOCKET        - Error selecting stream mode
//     D_NET_OK            - Connection established successfully
//
int C_CONNECT::StreamSocket( void )
{
   // Create a socket for this streamed connection
   iSocket = socket( AF_INET, SOCK_STREAM, 0 );
   if( iSocket -- -1 )
   {
      iSocket = 0;
      return D_NET_SOCKET;
   }

   return D_NET_OK;
}

//-----------
// RawSocket \
//-----------------------------------------------------------------------
// Description:
//     This method sets the socket interface to raw, which is typically
//     used for low-level data transfers such as Ping.
//
```

resource pool for other applications to use. Neglecting to call Close() at the end of a communication leaves the TCP/IP socket allocated; if this is done often enough, TCP/IP will eventually cease to function due to lack of resources. Always call Close() when you are finished with a connection.

```
//-------
// Close \
//------------------------------------------------------------------------
// Description:
//     This method closes the socket associated with the current
//     connection. This method should be called to terminate a
//     socket connection properly.
//
// Parameters:
//     none
//
// Returns:
//     none
//
void C_CONNECT::Close( void )
{
   // Shut down the connection
   shutdown( iSocket, 2 );

   // Close the socket
   soclose( iSocket );
}
```

With the connection and disconnection code out of the way, we can discuss the actual procedures for transmitting and receiving data. C_CONNECT supports methods for both types of high-level TCP/IP communication—User Datagram Protocol (UDP) and Transmission Control Protocol (TCP).

For TCP communications, C_CONNECT provides two basic methods, the first being Send(). Send() is a simple wrapper used to isolate derived classes and applications from the TCP/IP API. It accepts a single parameter, a pointer to the NULL-terminated string to be transferred. You must follow the rules of the protocol you are using when calling Send(). For example, if the protocol requires that transmitted data be suffixed by an "\r\n" sequence, then it is the responsibility of the caller to ensure that this done.

```
//------
// Send \
//------------------------------------------------------------------------
// Description:
//     This method sends the supplied string to the TCP/IP connection.
//
```

```
// Parameters:
//     szCommand                - The command string to be issued
//
// Returns:
//     The number of characters sent.
//
int C_CONNECT::Send( char *szCommand )
{
   return send( iSocket, szCommand, (short)strlen( szCommand ), 0 );
}
```

The second TCP method for data transfer is ReceiveBuffer(), which accepts a pointer to a data buffer followed by its size in bytes. ReceiveBuffer() will read from the network input buffer until the output buffer, szBuffer, is full or the network input buffer is empty. If the input buffer is empty when ReceiveBuffer() is called, the method will wait for data to arrive. For this reason, it is very important that network transfer operations generally occur from within separate threads of an application rather than in the main PM thread; otherwise, the program may tie up the system message queue while waiting for data to arrive.

```
//---------------
// ReceiveBuffer \
//-------------------------------------------------------------------------
// Description:
//     This method receives a specified maximum number of characters from
//     TCP/IP connection and stores them in the buffer pointed to by szBuffer.
//
// Parameters:
//     szBuffer         - Target buffer for the received characters
//     iSize            - Maximum number of characters that the buffer can hold
//
// Returns:
//     The number of characters received.
//
int C_CONNECT::ReceiveBuffer( char *szBuffer, int iSize )
{
   int     iResult;

   iResult = recv( iSocket, szBuffer, iSize, 0 );

   return iResult;
}
```

Data reception for stream sockets can be rather more complicated than simply placing a call to ReceiveBuffer(). The problem arises because the ReceiveBuffer() grabs whatever data is sitting in the input buffer regardless of line termination. The buffer may actually contain many lines of streamed data. This makes reading data somewhat complicated—it would be ideal if there were a method that the programmer could call to extract a complete carriage-return-delimited line from the network buffer. In this way the requirements imposed on the programmer could be drastically reduced.

The Receive() method meets these requirements. Actually, Receive() offers a fringe benefit—speed. When I started writing TCP/IP applications I fell into the same trap as most developers, including IBM. This was the logical assumption that the fastest way to find a line of text in the network input buffer was to read a byte at a time until I found a carriage return. Dumb move!

Receive() is the result of rewriting my input code several times; now it finally seems to be right. The C_CONNECT class maintains a large secondary buffer from which Receive() extracts data. When Receive() is invoked, it checks the network buffer and reads as much of it as possible in the secondary buffer. Then it examines the secondary buffer, determines where the next line termination occurs, and extracts the data to that point. The line termination is stripped and the line of text is returned to the code that called Receive().

This double buffering of input data may at first seem awkward, but makes extraction of streamed information much easier; it also improves performance considerably. Compare the time it takes to read an article with IBM's NR/2 versus NeoLogic News, and you will see the difference.

```
//---------
// Receive \
//----------------------------------------------------------------------------
// Description:
//     This method will receive one carriage-return-delimited line from the
//     TCP/IP network buffer. Upon detection, the carriage control is
//     removed and the buffer is NULL terminated.
//
// Parameters:
//     szBuffer            - Pointer to target area for the received line.
//
// Returns:
//     none
//
void C_CONNECT::Receive( char *szBuffer )
{
   char    szString[1025];
   int     iResult;

   // If there are no more CR-LFs in the buffer, we must have more data
   // to load
   iResult = 0;
   memset( szBuffer, 0, 1024 );

   if( szNetBufferPtr == 0 )
```

```
    {
        memset( szNetBuffer, 0, D_NET_BUFFER + 1 );
        szNetBufferPtr = szNetBuffer;
    }

    // If there are no more complete lines, read one in from the network
    if( !strstr( szNetBuffer, "\r" ) )
    {
        // Loop until we have at least one complete line
        do {
            // Get the next chunk of data from the server
            iResult = ReceiveBuffer( szNetBuffer + strlen( szNetBuffer ),
                                     D_NET_BUFFER - strlen( szNetBuffer ) );
        } while( iResult > 0 && ( !strstr( szNetBuffer, "\r" )
                                 || !strstr( szNetBuffer, "\n" ) ) );
    }

    if( strstr( szNetBuffer, "\r" )  || strstr( szNetBuffer, "\n" ) )
     {
        // Copy the line out of the network buffer
        strncpy( szString, szNetBuffer, 1024 );

        // Eliminate the line termination
        if( strstr( szString, "\r" ) )
            *strstr( szString, "\r" ) = 0;
        if( strstr( szString, "\n" ) )
            *strstr( szString, "\n" ) = 0;

        // Chop the line out of the buffer and shove everything over
        memmove( szNetBuffer, szNetBuffer + strlen( szString ),
                         D_NET_BUFFER - strlen( szString ) + 3 );

        // Get rid of the line termination
        if( *szNetBuffer == '\r' )
            memmove( szNetBuffer, szNetBuffer + 1, D_NET_BUFFER );
        if( *szNetBuffer == '\n' )
            memmove( szNetBuffer, szNetBuffer + 1, D_NET_BUFFER );

        memset( szNetBuffer + strlen( szNetBuffer ), 0,
                                 D_NET_BUFFER - strlen( szNetBuffer ) );

        strcpy( szBuffer, szString );
    }
}
```

For UDP communications there are also two methods implemented in C_CONNECT. SendTo() sends a raw datagram packet to the defined socket. SendTo() is a simple wrapper for the TCP/IP API call sendto().

```
//--------
// SendTo \
//----------------------------------------------------------------------------
// Description:
//     This method wraps the standard TCP/IP sendto() API.
//
// Parameters:
//     pbyBuffer                  - Pointer to buffer to be sent
//     sLength                    - Length of the buffer
//
// Returns:
//     The number of characters sent
//
int C_CONNECT::SendTo( char *pbyBuffer, short sLength )
{
   return sendto( iSocket, pbyBuffer, sLength, 0,
            (struct sockaddr *)&xtSocket, sizeof( struct sockaddr_in ) );
}
```

The complementary function to SendTo() is ReceiveFrom(), which accepts UDP packets from the specified socket. Like SendTo(), ReceiveFrom() wraps a standard TCP/IP API call, recvfrom().

```
//-------------
// ReceiveFrom \
//----------------------------------------------------------------------------
// Description:
//     This method wraps the standard TCP/IP recvfrom() API.
//
// Parameters:
//     pbyBuffer          - Pointer to buffer where received data will be written
//     sLength            - Size of the buffer
//     pxsFrom            - Socket from which data will be received
//
// Returns:
//     The number of bytes received or -1 for an error
//
int C_CONNECT::ReceiveFrom( char *pbyBuffer, short sLength,
                                      struct sockaddr_in *pxsFrom )
{
   int      iSize;

   iSize = sizeof( struct sockaddr_in );
   return recvfrom( iSocket, pbyBuffer, (short)sLength, 0,
                          (struct sockaddr *)pxsFrom, &iSize );
}
```

Many of the streaming protocols implemented with TCP/IP can transfer ASCII files. Typically, these files are transferred a line at a time and terminated by an "\r\n.\r\n" character sequence. This technique is used to transfer articles and overviews in the news protocol, read documents in Gopher, and even receive messages in the POP or SMTP mail protocols. Since transferring ASCII files is such a common exercise, C_CONNECT implements the LoadFile() method to accomplish this it. LoadFile() accepts a filename string; data is written to the specified file until the "\r\n.\r\n" character sequence is received.

```
//----------
// LoadFile \
//-------------------------------------------------------------------------
// Description:
//   This method will read until a \r\n.\r\n character sequence is
//   detected in the data in the specified text file. Many descendant
//   classes will need to perform this operation for command processing,
//   so the functionality has been added to the base class. This method will
//   receive one carriage-return-delimited line from the TCP/IP network
//   buffer. Upon detection, the carriage control is removed and the buffer
//   is NULL terminated. If the specified file exists, it will be overwritten.
//
// Last Revision Date:
//           94-Oct-01
//
// Parameters:
//     szFilename          - Pointer to filename where data will be written
//
void C_CONNECT::LoadFile( char *szFilename )
{
   char    *szBuffer;
   FILE    *hFile;
   int     iFlag;

   // Create the specified file
   hFile = fopen( szFilename, "w" );
   iFlag = 0;
   szBuffer = (char *)malloc( 2048 );

   // Loop until an end of data sequence has been detected
   while( !iFlag )
   {
      // Get a line from the network
      Receive( szBuffer );

      // If the line is an end of buffer marker, flag it for termination
      if( strcmp( szBuffer, "." ) == 0 )
      {
```

```
            iFlag = 1;
        }
        else
        {
            // Write the line to the output file
            fprintf( hFile, "%s\n", szBuffer );
        }
    }
    fclose( hFile );

    free( szBuffer );
}
```

Ping Class

The Ping protocol is used in many cases to test the condition of a connection. To accomplish this, Ping uses the ICMP protocol specified in RFC 792 to transmit data packets with checksums to a specified address. The other end of the connection bounces the data back to the originator, where the data is verified for checksum errors and data loss. Ping also evaluates the round-trip time of the message to test the condition of the network.

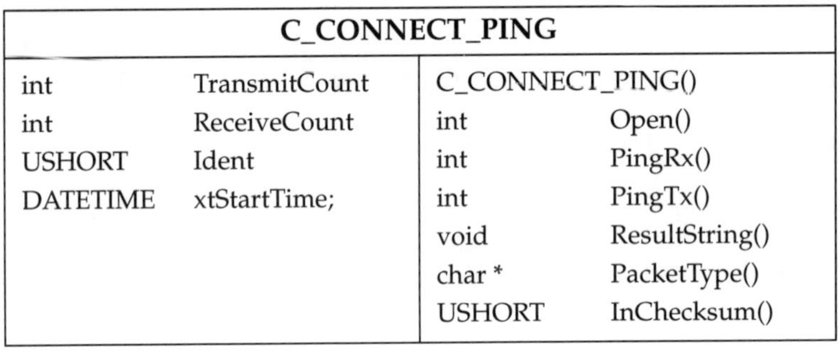

C_CONNECT_PING			
int	TransmitCount	C_CONNECT_PING()	
int	ReceiveCount	int	Open()
USHORT	Ident	int	PingRx()
DATETIME	xtStartTime;	int	PingTx()
		void	ResultString()
		char *	PacketType()
		USHORT	InChecksum()

Figure 7-3 C_CONNECT_PING class

The header file for C_CONNECT_PING is shown in Listing 7-2:

```
class C_CONNECT_PING : public C_CONNECT
{
    private:
        int       iTransmitCount;    // Packet number tx'ed
        USHORT    iIdent;            // Unique identifier for this Ping process
        DATETIME  xtStartTime;       // Start time of the Ping transmit

    public:
```

```
    _Export  C_CONNECT_PING( USHORT iIdentity, char *szConnectServer );
    int      _Export    Open( void );
    int      _Export    PingRx( BYTE *pbyPacket, char *szString );
    int      _Export    PingTx( BYTE *byPacket, int iLength );
    void     _Export    ResultString( char *szString,
                            char *buf, int cc, struct sockaddr_in *from );
    USHORT   _Export    InChecksum( USHORT *pbyAddr, int iLen );
};
```

Listing 7-2 NETPING.HPP - Class definition for C_CONNECT_PING

The C_CONNECT_PING class developed in this section provides a basic network interface for the Ping application presented in Part III. This class is derived from the C_CONNECT class presented previously; consequently, the constructor for this class calls the parent constructor, then initializes the attributes specific to the Ping class.

```
//----------------
// C_CONNECT_PING \
//--------------------------------------------------------------------------
// Description:
//     This constructor creates an instance of the C_CONNECT_PING class.
//
// Parameters:
//     iIdentity                - Identifying integer for this application
//     szConnectServer          - Pointer to domain name or IP string of server
//
// Returns:
//     none
//
// Author(s):
//     Steven Gutz
//
// Last Revision Date:
//     94-Oct-01
//
C_CONNECT_PING::C_CONNECT_PING( USHORT iIdentity, char *szConnectServer )
                                    : C_CONNECT( szConnectServer, 0 )
{

   iTransmitCount = 0;
   iIdent = iIdentity;
}
```

Ping uses the ICMP protocol operating directly on top of the IP level. For this reason the generic Open() method specified in C_CONNECT will not work. Ping needs to provide a more specific interface to open a connection to another host. Like the previously defined Open(), C_CONNECT_PING's Open() method first sets up the host attribute of the class. Open() then specifies the "ICMP" protocol that is used by Ping to transmit data, and also sets the raw transfer mode by calling RawSocket(). Notice that, unlike the parent class's Open(), the Open() method in C_CONNECT_PING does not call the connect() API from the TCP/IP library. This is because it works at a very low level requiring only a socket number and an IP address to start transferring data.

```
//------
// Open \
//--------------------------------------------------------------------------
// Description:
//     This method creates and opens a Ping connection to the IP specified
//     when this instance was constructed. If acquires the host information
//     and sets the protocol to ICMP, then creates a raw data connection.
//
// Parameters:
//     void
//
// Returns:
//     int                  - Result of the connection attempt
//
int C_CONNECT_PING::Open( void )
{
   int      iResult;

   // Fill in the host information
   iResult = FindHost();
   if( iResult != D_NET_OK )
       return iResult;

   // Set up the correct protocol
   iResult = Protocol( "icmp" );
   if( iResult != D_NET_OK )
       return iResult;

   // Connect to a raw data socket
   iResult = RawSocket();
   return iResult;
}
```

In order to transmit data, C_CONNECT_PING provides a PingTx() method which performs a number of operations to send a data packet. First, it creates and initializes an ICMP structure, setting the transmission packet count, and calculates the packet checksum. The packet that this method transfers is referenced by the pbyBuffer parameter passed into the method. In order to determine the round-trip time, Ping needs to know when a packet is transmitted, so PingTx() saves the current time, then calls SendTo() to send the packet immediately.

```
//--------
// PingTX \
//------------------------------------------------------------------------------
// Description:
//     This method sends a Ping packet to the host. It also updates the
//     packet transmission count used to track received packets and records
//     the starting time for the round-trip calculation.
//
// Parameters:
//     pbyPacket        - Pointer to a data area containing the data packet
//     iLength          - Size of the packet to be transmitted
//
// Returns:
//     int              - D_NET_OK if transmission was OK
//
int C_CONNECT_PING::PingTx( BYTE *pbyPacket, int iLength )
{
   int                 iResult;
   struct      icmp    *pxsICmp;

   // Populate the ICMP structure for transmission
   pxsICmp = (struct icmp *)pbyPacket;
   pxsICmp->icmp_type = ICMP_ECHO;
   pxsICmp->icmp_code = 0;
   pxsICmp->icmp_cksum = 0;
   pxsICmp->icmp_id = (UCHAR)iIdent;
   pxsICmp->icmp_seq = (UCHAR)iTransmitCount++;

   // Compute the packet checksum
   pxsICmp->icmp_cksum = InChecksum( (USHORT *)pxsICmp, iLength );

   // Get the start time for the ping TX
   DosGetDateTime( &xtStartTime );

   // Transmit the packet
   iResult = D_NET_RECV;

   if( SendTo( (char *)pbyPacket, iLength ) == iLength )
       iResult = D_NET_OK;
   return iResult;
}
```

The complementary operation to PingTx() is the PingRx() method. This method receives a packet from the instance's connection and determines the Ping result string, which contains any errors that have occurred and specifies the round-trip time for the packet.

```
//--------
// PingRX \
//-------------------------------------------------------------------------
// Description:
//      This method receives a Ping packet back from the host and formats
//      the appropriate result string for any errors that may have occurred.
//
// Parameters:
//      pbyPacket       - Pointer to a data area containing the data packet
//      szString        - Pointer area where the result string will be written
//
// Returns:
//      int             - Number of bytes received from the host.
//
int C_CONNECT_PING::PingRx( BYTE *pbyPacket, char *szString )
{
   int                  iCtr;
   int                  iResult;
   int                  sock_arr[5];
   struct sockaddr_in   xsFrom;

   iCtr = 0;
   strcpy( szString, "" );

   // Be willing to wait 5 seconds for a response
   sock_arr[0] = (short)Socket();
   iResult = select( (int *)sock_arr, 1, 0, 0, 5000L );
   if( iResult > 0 )
   {
      // Receive the packet from the host
      iCtr = ReceiveFrom( (char *)pbyPacket, D_NET_BUFFER, &xsFrom );

      // If there were no errors, format a Ping string to return to the caller
      if( iCtr >= 0 )
         ResultString( szString, (char *)pbyPacket, iCtr, &xsFrom );
   }

   return iCtr;
}
```

ResultString() is a helper method called by PingRx(). This method performs several error checks to verify that the packet is the correct length and belongs to the Ping socket that transmitted the packet. Assuming the packet belongs to this instance, the method acquires the system time and uses it to determine the round-trip time. Finally, it formats a result string that the PingRx() method returns to its caller.

```
//--------------
// ResultString \
//--------------------------------------------------------------------------
// Description:
//     This method calculates the round-trip time and formats a string
//     which indicates any errors that occurred during the Ping operation.
//
// Parameters:
//     szString        - Pointer area where the result string will be written
//     pbyPacket       - Pointer to a data area containing the data packet
//     iLength         - Size of the packet buffer
//     xsFrom          - Ping receive socket
//
// Returns:
//     void
//
void C_CONNECT_PING::ResultString( char *szString,
      char *pbyPacket, int iLength, struct sockaddr_in *xsFrom )
{
   char            *szPacketType;
   int             iHeaderLength;
   long            lStart;
   long            lEnd;
   DATETIME        xtEndTime;
   struct ip       *ip;
   struct icmp     *icp;
   struct in_addr  in;
   static char     *ttab[] = {
                   "Echo Reply", "ICMP 1", "ICMP 2",
                   "Dest Unreachable", "Source Quence",
                   "Redirect", "ICMP 6", "ICMP 7", "Echo",
                   "ICMP 9", "ICMP 10", "Time Exceeded",
                   "Parameter Problem", "Timestamp",
                   "Timestamp Reply", "Info Request",
                   "Info Reply"
   };

   in.s_addr = xsFrom->sin_addr.s_addr;
   xsFrom->sin_addr.s_addr = ntohl( xsFrom->sin_addr.s_addr );

   ip = (struct ip *)pbyPacket;
   iHeaderLength = (ip->ip_hl << 2) + 4;
   if( iLength < iHeaderLength + ICMP_MINLEN)
   {
      // Format the output string
      sprintf( szString, "packet too short (%d bytes) from %s",
                              iLength, inet_ntoa(in));
      return;
```

```
    }
    iLength -= iHeaderLength;
    icp = (struct icmp *)(pbyPacket + iHeaderLength);

    // Make sure this packet belongs to us
    if( icp->icmp_id == iIdent )
    {
        icp->icmp_type &= 0x0f;
        if( icp->icmp_type != ICMP_ECHOREPLY )
        {
            // Determine the packet type
            szPacketType = ttab[icp->icmp_type];
            // Format the output string
            sprintf( szString, "%d bytes from %s: icmp_type=%d (%s)",
                    iLength, inet_ntoa(in), icp->icmp_type,
                    szPacketType );
            return;
        }

        // Calculate the round-trip time
        DosGetDateTime( &xtEndTime );
        lStart = xtStartTime.hundredths + xtStartTime.seconds * 100 +
                xtStartTime.minutes * 6000 + xtStartTime.hours *
                                60 * 60000;
        lEnd = xtEndTime.hundredths + xtEndTime.seconds * 100 +
                xtEndTime.minutes * 6000 + xtEndTime.hours * 60
                                * 60000;
        lEnd -= lStart;

        // Format the output string
        sprintf( szString, "%d bytes from %s: icmp_seq=%d, time=%ldms",
                iLength, inet_ntoa(in), icp->icmp_seq, lEnd );
    }
    else
        strcpy( szString, "" );
}
```

The final method in C_CONNECT_PING is another helper method that determines the checksum for packets that will be transmitted with the PingTx() method. The algorithm is a simple calculation using a 32-bit accumulator to which sequential 16-bit words will be added.

News Class

The NNTP protocol is used to communicate with news servers. The protocol is fairly comprehensive but does have several limitations. For example, NNTP is unlike the FTP protocol in that there is no way to abort an operation once it has been initiated. This can be a real problem if you have mistakenly started to load a 5,000-line uuencoded binary. Also, NNTP does not support any form of data compression—all articles are transferred as single items containing uncompressed ASCII characters.

Although NNTP is showing its age, it is probably the most popular protocol on the Internet, with daily data transfers in the range of megabytes per day. It is a protocol that is impossible to ignore, and is actually one of the more straightforward applications one can build for TCP/IP.

Our support for NNTP has been developed in the C_CONNECT_NEWS class that is part of NETCLASS. The class structure follows in Figure 7-4:

C _CONNECT_NEWS	
	C_NEWS_CONNECT()
	int Open()
	void Close()
	int OpenPost()
	int ClosePost()
	int List()
	int ListNewsGroups()
	int ListNewGroups()
	int Overview()
	int Group()
	int First()
	int Next()
	int Article()
	int Body()
	int Head()

Figure 7-4 C_CONNECT_NEWS class

The C_CONNECT_NEWS class implements the protocol specified in RFC 977. This class will be used in the news application in Part III of this book. Like other network classes in NETCLASS, C_CONNECT_NEWS is derived from C_CONNECT and relies heavily on code from this parent class.

The header file for C_CONNECT_NEWS is shown in Listing 7-3:

```
// Standard TCP news port
#define    D_NEWS_PORT     119

class C_CONNECT_NEWS : public C_CONNECT
{
  private:
      int     iPostFlag;                 // Set if posting is permitted
```

```
    // Call the parent to open the socket
    iResult = C_CONNECT::Open();
    if( iResult >= D_NET_OK )
    {
        // Read the response from the server
        Receive( szBuffer );

        // Get the error result code
        iError = atoi( szBuffer );

        // If there was an error, flag it
        if( iError != 200 && iError != 201 )
        {
            iSocket = 0;
            return D_NET_CONNECT;
        }
    }

    // Connected OK
    return iError;
}
```

Once the application is finished with the NNTP connection, it should be closed. C_NEWS _CONNECT provides a Close() method to accomplish this. This method sends an NNTP "QUIT" command to the server, then calls the base class C_CONNECT::Close().

Although the "QUIT" command returns a response, the C_CONNECT_-NEWS object disregards it because it is about to close anyway. The string remaining in the network buffer will be discarded when the buffer is freed up, so we do not need to worry about memory leaks.

```
//---------
// Close() \
//-----------------------------------------------------------------------
// Description:
//     This method closes the news socket after communication is completed.
//     It send a QUIT command to the server to inform it of the shutdown
//     then calls the parent Close().
//
// Parameters:
//     none
//
// Returns:
//     none
//
void C_CONNECT_NEWS::Close( void )
{
```

```
    Send( "QUIT\r\n" );

    // Call the parent close to kill the socket
    C_CONNECT::Close();
}
```

When a client news program wants to post a new article to Usenet it needs to send some special commands to the server to prepare for the transfer. The C_CONNECT_NEWS class provides two methods of managing this. The first of these methods is OpenPost(). This method is actually quite simple—it issues a server "POST" command and fetches the response code. The server will respond with one of the following replies:

> 340 – Server is ready to receive the article to be posted
> 440 – Posting is prohibited for some installation-dependent reason.

Once a 340 response code has been received, the client can begin sending each line of the article text using the C_CONNECT::Send() method.

```
//------------
// OpenPost() \
//------------------------------------------------------------------------
// Description:
//     This method initiates a message posting. This is called any time
//     a new article is being posted to Usenet.
//
// Parameters:
//     none
//
// Returns:
//     none
//
int C_CONNECT_NEWS::OpenPost( void )
{
    char     szBuffer[1024];

    // Send the group command
    sprintf( szBuffer, "post\r\n" );
    Send( szBuffer );
    Receive( szBuffer );

    // Process the response
    return atoi( szBuffer );
}
```

When the article has been sent to the server, the client needs to terminate the transmission. This can be done by calling the C_CONNECT_NEWS::ClosePost() method. This method sends an "\r\n.\r\n" string to indicate the end of the transfer, then retrieves the server response code for the posting. Valid responses are as follows:

240 – Article posted OK
340 – Send article to be posted. End with "\r\n.\r\n"
440 – Posting not allowed
441 – Posting failed

```
//-------------
// ClosePost() \
//---------------------------------------------------------------------------
// Description:
//     This method is sent at the end of a posting operation.
//     It sends the "." terminator character and waits for a posting
//     response from the server.
//
// Parameters:
//     none
//
// Returns:
//     none
//
int C_CONNECT_NEWS::ClosePost( char *szResponse )
{
   char    szBuffer[1024];

   // Send the group command
   sprintf( szBuffer, "\r\n.\r\n" );
   Send( szBuffer );
   Receive( szBuffer );

   memset( szResponse, 0, 256 );
   strncpy( szResponse, szBuffer, 255 );

   // Process the response
   return atoi( szBuffer );
}
```

NNTP news servers provide a facility for clients to retrieve a list of all newsgroups currently maintained by the server. The C_CONNECT_NEWS::List() extracts this list from the server and writes it to the specified file name.

List() returns only a single result code:

215 List of newsgroups follows

The list of groups follows immediately, terminated by an "\r\n.\n\r" sequence. List() calls the C_CONNECT::LoadFile() method to read this information.

```
//--------
// List() \
//----------------------------------------------------------------------------
// Description:
//     This method retrieves a list of available newsgroups from the server
//     into the specified file. The file will be created or overwritten if
//     it already exists.
//
// Parameters:
//     szFilename      - File to which the list will be written
//
// Returns:
//     none
//
int C_CONNECT_NEWS::List( char *szFilename )
{
   char    szBuffer[1024];
   int     iResult;

   // Request the article
   sprintf( szBuffer, "list\r\n" );
   Send( szBuffer );
   Receive( szBuffer );

   // Get the response back from the server
   iResult = atoi( szBuffer );

   // If there was no error, load the response file
   if( iResult < 400 && iResult > 0 )
       LoadFile( szFilename );

   return iResult;
}
```

Most NNTP servers also provide a facility for the client to query a description list containing more detailed information about each group. Most news client programs do not support this capability, but you can use this command to retrieve a description list that can be displayed for the convenience of the user.

The ListNewsGroups() method uses the NNTP "LIST NEWSGROUPS" command. This is similar to the "LIST" command, for it compels the server to send the list terminated by a period. Again the C_CONNECT::LoadFile() method is called to write this information to the specified file.

```
//-----------------
// ListNewsGroups() \
//----------------------------------------------------------------------------
// Description:
//     This method retrieves a list of descriptions for newsgroups from the
```

```
//     server into the specified file. The file will be created or
//     overwritten if it already exists.
//
// Parameters:
//     szFilename      - File to which the list will be written
//
// Returns:
//     none
//
int C_CONNECT_NEWS::ListNewsGroups( char *szFilename )
{
   char     szBuffer[1024];
   int      iResult;

   // Request the article
   sprintf( szBuffer, "list newsgroups\r\n" );
   Send( szBuffer );
   Receive( szBuffer );

   // Get the response back from the server
   iResult = atoi( szBuffer );

   // If there was no error, load the response file
   if( iResult < 400 && iResult > 0 )
      LoadFile( szFilename );

   return iResult;
}
```

Since the group list loaded from a typical server can be upwards of 5000 groups, it is not efficient to load this from the server every time the user wants to see the list. It would be much more efficient to read only new groups added to the server since the last check. Fortunately, the developers of the NNTP protocol provided a "NEWSGROUPS" command that accepts a time stamp in the format:

```
NEWGROUPS date time [GMT] [<distributions>]
```

where date has the format: YYMMDD and time is formatted as HHMMSS in 24-hour form. Specifying "GMT" references the time stamp to GMT time. After receiving this command, the server responds with a response string followed immediately by the list, terminated by a period character. The "<distributions>" parameters determines the scope of the group search. For example, "<alt>" could be specified to search for new groups in the "alt" category.

C_CONNECT_NEWS provides a ListNewGroups() method that accepts the desired data stamp and a file name where the new group data will be written once retrieved.

```
//-----------------
// ListNewGroups() \
//-------------------------------------------------------------------------
// Description:
//     This method retrieves a list of new newsgroups since a specified date
//     and time from the server. This data is written into the specified
//     file. The file will be created or overwritten if it already exists.
//
// Parameters:
//     sedate              - Date/time string to use as a starting point
//     szFilename          - File to which the list will be written
//
// Returns:
//     none
//
int C_CONNECT_NEWS::ListNewsGroups( char *szDATE, char *szFilename )
{
   char    szBuffer[1024];
   int     iResult;

   // Request the article
   sprintf( szBuffer, "newgroups %s\r\n", szDate );
   Send( szBuffer );
   Receive( szBuffer );

   // Get the response back from the server
   iResult = atoi( szBuffer );

   // If there was no error, load the response file
   if( iResult < 400 && iResult > 0 )
       LoadFile( szFilename );

   return iResult;
}
```

Many news servers support several extensions to the NNTP command set that are not documented in RFC 977. The primary goal of these extensions is to improve performance by reducing the network activity required to complete a given task. One of these extensions is the "XOVER" command, and there are very few servers that do not support it.

XOVER is used to transfer the header information for a range of articles back to the client. The alternative is to use the "HEAD" command and parse each article header. The code to accomplish this must also be tolerant of expired or missing articles in the range. XOVER manages all of this automatically and returns an "\r\n.\r\n" terminated list of tab-delimited article information in the format:

```
<Subject><tab><Author><tab><Date><tab><Message ID><tab><References>
                                           <tab><Lines><tab><XRef>
```

C_CONNECT_NEWS provides the Overview() method; this accepts a starting and ending article number, forming the range of overview items that will be written one per line to a specified file. Once this data is retrieved from the news server, it is a relatively simple exercise to implement a parser to extract the required field information from the lines in the file.

Be aware that not all servers support the "XOVER" extension to the command set, so you always need to check the result code from Overview(). If XOVER is not supported, Overview() will return a number greater than or equal 400 (typically a >500 result to indicate an unimplemented command). There are other ways to find out the header information, as you will discover shortly.

```
//------------
// Overview() \
//---------------------------------------------------------------------------
// Description:
//     This method retrieves an article overview from the server and writes
//     to the specified file name. lStart and lEnd specify the range of
//     articles to overview.
//     Note: the overview command is not supported on all servers.
//
// Parameters:
//     lStart              - Starting message number for overview
//     lEnd                - Starting message number for overview
//     szFilename          - File to which the overview will be written
//
// Returns:
//     none
//
int C_CONNECT_NEWS::Overview( ULONG lStart, ULONG lEnd, char *szFilename )
{
   char    szBuffer[1024];
   int     iResult;

   // Request the article
   sprintf( szBuffer, "xover %ld-%ld\r\n", lStart, lEnd );
   Send( szBuffer );
   Receive( szBuffer );

   // Get the response back from the server
   iResult = atoi( szBuffer );

   // If there was no error, load the response file
   if( iResult < 400 && iResult > 0 )
       LoadFile( szFilename );

   return iResult;
}
```

Think of each newsgroup on the server as a separate directory. In fact, this is usually how a server stores individual article files. Like a subdirectory where you need to use the CHDIR (or CD) command, you likewise need to send the server a special command to select any given newsgroup; otherwise, you will not be allowed to read any of the articles it contains. This command is called "GROUP," and it accepts a newsgroup name as a parameter. For example:

```
GROUP comp.os.os2.announce
```

GROUP returns a response string that tells the client how many articles the group currently has and the range of message numbers for these articles. Since the total count returned by the server is generally an approximation, we can typically throw it away—if the exact total of articles is important to you, it is best to count them. The first and last message numbers, however, are always accurate, but note that the range is not necessarily consecutive. Articles can expire or get lost occasionally, so do not assume that the range implies a given number of articles. For example, it is perfectly valid for the server to return the range 100–275, although the server may contain only 50 articles.

The C_CONNECT_NEWS::Group() method selects the specified newsgroup from the server and returns the message number of the first and last articles in the group.

```
//---------
// Group() \
//--------------------------------------------------------------------------
// Description:
//     This method sends a GROUP command to the news server to select a new
//     group. The server returns the first and last article numbers in the group.
//
// Parameters:
//     szGroup                - Newsgroup to select
//     plFirstArticle         - Pointer to First article number returned
//     plLastArticle          - Pointer to Last article number returned
//
// Returns:
//     none
//
int C_CONNECT_NEWS::Group( char *szGroup,
       ULONG *plFirstArticle, ULONG *plLastArticle, ULONG *plTotal )
{
   char    szBuffer[1024];
   int     iResponse;
   ULONG   lTotal;

   // Send the group command
   sprintf( szBuffer, "group %s\r\n", szGroup );
   Send( szBuffer );
```

```
    Receive( szBuffer );

    // Process the response
    iResponse = atoi( szBuffer );
    if( iResponse > 0 && iResponse < 300 )
    {
        // Skip the unimportant parts
        atol( strtok( szBuffer, " " ) );

        // Get article information
        *plTotal = atol( strtok( NULL, " " ) );
        *plFirstArticle = atol( strtok( NULL, " " ) );
        *plLastArticle = atol( strtok( NULL, " " ) );
    }

    return iResponse;
}
```

NNTP servers can be set to maintain an internal message pointer that clients can use to control where they are positioned in the list of Usenet messages. The C_CONNECT_NEWS command implements two methods, the first of which is First().

First() sends a server STAT command with an article number to the server; the server responds by setting its internal article pointer accordingly. This method does not read the article—this can be achieved by issuing a HEAD, BODY, or ARTICLE command to the server.

```
//---------
// First() \
//---------------------------------------------------------------------------
// Description:
//     This method uses the internal indexing in the news server to select
//     the specified article in the current newsgroup.
//
// Parameters:
//     lArticle           - Article number to select
//
// Returns:
//     none
//
int C_CONNECT_NEWS::First( ULONG lArticle )
{
    char    szBuffer[1024];
    int     iResult;

    // Request the article
    sprintf( szBuffer, "stat %ld\r\n", lArticle );
    Send( szBuffer );
    Receive( szBuffer );
```

```
    // Get the response back from the server
    iResult = atoi( szBuffer );

    return iResult;
}
```

Once you have set the current article pointer, you must have some means by which to move around the message list. NNTP provides NEXT and PREV commands to manage this. I will not implement the PREV command in C_NEWS _CONNECT, but I will create a method to implement NEXT. The Next() method instructs the server to increment its internal article pointer.

In the absence of server support for the XOVER command described earlier, the combination of First() and Next() can be issued to achieve similar but significantly slower results.

```
//--------
// Next() \
//-------------------------------------------------------------------
// Description:
//      This method uses the internal indexing in the news server to select
//      the next article in the current newsgroup. The article number is
//      returned to the caller.
//
// Parameters:
//      plArticle           - Pointer to article number selected
//
// Returns:
//      none
//
int C_CONNECT_NEWS::Next( ULONG *plArticle )
{
    char    szBuffer[1024];
    int     iResult;

    // Request the article
    sprintf( szBuffer, "next\r\n" );
    Send( szBuffer );
    Receive( szBuffer );

    // Get the response back from the server
    iResult = atoi( szBuffer );

    // If there was no error, load the response file
    if( iResult < 400 && atoi( szBuffer ) > 0 )
        *plArticle = atol( szBuffer + 4 );

    return iResult;
}
```

To read an article, the C_CONNECT_NEWS class needs to issue an ARTICLE command to the server. To accomplish this, an Article() method has been implemented that reads an article to the specified file. This article file will consist of both a message header and the message text itself.

Article() accepts an article number to read; however, if the specified article number has a value of zero, the Article() method reads the article text indexed by the server's internal pointer.

```
//-----------
// Article() \
//--------------------------------------------------------------------------
// Description:
//     This method retrieves the article text for the specified article
//     number from the server and writes the data to the filename supplied
//     by the caller.
//
// Parameters:
//     lArticle             - Article number to retrieve
//     szFilename           - Point to filename where output will be written.
//
// Returns:
//     none
//
int C_CONNECT_NEWS::Article( ULONG lArticle, char *szFilename )
{
   char    szBuffer[1024];
   int     iResult;

   // Request the article
   if( lArticle > 0 )
      sprintf( szBuffer, "article %ld\r\n", lArticle );
   else
      strcpy( szBuffer, "article\r\n" );
   Send( szBuffer );
   Receive( szBuffer );

   // Get the response back from the server
   iResult = atoi( szBuffer );

   // If there was no error, load the response file
   if( iResult < 400 && atoi( szBuffer ) > 0 )
      LoadFile( szFilename );

   return iResult;
}
```

Depending on how you plan to implement your news client, you may not want to read the article headers, or there may be times when all you require is the message text proper. NNTP, and hence C_CONNECT_NEWS, supports a method, Body(), that retrieves the body of a specified article. Body() can also accept an article number of zero, in which case the body for the message pointed to by the server's internal message pointer is fetched into the specified output file.

```
//--------
// Body() \
//--------------------------------------------------------------------------
// Description:
//     This method retrieves the body text for the specified article number
//     from the server and writes the data to the filename supplied by the
//     caller. The header for the article is not retrieved by this method.
//
// Parameters:
//     lArticle        - Article number whose body is to be retrieved
//     szFilename      - Point to filename where output will be written.
//
// Returns:
//     none
//
int C_CONNECT_NEWS::Body( ULONG lArticle, char *szFilename )
{
   char    szBuffer[1024];
   int     iResult;

   // Request the article
   if( lArticle > 0 )
       sprintf( szBuffer, "body %ld\r\n", lArticle );
   else
       strcpy( szBuffer, "body\r\n" );
   Send( szBuffer );
   Receive( szBuffer );

   // Get the response back from the server
   iResult = atoi( szBuffer );

   // If there was no error, load the response file
   if( iResult < 400 && atoi( szBuffer ) > 0 )
       LoadFile( szFilename );

   return iResult;
}
```

Finally, we come to the last method in C_NEWS _CONNECT. The Head() member function implements the HEAD command to the server. Head() accepts an article number of zero and retrieves only the Usenet message header for an article. This method would be used to retrieve the header for each article in a newsgroup for servers that do not implement the XOVER command.

```
//--------
// Head() \
//-------------------------------------------------------------------------
// Description:
//     This method retrieves the header text for the specified article number
//     from the server and writes the data to the filename supplied by the
//     caller. The body for the article is not retrieved by this method.
//
// Parameters:
//     lArticle        - Article number whose header is to be retrieved
//     szFilename      - Point to filename where output will be written.
//
// Returns:
//     none
//
int C_CONNECT_NEWS::Head( ULONG lArticle, char *szFilename )
{
   char     szBuffer[10242];
   int      iResult;

   // Request the article
   if( lArticle > 0 )
      sprintf( szBuffer, "head %ld\r\n", lArticle );
   else
      strcpy( szBuffer, "head\r\n" );
   Send( szBuffer );
   Receive( szBuffer );

   // Get the response back from the server
   iResult = atoi( szBuffer );

   // If there was no error, load the response file
   if( iResult < 400 && atoi( szBuffer ) > 0 )
      LoadFile( szFilename );

   return iResult;
}
```

In this section we have implemented the C_CONNECT_NEWS class to support NNTP news servers. Every command supported by NNTP protocol specified in RFC 977 has not been implemented, and there are additional extensions, which do not appear in the RFC, that I have also elected to ignore. However, the basic framework is here; should you decide that some functionality you need is missing, you will hopefully have enough examples shown here to use as the basis for new support.

FTP Class

File Transfer Protocol (FTP) was originally developed to assist with file sharing between a client system and a typically larger server on the Internet. Among its many strengths, this protocol eliminates the incompatibilities common among the many file systems available today. Although FTP has undergone many enhancements since its inception, the basic file transfer structure has remained unchanged.

FTP is a bi-directional protocol, meaning that it can send commands and receive data at the same time. This can happen because FTP actually establishes two connections—a control connection for command transfers between the client and server, and a data connection to transfer files. The control connection is initiated during the initial interaction between the two hosts and lasts for the entire FTP session. Data connections are dynamic and are linked and disconnected as required to complete the file transfer.

Unlike the NNTP protocol we studied in the previous section, FTP has some distinct advantages. FTP clients can abort file transfers, a feature NNTP desperately needs. Also, the FTP protocol supports binary file transfers, rather than the uuencoded binaries required by the news protocol. This results in much more efficient data transfers.

The NETCLASS library offers a class to provide a simple interface to the FTP protocol. Most of the FTP command set defined in RFC 959 has been implemented, and any missing commands have been omitted solely because they are uncommon in the normal operation of an FTP client. Implementing support for these commands should pose no particular problem should they be required later.

The current C_CONNECT_FTP class was developed specifically for the client end of the FTP connection. So far, I have not dealt with the server side of the TCP/IP protocols, but armed with the knowledge built into NETCLASS, you should be able to develop suitable server classes and associated server applications. The C_CONNECT_FTP class is illustrated in Figure 7-5.

C _CONNECT_FTP			
C_MLE	*pxcMLE	C_FTP_CONNECT()	
int	iHash;	int	Open()
		void	Close()
		int	Send()
		void	Receive()
		int	Accept()
		int	Put()

```
//     iConnectPort              - Port number to use for the connection
//     pxcConsole                - Option MLE console window object
//
C_CONNECT_FTP::C_CONNECT_FTP( char *szConnectServer,
          int iConnectPort, C_MLE *pxcConsole )
                              : C_CONNECT( szConnectServer, iConnectPort )
{
   pxcMLE = pxcConsole;
   iHash = 0;

   // If an MLE control was specified, trun on hash marks
   if( pxcMLE )
      iHash = 1;
}
```

Like the NNTP class we looked at in the previous section, the FTP socket needs to be opened in order to establish a connection with the specified host. C_CONNECT_FTP provides an Open() method to perform this task.

Open() reuses the C_CONNECT::Open() code, then extends the functionality to complete the FTP connection and reads the response from the host, once connection has been established.

```
//------
// Open \
//------------------------------------------------------------------------
//
// Description:
//     This method opens the FTP connection with the server. It uses the
//     C_CONNECT::Open() method, then adds some FTP specific connection code.
//
// Parameters:
//     none
//
// Returns:
//     int                    - D_NET_OK if Open was successful
//
int C_CONNECT_FTP::Open( void )
{
   char    szBuffer[1024];
   int     iResult;
   int     iError;
   int     iFlag;

   // Default to an error result
   iError = D_NET_CONNECT;

   // Call the parent to open the socket
   iResult = C_CONNECT::Open();
```

```
    if( iResult >= D_NET_OK )
    {
        iFlag = 1;
        setsockopt( Socket(), (short)SOL_SOCKET, SO_OOBINLINE,
                                        (char *)&iFlag, sizeof( iFlag ) );
        do {
            memset( szBuffer, 0, 1024 );
            Receive( szBuffer );

            if( atoi( szBuffer ) > 400 || strlen( szBuffer ) < 4 )
            {
                return 421;
            }
        } while( szBuffer[3] == '-' );

        // Connected OK
        return D_NET_OK;
    }

    // Connected OK
    return iError;
}
```

The Close() functionality from C_CONNECT is also reused. C_CONNECT-_FTP overrides the Close() method defined in the parent class and, before calling this code, it sends an FTP "QUIT" command to the host.

```
//-------
// Close \
//------------------------------------------------------------------------
//
// Description:
//     This method closes the FTP connection.
//
// Parameters:
//     none
//
// Return:
//     none
//
void C_CONNECT_FTP::Close( void )
{
    // Send a quit command to end the conversation
    Send( "QUIT\r\n" );

    // Call the parent close to kill the socket
    C_CONNECT::Close();
}
```

The C_CONNECT_FTP class implements a Send() method to issue FTP commands to the host. If the MLE object was defined at the time the FTP class was instantiated, all data sent to the host is also echoed to the MLE console window. This is not necessarily a useful feature, since this will echo all command strings, including passwords and account information passed to the host—a potentially crippling problem if you plan to use this class in a complete FTP application.

```
//------
// Send \
//------------------------------------------------------------------------
//
// Description:
//     This method sends a command to the FTP server. It uses the
//     C_CONNECT::Send() method but adds hash marks to the MLE,
//     if available.
//
// Parameters:
//     szCommand               - Command to send to the server
//
// Return:
//     int                     - Result of the send operation
//
int C_CONNECT_FTP::Send( char *szCommand )
{
   int     iResult;

   // Write command to the console window if it is present
   if( pxcMLE )
       pxcMLE->Insert( szCommand );

   // Send the command to the server
   iResult = C_CONNECT::Send( szCommand );

   return iResult;
}
```

The C_CONNECT_FTP::Receive() method uses the Receive() code from its parent to collect any responses from the host. If the MLE console window has been defined, then all replies are echoed to the display.

Receive() collects responses from the server in a special way. The FTP specification requires that all responses will be preceded by a numerical error status, much like most other TCP/IP protocols. However, the RFC also states that any error value that is immediately followed by a "-" character indicates the presence of additional response text on subsequent lines. Receive() collects lines of text from the host connection until it finds a line that does not include the "-" after the error number.

```
//---------
// Receive \
//------------------------------------------------------------------------
//
// Description:
//     This method receives a string from the FTP server. It uses the
//     C_CONNECT::Receive() method, but adds the returned string to the
//     MLE, if available.
//
// Parameters:
//     szBuffer            - Pointer to target area for the received line.
//
// Returns:
//     none
//
void C_CONNECT_FTP::Receive( char *szBuffer )
{
   memset( szBuffer, 0, 256 );
   do {
       // Read a response from the FTP server
       C_CONNECT::Receive( szBuffer );

       // Display the line on the console if it is present
       if( pxcMLE )
       {
           pxcMLE->Insert( szBuffer );
           pxcMLE->Insert( "\n" );
       }

       // Repeat until we don't get a line continuation ie '230-'
   } while( ( strlen( szBuffer ) != 0 && !isdigit( *szBuffer ) ) ||
                                        *(szBuffer+3) == '-' );
}
```

I mentioned earlier that FTP actually involves two network connections. The Send() and Receive() methods manage the control connection; so far we have not discussed how data transfers are managed. C_CONNECT_FTP provides two methods of handling data manipulation. The first of these is Listen(), with an almost self-explanatory operation—it listens for a data connection from the host. However, a lot of specialized code is executed so we need to go into some detail.

The first thing Listen() does is to create a new socket to listen for the host. This socket is bound to a socket structure, and the TCP/IP API listen() function is called. The listen() function completes the socket-binding process and creates a connection request queue that will be used later in order to accept incoming connection requests. Once the listen() API returns, the code issues a PORT command to the host to complete the setup for the listener socket.

```
//--------
// Listen \
//-----------------------------------------------------------------------
//
// Description:
//     This method listens for a data connection from the server and, if
//     found, binds this connection to a socket so communication can occur.
//
// Parameters:
//     none
//
// Return:
//     int              - Data socket >0 if successful
//
int C_CONNECT_FTP::Listen( void )
{
   char     *a;
   char     *p;
   char     szString[1024];
   int      iSocket;
   int      iLength;
   int      iFlag = 1;
   struct       sockaddr_in      xtTempSocket;
   struct       sockaddr_in      xtListenSocket;

   // Connect to the news reader port
   xtListenSocket.sin_family = AF_INET;
   xtListenSocket.sin_port = htons( 0 );
   xtListenSocket.sin_addr.s_addr = 0;

   // Open a socket for this connection
   iSocket = socket( AF_INET, SOCK_STREAM, IPPROTO_TCP );
   if( iSocket == -1 )
       return D_NET_SOCKET;

   // Reuse any previous port that may already exist
   if( setsockopt( iSocket, SOL_SOCKET, SO_REUSEADDR, (char *)&iFlag,
                                                 sizeof( iFlag ) ) < 0 )
   {
       return D_NET_CONNECT;
   }

   // Bind the listener socket to a data connection
   if( bind( iSocket, (struct sockaddr *)&xtListenSocket,
                                     sizeof( struct sockaddr_in ) ) < 0 )
   {
       return -1;
   }
```

```
    // Get the name of the listener socket and save it
    iLength = sizeof( struct sockaddr_in );
    if( getsockname( iSocket, (struct sockaddr *)&xtListenSocket,
                                                        &iLength ) < 0 )
    {
        return D_NET_CONNECT;
    }

    // Listen for a data connection request from the server
    if( listen( iSocket, 1 ) != 0 )
    {
        soclose( iSocket );
    }

    // Inform remote host about the port we are using
    iLength = sizeof( struct sockaddr_in );
    getsockname( Socket(), (struct sockaddr *)&xtTempSocket, &iLength );
    a = (char *)&xtTempSocket.sin_addr;
    p = (char *)&xtListenSocket.sin_port;
    sprintf( szString, "PORT %d,%d,%d,%d,%d,%d\r\n",
                        (UCHAR)a[0], (UCHAR)a[1], (UCHAR)a[2],
                        (UCHAR)a[3], (UCHAR)p[0], (UCHAR)p[1] );
    Send( szString );
    Receive( szString );

    // Return the listen socket to the caller
    return iSocket;
}
```

To complement Listen(), C_CONNECT_FTP also implements an Accept() method responsible for completing a data link by accepting a connection on the socket setup by Listen(). Accept() first calls the TCP/IP accept() API to wait until a connection is established between client and server. The accept() call then returns a new data socket to the server, with which it communicates with the client.

Since C_CONNECT_FTP::Accept() is always used to transfer binary data, it then creates the binary file whose name was passed by the caller. All data is then retrieved from the host using the TCP/IP recv() function, and written to the file using a standard C fwrite().

Instead of the C file functions fopen(), fwrite(), and fclose(), you could rewrite Accept() to use C++ streams. I elected to use the standard C code so that C programmers could use this function without a complete rewrite.

If the console MLE window was specified when the object was created, hash marks will be displayed for each block of data received. Upon completion of the binary transfer, the data connection is destroyed, since it is no longer required.

```
//--------
// Accept \
//-----------------------------------------------------------------------
//
// Description:
//     This method accepts a block of binary data from the server and
//     writes it to the specified file. Data is retrieved via a data
//     connection initiated by the server.
//
// Parameters:
//     iSocket          - Control socket
//     szFile           - Pointer to out file where data will be written
//
// Return:
//     int              - Returns zero if successful
//
int C_CONNECT_FTP::Accept( int iSocket, char *szFile )
{
   char     *szBuffer;
   FILE     *hFile;
   int      iDataSocket;
   int      iResult;
   int      iLength;
   struct sockaddr_in      xtTempSocket;

   // Remove any old file that may be present
   DosForceDelete( (PSZ)szFile );

   // Accept a data socket from the server
   iLength = sizeof( struct sockaddr_in );
   iDataSocket = accept( iSocket, (sockaddr *)&xtTempSocket, &iLength );

   // Close the listener socket
   soclose( iSocket );
   if( iDataSocket < 0 )
       return iDataSocket;

   szBuffer = (char *)malloc( 8192 );

   // Read data into a file
   hFile = fopen( szFile, "w+b" );
   if( hFile )
   {
       do {
           // Receive a packet of information
           iResult = recv( (short)iDataSocket, szBuffer, 8192, 0 );
           if( iResult > 0 )
           {
               // Write the data to the output file
```

```
                fwrite( szBuffer, 1, iResult, hFile );
            }

            // If hash marking is on, then display hashes
            if( iHash && pxcMLE )
                pxcMLE->Insert( "#" );
        } while( iResult > 0 );
        fclose( hFile );
    }

    // If hash marking is on, then display a new line to end the hash marks
    if( iHash && pxcMLE )
        pxcMLE->Insert( "\n" );

    // Done with the data socket so dispose of it.
    soclose( iDataSocket );

    free( szBuffer );
    return 0;
}
```

The C_CONNECT defines a Close() method; however, this specifically closes the control connection. Since C_CONNECT_FTP creates some additional sockets, notably listener and data sockets, a new method is required to permit destruction of specific sockets.

SocketClose() performs this task by accepting a socket identifier, and calling the TCP/IP soclose() function to close it. Unlike C_CONNECT::Close(), SocketClose() does not call the shutdown(). C_CONNECT_FTP recycles sockets so there is no need to shut them down.

```
//-------------
// SocketClose \
//---------------------------------------------------------------------------
//
// Description:
//     This method closes a specified data socket.
//
// Parameters:
//     iSocket              - Data socket to close
//
// Return:
//     int                  - Always returns D_NET_OK
//
int C_CONNECT_FTP::SocketClose( int iSocket )
{
    soclose( iSocket );
    return D_NET_OK;
}
```

At the beginning of this section, I mentioned that the FTP protocol has provisions to abort operations between client and server. To accomplish this, the protocol supports what is termed "out-of-band" signaling, which lets the client send a high-priority message to the host.

C_CONNECT_FTP provides a special method called SendOOB, which uses the send() API to issue an out-of-band signal. Under normal operation, this method will not be used—typically, it is the exclusive domain of the ABOR() method that will be shown later.

```
//---------
// SendOOB \
//----------------------------------------------------------------------
//
// Description:
//     This method sends an out-of-band command to the FTP server.
//
// Parameters:
//     szCommand       - OOB command to issue
//
// Return:
//     int             - Result of send command
//
int C_CONNECT_FTP::SendOOB( char *szCommand )
{
   return send( Socket(), szCommand, (short)strlen( szCommand ), MSG_OOB );
}
```

Since the FTP protocol is designed specifically for transferring files, we should take a look at some of the mechanisms to accomplish this task. We have already examined the Accept() method that receives data from the server, but we have not seen a way to send files.

The Put() method in C_CONNECT_FTP performs this operation.. Put() creates a data socket by calling accept() to accept the connection set up by the host. Once the data connection is established, the requested file is opened and transmitted to the host. When the file transfer is complete, the data connection is closed.

```
//-----
// Put \
//----------------------------------------------------------------------
//
// Description:
//     This method transfers a file to the server using the specified
//     data socket.
//
// Parameters:
//     iSocket         - Data socket to use for transmission
//     szFile          - Name of file to transfer
```

```
//
// Return:
//     int             - 0 if successful
//
int C_CONNECT_FTP::Put( int iSocket, char *szFile )
{
    char    *szBuffer;
    FILE    *hFile;
    int     iDataSocket;
    int     iResult;
    int     iLength;
    struct sockaddr_in      xtTempSocket;

    // Accept a data connection from the server
    iLength = sizeof( struct sockaddr_in );
    iDataSocket = accept( iSocket, (sockaddr *)&xtTempSocket, &iLength );

    // Close the listener socket
    soclose( iSocket );
    if( iDataSocket < 0 )
        return iDataSocket;

    szBuffer = (char *)malloc( 8192 );

    // Read data into a file
    hFile = fopen( szFile, "rb" );
    if( hFile )
    {
        iResult = 1;
        while( iResult > 0 )
        {
            iResult = fread( szBuffer, 1, 8192, hFile );
            send( (short)iDataSocket, szBuffer, (short)iResult, 0 );

            // If hash marking is on, then display hashes
            if( iHash && pxcMLE )
                pxcMLE->Insert( "#" );
        }
        fclose( hFile );
    }

    // If hash marking is on, then display a new line
    if( iHash && pxcMLE )
        pxcMLE->Insert( "\n" );

    free( szBuffer );

    soclose( iDataSocket );
    return 0;
}
```

With the low-level FTP interface behind us, the remainder of the class is relatively simple. All the remaining code is used to implement the FTP command set, as specified by the RFC. Since all these commands operate in much the same way, all commands use the command FTPCommand() method; this sends the specified command using the control connection and receives the host response.

```
//------------
// FTPCommand \
//--------------------------------------------------------------------------
//
// Description:
//     This method sends an FTP command to the server and retrieves the
//     response string.
//
// Parameters:
//     szCommand       - Command to send
//
// Return:
//     none
//
void C_CONNECT_FTP::FTPCommand( char *szCommand )
{
   // Send an FTP command to the server
   Send( szCommand );

   // Get the command reply from the server
   Receive( szCommand );
}
```

SYST() implements the FTP SYST command, which returns the type of FTP server software running on the server. This can be used to help determine the type of file system, information that is useful if you plan to write an FTP client to parse directory listings and display them graphically.

```
//------
// SYST \
//--------------------------------------------------------------------------
//
// Description:
//     This method sends a SYST command to determine the server type.
//
// Parameters:
//     none
//
// Return:
//     int          - Result of the command
//
```

```
int C_CONNECT_FTP::SYST( void )
{
   char    szString[1024];

   // Send the SYST command and get the server response
   sprintf( szString, "SYST\r\n" );
   FTPCommand( szString );

   return atoi( szString );
}
```

The SITE command can be used to issue special server commands that are not standard to the FTP protocol. Some firewall security systems use SITE to establish a link through the firewall.

```
//------
// SITE \
//--------------------------------------------------------------------------
//
// Description:
//     This method sends a SITE command to issue server specific command.
//
// Parameters:
//     szText      - Specific server command to send
//
// Return:
//     int         - Result of the command
//
int C_CONNECT_FTP::SITE( char *szText )
{
   char    szString[1024];

   sprintf( szString, "SITE %s\r\n", szText );
   FTPCommand( szString );

   return atoi( szString );
}
```

The ACCT command sends some additional account information to the server. Some servers require this command be issued as part of the login process, and it may also be used as part of the site firewall security.

```
//------
// ACCT \
//--------------------------------------------------------------------------
//
// Description:
//     This method sends an ACCT command to issue any required account data.
```

```
//
// Parameters:
//     szText       - Account information
//
// Return:
//     int          - Result of the command
//
int C_CONNECT_FTP::ACCT( char *szText )
{
  char    szString[1024];

  sprintf( szString, "ACCT %s\r\n", szText );
  FTPCommand( szString );

  return atoi( szString );
}
```

The USER command is sent to the server as part of the login process. This command must be accompanied by the user name, and is usually the first command issued to a server.

```
//------
// USER \
//---------------------------------------------------------------------------
//
// Description:
//     This method sends a USER command to issue log in user name.
//
// Parameters:
//     szText       - Username
//
// Return:
//     int          - Result of the command
//
int C_CONNECT_FTP::USER( char *szText )
{
  char    szString[1024];

  sprintf( szString, "USER %s\r\n", szText );
  FTPCommand( szString );
  return atoi( szString );
}
```

PASS is normally the second command sent to a server. Most servers implement security requiring that a password be issued as part of the login process. FTP clients send a PASS command, accompanied by the password text, and the server verifies the account information.

```
//------
// PASS \
//---------------------------------------------------------------------------
//
// Description:
//     This method sends a PASS command to issue log in password.
//
// Parameters:
//     szText      - Password
//
// Return:
//     int         - Result of the command
//
int C_CONNECT_FTP::PASS( char *szText )
{
  char    szString[1024];

  sprintf( szString, "PASS %s\r\n", szText );
  FTPCommand( szString );
  return atoi( szString );
}
```

The TYPE command sets the type of file transfer to use between the client and the server. Valid TYPE parameters are:

A	Transfers will be performed using standard ASCII text.
E	EBCDIC file transfers. This is very uncommon today.
I	Files are transferred in binary mode.
L	Files are transferred according to a specified local byte size. This is another uncommon mode.

```
//------
// TYPE \
//---------------------------------------------------------------------------
//
// Description:
//     This method sends a TYPE command to set the transfer mode.
//
// Parameters:
//     szType      - Transfer type (I,A,E,L)
//
// Return:
//     int         - Result of the command
//
int C_CONNECT_FTP::TYPE( char *szType )
```

```
{
   char    szString[1024];

   // Set the transfer type
   sprintf( szString, "TYPE %s\r\n", szType );
   FTPCommand( szString );
   return atoi( szString );
}
```

To request the working directory, use the PWD() method. This returns the complete server directory as a NULL-terminated string.

```
//-----
// PWD \
//-----------------------------------------------------------------------------
//
// Description:
//     This method sends a PWD command to return the current directory.
//
// Parameters:
//     szDir       - Returned directory
//
// Return:
//     int         - Result of the command
//
int C_CONNECT_FTP::PWD( char *szDir )
{
   char    szString[1024];

   // Send the PWD command and get the server response
   sprintf( szString, "PWD\r\n" );
   FTPCommand( szString );

   // Return the working directory to the caller
   strcpy( szDir, "" );
   if( atoi( szString ) >= 250 && atoi( szString ) < 300 )
   {
       if( strstr( szString, "\"" ) )
       {
           strcpy( szDir, strstr( szString, "\"" ) + 1 );
           if( strstr( szDir, "\"" ) )
               *strstr( szDir, "\"" ) = 0;
       }

       // If the directory wasn't located then it may be enclosed in [] chars
       if( strlen( szDir ) == 0 && strstr( szString, "[" ) )
       {
           strcpy( szDir, szString + 4 );
```

```
         if( strstr( szDir, "]" ) )
            *(strstr( szDir, "]" ) + 1) = 0;
      }
   }

   return atoi( szString );
}
```

The CWD() method changes the working directory on the server. This directory string can be a full path name or a reference from the current working directory.

```
//-----
// CWD \
//-----------------------------------------------------------------------
//
// Description:
//    This method sends a CWD command to set the current work directory.
//
// Parameters:
//    szDir       - New working directory
//
// Return:
//    int         - Result of the command
//
int C_CONNECT_FTP::CWD( char *szDir )
{
   char    szString[1024];

   sprintf( szString, "CWD %s\r\n", szDir );
   FTPCommand( szString );
   return atoi( szString );
}
```

The RMD() method removes a directory from the server. Server security may prevent this command from being completed.

```
//------
// RMD \
//-----------------------------------------------------------------------
//
// Description:
//    This method sends an RMD command to remove a directory.
//
// Parameters:
//    szFile      - Directory to remove
//
// Return:
```

```
//    int         - Result of the command
//
int C_CONNECT_FTP::RMD( char *szFile )
{
  char    szString[1024];

  sprintf( szString, "RMD %s\r\n", szFile );
  FTPCommand( szString );
  return atoi( szString );
}
```

MKD() makes new directories on the server. The string passed to this method can consist of a full path or a relative offset from the current working directory.

```
//-----
// MKD \
//---------------------------------------------------------------------------
//
// Description:
//    This method sends an MKD command to create a directory.
//
// Parameters:
//    szFile      - Directory to create
//
// Return:
//    int         - Result of the command
//
int C_CONNECT_FTP::MKD( char *szFile )
{
  char    szString[1024];

  sprintf( szString, "MKD %s\r\n", szFile );
  FTPCommand( szString );
  return atoi( szString );
}
```

DELE() accepts either full path name or relative offset for a file on the server to be deleted. This operation may be prevented by server security.

```
//------
// DELE \
//---------------------------------------------------------------------------
//
// Description:
//    This method sends a DELE command to remove a file.
//
// Parameters:
```

```
//     szFile       - File to remove
//
// Return:
//     int          - Result of the command
//
int C_CONNECT_FTP::DELE( char *szFile )
{
   char    szString[1024];

   sprintf( szString, "DELE %s\r\n", szFile );
   FTPCommand( szString );
   return atoi( szString );
}
```

The DIR() method is used to return a directory listing from the server. The method accepts a parameter that specifies the full pathname including any wildcards. The directory list is then retrieved to the specified file. If the console MLE window was defined when the object was created, output is written to the display window rather than the file.

```
//-----
// DIR \
//--------------------------------------------------------------------------
//
// Description:
//     This method fetches a directory listing for the current directory
//     from the server.
//
// Parameters:
//     szWildCards      - Any filename wildcards used for the listing
//     szFile           - Output file for the listing
//
// Return:
//     int              - 0 if successful
//
int C_CONNECT_FTP::DIR( char *szWildcards, char *szFile )
{
   char    szString[1024];
   int     iListener;
   FILE    *hFile;

   // List for a reply connection
   iListener = Listen();

   // Send the command to the server
   if( !szWildcards || strlen( szWildcards ) == 0 )
       sprintf( szString, "LIST\r\n" );
   else
```

```
        sprintf( szString, "LIST %s\r\n", szWildcards );
    FTPCommand( szString );

    // Flag inaccessible directories
    if( atoi( szString ) > 500 || atoi( szString ) == 425 )
    {
        SocketClose( iListener );
        return atoi( szString );
    }

    if( Accept( iListener, szFile ) >= 0 )
    {
        // Display the directory if the MLE window is defined
        if( pxcMLE )
        {
            hFile = fopen( szFile, "rt" );
            if( hFile )
            {
                // Display each line of the directory in the console window
                while( !feof( hFile ) && fgets( szString, 1024, hFile ) )
                    pxcMLE->Insert( szString );

                fclose( hFile );

                DosForceDelete( szFile );
            }
        }

        Receive( szString );
        SocketClose( iListener );
        return atoi( szString );
    }
    SocketClose( iListener );
    return 0;
}
```

The ABOR() method is a special-purpose function. It can be used to abort an FTP operation and will close any data connections. This can be used to terminate a file transfer.

ABOR() sends a termination string using the SendOOB() out-of-band transmission method, and then simply waits for the server to acknowledge the abort operation on the control connection. The TCP/IP select() API waits up to 18,000 milliseconds (18 seconds) for the server to respond. If no response is received, the ABOR() method assumes that connection has been lost and continues as if the abort operation was successful.

```
//------
// ABOR \
//---------------------------------------------------------------------------
// Description:
//     This method implements the transfer abort functionality specified in
//     RFC 959.
//
int C_CONNECT_FTP::ABOR( void )
{
   SHORT   sock_arr[5];
   char    szString[1024];
   int     iResult;

   // Send the abort sequence
   sprintf( szString,"%c%c\r\n",255,244);
   Send( szString );
   sprintf( szString,"%c%c",255,242);
   SendOOB( szString );
   Send( "ABOR\r\n" );

   // Wait for the server to respond
   sock_arr[0] = (short)Socket();
   do {
       iResult = select( (int *)sock_arr, 1, 0, 0, 18000L );
       C_CONNECT::Receive( szString );
   } while( iResult > 0 && strlen( szString ) == 0 );

   return 0;
}
```

The RETR() method retrieves files from the server using the currently selected transfer mode. The code accepts both a source file name and a destination file name. This means that a file can be renamed during the transfer simply by specifying different name strings.

```
//------
// RETR \
//---------------------------------------------------------------------------
//
// Description:
//     This method sends a RETR command to retrieve a file.
//
// Parameters:
//     szSrcFile       - Source file to retrieve
//     szDstFile       - Local file location where retrieval will be written
//
// Return:
//     int             - Result of the command
```

```
//
int C_CONNECT_FTP::RETR( char *szSrcFile, char *szDstFile )
{
   char     szString[1024];
   int      iListener;

   iListener = Listen();
   sprintf( szString, "RETR %s\r\n", szSrcFile );
   FTPCommand( szString );

   if( atoi( szString ) > 500 )
      return 550;

   if( Accept( iListener, szDstFile ) >= 0 )
   {
      Receive( szString );

      SocketClose( iListener );
      return atoi( szString );
   }
   SocketClose( iListener );
   return 0;
}
```

To transfer a file from the local drive to the remote host, C_CONNECT_FTP implements a STOR() method. This simply invokes the Put() method (described previously) to transfer the specified source file to the location selected for the remote file. Like RETR(), different file names can be specified in order to rename the file during the file transfer.

```
//------
// STOR \
//-------------------------------------------------------------------------
//
// Description:
//     This method sends a STOR command to send a file to the server.
//
// Parameters:
//     szSrcFile       - Source file to send
//     szDstFile       - Remote file location where the file will be written
//
// Return:
//     int             - Result of the command
//
int C_CONNECT_FTP::STOR( char *szSrcFile, char *szDstFile )
{
   char     szString[1024];
   int      iListener;
```

```
    iListener = Listen();
    sprintf( szString, "STOR %s\r\n", szDstFile );
    FTPCommand( szString );

    if( atoi( szString ) > 500 )
        return 550;

    if( Put( iListener, szSrcFile ) >= 0 )
    {
        Receive( szString );
        SocketClose( iListener );
        return atoi( szString );
    }
    SocketClose( iListener );
    return 0;
}
```

To end the FTP session with the remote host, the client needs to call the QUIT() method. This forces the server to disconnect the control socket.

```
//------
// QUIT \
//--------------------------------------------------------------------------
//
// Description:
//     This method sends a QUIT command to end the conversation.
//
// Parameters:
//     none
//
// Return:
//     int          - Result of the command
//
int C_CONNECT_FTP::QUIT( void )
{
    char    szString[1024];

    // Send the QUIT command and get the server response
    sprintf( szString, "QUIT\r\n" );
    FTPCommand( szString );

    return atoi( szString );
}
```

The final command implemented in C_CONNECT_FTP is the NOOP() method. Typically, servers will automatically disconnect any connection that is idle for a specified amount of time. You can use NOOP() periodically to issue a command to "fool" the server into believing that the connection is busy. This method does nothing to affect file transfer or the general state of the connection.

```
//------
// NOOP \
//---------------------------------------------------------------------------------
//
// Description:
//     This method sends a NOOP command to perform "no operation".
//
// Parameters:
//     none
//
// Return:
//     int          - Result of the command
//
int C_CONNECT_FTP::NOOP(  void )
{
   char    szString[1024];

   // Send the NOOP command and get the server response
   sprintf( szString, "NOOP\r\n" );
   FTPCommand( szString );

   return atoi( szString );
}
```

The C_CONNECT_FTP class barely scratches the surface of the capabilities built into the FTP protocol. For example, no support for passive server-to-server file transfers has been implemented. This feature is crucial to some users.

We have not delved too deeply into the interaction between client and server. Each command issued by the client invokes a response from the server, but I have given little detail on response codes returned by the server. The following table summarizes some of the more common responses returned from the remote host. This is by no means a complete list.

125	Data connection already open
200	Command OK
211	System status or system help reply
212	Directory status
213	File status
214	Help message
215	NAME system type, where NAME is the name of the FTP server in use
220	Server ready for new user
221	Server closing control connection
225	Data connection open
226	Closing data connection
227	Entering passive mode

230	User logged in
331	User name OK, password required
332	Need account for log in
421	Service not available
425	Can't open data connection
426	Connection closed, transfer aborted
500	Syntax Error, command not recognized
501	Syntax error in command arguments
502	Command not implemented
503	Bad sequence of commands
504	Command not implemented for that parameter
530	Not logged in
532	Need account for storing files

For more details on the FTP protocol or response codes, refer to RFC 959.

Developing Other Network Classes

If you are building TCP/IP applications, you are going to want to write some new code to support other application protocols. For example, you may want to create a network class that implements the Internet Relay Chat (IRC) protocol.

This, of course, means that you need to know something about IRC and how it works, but also implies that you are prepared to dig into some lower-level socket programming. However, creating classes for new protocols should not intimidate you—we have already built several in this chapter, and you can use these as a basic template from which to create new classes. Whenever you consider creating new network classes, remember that much of your potential work has already been handled by the C_CONNECT class. Before you implement new code, be sure you understand the base network class to avoid reinventing some functionality that has already been implemented in C_CONNECT.

The base class should be able to address most of the low-level socket issues for any new protocol, for either the client or server side of a connection. Any new classes you develop should have a minimum of new code. Remember to reuse whenever possible!

Building a Connection Manager

There are some obvious problems with using TCP/IP in a multitasking environment. Although it is an almost trivial exercise to write multithreaded OS/2 applications, keep in mind that a TCP/IP connection is inherently single tasking. For example, if we write a program to connect to a news server and subsequently ask the server for a list of all available newsgroups, the network pipe between our application and the server cannot process anything else until the server finishes sending the list (a potentially time-consuming task). If we were writing Microsoft Windows 3.1 applications, this really would not be an issue, since Windows does not multitask very well anyway. In OS/2, however, we can effectively perform several tasks simultaneously, so we need to find a solution.

When I wrote NeoLogic News, I adopted an approach whereby the news client could create multiple connections to the server. This way, if one connection was busy and the user decided to initiate a new network task, the program could quickly accommodate the request. This approach was later "borrowed" by the NewsReader/2 people at IBM, although I am not sure they really grasped the full potential of multiple connections.

NeoLogic News uses a special piece of code called a connection manager; this monitors user requests for network access and provides one of several active news connections for the task. Although this code can be quite complex, what it amounts to is a supervisory process that monitors the activity on current connections, assigning the first free connection to the process that needs it. The goal in all this extra coding is to keep the user busy—we want our applications to offer remarkable response. This is not easy to achieve with a single connection.

In Part III, as part of the news program, we will implement a very simple connection manager. This will not be nearly as complex as the one implemented in the NeoLogic News product, but it will be sophisticated enough to demonstrate how to create an effective connection manager for a news client. You can take it from there, implementing something much more powerful without investing significant amounts of time.

The NNTP protocol demands that a connection be established and maintained for the entire user session. With a Gopher or FTP client, we can adopt a different kind of connection manager that is much easier to implement and understand. With these protocols, there is typically no permanent connection. A Gopher client can connect to a specified page of data, retrieve it, and then disconnect. The FTP protocol is similar, in that one connection is dedicated to one session, and therefore connection management is virtually self-controlled. Each time an instance of a Gopher connection is established, a physical connection is created and maintained, isolated from other connections. This means that we can write an application capable of requesting several pages simultaneously. More importantly, if one Gopher connection is busy downloading a large uuencoded binary, there is no reason to prevent the user from regaining access to the Gopher program to make other requests. Incidentally, the Gopher client provided in the IBM Warp Internet Access Kit does not offer this advantage, for some unexplained reason. The same thinking applies to the FTP protocol. The same FTP client should have the capability of connecting to several servers simultaneously, and of transferring files to or from any of these sources.

Chapter Summary

In this chapter, you have learned about the contents of the NETCLASS class library and how it interconnects with the TCP/IP API and run-time libraries. We have developed a base C_CONNECT network class and derived three of the more common protocols—Ping, News, and FTP. We have also discussed ways to expand this class library to incorporate other network protocols. It is hoped you will now be comfortable with the prospect of designing complete network classes for your own TCP/IP applications.

Finally, we discussed the concept of a connection manager class and why you might want one. Connection managers may be important to you if you are interested in creating applications that can perform more than a single network task at any given time. Performing multiple network activities is an excellent way to demonstrate a key benefit of OS/2—performance. You should seriously consider implementing a connection manager class for applications you develop.

The NETCLASS class library will be used to develop all the applications in Part III of this book. In order to ensure that you understand the concepts presented in this chapter, you could write some simple test code to make sure you understand what is happening inside the methods. Most development systems include very good debuggers—don't hesitate to use them if you need to.

Part III: Building Applications

Finally, we arrive at the third part of this book where we will start to build some practical applications. In order to get up to speed with the class libraries, the first application we will tackle will be an improved system editor. It is an ambitious project, but the result will be an application infinitely more useful than a sequence of increasingly complex "Hello World" programs.

With our indoctrination into PMCLASS and NVCLASS behind us, we will start to build some actual TCP/IP applications. We will start out with something very simple like Ping and work our way up to more intricate applications like news and FTP. Although these applications will be somewhat limited, I have purposely left lots of doors open to you with the hope that you will venture out on your own to add enhancements to my applications and eventually begin developing your own.

It has been a long road to this point, but we now have complete classes in place for just about everything we will need. As you will see, the applications will come together quite quickly because we have devoted so much time to creating solid class libraries.

Well, let's get started.

In this chapter

- ✓ Creating an improved system editor
- ✓ Implementing toolbars in applications
- ✓ Displaying dialog boxes from a resource file

8

An Improved Editor

Coding the Editor

I said earlier that, if we really wanted to, we could build an improved version of the OS/2 system editor, E. Since you are learning the basics of OS/2, Presentation Manager, and the class libraries, this offers you a good opportunity to build something useful and at the same time learn how all of this capability interrelates.

In this chapter, we will begin to build our first practical application. What we will try to achieve is to build an editor that will be of use later. Rather than inundate you with a lengthy source listing, I will instead start from a fundamental program framework and add functionality a piece at a time.

Our goal is to reproduce the functionality of E, including most of its menu operations. We will improve on E somewhat with the addition of an appealing and useful toolbar and some status information. We will also make our improved editor Workplace Shell aware by adding support for drag-and-drop colors and fonts, selected from the system palettes.

Figure 8-1 is an output sample of the program we are going to create in this section. Initially, the editor will in no way resemble this picture, but though we will start from humble beginnings, the editor will quickly take shape. You will see that with a good plan up front, incremental development is relatively simple.

Let's begin with a minimal program. This code simply creates a basic frame window that you can size and move around the desktop. You can also maximize or minimize it and it will appear in the WPS task list. It isn't a very fancy program now, but it will get better.

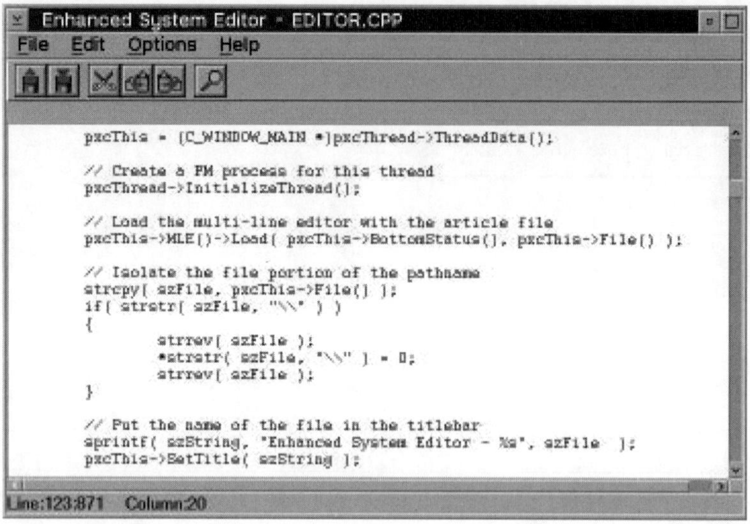

Figure 8-1 Enhanced editor

The first thing we need to do is create a module definition file. This isn't a strict requirement of developing a simple application, but larger programs like the completed editor will usually require one. The DEF file for the editor application is shown in Listing 8-1.

```
NAME            ImprovedEditor          WINDOWAPI
DESCRIPTION     'Improved OS/2 Editor - (c) 1995 by Steven Gutz'
DATA            MULTIPLE

STACKSIZE       16000
HEAPSIZE        16000

PROTMODE
```

Listing 8-1 EDITOR.DEF

Seems pretty straightforward, doesn't it? The first field, NAME, identifies the module as an "ImprovedEditor" and the WINDOWAPI indicates that this module is a PM application. WINDOWAPI causes the linker to build the EXE so that it informs OS/2 that the PM engine needs to be running when this application is started.

The DESCRIPTION field is a text description of what our program is. The field gets embedded in the final executable by the linker, so you can place your copyright notice here if you wish.

The DATA statement defines the default characteristics for data segments used by the program. In this case, data segments are shared amongst all running copies of the program.

The STACKSIZE statement specifies how many bytes of memory are to be reserved for the program stack. For PM applications the minimum stack size is around 4 Kbytes, but a larger stack is recommended—we'll use 16 K for the editor program and larger stacks in some of the other applications shown later.

The HEAPSIZE line defines the initial size of the free memory pool for the application. This area is used to store the automatic data created by the program or for any dynamic memory we allocate in our application. In our editor application we will use a 16K heap, but the applications developed later will increase this number substantially.

The final keyword in the editor DEF file is PROTMODE. This line indicates that the program is a 32-bit protected mode application. Since very few people are developing 16-bit OS/2 applications, the keyword is generally included in all cases, certainly in all DEF files for this book.

The basic editor program initially requires two header files; they will be used, although in expanded form, throughout the entire development process for our editor. The first of these is RC.HPP, as shown in Figure 8-2.

```
//--------------------
// Window Identifiers \
//------------------------------------------------------------------------
#define        ID_MAIN         1            // ID of main window

//------------------------------
// Main Window Menu Identifiers \
//------------------------------------------------------------------------

//--------------------------------
// Main Window Button Identifiers \
//------------------------------------------------------------------------

//---------------------
// Resource Identifiers \
//------------------------------------------------------------------------
```

Listing 8-2 RC.HPP

Currently, this header defines only a single item, ID_MAIN, which is the identifier for our main editor window. You will notice some other comment blocks in this file as well. These will be populated as we begin to enhance our editor.

Listing 8-3 shows the second header file. EDITOR.HPP is the header defining the window object for the main window. This class is pretty barren at the moment, containing only a constructor and destructor, but we will add to it as we go along. In the completed editor this file contains many additional class methods and attributes.

```
//--------------
// C_WINDOW_MAIN \
//-----------------------------------------------------------------------
// Derived from: C_WINDOW_STD
//
class C_WINDOW_MAIN : public C_WINDOW_STD
{
  public:
      C_WINDOW_MAIN( void );
      ~C_WINDOW_MAIN( void );
};

//----------------------------
// User defined window messages \
//-----------------------------------------------------------------------
```

Listing 8-3 EDITOR.HPP

Now let's take a look at the main program. EDITOR.CPP is also quite short at the moment, defining only three functions. It includes the constructor code for C_WINDOW_MAIN, which identifies the message table used by our main window to the parent C_WINDOW_STD object.

A destructor method is also provided. Currently, it has nothing to do, but it will have a very important function in later versions of our code.

```
//------------------
// OS/2 Conditionals \
//-----------------------------------------------------------------------
#define    INCL_DOS
#define    INCL_WIN

//-----------------
// Standard Headers \
//-----------------------------------------------------------------------
#include <os2.h>
#include <stdio.h>
#include <string.h>
#include <process.h>

//----------------
// NVCLASS Headers \
//-----------------------------------------------------------------------
#include <thread.hpp>
#include <threadpm.hpp>
#include <semev.hpp>
```

```
//-----------------
// PMCLASS Headers \
//-----------------------------------------------------------------------------
#include <app.hpp>
#include <window.hpp>
#include <winstd.hpp>
#include <winchild.hpp>
#include <status.hpp>
#include <button.hpp>
#include <tbar.hpp>
#include <mle.hpp>

//---------------------
// Application Headers \
//-----------------------------------------------------------------------------
#include "rc.hpp
#include <editor.hpp>

//-------------
// Global Data \
//-----------------------------------------------------------------------------
C_APPLICATION      xcApp;
C_WINDOW_MAIN      xcWindow;

//---------------------------
// Main Window Message Table \
//-----------------------------------------------------------------------------
DECLARE_MSG_TABLE( xtEditorMain )
   DECLARE_MSG( WM_PAINT, C_WINDOW_STD::MsgPaint )
END_MSG_TABLE

//-------------
// Constructor \
//-----------------------------------------------------------------------------
C_WINDOW_MAIN::C_WINDOW_MAIN( void ) : C_WINDOW_STD( xtEditorMain )
{
}

//-------------
// Destructor \
//-----------------------------------------------------------------------------
C_WINDOW_MAIN::~C_WINDOW_MAIN( void )
{
}

void main( void )
{
   // Register and create a new program window
   xcWindow.Register( "ImprovedEditor" );
```

```
    // Set the window characteristics
    xcWindow.WCF_SizingBorder();
    xcWindow.WCF_SysMenu();
    xcWindow.WCF_TaskList();
    xcWindow.WCF_ShellPosition();
    xcWindow.WCF_MinButton();
    xcWindow.WCF_MaxButton();
    xcWindow.WCF_TitleBar();

    // Create the window
    xcWindow.Create( ID_MAIN, "Improved System Editor" );
    xcWindow.Show();

    // Start the message loop
    xcApp.Run();
}
```

Listing 8-4 EDITOR.CPP

We took a brief look an a main() function similar to this one in the PMCLASS "Hello World" program. This code first registers our new window with the operating system, then defines the initial characteristics of the window. For example, this window has sizable borders, and some embellishments including a system menu, minimize and maximize buttons, as well as a title bar. Any instances of this window are given an initial size and position, as defined by Presentation Manager, and any instances of this window will appear in the WPS task list. Next, the window is created and displayed on the WPS desktop.

The final step in our main procedure is a call to xcApp.Run() to start a message loop for the editor so it can begin executing. The resulting output is similar to the "Hello World" example, so we need not review it here.

Handling Window Creation

The first thing we need to do is create a message handler that will get called whenever the main editor window is created. This will be used later to initialize our window object's attributes and set up any child objects that our applications need.

There are a few lines of code that we will need to insert into some of the existing source files. First of all, we need to add a new entry into the message table to mate the PM_CREATE message to our new MsgCreate() method. Edit the EDITOR.CPP file, adding in the message table:

```
DECLARE_MSG( PM_CREATE, C_WINDOW_MAIN::MsgCreate )
```

We then need to implement the new method. In EDITOR.HPP, add the following line to the public section of the class:

```
void    *MsgCreate( void *mp1, void *mp2 );
```

Finally, add the following new method code to EDITOR.CPP, as follows:

```
//-----------
// MsgCreate \
//---------------------------------------------------------------------
// Event:       PM_CREATE
// Cause:       Issued by OS when window is created
// Description:This method gets called when the window is initially created.
//              It initializes all of the visual aspects of the class.
void *C_WINDOW_MAIN::MsgCreate( void *mp1, void *mp2 )
{
   return FALSE;
}
```

For now, the MsgCreate function does not add any additional functionality. It does have a single line of code forcing a return value of FALSE. Window message handler methods must return a value, and the usual value is FALSE.

You can recompile the application with these new additions, but you would not observe any appreciable difference from the base executable. In the next section we'll change that.

Adding Status Bar Objects

One of the distinctions we will make in our editor, as compared with E, is the addition of some user feedback on the current states of things. The best way to accomplish this is to create a status bar where our application can display key pieces of information for us.

Our enhanced editor will actually implement two status bars because there are a few things that we want to display simultaneously, and we want to avoid confusing the user by jumbling this information on a single status line.

Since we will be changing the characteristics of the C_WINDOW_MAIN class, we first need to tell it about the new status bar attributes. In EDITOR.HPP add the following lines:

```
   private:
      C_STATUS    *pxcTopStatus;       // Pointer to top status bar
      C_STATUS    *pxcBottomStatus;    // Pointer to the bottom status bar
```

In the MsgCreate() method in EDITOR.CPP, add the following lines to create new instances of the status objects:

```
   // Create the status bars to display miscellaneous data
   pxcTopStatus = (C_STATUS *) new C_STATUS( this );
   pxcBottomStatus = (C_STATUS *) new C_STATUS( this );
```

Finally, because the objects are created dynamically, we need to ensure that the memory they use is deallocated if the main window is destroyed. To accomplish this, add the following lines to the C_WINDOW_MAIN destructor method:

```
// Free up the dynamic memory used for status bars
delete      pxcTopStatus;
delete      pxcBottomStatus;
```

The status bars are now in place and will get created when the main window is opened. If you run this code, however, you will still not notice any positive change to program output. Why? There are a couple of reasons. First of all, the client area of our window is the same color as the status bars, so the status lines are essentially invisible. Second, both status bars are at exactly the same position in the window and are the same size, so even in a best case scenario we would only be able to see one of them.

Don't panic yet, we will start sizing things once we get all the controls created. We still do not have an edit window in place, so we cannot perform any text editing. This is the next step.

Adding a Multiline Editor Object

So far our editor program is useless. We can display a main window, but we cannot actually edit anything because we have not yet implemented a multiline editor object. The steps to accomplishing this are similar to those taken to create status bars. All we need to do is add a few more lines of code.

Again, we need to update the class definition since we will be adding a new attribute. Edit EDITOR.HPP and insert the following line in the private section of the class.

```
C_MLE    *pxcMLE;                    // Pointer to the editor object
```

Now edit EDITOR.CPP and, in the MsgCreate() method, insert:

```
// Create a new multiline editor control
pxcMLE = (C_MLE *)new C_MLE( this, ID_MAIN_MLE );
```

This line creates a new dynamic instance of an MLE. Like the status line object, we need to ensure that this object's memory is returned to the heap before the window is closed. So, in the destructor for C_WINDOW_MAIN, we need to add the following code:

```
// Free up the multiline editor object
delete      pxcMLE;
```

One final item we need to address is the new definition made for the MLE creation line. Every control needs to have a distinct identifier, and in the case of pxcMLE we have introduced ID_MAIN_MLE, which we have to define somewhere in the code. We will do this in RC.HPP immediately after the ID_MAIN definition.

```
#define        ID_MAIN_MLE2              // ID of the MLE object
```

Sizing Up

In spite of the fact that most of our objects have been created, the program still does not operate correctly. If you run the updated executable you will notice a very small object in the lower corner of the client area possessing a vertical and horizontal scrollbar. This is actually the MLE we just created. But what good is it?

When the MLE was created it was assigned default size and position values by the PMCLASS code. These values are not acceptable; we have to resize the control in order to make it suitable for use. What we really want is to have our status bars span the width of the main window and sit at the top and bottom of the client area, and we want our MLE control to extend to the remainder of the client area. When the user moves or resizes the main window all the controls should scale with it. How can we achieve this?

Fortunately, Presentation Manager can help our application out by telling it exactly when the user has resized the main frame window. PM sends our application a WM_SIZE message, and all we need to do is intercept this message and size the status bars and MLE control.

Since we are going to watch for a new window message, we need to repeat the steps we took to add the MsgCreate() method. In EDITOR.HPP we will add a new method prototype to the public section of the class.

```
void    *MsgSize( void *mp1, void *mp2 );
```

Then, in EDITOR.CPP, we can add a new entry into the message table.

```
DECLARE_MSG( WM_SIZE,C_WINDOW_MAIN::MsgSize )
```

Finally, we need to create the new method to handle window sizing. In EDITOR.CPP, add the following method code.

```
//---------
// MsgSize \
//-----------------------------------------------------------------------
// Event:       WM_SIZE
// Cause:       Issued by OS when window is resized
// Description:This method is called any time PM decides the window needs
```

```
//          to be resized. It determines the new window dimensions and
//          resizes the visual components accordingly.
//
void *C_WINDOW_MAIN::MsgSize( void *mp1, void *mp2 )
{
   int      iCX;
   int      iCY;

   // Determine the new size of the client area
   C_WINDOW::GetSize( &iCX, &iCY );

   // Stretch the top status across the entire window
   iCY -= 20;
   pxcTopStatus->SetSizePosition( 0, iCY, iCX, 20 );

   // Make the container window use whatever space is left minus the height
   // of the second status bar
   pxcMLE->SetSizePosition( 0, 20, iCX, iCY - 20 );

   // Draw the final status bar in the lower region of the window
   pxcBottomStatus->SetSizePosition( 0, 0, iCX, 20 );

   return FALSE;
}
```

Believe it or not, a large portion of our editor is now completed. Recompile the application and run the executable and you will see what I mean. Notice that the upper and lower status bars are in place and sandwich the large MLE window.

Using the mouse, click the left mouse button while the pointer is within the boundaries of the MLE window. You can type text and select text with the mouse. If you know the shortcut keys for copying and cutting text, you can interact with the clipboard.

Adding a Menu

So far, our enhanced editor still lacks some significant features that prevent it from being a serious competitor to E. For example, there is no way to save or load text and only an inconvenient method by which we can use the clipboard features. What we need to create is a menu from which program operations can be selected. This is accomplished by creating a resource script.

A resource script is a text file that can be used to add resources to a program's EXE file. These resources can take the form of binary items, such as icons, mouse pointers, and bitmaps. Menu templates and keyboard accelerators are usually also implemented in the resource file (RC). You can build all of these things with code if you wish, but an RC file saves hours of coding work.

Once the RC file is completed, you use a tool supplied by the compiler vendor called the Resource Compiler, which compiles the script into a binary file with a .RES extension. This RES file is bound to the EXE file by the linker. You will have to make sure this RC file gets compiled and linked into the program executable. Since this is compiler specific, I have not shown the project or MAKE files for this entire project. I am assuming you have some experience with these, but if not, look at the final project or MAKE file for this program on the companion disk. It will give you some insight into what is required.

The following listing contains the initial RC file for our enhanced editor.

```
#include <os2.h>
#include "rc.hpp"

MENU ID_MAIN
BEGIN
   SUBMENU "~File", DM_FILE
   BEGIN
       MENUITEM "~New...", DM_FILE_NEW
       MENUITEM "~Open...", DM_FILE_OPEN
       MENUITEM SEPARATOR
       MENUITEM "~Save...", DM_FILE_SAVE
       MENUITEM "Save ~as...", DM_FILE_SAVEAS
   END

   SUBMENU "~Edit", DM_EDIT
   BEGIN
       MENUITEM "~Undo\aAlt+Backspace", DM_EDIT_UNDO
       MENUITEM SEPARATOR
       MENUITEM "Cu~t\aShift+Del", DM_EDIT_CUT
       MENUITEM "~Copy\aCtrl+Ins", DM_EDIT_PASTE
       MENUITEM "~Paste\aShift+Ins", DM_EDIT_PASTE
       MENUITEM "Cl~ear\aDel", DM_EDIT_CLEAR
       MENUITEM SEPARATOR
       MENUITEM "~Find...\aCtrl+F", DM_EDIT_FIND
       MENUITEM "Select ~all", DM_EDIT_SELECT
   END

   SUBMENU "~Options", DM_OPTIONS
   BEGIN
       SUBMENU "~Word wrap", DM_OPTIONS_WRAP
       BEGIN
           MENUITEM "~On", DM_OPTIONS_WRAP_ON
           MENUITEM "O~ff", DM_OPTIONS_WRAP_OFF
       END
   END

   SUBMENU "~Help", DM_HELP
```

```
   BEGIN
      MENUITEM "Help ~index...", DM_HELP_INDEX
      MENUITEM "~General help...", DM_HELP_GENERAL
      MENUITEM "~Using help...", DM_HELP_USING
      MENUITEM "~Keys help...", DM_HELP_KEYS
      MENUITEM SEPARATOR
      MENUITEM "~Product information...", DM_HELP_INFO
   END
END

ACCELTABLE ID_MAIN PRELOAD MOVEABLE
BEGIN
   VK_BACKSPACE,       DM_EDIT_UNDO,       VIRTUALKEY, ALT
   VK_DELETE,          DM_EDIT_CUT,        VIRTUALKEY, SHIFT
   VK_INSERT,          DM_EDIT_COPY,       VIRTUALKEY, CONTROL
   VK_INSERT,          DM_EDIT_PASTE,      VIRTUALKEY, SHIFT
   VK_DELETE,          DM_EDIT_CLEAR,      VIRTUALKEY
   "f",            DM_EDIT_FIND,       CHAR,   CONTROL
END
```

Listing 8-5 EDITOR.RC

In Listing 8-5, a menu had been created, as well as an accelerator table for the menu. You will note that this menu is remarkably similar to one in E (actually, I patterned this menu after E's). You will notice that I have dropped the font and color selection items from the "Options." I did this because we are not going to require them for our completed editor. Our application will be WPS-compliant, so it will support drag-and-drop changes from the system palettes.

All of the menu options in the RC had an associated identifier which must be defined. The RC includes our RC.HPP for this reason, and we will define these identifiers there. Add the following to the "Main Window Menu Identifiers" section of RC.HPP.

```
#define       DM_FILE                  100
#define       DM_FILE_NEW              101
#define       DM_FILE_OPEN             102
#define       DM_FILE_SAVE             103
#define       DM_FILE_SAVEAS           104
#define       DM_EDIT                  200
#define       DM_EDIT_UNDO             201
#define       DM_EDIT_CUT              202
#define       DM_EDIT_COPY             203
#define       DM_EDIT_PASTE            204
#define       DM_EDIT_CLEAR            205
#define       DM_EDIT_FIND             206
#define       DM_EDIT_SELECT           207
#define       DM_OPTIONS               300
```

```
#define        DM_OPTIONS_WRAP          301
#define        DM_OPTIONS_WRAP_ON       302
#define        DM_OPTIONS_WRAP_OFF      303
#define        DM_HELP                  400
#define        DM_HELP_INDEX            401
#define        DM_HELP_GENERAL          402
#define        DM_HELP_USING            403
#define        DM_HELP_KEYS             404
#define        DM_HELP_INFO             405
```

Finally, we need to tell the main window that it now has a menu to load when it gets instantiated. This is a simple matter of adding the following line to the main() function of EDITOR.CPP. Add this to the end of the characteristics implemented previously.

```
xcWindow.WCF_Menu();
```

Now, if you compile and run the program, you'll start to see something that actually looks like E. It still isn't very functional, though. We'll start adding some "meat" to the program soon.

Adding a Toolbar

The final user interface issue we need to address is the toolbar. Toolbars are easy to create; however, they can be time-consuming. If you are like me (or any other typical programmer), you lack artistic skills. Since you will be building lots of button images, this is an important consideration. The button faces (for the up, down, and disabled states) need to be designed and implemented using ICONEDIT, a standard OS/2 tool. I'll provide the button graphics for this program, so all you need to do is implement a little code.

First, we need to create the toolbar object. Listing 8-6 contains the TBARTOP.HPP file, which defines the new toolbar object.

```
class C_TOOLBAR_TOP : public C_TOOLBAR
{
   public:
       C_TOOLBAR_TOP( C_WINDOW *pxcParentObj, C_STATUS *pxcStatus );
       void    Control( ULONG mp1 );
};

// Main Toolbar Identifier
#define        D_TOP_TBAR          50

// Main Toolbar button IDs
#define        DB_OPEN             100
#define        DB_SAVE             101
```

```
#define        DB_CUT              102
#define        DB_COPY             103
#define        DB_PASTE            104
#define        DB_FIND             105
```

Listing 8-6 TBARTOP.HPP

The TBARTOP.CPP file is shown in Listing 8-7.

```
//--------------------
// OS/2 Conditionals \
//-------------------------------------------------------------------------
#define INCL_DOS
#define INCL_WIN
#define INCL_GPI

//-------------------
// Standard Headers \
//-------------------------------------------------------------------------
#include <os2.h>
#include <stdio.h>
#include <stdlib.h>

//-----------------
// PMCLASS Headers \
//-------------------------------------------------------------------------
#include <app.hpp>
#include <window.hpp>
#include <winstd.hpp>
#include <winchild.hpp>
#include <status.hpp>
#include <button.hpp>
#include <tbar.hpp>

//---------------------
// Application Headers \
//-------------------------------------------------------------------------
#include <tbartop.hpp>
#include "rc.hpp"

//-------------
// Constructor \
//-------------------------------------------------------------------------
C_TOOLBAR_TOP::C_TOOLBAR_TOP( C_WINDOW *pxcParentObj, C_STATUS *pxcStatus )
                            : C_TOOLBAR( pxcParentObj, D_TOP_TBAR, 40 )
{
   DECLARE_BUTTON_TABLE( xtButtons )
       DECLARE_BUTTON( DB_OPEN, DB_OPEN_UP, DB_OPEN_DN, 0,
```

```
                            "Open a file", 8, 4 )
        DECLARE_BUTTON( DB_SAVE, DB_SAVE_UP, DB_SAVE_DN, 0,
                            "Save a file", 40, 4 )
        DECLARE_BUTTON( DB_CUT, DB_CUT_UP, DB_CUT_DN, 0,
                            "Cut selected text", 80, 4 )
        DECLARE_BUTTON( DB_COPY, DB_COPY_UP, DB_COPY_DN, 0,
                            "Copy selected text", 112, 4 )
        DECLARE_BUTTON( DB_PASTE, DB_PASTE_UP, DB_PASTE_DN, 0,
                            "Paste text from the clipboard", 144, 4 )
        DECLARE_BUTTON( DB_FIND, DB_FIND_UP, DB_FIND_DN, 0,
                        "Display the text search/replace dialog", 184, 4 )
END_BUTTON_TABLE

    // Set the status bar object used by the toolbar
    Status( pxcStatus );

    // Add some toolbar buttons
    CreateButtons( xtButtons );
}

//---------
// Control \
//---------------------------------------------------------------------------
void C_TOOLBAR_TOP::Control( ULONG mp1 )
{
    // Button-Command cross reference
    DECLARE_BUTTON_CMD_TABLE( xtCommandLookup )
        DECLARE_BUTTON_CMD( DB_OPEN, DM_FILE_OPEN )
        DECLARE_BUTTON_CMD( DB_SAVE, DM_FILE_SAVE )
        DECLARE_BUTTON_CMD( DB_CUT, DM_EDIT_CUT )
        DECLARE_BUTTON_CMD( DB_COPY, DM_EDIT_COPY )
        DECLARE_BUTTON_CMD( DB_PASTE, DM_EDIT_PASTE )
        DECLARE_BUTTON_CMD( DB_FIND, DM_EDIT_FIND )
    END_BUTTON_CMD_TABLE

    // Call the parent controller to process the items
    C_TOOLBAR::Control( mp1, xtCommandLookup );
}
```

Listing 8-7 TBARTOP.CPP

To the private section of C_WINDOW_MAIN in EDITOR.HPP, add:

```
C_TOOLBAR_TOP    *pxcTBar;         // Pointer to toolbar object
```

Add the following code to the "Main Window Button Identifiers" section in RC.HPP:

```
#define     DB_OPEN_UP          1000
#define     DB_OPEN_DN          1001
#define     DB_SAVE_UP          1002
#define     DB_SAVE_DN          1003
#define     DB_CUT_UP           1004
#define     DB_CUT_DN           1005
#define     DB_COPY_UP          1006
#define     DB_COPY_DN          1007
#define     DB_PASTE_UP         1008
#define     DB_PASTE_DN         1009
#define     DB_FIND_UP          1010
#define     DB_FIND_DN          1011
```

To EDITOR.RC, add the new pointer resources.

```
POINTER     DB_OPEN_UP      "./buttons/loadup.ptr"
POINTER     DB_OPEN_DN      "./buttons/loaddn.ptr"
POINTER     DB_SAVE_UP      "./buttons/saveup.ptr"
POINTER     DB_SAVE_DN      "./buttons/savedn.ptr"
POINTER     DB_COPY_UP      "./buttons/copyup.ptr"
POINTER     DB_COPY_DN      "./buttons/copydn.ptr"
POINTER     DB_CUT_UP       "./buttons/cutup.ptr"
POINTER     DB_CUT_DN       "./buttons/cutdn.ptr"
POINTER     DB_PASTE_UP     "./buttons/pasteup.ptr"
POINTER     DB_PASTE_DN     "./buttons/pastedn.ptr"
POINTER     DB_FIND_UP      "./buttons/srchup.ptr"
POINTER     DB_FIND_DN      "./buttons/srchdn.ptr"
```

In EDITOR.CPP, there are a number of changes to make. First we need to include the toolbar class definition, by adding a new header file to our list of includes. Add the following line immediately after the line that includes the RC.HPP header file.

```
#include <tbartop.hpp>
```

To the C_WINDOW_MAIN destructor, add the following lines in order to ensure that the toolbar memory is returned to the heap when the window is destroyed.

```
    // Free up the toolbar object
    delete      pxcTBar;
```

To create the toolbar, add the following lines to the MsgCreate() method.

```
    // Create a toolbar control
    pxcTBar = (C_TOOLBAR_TOP *)new C_TOOLBAR_TOP( this, pxcTopStatus );
```

In order to ensure that the toolbar is displayed and correctly resized when the main window size is changed, we need to add a bit of code. To accomplish this, some source needs to be added to the MsgSize() method. Immediately after the call to C_WINDOW::QuerySize(), add the following lines.

```
// Stretch the toolbar across the entire window
iCY -= 40;
pxcTBar->SetSizePosition( 0, iCY, iCX, 40 );
```

An important aspect of toolbars is that they are controls, and as such, generate a WM_CONTROL message that the owner window must intercept and process. To do this, we need to add a new message processor method for WM_CONTROL.

To EDITOR.HPP, add a new method prototype to the public section of the class, as follows:

```
void    *MsgControl( void *mp1, void *mp2 );
```

Then add the new message to the message table in EDITOR.CPP.

```
DECLARE_MSG( WM_CONTROL,C_WINDOW_MAIN::MsgControl )
```

Finally, add a method to process the WM_CONTROL messages. This method detects messages from the toolbar buttons and tells the toolbar object to convert these to WM_COMMAND messages by calling the Control() method.

```
//------------
// MsgControl \
//---------------------------------------------------------------------------
// Event:      WM_CONTROL
// Cause:      Issued by OS for control functions (Toolbar interaction)
//
void *C_WINDOW_MAIN::MsgControl( void *mp1, void *mp2 )
{
   switch( SHORT1FROMMP( mp1 ) )
   {
      case D_TOP_TBAR:
         pxcTBar->Control( (ULONG)mp1 );
         break;
   }
   return FALSE;
}
```

You can now add TBARTOP.CPP to your project or MAKE file and rebuild the executable. Run the program and you will see the toolbar immediately below the program menu. You can position the mouse over a button to see the fly-over text appear in the top status bar and you can click buttons to observe the change in appearance. The toolbar is now fully active, as are all of the menu options. What is missing are the command processors for each of these items. In the remainder of this chapter, we will begin adding these items to complete the editor.

Processing WM_COMMAND Messages

I will warn you now that this section contains a lot of code. So far we have not processed any menu or toolbar button operations, and without this capability our editor will never be useful. In this section we will add the capability to process all of the window commands.

We are going to create a dummy method for each option on the main menu. The result is a lot of empty code, but this is necessary for us to proceed with implementing the code for the options.

The first thing we will need to do is create a command table and tell the PMCLASS engine about it, so it knows where the method for each command message is located. The command table is virtually identical to the message table we have been using in this application. In EDITOR.CPP, add the following table immediately following the message table at the top of the file.

```
//---------------------------
// Main Window Command Table \
//---------------------------------------------------------------------------
DECLARE_COMMAND_TABLE( xtCommandMain )
   DECLARE_COMMAND( DM_FILE_NEW,          C_WINDOW_MAIN::CmdFileNew )
   DECLARE_COMMAND( DM_FILE_OPEN,         C_WINDOW_MAIN::CmdFileOpen )
   DECLARE_COMMAND( DM_FILE_SAVE,         C_WINDOW_MAIN::CmdFileSave )
   DECLARE_COMMAND( DM_FILE_SAVEAS,       C_WINDOW_MAIN::CmdFileSaveAs )
   DECLARE_COMMAND( DM_EDIT_UNDO,         C_WINDOW_MAIN::CmdEditUndo )
   DECLARE_COMMAND( DM_EDIT_CUT,          C_WINDOW_MAIN::CmdEditCut )
   DECLARE_COMMAND( DM_EDIT_COPY,         C_WINDOW_MAIN::CmdEditCopy )
   DECLARE_COMMAND( DM_EDIT_PASTE,        C_WINDOW_MAIN::CmdEditPaste )
   DECLARE_COMMAND( DM_EDIT_CLEAR,        C_WINDOW_MAIN::CmdEditClear )
   DECLARE_COMMAND( DM_EDIT_FIND,         C_WINDOW_MAIN::CmdEditFind )
   DECLARE_COMMAND( DM_EDIT_SELECT,       C_WINDOW_MAIN::CmdEditSelect )
   DECLARE_COMMAND( DM_OPTIONS_WRAP_ON,   C_WINDOW_MAIN::CmdOptionsWrapOn )
   DECLARE_COMMAND( DM_OPTIONS_WRAP_OFF,  C_WINDOW_MAIN::CmdOptionsWrapOff )
   DECLARE_COMMAND( DM_HELP_INDEX,        C_WINDOW_MAIN::CmdHelpIndex )
   DECLARE_COMMAND( DM_HELP_GENERAL,      C_WINDOW_MAIN::CmdHelpGeneral )
   DECLARE_COMMAND( DM_HELP_USING,        C_WINDOW_MAIN::CmdHelpUsing )
   DECLARE_COMMAND( DM_HELP_KEYS,         C_WINDOW_MAIN::CmdHelpKeys )
   DECLARE_COMMAND( DM_HELP_INFO,         C_WINDOW_MAIN::CmdHelpInfo )
END_MSG_TABLE
```

We have to let the parent window of C_WINDOW_MAIN know that we are now going to process our own command messages, so to the constructor add the following lines.

```
// Enable the required command handlers for this window
CommandTable( xtCommandMain );
```

For each entry in the command table we need to create a command method. This why I warned you that there would be lots of code. At present, each of these methods will be empty, returning only a FALSE value to the window manager. We will begin populating these items in the next section.

```
//-----------
// CmdFileNew \
//---------------------------------------------------------------------
// Event:      DM_FILE_NEW
// Cause:      User selects the File/New menu option
//
void *C_WINDOW_MAIN::CmdFileNew( void *mp1, void *mp2 )
{
   return FALSE;
}

//------------
// CmdFileOpen \
//---------------------------------------------------------------------
// Event:      DM_FILE_OPEN
// Cause:      User selects the File/Open menu option
//
void *C_WINDOW_MAIN::CmdFileOpen( void *mp1, void *mp2 )
{
   return FALSE;
}

//------------
// CmdFileSave \
//---------------------------------------------------------------------
// Event:      DM_FILE_SAVE
// Cause:      User selects the File/Save menu option
//
void *C_WINDOW_MAIN::CmdFileSave( void *mp1, void *mp2 )
{
   return FALSE;
}
```

```
//---------------
// CmdFileSaveAs \
//---------------------------------------------------------------------------
// Event:       DM_FILE_SAVEAS
// Cause:       User selects the File/SaveAs menu option
//
void *C_WINDOW_MAIN::CmdFileSaveAs( void *mp1, void *mp2 )
{
   return FALSE;
}

//-------------
// CmdEditUndo \
//---------------------------------------------------------------------------
// Event:       DM_EDIT_UNDO
// Cause:       User selects the Edit/Undo menu option
//
void *C_WINDOW_MAIN::CmdEditUndo( void *mp1, void *mp2 )
{
   return FALSE;
}

//------------
// CmdEditCut \
//---------------------------------------------------------------------------
// Event:       DM_EDIT_CUT
// Cause:       User selects the Edit/Cut menu option
//
void *C_WINDOW_MAIN::CmdEditCut( void *mp1, void *mp2 )
{
   return FALSE;
}

//-------------
// CmdEditCopy \
//---------------------------------------------------------------------------
// Event:       DM_EDIT_COPY
// Cause:       User selects the Edit/Copy menu option
//
void *C_WINDOW_MAIN::CmdEditCopy( void *mp1, void *mp2 )
{
   return FALSE;
}

//-------------
// CmdEditPaste \
//---------------------------------------------------------------------------
// Event:       DM_EDIT_PASTE
// Cause:       User selects the Edit/Paste menu option
```

```
//
void *C_WINDOW_MAIN::CmdEditPaste( void *mp1, void *mp2 )
{
   return FALSE;
}

//--------------
// CmdEditClear \
//--------------------------------------------------------------------------
// Event:      DM_EDIT_CLEAR
// Cause:      User selects the Edit/Clear menu option
//
void *C_WINDOW_MAIN::CmdEditClear( void *mp1, void *mp2 )
{
   return FALSE;
}

//-------------
// CmdEditFind \
//--------------------------------------------------------------------------
// Event:      DM_EDIT_FIND
// Cause:      User selects the Edit/Find menu option
//
void *C_WINDOW_MAIN::CmdEditFind( void *mp1, void *mp2 )
{
   return FALSE;
}

//---------------
// CmdEditSelect \
//--------------------------------------------------------------------------
// Event:      DM_EDIT_SELECT
// Cause:      User selects the Edit/Select menu option
//
void *C_WINDOW_MAIN::CmdEditSelect( void *mp1, void *mp2 )
{
   return FALSE;
}

//------------------
// CmdOptionsWrapOn \
//--------------------------------------------------------------------------
// Event:      DM_EDIT_WRAP_ON
// Cause:      User selects the Options/Wrap/On menu option
//
void *C_WINDOW_MAIN::CmdOptionsWrapOn( void *mp1, void *mp2 )
{
   return FALSE;
}
```

```
//-------------------
// CmdOptionsWrapOff \
//--------------------------------------------------------------------------------
// Event:      DM_EDIT_WRAP_OFF
// Cause:      User selects the Options/Wrap/Off menu option
//
void *C_WINDOW_MAIN::CmdOptionsWrapOff( void *mp1, void *mp2 )
{
   return FALSE;
}

//--------------
// CmdHelpIndex \
//--------------------------------------------------------------------------------
// Event:      DM_HELP_INDEX
// Cause:      User selects the Help/Index menu option
//
void *C_WINDOW_MAIN::CmdHelpIndex( void *mp1, void *mp2 )
{
   return FALSE;
}

//----------------
// CmdHelpGeneral \
//--------------------------------------------------------------------------------
// Event:      DM_HELP_General
// Cause:      User selects the Help/General menu option
//
void *C_WINDOW_MAIN::CmdHelpGeneral( void *mp1, void *mp2 )
{
   return FALSE;
}

//--------------
// CmdHelpUsing \
//--------------------------------------------------------------------------------
// Event:      DM_HELP_USING
// Cause:      User selects the Help/Using menu option
//
void *C_WINDOW_MAIN::CmdHelpUsing( void *mp1, void *mp2 )
{
   return FALSE;
}

//-------------
// CmdHelpKeys \
//--------------------------------------------------------------------------------
// Event:      DM_HELP_KEYS
```

```
// Cause:      User selects the Help/Keys menu option
//
void *C_WINDOW_MAIN::CmdHelpKeys( void *mp1, void *mp2 )
{
   return FALSE;
}

//-------------
// CmdHelpInfo \
//--------------------------------------------------------------------
// Event:      DM_HELP_INFO
// Cause:      User selects the Help/Index menu option
//
void *C_WINDOW_MAIN::CmdHelpInfo( void *mp1, void *mp2 )
{
   return FALSE;
}
```

Finally, prototype the new methods in EDITOR.HPP by adding the following lines to the public section of the class.

```
// Command Processor Methods
void    *CmdFileNew( void *mp1, void *mp2 );
void    *CmdFileOpen( void *mp1, void *mp2 );
void    *CmdFileSave( void *mp1, void *mp2 );
void    *CmdFileSaveAs( void *mp1, void *mp2 );
void    *CmdEditUndo( void *mp1, void *mp2 );
void    *CmdEditCut( void *mp1, void *mp2 );
void    *CmdEditCopy( void *mp1, void *mp2 );
void    *CmdEditPaste( void *mp1, void *mp2 );
void    *CmdEditClear( void *mp1, void *mp2 );
void    *CmdEditFind( void *mp1, void *mp2 );
void    *CmdEditSelect( void *mp1, void *mp2 );
void    *CmdOptionsWrapOn( void *mp1, void *mp2 );
void    *CmdOptionsWrapOff( void *mp1, void *mp2 );
void    *CmdHelpIndex( void *mp1, void *mp2 );
void    *CmdHelpGeneral( void *mp1, void *mp2 );
void    *CmdHelpUsing( void *mp1, void *mp2 );
void    *CmdHelpKeys( void *mp1, void *mp2 );
void    *CmdHelpInfo( void *mp1, void *mp2 );
```

From this point on, we will take much bigger steps. You should be feeling quite comfortable with the PMCLASS library now, so in the next section I will introduce the NVCLASS, as we start to create threads for loading and saving files.

Loading and Saving Files

Although our enhanced editor program now looks like a complete program, it still lacks the ability to save or load files. In this section we will add this capability, and although I will introduce you to the thread handling provided by the NVCLASS library, the complexity of the code will not increase significantly.

Add the following new attributes to the EDITOR.HPP file, in the private section of the class. These lines prepare for setting up additional threads to load and save the file and specify the file name on which the editor will be working.

```
C_THREAD_PM     xcLoadThread;       // Pointer to a PM aware thread
C_THREAD_PM     xcSaveThread;       // Pointer to a PM aware thread
char            szFile[512];        // String containing current file
```

Also, in preparation for multithreading, we need to create a few inline methods to permit access to some of the C_WINDOW_MAIN class's attributes. To the public section of the class definition add:

```
// Inline methods
C_STATUS    *BottomStatus( void )   { return pxcBottomStatus; };
C_MLE       *MLE( void )            { return pxcMLE; };
char        *File( void )           { return szFile; };
```

Now we will create the two thread functions we need to perform the saving and loading operations. When describing the MLE saving and loading processes earlier in this book, I pointed out that these operations should always occur on a separate thread simply because they can take significantly longer than the 1⁄10 second that PM programming style guidelines recommend.

Add the following two thread functions to EDITOR.CPP immediately after the command table near the top of the program.

```
//---------------
// FileLoadThread \
//-----------------------------------------------------------------------
void _Optlink FileLoadThread( void *pvData )
{
   C_WINDOW_MAIN    *pxcThis;
   C_THREAD_PM      *pxcThread;

   // Get a point to the main window object
   pxcThread = (C_THREAD_PM *)pvData;
   pxcThis = (C_WINDOW_MAIN *)pxcThread->ThreadData();

   // Create a PM process for this thread
   pxcThread->InitializeThread();

   // Load the multiline editor with the article file
```

```
    pxcThis->MLE()->Load( pxcThis->BottomStatus(), pxcThis->File() );

    // Terminate the thread
    pxcThread->TerminateThread();
}

//----------------
// FileSaveThread \
//-----------------------------------------------------------------------------
void _Optlink FileSaveThread( void *pvData )
{
    C_WINDOW_MAIN    *pxcThis;
    C_THREAD_PM      *pxcThread;

    // Get a point to the main window object
    pxcThread = (C_THREAD_PM *)pvData;
    pxcThis = (C_WINDOW_MAIN *)pxcThread->ThreadData();

    // Create a PM process for this thread
    pxcThread->InitializeThread();

    // Load the multiline editor with the article file
    pxcThis->MLE()->Save( pxcThis->BottomStatus(), pxcThis->File() );

    // Terminate the thread
    pxcThread->TerminateThread();
}
```

Notice in the thread functions that the action part of the code is really just a single line, as I said in a previous chapter. The rest of the thread code just sets up and tears down the thread.

Somehow we now need to start these threads; the way to do this is by adding code to three of the command handlers created in the last section. First we will add code to load a file. The PMCLASS library does not currently offer an object to present a file dialog, which is a drawback, but we can use this opportunity to examine how to integrate true PM API code into a program written with the classes. You can implement file dialog classes later, if you wish.

To the CmdFileOpen() method in EDITOR.CPP, add the following lines before the return statement. This code creates and displays a standard OS/2 file dialog, permitting the user to select a file for loading. Assuming the user then selects the dialog's OK button, the selected file is saved in the szFile class attribute and the load thread is started.

```
    FILEDLG      fild;
    HWND         hDlgWnd;

    // Use the OS/2 API to query the user for a file
```

```
memset( &fild, 0, sizeof(FILEDLG) );
fild.cbSize = sizeof(FILEDLG);
fild.fl = FDS_CENTER | FDS_OPEN_DIALOG;
fild.pszTitle = "Open file";
strcpy( fild.szFullFile, "*.*" );
hDlgWnd = WinFileDlg( HWND_DESKTOP, Window(), &fild );
if( hDlgWnd && ( fild.lReturn == DID_OK ) )
{
    // Get the filename we're supposed to load
    strcpy( szFile, fild.szFullFile );

    // Begin a thread to load the file
    xcLoadThread.Create( FileLoadThread, 40000, this );
}
```

The code for the CmdFileSave() method is much simpler. The editor already knows the name of the file, so it does not have to query the user again. Instead, it can simply start the save thread, as shown in the following lines.

```
// Begin a thread to Save the file
xcLoadThread.Create( FileSaveThread, 40000, this );
```

The CmdFileSaveAs() method is similar to the loading function. By selecting this operation, the user has elected to save the file under a different name, so once again the editor needs to display a standard file dialog to permit the user to set the file name. The SaveAs code is shown below.

```
FILEDLG     fild;
HWND        hDlgWnd;


// Use the OS/2 API to query the user for a file
memset( &fild, 0, sizeof(FILEDLG) );
fild.cbSize = sizeof(FILEDLG);
fild.fl = FDS_CENTER | FDS_SAVEAS_DIALOG;
fild.pszTitle = "Save file as";
strcpy( fild.szFullFile, "*.*" );
hDlgWnd = WinFileDlg( HWND_DESKTOP, Window(), &fild );
if( hDlgWnd && ( fild.lReturn == DID_OK ) )
{
    // Get the filename we're supposed to load
    strcpy( szFile, fild.szFullFile );

    // Begin a thread to load the file
    xcSaveThread.Create( FileSaveThread, 40000, this );
}
```

If you compile and run the editor executable now, you will see that it works. You can load files, edit them, and save them back to disk. All that remains to mimic the existing E functionality is to implement the Edit menu options. We will start this in the next section.

Adding Clipboard Interaction and Word Wrap

Looking back at the chapter describing the PMCLASS MLE code, we are reminded that the C_MLE class that is used in the editor already has the capability of interacting with the OS/2 clipboard. All we really need to do, then, is associate these operations with a specific command handler method.

For example, to implement the "undo" operation, add the following lines to the CmdEditUndo() method.

```
// Undo the last editor operation
pxcMLE->Undo();
```

The remainder of the editor functions are similar in implementation. To CmdEditCut(), add:

```
// Remove the selected text and place it on the clipboard
pxcMLE->Cut();
```

To CmdEditCopy(), add:

```
// Copy the selected text and place it on the clipboard
pxcMLE->Copy();
```

To CmdEditPaste(), add:

```
// Paste the contents of the clipboard into the file
pxcMLE->Paste();
```

To CmdEditClear(), add:

```
// Clear the current selection
pxcMLE->Clear();
```

And, finally, to CmdEditSelectAll(), add the following lines:

```
// Select all data in the MLE
pxcMLE->Select( 0 , pxcMLE->BufferLength() );
```

We might as well implement the word wrap options in this section as well, since they are similar to the clipboard operations. To turn word wrap on, the program calls CmdOptionsWrapOn()—its code follows.

```
// Enable word wrapping
pxcMLE->WordWrap( TRUE );
```

To toggle wrapping off, add the following lines to CmdOptionsWrapOff().

```
// Disable word wrapping
pxcMLE->WordWrap( FALSE );
```

I have deliberately ignored the Find menu option because it involves rather more complex code. If we want to mimic E's text searching, then we will need to create a dialog box to manage this operation. We will examine the use of dialogs next, starting with the Product Information dialog shown in the following section.

Loading Dialogs

We know that to polish an application we should create a product information window or About box. This is a window, usually created in the resource script, that displays some important data about an application. Since the product information dialog is probably the least complex of all dialogs, we will start by implementing it within our enhanced editor.

First, we need to use a dialog editor to create a new window that will have the finished appearance shown in Figure 8-2. I have elected to create a very rudimentary dialog for this application. I could have easily added graphics to the window or a copy of the program icon, but for now let's keep it simple.

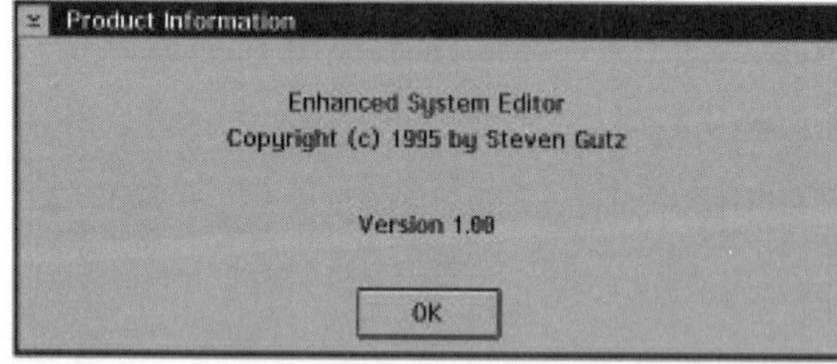

Figure 8-2 Enhanced editor product information dialog

To create this dialog, add this text to the end of the EDITOR.RC file:

```
DLGTEMPLATE ID_PROD_INFO
BEGIN
   DIALOG "Product Information", 100, 17, 40, 292, 87, WS_VISIBLE,
                                              FCF_SYSMENU | FCF_TITLEBAR
```

```
   BEGIN
      DEFPUSHBUTTON "OK", DID_OK, 121, 4, 51, 14
      CONTROL "Enhanced System Editor", 101, 4, 65, 283, 8, WC_STATIC, SS_TEXT |
               DT_CENTER | DT_TOP | DT_MNEMONIC | WS_VISIBLE | WS_GROUP
      CONTROL "Copyright (c) 1995 by Steven Gutz", 102, 4, 55, 283, 8, WC_STATIC,
               SS_TEXT | DT_CENTER | DT_TOP | DT_MNEMONIC | WS_VISIBLE | WS_GROUP
      CONTROL "Version 1.00", 103, 4, 31, 283, 8, WC_STATIC, SS_TEXT | DT_CENTER |
                DT_TOP | DT_MNEMONIC | WS_VISIBLE | WS_GROUP
   END
END
```

The ID_PROD_INFO identifier also needs to be defined. Add the following line to the RC.HPP file in the same location as the other window identifiers previously inserted.

```
#define    ID_PROD_INFO3// ID of product information dialog
```

In order to invoke a resource from the executable, we need to associate it with a class of some sort. Fortunately, PMCLASS offers the C_DIALOG class. From this we can derive a new object specifically designed to handle the product information dialog. This new class C_DIALOG_ABOUT is defined in PRODINFO.HPP, shown in Listing 8-8. The C++ source file appears in Listing 8-9.

```
//----------------
// C_DIALOG_ABOUT \
//------------------------------------------------------------------------
// Derived from: C_DIALOG
//
class C_DIALOG_ABOUT : public C_DIALOG
{
   public:
      C_DIALOG_ABOUT::C_DIALOG_ABOUT( C_WINDOW *pxcParentObj, int iID );

      // Message processors
      void *  MsgCreate( void *mp1, void *mp2 );

      // Command Processors
      void *  CmdOK( void *mp1, void *mp2 );
};
```

Listing 8-8 PRODINFO.HPP

```
//-------------------
// OS/2 Conditionals \
//------------------------------------------------------------------------
#define    INCL_DOS
#define    INCL_WIN
```

```
//------------------
// Standard Headers \
//------------------------------------------------------------------------------
#include <os2.h>
#include <stdio.h>

//-----------------
// PMCLASS Headers \
//------------------------------------------------------------------------------
#include <app.hpp>
#include <window.hpp>
#include <winstd.hpp>
#include <winchild.hpp>
#include <dialog.hpp>
#include <edit.hpp>
#include <status.hpp>
#include <button.hpp>
#include <tbar.hpp>
#include <mle.hpp>
#include <log.hpp>

//---------------------
// Application Headers \
//------------------------------------------------------------------------------
#include "rc.hpp"
#include <prodinfo.hpp>

//---------------------------
// Main Window Message Table \
//------------------------------------------------------------------------------
DECLARE_MSG_TABLE( xtEditorProdInfo )
   DECLARE_MSG( PM_CREATE,      C_DIALOG_ABOUT::MsgCreate )
END_MSG_TABLE

//----------------------------
// About Window Command Table \
//------------------------------------------------------------------------------
DECLARE_COMMAND_TABLE( xtCommandAbout )
   DECLARE_COMMAND( DM_OK,C_DIALOG_ABOUT::CmdOK )
END_COMMAND_TABLE

//-------------
// Constructor \
//------------------------------------------------------------------------------
C_DIALOG_ABOUT::C_DIALOG_ABOUT( C_WINDOW *pxcParentObj, int iID )
                        : C_DIALOG( pxcParentObj, xtEditorProdInfo )
{
   // Enable the required handlers for this window
```

```
   CommandTable( xtCommandAbout );

   // Create the physical dialog
   Create( iID );

   // Begin processing the about box
   Process();
}

//-----------
// MsgCreate \
//--------------------------------------------------------------------------
// Event:       PM_CREATE
// Cause:       Issued by OS when window is created
// Description:This method gets called when the window is initially created.
//
void *C_DIALOG_ABOUT::MsgCreate( void *mp1, void *mp2 )
{
   DosBeep( 100, 100 );

   return FALSE;
}

//-------
// CmdOK \
//--------------------------------------------------------------------------
// Event:       DM_OK
// Cause:       User selects the OK button-
//
void *C_DIALOG_ABOUT::CmdOK( void *mp1, void *mp2 )
{
   // Close this dialog
   Close( FALSE );

   return FALSE;
}
```

Listing 8-9 PRODINFO.CPP

In EDITOR.CPP we need to add some additional code to invoke the dialog when the user selects the product information menu option. The method that manages this option is CmdHelpInfo(); to that method, add the following lines to create the About Box.

```
   // Create an instance of the about dialog
   C_DIALOG_ABOUT  xcAbout( this, ID_PROD_INFO );
```

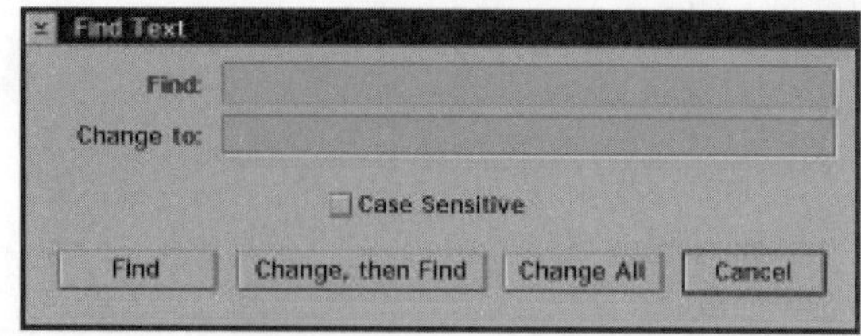

As you can see from Listing 8-9, a dialog box from a resource file is processed almost identically with any other window object. Message tables and command tables are still used and the format of the handler methods is exactly the same. Contrast this to the normal OS/2 API, which has subtle differences in the way dialogs are managed that make it confusing to new programmers.

Search and Replace

Although the enhanced editor can now manipulate files, and is actually quite an effective editor, it still lacks the ability to search for text strings, and is also missing the capability of replacing one string of text with another. In this section we will implement a new dialog box and some code to implement this feature. This dialog is shown in Figure 8-3.

Figure 8-3 Find text dialog box

The first step in the process is to create this dialog in resource script language. Edit EDITOR.RC, adding the following script.

```
DLGTEMPLATE ID_FIND_DIALOG
BEGIN
   DIALOG "Find Text", 100, 24, 52, 292, 77, WS_VISIBLE, FCF_SYSMENU | FCF_TITLEBAR
   BEGIN
      PUSHBUTTON "Cancel", DID_CANCEL, 231, 9, 51, 12
      CONTROL "Find:", 101, 4, 62, 58, 8, WC_STATIC, SS_TEXT | DT_RIGHT | DT_TOP |
                           DT_MNEMONIC | WS_VISIBLE | WS_GROUP
      CONTROL "", 102, 71, 62, 213, 9, WC_ENTRYFIELD, ES_LEFT | ES_AUTOSCROLL |
                           ES_MARGIN | WS_VISIBLE | WS_GROUP | WS_TABSTOP
      CONTROL "Change to:", 103, 4, 48, 58, 8, WC_STATIC, SS_TEXT | DT_RIGHT |
                           DT_TOP | DT_MNEMONIC | WS_VISIBLE | WS_GROUP
      CONTROL "", 104, 71, 48, 213, 9, WC_ENTRYFIELD, ES_LEFT | ES_AUTOSCROLL |
                           ES_MARGIN | WS_VISIBLE | WS_GROUP | WS_TABSTOP
      CONTROL "Case Sensitive", 105, 107, 28, 96, 10, WC_BUTTON, BS_AUTOCHECKBOX |
                           WS_VISIBLE | WS_GROUP | WS_TABSTOP
      CONTROL "Find", 106, 11, 9, 57, 12, WC_BUTTON, BS_PUSHBUTTON | WS_VISIBLE |
                           WS_GROUP | WS_TABSTOP
      CONTROL "Change All", 108, 168, 9, 57, 12, WC_BUTTON, BS_PUSHBUTTON |
                           WS_VISIBLE | WS_GROUP | WS_TABSTOP
```

```
      CONTROL "Change, then Find", 107, 74, 9, 89, 12, WC_BUTTON, BS_PUSHBUTTON |
                        WS_VISIBLE | WS_GROUP | WS_TABSTOP
   END
END
```

Now edit the RC.HPP file, adding the new window definition.

```
#define    ID_FIND_DIALOG4             // ID of the Find dialog
```

Also add definitions for all the new controls introduced by this dialog, as shown in the following segment.

```
#define        DM_CANCEL               2
#define        DM_FIND                 106
#define        DM_CHANGE_FIND          107
#define        DM_CHANGE_ALL           108
#define        DC_CASE_SENSITIVE       105
#define        DE_FIND_TEXT            102
#define        DE_CHANGE_TEXT          104
```

As usual, we will need to create a new source file to support this new object C_DIALOG_FIND. To accompany this, we will also create a new header file to define the class. Listing 8-10 shows the new header file, and Listing 8-11 shows the accompanying C++ source for the C_DIALOG_FIND class. I will not be detailing these files because they are just a rehash of things we have already seen. The one new item is the reference to ParentObject(). This is a method, which every child class provides, that returns a pointer to the owner object (i.e., the object that created the dialog).

```
//---------------
// C_DIALOG_FIND \
//-------------------------------------------------------------------------
// Derived from: C_DIALOG
//
class C_DIALOG_FIND : public C_DIALOG
{
   private:
       C_WINDOW_STD        *pxcParent;              // Pointer to owner window

   public:
       C_DIALOG_FIND::C_DIALOG_FIND( C_WINDOW *pxcParentObj, int iID );

       // Message processors
       void *      MsgCreate( void *mp1, void *mp2 );

       // Command Processors
       void *      CmdFind( void *mp1, void *mp2 );
```

```
        void *      CmdChangeFind( void *mp1, void *mp2 );
        void *      CmdChangeAll( void *mp1, void *mp2 );
        void *      CmdCancel( void *mp1, void *mp2 );
};
```

Listing 8-10 FINDDLG.HPP

```
//-------------------
// OS/2 Conditionals \
//-----------------------------------------------------------------------------
#define         INCL_DOS
#define         INCL_WIN

//------------------
// Standard Headers \
//-----------------------------------------------------------------------------
#include <os2.h>
#include <stdio.h>
#include <string.h>
#include <process.h>

//-----------------
// NVCLASS Headers \
//-----------------------------------------------------------------------------
#include <thread.hpp>
#include <threadpm.hpp>
#include <semev.hpp>

//-----------------
// PMCLASS Headers \
//-----------------------------------------------------------------------------
#include <app.hpp>
#include <window.hpp>
#include <winstd.hpp>
#include <winchild.hpp>
#include <dialog.hpp>
#include <edit.hpp>
#include <status.hpp>
#include <button.hpp>
#include <tbar.hpp>
#include <mle.hpp>
#include <log.hpp>

//---------------------
// Application Headers \
//-----------------------------------------------------------------------------
#include "rc.hpp"
#include <tbartop.hpp>
```

```
#include <finddlg.hpp>
#include <editor.hpp>

//----------------------------
// Main Window Message Table \
//---------------------------------------------------------------------------
DECLARE_MSG_TABLE( xtEditorFind )
   DECLARE_MSG( PM_CREATE,      C_DIALOG_FIND::MsgCreate )
END_MSG_TABLE

//----------------------------
// About Window Command Table \
//---------------------------------------------------------------------------
DECLARE_COMMAND_TABLE( xtCommandFind )
   DECLARE_COMMAND( DM_FIND,            C_DIALOG_FIND::CmdFind )
   DECLARE_COMMAND( DM_CHANGE_FIND,     C_DIALOG_FIND::CmdChangeFind )
   DECLARE_COMMAND( DM_CHANGE_ALL,      C_DIALOG_FIND::CmdChangeAll )
   DECLARE_COMMAND( DM_CANCEL,          C_DIALOG_FIND::CmdCancel )
END_COMMAND_TABLE

//-------------
// Constructor \
//---------------------------------------------------------------------------
C_DIALOG_FIND::C_DIALOG_FIND( C_WINDOW *pxcParentObj, int iID )
                        : C_DIALOG( pxcParentObj, xtEditorFind )
{
   // Enable the required handlers for this window
   CommandTable( xtCommandFind );

   // Create the physical dialog
   Create( iID );

   // Begin processing the dialog box
   Process();
}

//-----------
// MsgCreate \
//---------------------------------------------------------------------------
// Event:       PM_CREATE
// Cause:       Issued by OS when window is created
// Description:This method gets called when the window is initially created.
//              It initializes all of the visual aspects of the class.
void *C_DIALOG_FIND::MsgCreate( void *mp1, void *mp2 )
{
   C_EDIT       *pxcEdit;

   // Get the find text
```

```
   pxcEdit = (C_EDIT *) new C_EDIT( (C_DIALOG *)this, DE_FIND_TEXT );

   WinSetFocus( HWND_DESKTOP, pxcEdit->Window() );

   // Dispose of the edit field object
   delete pxcEdit;

   return (void *)TRUE;
}

//---------
// CmdFind \
//-----------------------------------------------------------------------------
// Event:      DM_FIND
// Cause:      User selects the Find button
//
void *C_DIALOG_FIND::CmdFind( void *mp1, void *mp2 )
{
   char        szString[256];
   C_EDIT      *pxcFind;
   int         iCase;

   // Determine the case sensitivity flag
   iCase = (int)WinSendDlgItemMsg( Window(), DC_CASE_SENSITIVE,
                                             BM_QUERYCHECK, 0, 0 );
   ParentObject()->SendMsg( PM_FIND_SET_CASE, (void *)iCase, 0 );

   // Get the find text
   pxcFind = (C_EDIT *) new C_EDIT( (C_DIALOG *)this, DE_FIND_TEXT );

   // Send a message to our parent telling it to find the next instance
   // of this text
   pxcFind->GetText( szString, 256 );
   ParentObject()->SendMsg( PM_FIND, (void *)szString, 0 );

   // Dispose of the edit field object
   delete pxcFind;

   return FALSE;
}

//---------------
// CmdChangeFind \
//-----------------------------------------------------------------------------
// Event:      DM_CHANGE_FIND
// Cause:      User selects the "Change then Find" button
//
void *C_DIALOG_FIND::CmdChangeFind( void *mp1, void *mp2 )
```

```
{
   char     szChange[256];
   char     szString[256];
   C_EDIT   *pxcFind;
   C_EDIT   *pxcChange;
   int      iCase;

   // Determine the case sensitivity flag
   iCase = (int)WinSendDlgItemMsg( Window(), DC_CASE_SENSITIVE,
                                                   BM_QUERYCHECK, 0, 0 );
   ParentObject()->SendMsg( PM_FIND_SET_CASE, (void *)iCase, 0 );

   // Get the find text
   pxcFind = (C_EDIT *) new C_EDIT( (C_DIALOG *)this, DE_FIND_TEXT );
   pxcChange = (C_EDIT *) new C_EDIT( (C_DIALOG *)this, DE_CHANGE_TEXT );

   // Send a message to our parent telling it to change then find
   pxcFind->GetText( szString, 256 );
   pxcChange->GetText( szChange, 256 );
   ParentObject()->SendMsg( PM_CHANGE_FIND,
                        (void *)szString, (void *)szChange );

   // Dispose of the edit field objects
   delete pxcFind;
   delete pxcChange;

   return FALSE;
}

//-----------
// CmdChange \
//--------------------------------------------------------------------------
// Event:      DM_CHANGE_ALL
// Cause:      User selects the ChangeAll button
//
void *C_DIALOG_FIND::CmdChangeAll( void *mp1, void *mp2 )
{
   char     szChange[256];
   char     szString[256];
   C_EDIT   *pxcFind;
   C_EDIT   *pxcChange;
   int      iCase;

   // Determine the case sensitivity flag
   iCase = (int)WinSendDlgItemMsg( Window(), DC_CASE_SENSITIVE,
                                                   BM_QUERYCHECK, 0, 0 );
   ParentObject()->SendMsg( PM_FIND_SET_CASE, (void *)iCase, 0 );
```

```
   // Get the find text
   pxcFind = (C_EDIT *) new C_EDIT( (C_DIALOG *)this, DE_FIND_TEXT );
   pxcChange = (C_EDIT *) new C_EDIT( (C_DIALOG *)this, DE_CHANGE_TEXT );

   // Send a message to our parent telling it to change all
   pxcFind->GetText( szString, 256 );
   pxcChange->GetText( szChange, 256 );
   ParentObject()->SendMsg( PM_CHANGE_ALL,
                            (void *)szString, (void *)szChange );

   // Dispose of the edit field objects
   delete pxcFind;
   delete pxcChange;

   return FALSE;
}

//-----------
// CmdCancel \
//---------------------------------------------------------------------------
// Event:     DM_CANCEL
// Cause:     User selects the Cancel button
//
void *C_DIALOG_FIND::CmdCancel( void *mp1, void *mp2 )
{
   // Close this dialog
   Close( FALSE );

   return FALSE;
}
```

Listing 8-11 FINDDLG.CPP

The C_DIALOG_FIND object communicates with C_WINDOW_MAIN, and it is this parent that actually performs most of the work associated with the searching and replacing of text strings. To implement this, a number of changes to the existing source need to be performed.

To EDITOR.HPP, add the following lines to the public section of the class.

```
void    *MsgFindSetCase( void *mp1, void *mp2 );
void    *MsgFind( void *mp1, void *mp2 );
void    *MsgChangeFind( void *mp1, void *mp2 );
void    *MsgChangeAll( void *mp1, void *mp2 );
```

In the class definition we have also introduced a new attribute to keep track of the case sensitivity of any searches that are performed. To the private section of the class, add the line:

```
    int             iCaseSensitive;      // Set if searches are to be cased
```

Then, in EDITOR.CPP, add new entries into the message table, as shown in the following code snippet.

```
   DECLARE_MSG( PM_FIND,                  C_WINDOW_MAIN::MsgFind )
   DECLARE_MSG( PM_FIND_SET_CASE,         C_WINDOW_MAIN::MsgFindSetCase )
   DECLARE_MSG( PM_CHANGE_FIND,           C_WINDOW_MAIN::MsgChangeFind )
   DECLARE_MSG( PM_CHANGE_ALL,            C_WINDOW_MAIN::MsgChangeAll )
```

This naturally mandates the definition of methods for these new messages. These are shown as follows:

```
//---------
// MsgFind \
//-------------------------------------------------------------------------
// Event:       PM_FIND
// Cause:       Issued by the Find dialog when a find is required
// Description:This method searches the MLE from the current cursor location
//              for the string supplied in mp1.
void *C_WINDOW_MAIN::MsgFind( void *mp1, void *mp2 )
{
   char    *szFind;

   // Get the find string passed to us
   szFind = (char *)mp1;

   pxcMLE->FindFromCursor( szFind, iCaseSensitive );

   return FALSE;
}

//----------------
// MsgFindSetCase \
//-------------------------------------------------------------------------
// Event:       PM_FIND_SET_CASE
// Cause:       Issued by the Find dialog to set case sensitivity flag
// Description:This method accepts a value in mp1 which is used to determine
//              if case sensitivity is used for searches and replacements.
void *C_WINDOW_MAIN::MsgFindSetCase( void *mp1, void *mp2 )
{
   // Determine the case sensitivity flag
   if( mp1 )
       iCaseSensitive = 1;
   else
       iCaseSensitive = 0;

   return FALSE;
}
```

```
//---------------
// MsgChangeFind \
//-----------------------------------------------------------------------------
// Event:       PM_CHANGE_FIND
// Cause:       Issued by the Find dialog when a "change then find" is required
// Description:This method changes the current selection to the string
//              pointed to by mp2, then searches the MLE from the current
//              cursor location for the string supplied in mp1.
void *C_WINDOW_MAIN::MsgChangeFind( void *mp1, void *mp2 )
{
   char     *szFind;
   char     *szChange;

   // Get the find and change strings string passed to us
   szFind = (char *)mp1;
   szChange = (char *)mp2;

   pxcMLE->Insert( szChange );
   pxcMLE->FindFromCursor( szFind, iCaseSensitive );

   return FALSE;
}

//--------------
// MsgChangeAll \
//-----------------------------------------------------------------------------
// Event:       PM_CHANGE_ALL
// Cause:       Issued by the Find dialog when a "change all" is required
// Description:This method changes all instances of MLE text, matching
//              the string supplied in mp1 with the string supplied in mp2.
void *C_WINDOW_MAIN::MsgChangeAll( void *mp1, void *mp2 )
{
   char     *szFind;
   char     *szChange;

   // Get the find and change strings string passed to us
   szFind = (char *)mp1;
   szChange = (char *)mp2;

   pxcMLE->ChangeAll( szFind, szChange, iCaseSensitive );

   return FALSE;
}
```

After placing the FILEDLG.CPP file in your project or MAKE file and rebuilding the application, you should be able to run the executable and search for text and/or replace text. Although there is quite a lot of code in this section, it isn't that complex and, since by now you should be quite an expert with PMCLASS, you should be able to negotiate it easily.

Final Embellishments

A number of features can be added to the enhanced editor. For example, code is required to detect changes in the editor text and to warn the user if an attempt is made to exit without saving the file. This code should automatically call the Save or SaveAs methods as required to make sure the file is saved automatically.

Most editors, including E, display the file name of the file being edited in the application title bar so users know what is active. This is coded in the final enhanced editor, which can be found on the companion disk.

Other important aspects of the code that have not been detailed thus far are the ability to save and restore color and font changes, and to preserve the size and position of the editor window between sessions. The program has supported drag-and-drop changes from the start; however, any changes have not been permanently stored. To accomplish this, INI file support must be implemented. On program start the INI file should be referenced to obtain the appropriate values, and at exit these values should be saved back to the INI file. The final editor code implements this capability.

Another useful feature that you will not see in E is a display of the current line count or the column number for the cursor. In the final version of the enhanced editor, I have implemented an attempt at this by intercepting the WM_CHAR messages sent to the main window. These messages are issued by PM each time a key is pressed in the Multiline Edit control. The limitation of this code in its current form is its inability to update the lower status line when the mouse is clicked. If you click to a location in the editor, the line/column display will not get updated until you press a key. This isn't a big limitation, but it is something of which you should be aware. Feel free to dig into the code to correct this limitation.

These missing features are implemented in the final version of the enhanced editor executable. If you are interested in figuring out what has been done in the final version, take a look at the source code on the companion disk.

Chapter Summary

In this chapter, we have implemented a complete editor program offering several features not found in the standard OS/2 editor, E. You should now have a more complete understanding of the logic that has been implemented in the class libraries from Part II of this book.

We have, for the most part, covered everything you need to know to write complete and effective applications using PMCLASS and NVCLASS. In the final chapters, we will begin implementing applications using the experience gained by creating the enhanced editor. As you will see, introduction of TCP/IP networking classes does not necessarily complicate the design of a program. You will find that the network applications in following chapters are only slightly more complicated than what you have already seen and implemented in the enhanced editor.

In this chapter

- ✓ Implementing a simple Ping application
- ✓ Integrating Ping with a PM application

9

A Simple PM Ping

Ping Main Program

The best place to start programming for TCP/IP is probably a simple Ping program. The concepts of Ping are easier to understand and the user interface code should be shorter than for any of the other programs we will build in this book.

Though I have elected not to implement help for the Ping program, the help menu does provide a "product information" option that is implemented in order display an information box. The program also implements a second dialog box used to input new server information. This code creates a window with an edit control, so you can learn how to interact with the C_EDIT class from the PMCLASS visual class library. The enhanced editor shown in the previous chapter used this object, but I did not go into much detail about it there. We will take a more comprehensive look at it here.

The PING.CPP source, shown in Listing 9-1, is the main start-up code for the Ping program; there are several additional modules that are also shown in their entirety. I will discuss individual routines and global data after each listing, if appropriate, in order to point out any technical issues that might be of interest in understanding the flow of the program.

```
//-------------------
// OS/2 Conditionals \
//----------------------------------------------------------------------------
#define    INCL_DOS
#define    INCL_WIN
```

```
//------------------
// Standard Headers \
//----------------------------------------------------------------------------
#include <os2.h>
#include <stdio.h>
#include <string.h>
#include <process.h>


//-----------------
// PMCLASS Headers \
//----------------------------------------------------------------------------
#include <app.hpp>
#include <window.hpp>
#include <winstd.hpp>
#include <winchild.hpp>
#include <dialog.hpp>
#include <edit.hpp>
#include <status.hpp>
#include <button.hpp>
#include <tbar.hpp>
#include <mle.hpp>
#include <contain.hpp>
#include <log.hpp>


//-----------------
// NVCLASS Headers \
//----------------------------------------------------------------------------
#include <thread.hpp>
#include <threadpm.hpp>


//------------------
// NETCLASS Headers \
//----------------------------------------------------------------------------
#include <net.hpp>
#include <netping.hpp>


//---------------------
// Application Headers \
//----------------------------------------------------------------------------
#include "ping.rch"
#include "tbartop.hpp"
#include "address.hpp"
#include "about.hpp"
#include "ping.hpp"
```

```
//------------
// Global Data \
//-------------------------------------------------------------------------
C_APPLICATION      xcApp;
C_WINDOW_MAIN      xcWindow;

//-------------------------
// Main Window Message Table \
//-------------------------------------------------------------------------
DECLARE_MSG_TABLE( xtMsgMain )
   DECLARE_MSG( PM_CREATE,              C_WINDOW_MAIN::MsgCreate )
   DECLARE_MSG( PM_DONE,                C_WINDOW_MAIN::MsgDone )
   DECLARE_MSG( WM_CLOSE,               C_WINDOW_MAIN::MsgClose )
   DECLARE_MSG( WM_DESTROY,             C_WINDOW_MAIN::MsgDestroy )
   DECLARE_MSG( WM_SIZE,                C_WINDOW_MAIN::MsgSize )
   DECLARE_MSG( WM_CONTROL,             C_WINDOW_MAIN::MsgControl )
   DECLARE_MSG( WM_PAINT,               C_WINDOW_STD::MsgPaint )
END_MSG_TABLE

//-------------------------
// Main Window Command Table \
//-------------------------------------------------------------------------
DECLARE_COMMAND_TABLE( xtCommandMain )
   DECLARE_COMMAND( DM_EXIT,            C_WINDOW_MAIN::CmdExit )
   DECLARE_COMMAND( DM_CONNECT,         C_WINDOW_MAIN::CmdConnect )
   DECLARE_COMMAND( DM_INFO,            C_WINDOW_MAIN::CmdHelpInfo )
END_MSG_TABLE

//-----------
// PingThread \
//-------------------------------------------------------------------------
void _Optlink PingThread( void *pvData )
{
   char            szString[256];
   BYTE            byPacket[100];
   int             iResult;
   C_WINDOW_MAIN   *pxcThis;
   C_THREAD_PM     *pxcThread;

   // Get a pointer to the main window object
   pxcThread = (C_THREAD_PM *)pvData;
   pxcThis = (C_WINDOW_MAIN *)pxcThread->ThreadData();

   // Create a PM process for this thread
   pxcThread->InitializeThread();

   // Create an instance of a Ping networking object
   C_CONNECT_PING xcPingPort( 1, pxcThis->ServerAddress() );
```

```
// Open the Ping channel
iResult = xcPingPort.C_CONNECT_PING::Open();
if( iResult == D_NET_OK )
{
    // Loop until the user stops this thread
    while( !pxcThis->ExitFlag() )
    {
        // Transmit a Ping to the other end of the connection
        memset( byPacket, 0xff, 100 );
        iResult = xcPingPort.PingTx( byPacket, 64 );
        if( iResult == D_NET_OK )
        {
            // Receive the Ping results
            memset( byPacket, 0xff, 100 );
            strcpy( szString, "" );
            xcPingPort.PingRx( byPacket, szString );

            // Print the Ping results to the MLE
            if( strlen( szString ) )
            {
                strcat( szString, "\r\n" );
                pxcThis->MLE()->Insert( szString );
            }

            // Sleep for a second before we ping again
            DosSleep( 1000 );
        }
        else
        {
            // Tell the user that something is amiss
            WinMessageBox( HWND_DESKTOP, pxcThis->Window(),
                    "PING transmission error - aborting", D_APPNAME,
                                            0, MB_OK | MB_ICONHAND );

            // Force the window to close
            pxcThis->ExitFlag( 1 );
        }
    }

    // Close the Ping port
    xcPingPort.Close();
}
else
{
    // Tell the user that we couldn't find the selected host
    WinMessageBox( HWND_DESKTOP, pxcThis->Window(),
        "Couldn't Open PING socket", D_APPNAME, 0,
                                            MB_OK | MB_ICONHAND );
}
```

```
    // Terminate the thread
    pxcThread->TerminateThread();
}

//-------------
// Constructor \
//------------------------------------------------------------------------
C_WINDOW_MAIN::C_WINDOW_MAIN( void ) : C_WINDOW_STD( xtMsgMain )
{
    // Enable the required handlers for this window
    CommandTable( xtCommandMain );
}

//-----------
// MsgCreate \
//------------------------------------------------------------------------
// Event:       WM_CREATE
// Cause:       Issued by OS when window is created
//
void *C_WINDOW_MAIN::MsgCreate( void *mp1, void *mp2 )
{
    // Create a status bar to display miscellaneous data
    xcStatus = (C_STATUS *) new C_STATUS( this );

    // Create a toolbar control
    xcTBar = (C_TOOLBAR_TOP *)new C_TOOLBAR_TOP( this, xcStatus );

    // Create a container control
    xcMLE = (C_MLE *)new C_MLE( this, D_ID_MLE );

    // Set the color and font for the container
    xcMLE->SetFont( "Helv", 10 );
    xcMLE->SetForegroundColor( 255, 255, 255 );
    xcMLE->SetBackgroundColor( 0, 0, 128 );

    // Initialize the instance attributes
    iMustExit = 0;
    strcpy( szServerAddress, "" );

    // Make the window visible
    Show();

    return FALSE;
}

//----------
// MsgClose \
//------------------------------------------------------------------------
// Event:       WM_CLOSE
```

```
// Cause:      Issued by OS when window is closed
//
void *C_WINDOW_MAIN::MsgClose( void *mp1, void *mp2 )
{
   // Application was told to close, so post a QUIT message to the OS
   PostMsg( WM_QUIT, 0, 0 );
   return FALSE;
}

//------------
// MsgDestroy \
//-------------------------------------------------------------------------
// Event:      WM_DESTROY
// Cause:      Issued by OS when window is destroyed
//
void *C_WINDOW_MAIN::MsgDestroy( void *mp1, void *mp2 )
{
   // Get rid of the dynamic memory we allocated
   delete  xcStatus;
   delete  xcTBar;

   return FALSE;
}

//---------
// MsgSize \
//-------------------------------------------------------------------------
// Event:      WM-SIZE
// Cause:      Issued by OS when window is resized
//
void *C_WINDOW_MAIN::MsgSize( void *mp1, void *mp2 )
{
   int     iCX;
   int     iCY;

   // Determine the size of the client area
   C_WINDOW::GetSize( &iCX, &iCY );

   // Stretch the toolbar and status windows so they use the entire window
   iCY -= 40;
   xcTBar->SetSizePosition( 0, iCY, iCX, 40 );
   iCY -= 25;
   xcStatus->SetSizePosition( 0, iCY, iCX, 25 );

   // Make the MLE take up the remainder of the client area space
   xcMLE->SetSizePosition( 0, 0, iCX, iCY );

   return FALSE;
}
```

```
//------------
// MsgControl \
//---------------------------------------------------------------------------
// Event:      WM_CONTROL
// Cause:      Issued by OS for control functions (Toolbar interaction)
//
void *C_WINDOW_MAIN::MsgControl( void *mp1, void *mp2 )
{
  switch( SHORT1FROMMP( mp1 ) )
  {
      case D_TOP_TBAR:
          xcTBar->Control( (ULONG)mp1 );
          break;
  }
  return FALSE;
}

//---------
// MsgDone \
//---------------------------------------------------------------------------
// Event:      PM_DONE
// Cause:      Issued by the connection dialog when a new connection
//             has been selected. Also issued by main() if user specifies
//             a command line address.
void *C_WINDOW_MAIN::MsgDone( void *mp1, void *mp2 )
{
  char    szString[256];

  // Format the window title correctly
  xcStatus->Text( "Pinging %s", (char *)mp1 );

  // Get the selected server from the caller
  strcpy( szServerAddress, (char *)mp1 );

  // Terminate the existing thread if it is running
  iMustExit = 1;
  xcPingThread.WaitIndefinite();

  iMustExit = 0;

  sprintf( szString, "\r\nPinging %s\r\n", szServerAddress );
  xcMLE->Insert( szString );

  // Begin a thread to Ping servers
  xcPingThread.Create( PingThread, 40000, this );

  return FALSE;
}
```

```
//---------
// CmdExit \
//-------------------------------------------------------------------------
// Event:     DM_EXIT
// Cause:     User selects the exit menu option
//
void *C_WINDOW_MAIN::CmdExit( void *mp1, void *mp2 )
{
   // If the user picks "Exit" from the main menu, close the program
   SendMsg( WM_CLOSE, 0, 0 );
   return FALSE;
}

//------------
// CmdConnect \
//-------------------------------------------------------------------------
// Event:     DM_CONNECT
// Cause:     User selects the connect option or toolbar button
//
void *C_WINDOW_MAIN::CmdConnect( void *mp1, void *mp2 )
{
   // Create an instance of the address dialog
   C_DIALOG_ADDRESS xcAddress( this, D_DIALOG_ADDRESS );

   // Tell the window who its parent is so it can talk back
   xcAddress.SendMsg( PM_PARENT, this, 0 );

   // Process the dialog
   xcAddress.Process();

   return FALSE;
}

//-------------
// CmdHelpInfo \
//-------------------------------------------------------------------------
// Event:     DM_INFO
// Cause:     User selects the Product Information menu option
//
void *C_WINDOW_MAIN::CmdHelpInfo( void *mp1, void *mp2 )
{
   // Create an instance of the about dialog
   C_DIALOG_ABOUT      xcAbout( this, D_DIALOG_ABOUT );
   return FALSE;
}

void main( int iArgCount, char *szArgV[] )
{
```

```
    // Register the application window
    xcWindow.Register( "Ping" );

    // Create a new program window
    xcWindow.WCF_Standard();
    xcWindow.Create( ID_WINDOW, "Ping - Control Panel " );

    // Process any command line arguments
    if( iArgCount > 1 )
    {
        // Pass in the command-line argument
        xcWindow.PostMsg( PM_DONE, szArgV[1], 0 );
    }

    // Start the message loop
    xcApp.Run();
}
```

Listing 9-1 PING.CPP

The first thing I should mention is the global variable list defined for this program. I really dislike the use of excessive global data so I make extreme attempts to avoid it. You will discover, however, that building a Presentation Manager program that is free of global variables is all but impossible. All message and command tables defined in Ping are global, but they are constant. We never change them, so there really are not much of a concern in global memory space. There are two globally instantiated classes in Ping, as shown below.

```
C_APPLICATION       xcApp;
C_WINDOW_MAIN       xcWindow;
```

The first is an instance of the application class. All of the programs in this part of the book will create an instance of C_APPLICATION which, as we discussed in Part II, looks after getting the Presentation Manager engine up and running, and also manages the termination of the program when the user exits.

The second global class is actually an instance of the main window. We didn't really need to make this class global, but it does simplify the code to do so. The C++ language provides excellent protection of data, so we do not need to concern ourselves too much with a globally defined class. However, always be aware of possible data conflicts if there is any possibility that two separate threads might attempt access to the same data from any global area.

Near the top of the PING.CPP file, you will see two odd-looking table definitions. The first table is a list of messages and their equivalent parser methods. As we discussed earlier, each window class must provide a parser method for each message it cares about; this is done by defining a message table like the one shown below. Large, uncontrollable window procedures are avoided and the code becomes clearer. In the case of the Ping window, seven window messages are intercepted.

```
DECLARE_MSG_TABLE( xtMsgMain )

   DECLARE_MSG( PM_CREATE,          C_WINDOW_MAIN::MsgCreate )
   DECLARE_MSG( PM_DONE,            C_WINDOW_MAIN::MsgDone )
   DECLARE_MSG( WM_CLOSE,           C_WINDOW_MAIN::MsgClose )
   DECLARE_MSG( WM_DESTROY,         C_WINDOW_MAIN::MsgDestroy )
   DECLARE_MSG( WM_SIZE,            C_WINDOW_MAIN::MsgSize )
   DECLARE_MSG( WM_CONTROL,         C_WINDOW_MAIN::MsgControl )
   DECLARE_MSG( WM_PAINT,           C_WINDOW_STD::MsgPaint )
END_MSG_TABLE
```

The second table contains a listing of all the command messages we care about. Command messages are those messages that are sent from menu selections or toolbar button presses. Since Ping is very simple, there are only three possible commands it can send, and we will provide a processor for each of them.

```
DECLARE_COMMAND_TABLE( xtCommandMain )
   DECLARE_COMMAND( DM_EXIT,        C_WINDOW_MAIN::CmdExit )
   DECLARE_COMMAND( DM_CONNECT,     C_WINDOW_MAIN::CmdConnect )
   DECLARE_COMMAND( DM_INFO,        C_WINDOW_MAIN::CmdHelpInfo )
END_MSG_TABLE
```

Now let's take a look at the main() routine:

```
void main( int iArgCount, char *szArgV[] )
{
   // Register the application window
   xcWindow.Register( "Ping" );

   // Create a new program window
   xcWindow.WCF_Standard();
   xcWindow.Create( ID_WINDOW, "Ping" );

   // Process any command line arguments
   if( iArgCount > 1 )
   {
      // Pass in the command-line argument
      xcWindow.PostMsg( PM_DONE, szArgV[1], 0 );
   }

   // Start the message loop
   xcApp.Run();
}
```

The very first thing Ping does when it starts is register its new window type with the operating system. Then it sets the window's characteristics (i.e., a standard window with a menu, sizable borders, etc.) and calls the Create() method to actually create the window from its predetermined parameters. This prompts the operating system to send the window a PM_CREATE message.

The next part of main() attempts to determine if the user provided a command-line parameter. Ping assumes that any parameter provided on the command line is a server address, and sends the window a PM_DONE message. This message to the window indicates that it should stop any Ping process that is currently active and start a new one.

Finally, main() calls the Run() method from the instance of C_APPLICATION. This starts an internal message loop in the program so its windows can start processing messages. The first message that any C_WINDOW based window receives is PM_CREATE.

The processor method for the PM_CREATE message in the main Ping window looks like this:

```
void *C_WINDOW_MAIN::MsgCreate( void *mp1, void *mp2 )
{
   // Create a status bar to display miscellaneous data
   xcStatus = (C_STATUS *) new C_STATUS( this );

   // Create a toolbar control
   xcTBar = (C_TOOLBAR_TOP *)new C_TOOLBAR_TOP( this, xcStatus );

   // Create a container control
   xcMLE = (C_MLE *)new C_MLE( this, D_ID_MLE );

   // Set the color and font for the container
   xcMLE->SetFont( "10.Helv" );
   xcMLE->SetForegroundColor( 255, 255, 255 );
   xcMLE->SetBackgroundColor( 0, 0, 128 );

   // Initialize the instance attributes
   iMustExit = 0;
   strcpy( szServerAddress, "" );

   // Make the window visible
   Show();

   return FALSE;
}
```

After the window is created, the MsgCreate() method creates an instance of a status line, xcStatus, and an instance of a toolbar class, xcTBar. In all the applications in this book, these objects will typically be created first, since every program has a toolbar and status line at the top of its main window (at least). As you will see, however, these controls are not limited to the main window, and you will see several examples later where a child window also has a toolbar.

The MsgCreate() method also creates an instance of a multiline edit control (xcMLE), used by the program to display the pinging information. The MLE foreground and background colors are also set. Like all windows in OS/2, the MLE will support drag-and-drop color; however, I have elected not to support any facility for saving these changes. You will find out how to save this information in an INI file later.

The last line of code in the creation method is a call to the Show() routine. This makes the window visible on the OS/2 desktop. Note that the dimensions and position of the application window are automatically determined by the operating system because we defined this window as a standard display type. In other programs in this book we will find out more about sizing and positioning an application window.

Another key message processor in the Ping program is the MsgSize() method; this is called any time the WM_SIZE message is sent to the window. This method must acquire the new size of the window and resize the toolbar and status bar accordingly, so that they span the full width of the window. Finally, the method resizes the MLE control to occupy the remaining space in the program window.

```
void *C_WINDOW_MAIN::MsgSize( void *mp1, void *mp2 )
{
    int     iCX;
    int     iCY;

    // Determine the size of the client area
    QuerySize( &iCX, &iCY );

    //Stretch the toolbar and status windows so they use the entire window
    iCY -= 40;
    xcTBar->SetSizePosition( 0, iCY, iCX, 40 );
    iCY -= 25;
    xcStatus->SetSizePosition( 0, iCY, iCX, 25 );

    // Make the MLE take up the remainder of the client area space
    xcMLE->SetSizePosition( 0, 0, iCX, iCY );

    return FALSE;
}
```

So far, I have not mentioned any of the networking aspects of Ping. This isn't because there is some sort of magic involved; rather, the network interface for Ping is so small that it is almost insignificant to the whole program. The pinging network code is encapsulated in a thread that runs independently of the user interface. When the main window receives the PM_DONE message, it executes the MsgDone() method.

This method informs any currently executing Ping thread that it must stop. It does this by setting the iMustExit attribute and waits for the current thread (if any) to stop. It then sets the new Ping address and starts a new network thread.

```
void *C_WINDOW_MAIN::MsgDone( void *mp1, void *mp2 )
{
    char    szString[256];

    // Format the window title correctly
    xcStatus->Text( "Pinging %s", (char *)mp1 );

    // Get the selected server from the caller
    strcpy( szServerAddress, (char *)mp1 );

    // Terminate the existing thread if it is running
    iMustExit = 1;
    xcPingThread.WaitIndefinite();

    iMustExit = 0;

    sprintf( szString, "\r\nPinging %s\r\n", szServerAddress );
    xcMLE->Insert( szString );

    // Begin a thread to Ping servers
    xcPingThread.Create( PingThread, 40000, this );

    return FALSE;
}
```

The Ping thread is much easier to manage than a standard OS/2 thread. As was pointed out in the discussion of the C_THREAD class in the previous part, the thread function for a C_THREAD class is slightly different than it would be for a standard OS/2 thread. In a normal thread function, the void parameter passed in contains a pointer to whatever you supplied in the _beginthread() function. In a thread function for C_THREAD class, the parameter passed to the thread function is a pointer to the thread instance. The data structure that is passed into the thread can be retrieved by using the ThreadData() method.

The PingThread() code retrieves the thread instance and the data structure, as follows:

```
    // Get a pointer to the main window object
    pxcThread = (C_THREAD_PM *)pvData;
    pxcThis = (C_WINDOW_MAIN *)pxcThread->ThreadData();
```

Since this thread will send window messages, it also needs to set a message queue.

```
// Create a PM process for this thread
pxcThread->InitializeThread();
```

Now the thread can create an instance of a new C_CONNECT_PING class to ping the specified address. After the instance creation, the connection is opened while appropriate error detection is taking place.

```
// Create a instance of a Ping networking object
C_CONNECT_PING xcPingPort( 1, pxcThis->ServerAddress() );

// Open the Ping channel
iResult = xcPingPort.C_CONNECT_PING::Open();
```

Once a connection has been established, the thread loops at one-second intervals, synchronously transmitting and receiving 64-byte packets. This loop terminates when the ExitFlag() method returns a true value, indicating that the creator of the thread wishes to terminate the connection.

```
    // Loop until the user stops this thread
    while( !pxcThis->ExitFlag() )
    {
        // Transmit a Ping to the other end of the connection
        memset( byPacket, 0xff, 100 );
        iResult = xcPingPort.PingTx( byPacket, 64 );
        if( iResult == D_NET_OK )
        {
            // Receive the Ping results
            memset( byPacket, 0xff, 100 );
            strcpy( szString, "" );
            xcPingPort.PingRx( byPacket, szString );

            // Print the Ping results to the MLE
            if( strlen( szString ) )
            {
                strcat( szString, "\r\n" );
                pxcThis->MLE()->Insert( szString );
            }

            // Sleep for a second before we ping again
            DosSleep( 1000 );
        }
        else
        {
            // Tell the user that something is amiss
            WinMessageBox( HWND_DESKTOP, pxcThis->Window(),
                    "PING transmission error - aborting", D_APPNAME,
                                        0, MB_OK | MB_ICONHAND );
```

```
            // Force the window to close
            pxcThis->ExitFlag( 1 );
         }
      }
```

Once the loop ends, the Ping connection is closed and the thread ends.

```
      // Close the Ping port
      xcPingPort.Close();
```

Since this thread called the PM initialization method when it started, it must call the TerminateThread() method to dispose of the PM message queue it created.

```
   // Terminate the thread
   pxcThread->TerminateThread();
}
```

When you select the connection menu option or click on Ping's sole toolbar button, you invoke the CmdConnect() method. Though this method is relatively straightforward, I will describe it because it demonstrates an important concept. This concept is the use of dialog resources. The method creates an instance of a C_DIALOG_ADDRESS class. This class will be described shortly, but for now we will just assume that this dialog has been created and stored in the resource file compiled into the Ping executable.

The address dialog permits the user to enter a new Ping address; in order for Ping to connect to this address, the dialog must send the main window the address the user entered. To accomplish this feat, the dialog must know who its parent is. After creating an instance of the dialog, the main window sends the dialog a message containing a pointer to the main window class.

```
void *C_WINDOW_MAIN::CmdConnect( void *mp1, void *mp2 )
{
   // Create an instance of the address dialog
   C_DIALOG_ADDRESS xcAddress( this, D_DIALOG_ADDRESS );

   // Tell the window who its parent is so it can talk back
   xcAddress.SendMsg( PM_PARENT, this, 0 );

   // Process the dialog
   xcAddress.Process();

   return FALSE;
}
```

Finally, the CmdConnect() command processor starts the dialog by calling its processor method.

I won't go into the other methods in the main window class for Ping here; they are, for the most part, self-explanatory, and you should be able to understand these methods without much difficulty.

Getting Ping Addresses

Since I explained the CmdConnection() method in the previous section, we should go into some detail on the C_DIALOG_ADDRESS class that it uses in order to obtain IP addresses from the user. The complete code for this class is shown in Listing 9-2.

```
//------------------
// OS/2 Conditionals \
//-------------------------------------------------------------------------
#define    INCL_DOS
#define    INCL_WIN

//-----------------
// Standard Headers \
//-------------------------------------------------------------------------
#include <os2.h>
#include <stdio.h>
#include <string.h>

//----------------
// PMCLASS Headers \
//-------------------------------------------------------------------------
#include <app.hpp>
#include <window.hpp>
#include <winstd.hpp>
#include <winchild.hpp>
#include <dialog.hpp>
#include <edit.hpp>
#include <status.hpp>
#include <button.hpp>
#include <tbar.hpp>
#include <mle.hpp>
#include <log.hpp>

//----------------
// NVCLASS Headers \
//-------------------------------------------------------------------------
#include <thread.hpp>
#include <threadpm.hpp>
```

```
//--------------------
// Application Headers \
//-------------------------------------------------------------------------
#include "ping.rch"
#include "tbartop.hpp"
#include "address.hpp"
#include "ping.hpp"

//---------------------------
// Address Window Message Table \
//-------------------------------------------------------------------------
DECLARE_MSG_TABLE( xtMsgAddress )
   DECLARE_MSG( PM_CREATE,          C_DIALOG_ADDRESS::MsgInitDlg )
   DECLARE_MSG( WM_DESTROY,         C_DIALOG_ADDRESS::MsgDestroy )
   DECLARE_MSG( PM_PARENT,          C_DIALOG_ADDRESS::MsgParent )
END_MSG_TABLE

//---------------------------
// Address Window Command Table \
//-------------------------------------------------------------------------
DECLARE_COMMAND_TABLE( xtCommandAddress )
   DECLARE_COMMAND( DM_CANCEL,      C_DIALOG_ADDRESS::CmdCancel )
   DECLARE_COMMAND( DM_OK,          C_DIALOG_ADDRESS::CmdOK )
END_COMMAND_TABLE

//------------
// Constructor \
//-------------------------------------------------------------------------
C_DIALOG_ADDRESS::C_DIALOG_ADDRESS( C_WINDOW *pxcParentObj, int iID )
                              : C_DIALOG( pxcParentObj, xtMsgAddress )
{
   // Enable the required handlers for this window
   CommandTable( xtCommandAddress );

   Create( iID );
}

//-----------
// MsgInitDlg \
//-------------------------------------------------------------------------
// Event:      PM_CREATE
// Cause:      Issued by OS when dialog is created
//
void *C_DIALOG_ADDRESS::MsgInitDlg( void *mp1, void *mp2 )
{
   pxcEditAddress = (C_EDIT *) new C_EDIT( (C_DIALOG *)this, DE_ADDRESS );

   // Set the text limit of the address field
   pxcEditAddress->SendMsg( EM_SETTEXTLIMIT, MPFROMSHORT( 256 ), 0);
```

```
    // Give the edit window the focus
    pxcEditAddress->SetFocus();

    // Prevent the default window procedure from executing
    return (MRESULT)TRUE;
}

//------------
// MsgDestroy \
//---------------------------------------------------------------------------
// Event:      WM_DESTROY
// Cause:      Issued by OS when window is destroyed
//
void *C_DIALOG_ADDRESS::MsgDestroy( void *mp1, void *mp2 )
{
    // Dispose of the dynamic memory used by this object
    delete pxcEditAddress;

    return FALSE;
}

//-----------
// MsgParent \
//---------------------------------------------------------------------------
// Event:      PM_PARENT
// Cause:      Issued by parent to identify itself to this child
//
void *C_DIALOG_ADDRESS::MsgParent( void *mp1, void *mp2 )
{
    // Save the pointer to the parent window object
    pxcParent = (C_WINDOW *)mp1;

    return FALSE;
}

//-----------
// CmdCancel \
//---------------------------------------------------------------------------
// Event:      DM_CANCEL
// Cause:      User selects the Cancel button
//
void *C_DIALOG_ADDRESS::CmdCancel( void *mp1, void *mp2 )
{
    // Close this dialog
    Close( FALSE );

    return FALSE;
}
```

```
//-------
// CmdOK \
//---------------------------------------------------------------------------
// Event:      DM_OK
// Cause:      User selects the OK button
//
void *C_DIALOG_ADDRESS::CmdOK( void *mp1, void *mp2 )
{
   char    szString[256];

   // Tell the parent what server was picked
   pxcEditAddress->GetText( szString, 256 );

   // Tell the window who its parent is so it can talk back
   if( strlen( szString ) > 0 )
       pxcParent->SendMsg( PM_DONE, szString, 0 );

   // Close this dialog
   Close( FALSE );

   return FALSE;
}
```

Listing 9-2 ADDRESS.CPP

The ADDRESS.CPP file begins much like the PING.CPP file we discussed previously. It creates a message table and a command table to handle all the important window messages and commands that the dialog needs to process.

When an instance of this dialog is created, the constructor is called. In addition to calling the code from the parent constructor, the C_DIALOG_ADDRESS constructor also sets the command table for the dialog and calls the Create() method supplying the resource identifier, so the PMCLASS class window manager knows that the dialog is to be loaded from the Ping executable, as opposed to being created dynamically.

```
C_DIALOG_ADDRESS::C_DIALOG_ADDRESS( C_WINDOW *pxcParentObj, int iID )
                              : C_DIALOG( pxcParentObj, xtMsgAddress )
{
   // Enable the required handlers for this window
   CommandTable( xtCommandAddress );

   Create( iID );
}
```

In describing the PING.CPP code, I mentioned the CmdConnect() method and how it creates an instance of the C_DIALOG_ADDRESS class. Before processing, the main window sends a PM_PARENT message to the address dialog. This invokes the MsgParent method which, as shown below, populates the pxcParent class attribute, with the window pointer specified in the mp1 parameter.

```
void *C_DIALOG_ADDRESS::MsgParent( void *mp1, void *mp2 )
{
   // Save the pointer to the parent window object
   pxcParent = (C_WINDOW *)mp1;

   return FALSE;
}
```

Once the user enters an address and presses the dialog's OK button, the command processor method, CmdOK(), is called. This routine retrieves the current text value of the address field by calling the GetText() for the edit window.

```
   // Tell the parent what server was picked
   pxcEditAddress->GetText( szString, 256 );
```

If the field contains a string, which is assumed to be an address, it sends a PM_DONE message and the address string back to the main window object. As we saw earlier, the PM_DONE message starts a new Ping connection.

```
   // Tell the window who its parent is so it can talk back
   if( strlen( szString ) > 0 )
       pxcParent->SendMsg( PM_DONE, szString, 0 );
```

Once the PM_DONE message has been sent, the dialog can be closed. This is accomplished with a call to the Close() method.

```
   // Close this dialog
   Close( FALSE );
```

Ping Product Information Dialog

The Ping program has code to present the user with one more dialog box, the product information dialog. Each program you write should have a product information dialog in order to describe your program, present a copyright notice, etc.

```
//-------------------
// OS/2 Conditionals \
//-----------------------------------------------------------------------
#define    INCL_DOS
#define    INCL_WIN

//------------------
// Standard Headers \
//-----------------------------------------------------------------------
```

```
#include <os2.h>
#include <stdio.h>

//-----------------
// PMCLASS Headers \
//--------------------------------------------------------------------------
#include <app.hpp>
#include <window.hpp>
#include <winstd.hpp>
#include <winchild.hpp>
#include <dialog.hpp>
#include <edit.hpp>
#include <status.hpp>
#include <button.hpp>
#include <tbar.hpp>
#include <mle.hpp>
#include <log.hpp>

//---------------------
// Application Headers \
//--------------------------------------------------------------------------
#include "ping.rch"
#include "about.hpp"

//---------------------------
// About Window Message Table \
//--------------------------------------------------------------------------
DECLARE_MSG_TABLE( xtMsgAbout )
   DECLARE_MSG( PM_CREATE,          C_DIALOG_ABOUT::MsgInitDlg )
END_MSG_TABLE

//---------------------------
// About Window Command Table \
//--------------------------------------------------------------------------
DECLARE_COMMAND_TABLE( xtCommandAbout )
   DECLARE_COMMAND( DM_OK,          C_DIALOG_ABOUT::CmdOK )
END_COMMAND_TABLE

//-------------
// Constructor \
//--------------------------------------------------------------------------
C_DIALOG_ABOUT::C_DIALOG_ABOUT( C_WINDOW *pxcParentObj, int iID )
                               : C_DIALOG( pxcParentObj, xtMsgAbout )
{
   // Enable the required handlers for this window
   CommandTable( xtCommandAbout );

   // Create the physical dialog
```

```
   Create( iID );

   // Begin processing the about box
   Process();
}

//------------
// MsgInitDlg \
//--------------------------------------------------------------------------
// Event:      PM_CREATE
// Cause:      Issued by OS when dialog is created
//
void *C_DIALOG_ABOUT::MsgInitDlg( void *mp1, void *mp2 )
{
   char    szString[256];

   // Create an edit control instance and associate it with the version
   // string in the dialog (ID 105)
   pxcEditVersion = (C_EDIT *) new C_EDIT( (C_DIALOG *)this, 105 );

   // Format the real version string and insert it into the dialog
   sprintf( szString, "Version: %s", D_VERSION );
   pxcEditVersion->SetText( szString );

   // We can dispose of the edit control object now
   delete pxcEditVersion;

   return FALSE;
}

//-------
// CmdOK \
//--------------------------------------------------------------------------
// Event:      DM_OK
// Cause:      User selects the OK button
//
void *C_DIALOG_ABOUT::CmdOK( void *mp1, void *mp2 )
{
   // Close this dialog
   Close( FALSE );

   return FALSE;
}
```

Listing 9-3 ABOUT.CPP

The code for the Ping About box is shown in Listing 9-3; as you can see, it is quite straightforward. By now you should recognize the message and command tables. The only method of any real interest in the ABOUT.CPP source is the code used to process the MsgInitDlg method. This method creates an instance of an edit control that points to the version number text in the dialog box.

```
// Create an edit control instance and associate it with the version
// string in the dialog (ID 105)
pxcEditVersion = (C_EDIT *) new C_EDIT( (C_DIALOG *)this, 105 );
```

Once we have this instance, we can use it to set the version number string in the dialog. We set the version number this way, rather than hard coding it into the dialog, so we do not have to maintain version numbers in several places in the code. We can simply define a compiler definition, D_VERSION, and reference it whenever we need to display or examine the application version number.

```
// Format the real version string and insert it into the dialog
sprintf( szString, "Version: %s", D_VERSION );
pxcEditVersion->SetText( szString );
```

Once the version number text has been set, we need to dispose of the dynamic instance of the edit control in order free up the memory it uses. The delete statement forces the instance to call its class destructor.

```
// We can dispose of the edit control object now
delete pxcEditVersion;
```

The Ping Toolbar

The Ping toolbar is last item in Ping that we need to discuss. The Ping application provides a toolbar, albeit a simple one. This toolbar supports one button, the connect operation the user can press to select different Ping addresses. The entire source module for the main toolbar follows in Listing 9-4.

We discussed the code to implement a toolbar in the previous chapter, so we need not review it in any great detail here.

```
//-------------------
// OS/2 Conditionals \
//---------------------------------------------------------------------------
#define INCL_DOS
#define INCL_WIN
#define INCL_GPI

//------------------
// Standard Headers \
//---------------------------------------------------------------------------
#include <os2.h>
```

```
#include <stdio.h>
#include <stdlib.h>

//-----------------
// PMCLASS Headers \
//------------------------------------------------------------------------
#include <app.hpp>
#include <window.hpp>
#include <winstd.hpp>
#include <winchild.hpp>
#include <status.hpp>
#include <button.hpp>
#include <tbar.hpp>

//---------------------
// Application Headers \
//------------------------------------------------------------------------
#include "tbartop.hpp"
#include "ping.rch"

//-------------
// Constructor \
//------------------------------------------------------------------------
C_TOOLBAR_TOP::C_TOOLBAR_TOP( C_WINDOW *pxcParentObj, C_STATUS *pxcStatus )
                              : C_TOOLBAR( pxcParentObj, D_TOP_TBAR, 40 )
{
   DECLARE_BUTTON_TABLE( xtButtons )
       DECLARE_BUTTON( DB_CONNECT, DB_CONNECT_UP, DB_CONNECT_DN, 0,
                              "Ping a new host...", 8, 4 )
   END_BUTTON_TABLE

   // Set the status bar object used by the toolbar
   Status( pxcStatus );

   // Add some toolbar buttons
   CreateButtons( xtButtons );
}

//---------
// Control \
//------------------------------------------------------------------------
void C_TOOLBAR_TOP::Control( ULONG mp1 )
{
   // Button-Command cross reference
   DECLARE_BUTTON_CMD_TABLE( xtCommandLookup )
       DECLARE_BUTTON_CMD( DB_CONNECT, DM_CONNECT )
   END_BUTTON_CMD_TABLE
```

```
    // Call the parent controller to process the items
    C_TOOLBAR::Control( mp1, xtCommandLookup );
}
```

Listing 9-4 TBARTOP.CPP

Chapter Summary

In this chapter, we have built a very simple Ping application using code mostly from the C++ class libraries created earlier, along with some "glue" code to hold everything together. This Ping program is a fully functional Presentation Manager application from start to finish, and if you have seen the Ping provided in the Neo-Logic Network Suite, you will notice some remarkable similarities. In reality, Neo-Logic Ping uses virtually the same code base as the application presented in this chapter. Now you know how we wrote it—you have the source (almost)!

The Ping presented here is not without its own idiosyncrasies. For example, it pings synchronously (i.e., it sends a packet and expects it to return). A lost packet can hang the transmission even though the system you are pinging may still be functioning normally. If you want to avoid this limitation, you need to look at a function out of the TCP/IP API call select() that will allow you to set and detect a time-out. You can then modify the C_NETWORK_PING code to recognize a time-out as a lost packet and display this information to the user. Also, the Ping presented here does not provide any historical statistics regarding packet loss or long-term efficiency. All it will tell you about is instantaneous round-trip time for a packet.

In this chapter

- Implementing a simple NNTP news reader
- Using connection managers
- Suggested program enhancements

10

A Simple News Client

Goals for the News Client Application

With the enhanced editor and Ping code behind us, we can now advance to something a little more complicated. The NNTP news reader we will create in this chapter will integrate the network interface and the PMCLASS code into a complex application featuring multiple windows and multiple network connections.

Many applications being written today consist of a completely encapsulated user interface with a central application window and enclosed child windows. The news application will be a little different. The main program will consist of a control panel only. The other child windows for listing available server groups and subscriptions, as well as the message listings and articles, will all be managed as separate windows not constrained to a single parent window.

Each window is created as a separate object within the code, and since the WorkPlace Shell is an object-oriented interface, we will treat each window as a distinct display element. This technique is now coming into vogue with the advent of object frameworks such as Taligent and OpenDoc. The reasons for this are obvious. Studies have shown that this is how people work. Users would like a window to have a single function, and all configuration and management of that window should reside within the window.

Secondly, understanding how people work helps encapsulate and greatly simplifies the coding task. As a developer, you no longer have to worry about how the visual actions of one window affect another. Take tiling in a multiple document interface (MDI) application, for example. If the user has several MDI windows open and elects to tile them, the display of each of these windows is likely to be affected—perhaps in a way that is undesirable for the user. Using completely separate windows, we eliminate this problem and make our own programming job a lot easier.

Figure 10-1 illustrates the WPS desktop during a typical session with the news reader we will build in this chapter. Each window is completely disconnected from its relatives, and can be moved, resized, restyled (undergo font and color changes) independently of any other window on the desktop.

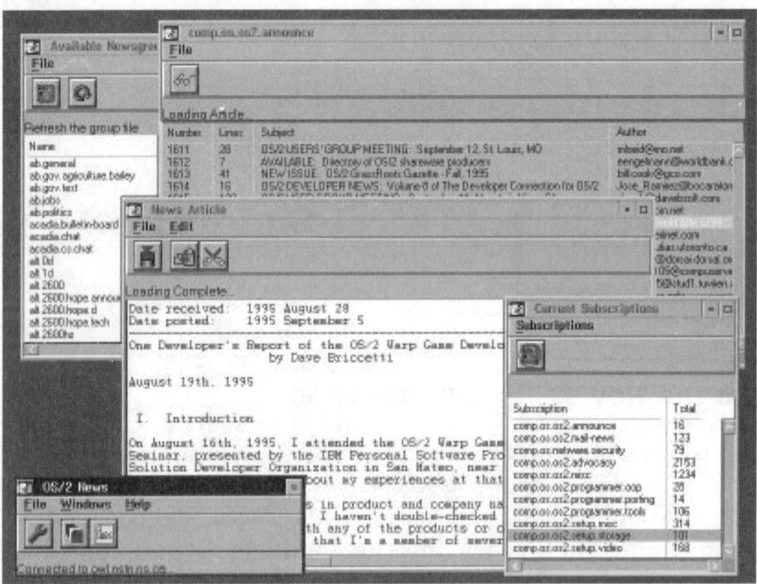

Figure 10-1 News sample program output

This is probably a good time to "burst your bubble" regarding what you will get from this chapter. I've referred to the NeoLogic News program a few times; if you are familiar with this shareware application, then you will realize that it contains a lot of functionality. If you have hopes of getting the source for NeoLogic News in this chapter, you will be disappointed.

The truth about the news application in this chapter is that it suffers from considerable limitations. I will explain these in detail at the end of the chapter; briefly, you will receive no capability of posting messages in this application—news is strictly a news "reader." There is also no way to print, save, or copy news articles, and no way to keep track of what you have viewed and what articles you have not seen before. It sounds as if this program is virtually useless, but in reality it will show you the basic interface to news servers, and demonstrate some advanced features that you will find in few other news programs.

I will leave the extensions as an exercise for you. If you remember the basic concepts of object orientation, you will have little difficulty attaching new features to this program to suit your own requirements.

Most of the code you will find in this news example has been discussed in detail in previous chapters, so we will skip those portions of the code which have been reused. There are, however, lots of new things to learn in this chapter, and we will start by developing a connection manager for our news client.

Building a News Connection Manager

As explained in Chapter 7, the inherent problem with interfacing an OS/2 application to TCP/IP is that the program can multitask, while the network connection cannot. The program could make a network request and put the whole application on hold while it waits for the server to respond, but this would result in the user sitting idle for long periods of time.

The alternative is to make several connections to the server so that multiple network tasks can occur in parallel. For example, with three connections to the server, one could be loading the list of available newsgroups, which is a lengthy task, while the user could be reading articles on another, and still another connection could be updating subscriptions. In theory you could make many connections and the user would never have to wait for any significant amount of time.

Realize, however, that there are limitations on network bandwidth and on the server itself. The administrator of the server will likely limit the total number of concurrent connections, and the throughput you can achieve depends very much upon the rate at which your network runs. A 14.4K SLIP or PPP data link would offer little benefit in supporting 30 news server connections. Through experimentation, I have discovered that in most environments two or three server connections is sufficient for satisfactory client performance.

Now that you understand what multitasking and multiconnection applications can do, you are possibly questioning how this goal can be achieved. The solution, of course, is to break the network interface out of the program mainstream and create a new class to manage all server interaction.

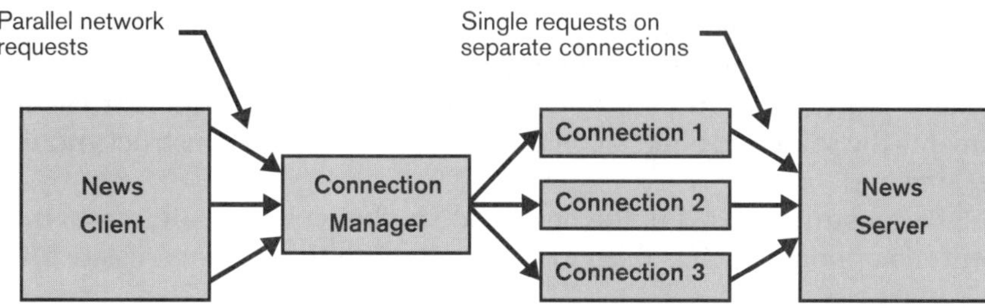

Figure 10-2 Connection manager functionality

Figure 10-2 illustrates how the connection manager functions. The client code at the left creates an instance of the connection manager layer and, in this case, specifies three connections. The connection manager creates the connections to the server, which now believes it has three separate clients connected.

When the multithreaded client requires a connection, it requests a free one from the connection manager, which finds the first idle connection and returns it to the requester to accomplish its task. Once the requesting thread is finished with the connection, it informs the connection manager, and the server connection is returned to the connection pool to wait use for another task. In the event that a thread of the news client requests a connection and they are all busy, the connection manager makes the client thread wait by setting a semaphore to trigger when the connection becomes idle.

The connection manager class is illustrated in Figure 10-3.

C_CONNECT_MGR			
int	iConnections	C_CONNECT_MGR()	
int	iConnectionCount	~C_CONNECT_MGR( )	
char	szNewsServer[256]	void	Close()
int	iNewsPort;	void	Initialize()
C_SEM_EVENT	hSemConMgr	int	Connect()
C_NEWS_CONNECT	*pxcConnect	void	Disconnect()
		int	FreeConnections()
		char	*Server()
		int	Port()
		int	Connections()
		int	Connection()
		int	MaxConnections()
		void	IncrementConnectionCount()
		C_NEWS_CONNECT *Connection()	

Figure 10-3 C_CONNECT_MGR class

C_CONNECT_MGR provides two constructors; however, the news client uses only one of them, so for now we will ignore the first member. The unused constructor is provided in case you want to implement a different client, and implements the same code and a combination of the second construct and the Initialize() method.

The constructor used in the news code is shown below; all it does is create an event semaphore which is used to detect when all the connections are busy.

```
//------------
// Constructor \
//------------------------------------------------------------------------
C_CONNECT_MGR::C_CONNECT_MGR( void )
{
   // Create an event semaphore to track the state of the connection manager
   hSemConMgr.Create();
   hSemConMgr.Open();
   hSemConMgr.Post();
}
```

The destructor for the connection manager is responsible for closing all the connections with the news server. To each one of the connection instances, the destructor issues a call to the Close() method, which destroys the connection and disposes of the TCP/IP socket used for communications. For more detail on the process involved in Close(), look at the C_CONNECT_NEWS class previously implemented in Chapter 7.

```
//-----------
// Destructor \
//------------------------------------------------------------------------
C_CONNECT_MGR::~C_CONNECT_MGR( void )
{
   int     iCtr;

   // Open each connection
   iCtr = iConnectionCount - 1;
   while( iCtr >= 0 )
   {
      // Close the server connection
      (pxcConnect + iCtr )->Close();
      iCtr--;
   }

   // Get rid of the network object
   delete pxcConnect;
}
```

Creating an instance of the connection manager using the void constructor is not sufficient to establish connections to the news server. The Initialize method provides this functionality. Initialize() accepts a specified number of connections and a server address, as well as a TCP/IP port to use for the communications.

The method creates an instance of the C_CONNECT_NEWS class for each connection, initializes the connection object, and attempts to open each connection with the server. Finally, using an attribute internal to C_CONNECT_MGR, Initialize() sets the activity state of each connection to an idle indicator.

```
//------------
// Initialize \
//-----------------------------------------------------------------------
//
// Description:
//     This method establishes a connection instance for each of the
//     required server connections and initializes each of them.
//
// Parameters:
//     iConCount       - Number of server connections to create
//     szServer        - Address of the news server
//     iPort           - TCP/IP port number to use for connections
//
// Returns:
//     void
//
void  C_CONNECT_MGR::Initialize( int iConCount, char *szServer, int iPort )
{
   int     iResult;
   int     iCtr;

   // Save the attributes
   iConnections = iConCount;
   iConnectionCount = 0;
   strcpy( szNewsServer, szServer );
   iNewsPort = iPort;

   // Create the specified number of connection instances
   pxcConnect = (C_CONNECT_NEWS *)new C_CONNECT_NEWS[iConnections];

   // Initialize each connection
   for( iCtr = 0; iCtr < MaxConnections(); iCtr++ )
   {
       // Initialize the news server connection
       (pxcConnect+iCtr)->Initialize( Server(), Port() );
   }

   // Open each connection
   for( iCtr = 0; iCtr < MaxConnections(); iCtr++ )
   {
       // Open the connection
       iResult = (pxcConnect+iCtr)->Open();
       if( iResult >= D_NET_OK )
       {
           // Say that we have a connection open
           IncrementConnectionCount();
       }

       // Indicate that the connection is initially idle
```

```
        (pxcConnect+iCtr)->Busy( 0 );
    }
}
```

The connection manager code permits requesting threads to close a connection. The Close() method sends a "close" message to the connection object and marks the state of the connection as idle. Use of this method is not recommended unless you are sure you know what you are doing. Closing a connection outside the connection manager will prevent any other thread from accessing that connection. It is used mainly for error control in the client code—if the news client determines that a problem exists on a specific connection, it can be shut down and still allow the other connections to continue operating normally.

```
//-------
// Close \
//-------------------------------------------------------------------------
//
// Description:
//      This method closes the specified news server connection.
//
// Parameters:
//      iConnection         - Connection to close
//
// Returns:
//      void
//
void  C_CONNECT_MGR::Close( int iConnection )
{
    // Close the connection
    (pxcConnect+iConnection)->Close();

    // Indicate that it is not longer busy
    (pxcConnect+iConnection)->Busy( 0 );

    // Reduce the number of available connections
    if( iConnectionCount > 0 )
        iConnectionCount--;
}
```

When the client application needs to access the server, it calls the C_CONNECT_MGR::Connect() method to request a connection. This member function waits for a free connection, if none is available, by referencing the semaphore assigned to this duty. Assuming a connection is idle, its offset number is returned to the caller and the connection is marked as "busy."

If all connections are currently busy, the method will loop at half-second intervals until a connection becomes available. This is a potential problem point in the code; though, after many hours of testing, I was not able to hang the program in this code, it should be approached with caution.

```
//---------
// Connect \
//------------------------------------------------------------------------
//
// Description:
//     This method returns connection from the idle connection pool to the
//     caller. The connection is marked as busy, and the calling function is
//     responsible for disconnecting when its task is complete.
//
// Parameters:
//     none
//
// Returns:
//     int          - >=0 connection for use. <0 no connection available
//
int    C_CONNECT_MGR::Connect( void )
{
   int      iCtr;
   ULONG    lCount;

   // Wait for a free connection
   hSemConMgr.WaitIndefinite();
   hSemConMgr.Reset( &lCount );

   do {
       // Look at each connection
       for( iCtr = 0; iCtr < iConnections; iCtr++ )
       {
           // Is the connection busy?
           if( (pxcConnect+iCtr)->Socket() && !(pxcConnect+iCtr)->Busy() )
           {
               // Not busy, so we'll use it. Mark as busy.
               (pxcConnect+iCtr)->Busy( 1 );

               // Return the connection number that was connected
               hSemConMgr.Post();
               return iCtr;
           }
       }

       // Wait around a while until a connection becomes free
       DosSleep( 500 );
   } while( 1 == 1 );

   // The program should never get here, but return something to keep the
   // compiler happy
   return -1;
}
```

The requesting code can determine the number of idle connections in the connection manager using the FreeConnections() method. This is useful if you want to build a thread that uses more than one connection to "gang up" on a task. In NeoLogic News, I used this type of code to allow several connections to update subscriptions, while leaving one connection free to read articles or perform other tasks. To accomplish this, I monitored the number of free connections using FreeConnections() to make sure there was always one free for other user demands.

```
//-----------------
// FreeConnections \
//---------------------------------------------------------------------------
//
// Description:
//     This method returns the number of currently idle connections.
//
// Parameters:
//     none
//
// Returns:
//     int             - The number of free connections.
//
intC_CONNECT_MGR::FreeConnections( void )
{
   int     iCtr;
   int     iFreeCtr;

   iFreeCtr = 0;

   // Check each connection
   for( iCtr = 0; iCtr < iConnections; iCtr++ )
   {
      // If the connection is idle, count it.
      if( (pxcConnect+iCtr)->Socket() && !(pxcConnect+iCtr)->Busy() )
         iFreeCtr++;
   }

   // Return the number of free connections
   return iFreeCtr;
}
```

Since a thread cannot keep a connection allocated forever, it must have some procedure in place to return the connection to the connection manager's free pool. The Disconnect() method implements this capability by simply marking the connection's operational state back to an "idle."

```
//------------
// Disconnect \
//------------------------------------------------------------------------------
//
// Description:
//     This method returns the specified connection to the idle connection
//     pool for use by other processes.
//
// Parameters:
//     iConnect            - Connection to return to the pool
//
// Returns:
//     none
//
void C_CONNECT_MGR::Disconnect( int iConnect )
{
   // Mark the connection as idle
   (pxcConnect+iConnect)->Busy( 0 );
}
```

The header file for the connection manager code also contains a number of simple inline functions that mostly return class attribute values.

```
C_CONNECT_NEWS *Connection( int iConnect )
                                       { return pxcConnect+iConnect; };
int     FreeConnections( void );
char    *Server( void )                { return szNewsServer; };
int     Port( void )                   { return iNewsPort; };
int     Connection( void )             { return iConnectionCount; };
int     MaxConnections( void )         { return iConnections; };
void    IncrementConnectionCount( void ){ iConnectionCount++; };
```

The connection manager is now behind us. I hope you've sifted through the source because it is the key to making the news client more efficient than most similar applications, and it demonstrates some very important advantages of OS/2 over other environments such as Windows (except NT).

In the next section you will see how the connection manager layer is integrated into the news client, and the advantages of the connection manager will become clear.

Starting Up a News Client

Now that we have established a method for communicating with a news server, we can begin to create a real applications to read news. The first step is obviously the creation of a main() procedure and, since we want to make our news client a Presentation Manager application, we need to create a main window.

Most of the code for the main window need not be reviewed here, since it is quite similar to the enhanced editor and Ping which we built earlier. I will, however, explain some of the new features we have not seen previously.

One of the key features of the news client is that all activity in the program is controlled by the C_WINDOW_MAIN class. This means that in many cases the main window object simply acts as a message relay. For example, when the user subscribes to a new group, the available groups window sends a message to the main window object, which in turn sends a message to the subscription window. This technique simplifies the overall design and helps with program maintenance. If you do find a problem, you can usually track it down to a message handler in C_WINDOW_MAIN, since interaction between the other windows is nonexistent.

Figure 10-4 contains a message diagram that graphically explains how the program interacts with the user and its various internal parts. You should be able to use this diagram when referencing the C_WINDOW_MAIN source that follows. For the sake of simplicity, the diagram does not show every message passed. In particular, the WM_CLOSE messages have been eliminated in step 6.

1. The user has executed the program. News makes a connection to the server, then creates and displays the subscription window. The subscription window is populated with data from the user's subscription file and is updated with the most recent article counts from the server.
2. The user elects to display the list of available groups. News creates the group window, and populates it based on information available either from the news server or from the GROUPS.GRP file on disk.
3. The user subscribes to a new group. The group window issues a PM_GRP_SUBSCRIBE message to the main window. C_WINDOW_MAIN notifies the subscription window that a new group has been added to the subscription list.
4. The user wants to view a list of subjects, so he selects a group displayed in the subscription window. The subscription window issues a PM_SUB_READ message to the main window, which creates a new instance of C_WINDOW_MESSAGE and prompts that window to load a list of subjects from the server for the specified group.
5. The user finds an article he wants to read. He selects the article's subject from the message list window, which prompts it to send a PM_ART_READ message to the main window. C_WINDOW_MAIN creates a new instance of the article viewer class and instructs it to load the article from the server and display it.
6. The user closes the application. The main window sends a WM_CLOSE message to each of the other windows if they are open. Each window responds with an acknowledgment. After all child windows have been notified, the main window sends a WM_QUIT message to close the application.

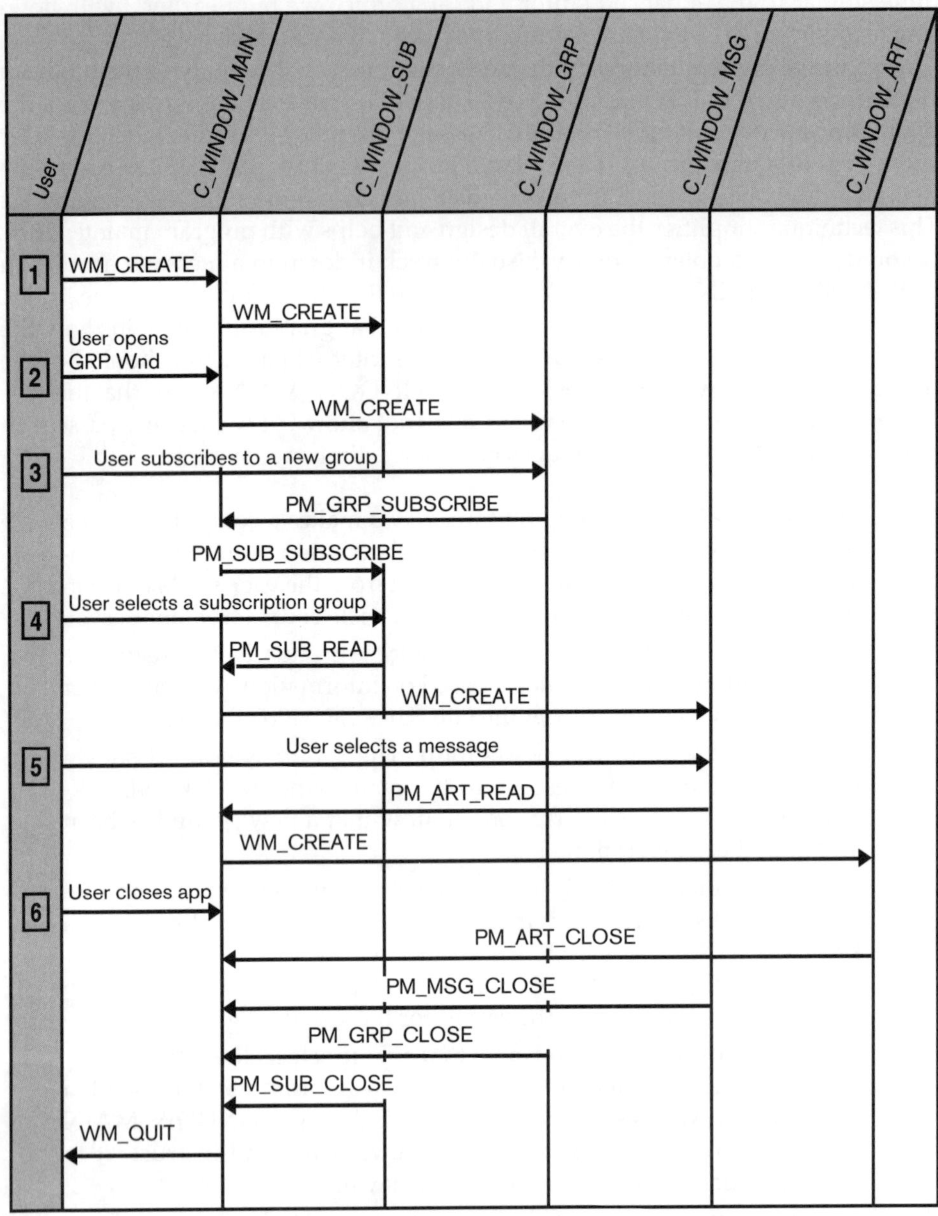

Figure 10-4 News message flow

Before we begin looking at the code, let's address the global variables used by news. I dislike global variables, so I want to try to justify their use in the news client. All the global data is in the form of classes that are instantiated at program startup and are not really variable. The objects are created and referenced by many parts of the code, but for the purposes of this discussion all the global classes are really constants that get assigned at run time.

```
//-------------
// Global Data \
//-----------------------------------------------------------------------------
C_APPLICATION       xcApp;                  // Application instance
C_WINDOW_MAIN       xcWindow;               // Main window instance
C_CONNECT_MGR       *pxcMgr;                // Connection Manager Instance
C_LOG               *pxcLog;                // Debug log instance
```

Since the entire source for news is included on the companion disk, I'm not going to drag you through every line, especially since much of the code is similar to that used in previous chapters. However, we will look at some of the key components starting with the main() procedure.

```
void main( int argc, char *argv[] )
{
   // Create a debugging log file
   pxcLog = (C_LOG *)new C_LOG( "news.log", 1 );
   pxcLog->Open();

   // Register the application window
   xcWindow.Register( "OS/2 News" );
   xcWindow.WCF_Icon();
   xcWindow.WCF_SysMenu();
   xcWindow.WCF_Menu();
   xcWindow.WCF_TitleBar();
   xcWindow.WCF_MinButton();
   xcWindow.WCF_TaskList();
   xcWindow.WCF_DialogBorder();
   xcWindow.Create( ID_WINDOW, "OS/2 News" );

   // Create the news connections
   pxcLog->Write( "Main:Creating Connection Manager" );
   pxcMgr = (C_CONNECT_MGR *)new C_CONNECT_MGR;
   pxcLog->Write( "Main:Created Connection Manager" );

   // Set the news server
   xcWindow.SetServer( argv[1] );

   // Start the message loop
   xcApp.Run();
```

```
    // Destroy the news connections
    delete pxcMgr;

    // Close and free the debug log
    pxcLog->Write( "NEWS:Closing Log" );
    pxcLog->Close();
    delete pxcLog;
}
```

The first two lines of code in main() are something we have not seen in the previous applications. These lines set up a debugging log file called NEWS.LOG, which will receive a dump of some key process information for news. These lines create an instance of a debug log and open it.

```
// Create a debugging log file
pxcLog = (C_LOG *)new C_LOG( "news.log", 1 );
pxcLog->Open();
```

At the end of the main() procedure, we reverse this process by closing the log and destroying the instance.

```
// Close and free the debug log
pxcLog->Write( "NEWS:Closing Log" );
pxcLog->Close();
delete pxcLog;
```

The Write() operation writes the enclosed string to the log file. This is useful for determining why an application is malfunctioning. Note that C_LOG::Write() functions much like the C printf() procedure, in that you can enclose print formatting to display the values of variables used in the application.

```
pxcLog->Write( "The value of x is %ld", x );
```

Before the application message loop is started, main() also does something else that we have not seen before. It executes the following line:

```
// Create the news connections
pxcMgr = (C_CONNECT_MGR *)new C_CONNECT_MGR;
```

This line of code creates an instance of the connection manager that we examined in the previous section. The program has not yet connected to the server—all we have done is reserve space for the connection manager.

Immediately before the message loop is started, we send the main window a server address.

```
// Set the news server
xcWindow.SetServer( argv[1] );
```

The news program requires that a server IP or domain name string be specified on the command line. This string is sent to the main window, which has the responsibility for connecting to the server. The news program currently does not provide any form of error checking to ensure that an address has been added to the command line. I will leave this for you to correct.

Once the program drops out of the message loop, main() resumes control and needs to remove the dynamic memory used by the connection manager. It makes the following call to destroy the connection manager object and free up its memory.

```
// Destroy the news connections
delete pxcMgr;
```

The main window for news is an object based on the PMCLASS C_WINDOW_STD class; from our past experience we know that we need to supply a message table, shown below. The methods it references need not be reviewed here; although I will go into detail for some of them, the majority are copies of what we have already seen in previous applications.

```
//--------------------------
// Main Window Message Table \
//------------------------------------------------------------------------
DECLARE_MSG_TABLE( xtMsgMain )
   DECLARE_MSG( PM_CREATE,             C_WINDOW_MAIN::MsgCreate )
   DECLARE_MSG( PM_GROUP_CLOSE,        C_WINDOW_MAIN::MsgGroupClose )
   DECLARE_MSG( PM_GROUP_SUBSCRIBE,    C_WINDOW_MAIN::MsgGroupSubscribe )
   DECLARE_MSG( PM_SUB_CLOSE,          C_WINDOW_MAIN::MsgSubscriptionClose )
   DECLARE_MSG( PM_SUB_READ,           C_WINDOW_MAIN::MsgSubscriptionRead )
   DECLARE_MSG( PM_MSG_CLOSE,          C_WINDOW_MAIN::MsgMessageClose )
   DECLARE_MSG( PM_MSG_READ,           C_WINDOW_MAIN::MsgMessageRead )
   DECLARE_MSG( PM_ART_CLOSE,          C_WINDOW_MAIN::MsgArticleClose )
   DECLARE_MSG( PM_CONNECT,            C_WINDOW_MAIN::MsgConnect )
   DECLARE_MSG( WM_CLOSE,              C_WINDOW_MAIN::MsgClose )
   DECLARE_MSG( WM_SIZE,               C_WINDOW_MAIN::MsgSize )
   DECLARE_MSG( WM_CONTROL,            C_WINDOW_MAIN::MsgControl )
   DECLARE_MSG( WM_PAINT,              C_WINDOW_STD::MsgPaint )
END_MSG_TABLE
```

C_WINDOW_MAIN also supports some menu and toolbar commands, so we have also implemented a command table.

```
//--------------------------
// Main Window Command Table \
//------------------------------------------------------------------------
DECLARE_COMMAND_TABLE( xtCommandMain )
   DECLARE_COMMAND( DM_GROUPS,             C_WINDOW_MAIN::CmdGroups )
   DECLARE_COMMAND( DM_SUBSCRIPTIONS,      C_WINDOW_MAIN::CmdSubscriptions )
```

```
    DECLARE_COMMAND( DM_EXIT,                   C_WINDOW_MAIN::CmdExit )
    DECLARE_COMMAND( DM_INFO,                   C_WINDOW_MAIN::CmdHelpInfo )
END_MSG_TABLE
```

The constructor for C_WINDOW_MAIN assigns the message and command tables and additionally initializes the attributes used by the instance.

```
//-------------
// Constructor \
//---------------------------------------------------------------------------
//
// Description:
//     This constructor initializes the main window class for the editor.
//     It zeroes the class attributes and sets up the command handler and
//     server address.
//
// Parameters:
//     szServer             - Address of the news server
//
C_WINDOW_MAIN::C_WINDOW_MAIN( void ) : C_WINDOW_STD( xtMsgMain )
{
    // Initialize all child objects
    pxcTBar = 0;
    pxcStatus = 0;
    pxcMenu = 0;
    pxcGroups = 0;
    pxcSubs = 0;
    pxcMsg = 0;
    pxcArticle = 0;

    // Enable the required command handler for this window
    CommandTable( xtCommandMain );

    // Set the server address
    strcpy( szServerAddress, "" );
}
```

The destructor for the main window object is similar to the one we implemented for the enhanced editor. It simply deallocates the space used by all the child window objects.

```
//-------------
// Destructor \
//---------------------------------------------------------------------------
//
// Description:
//     The destructor frees up all the dynamically allocated objects
//     and attributes used by this instance.
//
```

```
C_WINDOW_MAIN::~C_WINDOW_MAIN( void )
{
   pxcLog->Write( "~C_WINDOW_MAIN:Start" );

   delete pxcTBar;
   delete pxcStatus;
   delete pxcMenu;

   delete pxcGroups;
   delete pxcSubs;
   delete pxcMsg;
   delete pxcArticle;

   pxcLog->Write( "~C_WINDOW_MAIN:End" );
}
```

The MsgCreate() is called when the window receives a WM_CREATE message and sets up the characteristics of the window. Since there is a lot of new code in this method, we should spend some time studying it.

```
//-----------
// MsgCreate \
//---------------------------------------------------------------------------
// Event:       WM_CREATE
// Cause:       Issued by OS when window is created
// Description:This method gets called when the window is initially created.
//              It initializes all the visual aspects of the class.
//
void *C_WINDOW_MAIN::MsgCreate( void *mp1, void *mp2 )
{
   char    szX[10];
   char    szY[10];

   // Create a status bar to display miscellaneous data
   pxcStatus = (C_STATUS *) new C_STATUS( this );

   // Create a toolbar control
   pxcTBar = (C_TOOLBAR_TOP *)new C_TOOLBAR_TOP( this, pxcStatus );

   // Keep track of the main menu so we can enable/disable items
   pxcMenu = (C_MENU *)new C_MENU( this );

   // Load parameters out of the INI file
   C_INI_USER xcIni( "BookNews" );
   xcIni.Open();
   xcIni.Read( "MainX", szX, "0", 10 );
   xcIni.Read( "MainY", szY, "0", 10 );
   xcIni.Close();
```

```
    // Make the window look like a control panel
    SetSizePosition( atoi( szX ), atoi( szY ), xcApp.DesktopWidth() / 10 * 4,
            xcApp.DialogBorderHeight() * 2 + xcApp.TitleBarHeight() +
                                              xcApp.MenuHeight() + 65 );

    // Make the window visible
    Show();

    // Disable menu options so the user can't select information
    // until we're connected
    pxcMenu->DisableItem( DM_WINDOWS );

    // Disable the toolbar buttons until we're connected
    pxcTBar->ButtonEnable( DB_WND_GRP, FALSE );
    pxcTBar->ButtonEnable( DB_WND_SUB, FALSE );

    // Begin a thread to open all the news connections
    xcConnectThread.Create( ConnectThread, 40000, this );

    return FALSE;
}
```

The first new code we see are the lines that load the previous window states from the OSUSR.INI file. MsgMain() creates an instance of C_INI_USER and opens it in order to retrieve the last known X,Y coordinates of the main control panel. Since the size of this window is fixed, we do not need to save the width and height dimensions.

```
    // Load parameters out of the INI file
    C_INI_USER xcIni( "BookNews" );
    xcIni.Open();
    xcIni.Read( "MainX", szX, "0", 10 );
    xcIni.Read( "MainY", szY, "0", 10 );
    xcIni.Close();
```

Something else that is new is the code to disable the "Windows" menu item, and the toolbar buttons used to display the available groups window and the subscription window. Since both of these windows require network access, we need to prevent the user from opening these windows until we are connected to the news server.

```
    // Disable menu options so the user can't select information
    // until we're connected
    pxcMenu->DisableItem( DM_WINDOWS );

    // Disable the toolbar buttons until we're connected
    pxcTBar->ButtonEnable( DB_WND_GRP, FALSE );
    pxcTBar->ButtonEnable( DB_WND_SUB, FALSE );
```

Finally, the MsgCreate() method starts a thread to initialize the connection manager.

```
// Begin a thread to open all the news connections
xcConnectThread.Create( ConnectThread, 40000, this );
```

The ConnectThread() thread function calls the Initialize() method for the connection manager instance and displays the connection status in the main window's status line. If the connection manager fails to establish a server connection, the program does not allow further processing to occur, and the user's only option is to exit the program.

Assuming a successful connection was established to the server, the thread issues a PM_CONNECT message to the main window.

```
//---------------
// ConnectThread \
//------------------------------------------------------------------------
//
// Description:
//    This thread function creates a connection to the news server. If
//    successful, it sends a PM_CONNECT message back to the main window class.
//
void _Optlink ConnectThread( void *pvData )
{
   C_WINDOW_MAIN    *pxcThis;
   C_THREAD_PM      *pxcThread;

   // Get a point to the main window object
   pxcThread = (C_THREAD_PM *)pvData;
   pxcThis = (C_WINDOW_MAIN *)pxcThread->ThreadData();

   // Create a PM process for this thread
   pxcThread->InitializeThread();

  pxcThis->Status()->Text( "Connecting to %s...", pxcThis->ServerAddress() );
  pxcMgr->Initialize( D_MAX_CONNECT, pxcThis->ServerAddress(), D_NEWS_PORT );

   // If there was an error, tell the user about it
   if( pxcMgr->Connections() <= 0 )
   {
       // Tell the user that the connection failed
       WinMessageBox( HWND_DESKTOP, pxcThis->Window(),
               "News could not connect to the server",
                                  "News", 0, MB_OK | MB_ICONHAND );

       pxcThis->Status()->Text( "Not connected" );
   }
```

```
   else
   {
      // Tell the main window that there were no errors - we're online!
      pxcThis->PostMsg( PM_CONNECT, 0, 0 );
   }

   // Terminate the thread
   pxcThread->TerminateThread();
}
```

This PM_CONNECT message is managed by the MsgConnect() method. This method enables the "Windows" menu item and toolbar buttons, and then issues a DM_SUBSCRIPTION command to display the subscription window.

```
//-----------
// MsgConnect \
//--------------------------------------------------------------------------
// Event:      PM_CONNECT
// Cause:      Issued by the connection thread when a connection has been
//             established
//
void *C_WINDOW_MAIN::MsgConnect( void *mp1, void *mp2 )
{
   // Tell the user he is connected
   pxcStatus->Text( "Connected to %s...", ServerAddress() );

   // Enable menu options so the user can select information
   pxcMenu->EnableItem( DM_WINDOWS );

   // Enable the toolbar buttons
   pxcTBar->ButtonEnable( DB_WND_GRP, TRUE );
   pxcTBar->ButtonEnable( DB_WND_SUB, TRUE );

   // Give the user some audible feedback to say that we've connected
   DosBeep( 100, 100 );

   // Since we are now connected, open the subscription window and tell
   // it to update.
   SendMsg( WM_COMMAND, (void *)DM_SUBSCRIPTIONS, 0 );

   return FALSE;
}
```

When the DM_SUBSCRIPTION command is received, the CmdSubscriptions() method is called. It creates an instance of the subscription window class and sends it a PM_POPULATE message to begin loading the subscriptions.

```
//------------------
// CmdSubscriptions \
//--------------------------------------------------------------------------
// Event:      DM_SUBSCRIPTION
// Cause:      User selects the Window/Subscriptions option in order to
//             display the list of available groups supported by the server.
//
void *C_WINDOW_MAIN::CmdSubscriptions( void *mp1, void *mp2 )
{
   // Only permit the user to open a sub window if it isn't already open
   if( !pxcSubs )
   {
      // Create a new instance of the groups window
      pxcSubs = (C_WINDOW_SUBSCRIPTION *)new C_WINDOW_SUBSCRIPTION;

      // Set up groups window
      pxcSubs->Register( "Subscriptions" );
      pxcSubs->WCF_Standard();
      pxcSubs->Create( ID_SUBSCRIPTIONS, "Current Subscriptions" );

      // Tell the group window that this is its parent
      pxcSubs->SendMsg( PM_PARENT, (void *)this, 0 );

      // Tell the group window to populate
      pxcSubs->SendMsg( PM_POPULATE, 0, 0 );
   }
   else
   {
      // Otherwise give the user focus to the existing window
      pxcSubs->Show();
   }
   return FALSE;
}
```

If the user closes the subscription window, a PM_SUB_CLOSE message is sent to the main window to notify it of the action. The instance of the subscription window is then destroyed.

```
//----------------------
// MsgSubscriptionClose \
//--------------------------------------------------------------------------
// Event:      PM_SUB_CLOSE
// Cause:      Issued by the subscription window when the user closes it
//
void *C_WINDOW_MAIN::MsgSubscriptionClose( void *mp1, void *mp2 )
{
   // Delete the current subscription window
   delete pxcSubs;
```

```
    pxcSubs = 0;

    return FALSE;
}
```

When the user clicks the "groups" toolbar button or menu selection, the groups windows is created. This invokes the CmdGroups() method, which creates a new instance of the groups window class and issues a PM_POPULATE message to it. This code is almost a duplicate of the subscription startup code.

```
//-----------
// CmdGroups \
//-------------------------------------------------------------------------
// Event:      DM_GROUPS
// Cause:      User selects the Window/Groups option in order to display the
//             list of available groups supported by the server.
//
void *C_WINDOW_MAIN::CmdGroups( void *mp1, void *mp2 )
{
    // Only permit the user to open a groups window if it isn't already open
    if( !pxcGroups )
    {
        // Create a new instance of the groups window
        pxcGroups = (C_WINDOW_GROUP *)new C_WINDOW_GROUP;

        // Set up the available groups window
        pxcGroups->Register( "Groups" );
        pxcGroups->WCF_Standard();
        pxcGroups->Create( ID_GROUPS, "Available Newsgroups" );

        // Tell the group window that this is its parent
        pxcGroups->SendMsg( PM_PARENT, (void *)this, 0 );

        // Tell the group window to populate
        pxcGroups->SendMsg( PM_POPULATE, 0, 0 );
    }
    else
    {
        // Otherwise give the user focus to the existing window
        pxcGroups->Show();
    }
    return FALSE;
}
```

Like the subscription window, when the group window is closed it sends a message back to the main window manager. The PM_GROUP_CLOSE message causes the MsgGroupClose() method to be activated, which destroys the group window instance.

```
//---------------
// MsgGroupClose \
//------------------------------------------------------------------------
// Event:      PM_GROUP_CLOSE
// Cause:      Issued by the group window when the user closes it
//
void *C_WINDOW_MAIN::MsgGroupClose( void *mp1, void *mp2 )
{
   // Close and Delete the current group window
   delete pxcGroups;
   pxcGroups = 0;

   return FALSE;
}
```

The groups window has an additional purpose that generates a different window message. The groups window permits the user to select new newsgroups to which a subscription will be made. For each group that the user subscribes to, the group window will send a PM_GROUP_SUBSCRIBE message. Though the main window is not responsible for subscribing to newsgroups, it is the central control for the application. The group window knows nothing about the subscription process, so the main window acts as a messenger.

When a PM_GROUP_SUBSCRIBE message is received in the message queue, the main window generates a PM_SUB_SUBSCRIBE for the subscription window, attaching the names of the new groups.

```
//-------------------
// MsgGroupSubscribe \
//------------------------------------------------------------------------
// Event:      PM_GROUP_SUBSCRIBE
// Cause:      Issued by the group window when the user subscribes to a group.
// Description:This method is invoked any time a group is subscribed to.
//             The mp1 parameter contains a pointer to the group name string
//             being subscribed.
//
void *C_WINDOW_MAIN::MsgGroupSubscribe( void *mp1, void *mp2 )
{
   // Tell the subscription window about the new group
   pxcSubs->SendMsg( PM_SUB_SUBSCRIBE, mp1, 0 );

   return FALSE;
}
```

If the user selects a group from the subscription, this notifies news that the user wishes to read the list of subjects from that group. The subscription window sends a PM_SUB_READ message to the main window handler.

MsgSubscriptionRead() determines the name of the group to be read, creates an instance of a message list window, and instructs this new window to populate itself with information from the server.

```
//----------------------
// MsgSubscriptionRead \
//-----------------------------------------------------------------------------
// Event:      PM_SUB_READ
// Cause:      Issued by the subscription window when the user wants to
//             read a subscription.
// Description:This method is called any time the user selects a subscription
//             to read. This will create an instance of a message list window
//             and display the subscription contents.
//
void *C_WINDOW_MAIN::MsgSubscriptionRead( void *mp1, void *mp2 )
{
   char    *szGroup;
   char    szString[64];

   // Determine which group is being displayed
   szGroup = (char *)mp1;
   pxcLog->Write( "MsgSubscriptionRead:Group=%s", szGroup );

   // Only permit the user to open a groups window if it isn't already open
   if( !pxcMsg )
   {
       // Create a new instance of the groups window
       pxcMsg = (C_WINDOW_MESSAGE *)new C_WINDOW_MESSAGE;

       // Set up message window
       pxcMsg->Register( "Message" );
       pxcMsg->WCF_Standard();
       pxcMsg->Create( ID_MESSAGES, "Message List" );

       // Tell the message window that this is its parent
       pxcMsg->SendMsg( PM_PARENT, (void *)this, 0 );

       // Tell the message window to populate for the given group in mp1
       pxcMsg->SendMsg( PM_POPULATE, mp1, 0 );
   }
   else
   {
       // Otherwise give the user focus to the existing window
       pxcMsg->Show();
   }

   return FALSE;
}
```

When the user closes a message window, a PM_MSG_CLOSE message is sent to the main window that invokes the MsgMessageClose() method. This destroys the instance of the message list window and deallocates the memory it was using.

```
//-----------------
// MsgMessageClose \
//--------------------------------------------------------------------------
// Event:       PM_MSG_CLOSE
// Cause:       Issued by the message window when the user closes it
//
void *C_WINDOW_MAIN::MsgMessageClose( void *mp1, void *mp2 )
{
   // Delete the current message window
   delete pxcMsg;
   pxcMsg = 0;

   return FALSE;
}
```

If the user selects a subject from the message list, news is notified that an article should be displayed. This starts the MsgMessageRead() method, which manages creation of an article window and instructs the new window to load a specific article number requested by the message list window when the item was selected.

```
//----------------
// MsgMessageRead \
//--------------------------------------------------------------------------
// Event:       PM_MSG_READ
// Cause:       Issued by the message window when the user wants to read
//              an article.
// Description:This method is called any time the user selects an article
//              to read. This will create an instance of an article window
//              and display the article supplied in mp1 to the viewer.
//
void *C_WINDOW_MAIN::MsgMessageRead( void *mp1, void *mp2 )
{
   pxcLog->Write( "MsgMessageRead:File=%s", (char *)mp1 );

   // Only permit the user to open a window if it isn't already open
   if( !pxcArticle )
   {
      // Create a new instance of the groups window
      pxcArticle = (C_WINDOW_ARTICLE *)new C_WINDOW_ARTICLE;

      // Set up article window
```

```
        pxcArticle->Register( "Article" );
        pxcArticle->WCF_Standard();
        pxcArticle->Create( ID_ARTICLE, "News Article" );

        // Tell the message window that this is its parent
        pxcArticle->SendMsg( PM_ART_PARENT, (void *)this, 0 );

        // Tell the article window to populate for the given article in mp1
        pxcArticle->SendMsg( PM_ART_POPULATE, mp1, 0 );
    }
    else
    {
        // Otherwise give the user focus to the existing window
        pxcArticle->Show();
    }

    return FALSE;
}
```

As you have probably come to expect by now, when the user closes an article viewer window, a message is sent back to the main window handler. PM_ART_CLOSE causes the MsgArticleClose() method to be called, which destroys the article window instance.

```
//-----------------
// MsgArticleClose \
//-----------------------------------------------------------------------------
// Event:      PM_ART_CLOSE
// Cause:      Issued by the article window when the user closes it
//
void *C_WINDOW_MAIN::MsgArticleClose( void *mp1, void *mp2 )
{
    // Delete the current article window
    delete pxcArticle;
    pxcArticle = 0;

    return FALSE;
}
```

The final method we are going to examine in the C_WINDOW_MAIN class is MsgClose(), which is called when the user closes the main window by either double-clicking the mouse on the system menu button or by selecting the "Exit" menu item.

```
//----------
// MsgClose \
//--------------------------------------------------------------------------
// Event:      WM_CLOSE
// Cause:      Issued by OS when window is closed
//
void *C_WINDOW_MAIN::MsgClose( void *mp1, void *mp2 )
{
   char    szString[80];
   int     iX;
   int     iY;
   int     iW;
   int     iL;

   // Get all the savable parameters
   GetSizePosition( &iX, &iY, &iW, &iL );

   // Save parameters into the INI file
   C_INI_USER xcIni( "BookNews" );
   xcIni.Open();
   sprintf( szString, "%d", iX );
   xcIni.Write( "MainX", szString );
   sprintf( szString, "%d", iY );
   xcIni.Write( "MainY", szString );
   xcIni.Close();

   // Debug
   pxcLog->Write( "NEWS:WM_CLOSE:Start" );

   // If there is a groups window open, close it and destroy
   if( pxcGroups )
       pxcGroups->SendMsg( WM_CLOSE, 0, 0 );

   // If there is a subscriptions window open, close it and destroy
   if( pxcSubs )
       pxcSubs->SendMsg( WM_CLOSE, 0, 0 );

   // If there is a message window open, close it and destroy
   if( pxcMsg )
       pxcMsg->SendMsg( WM_CLOSE, 0, 0 );

   // If there is an article window open, close it and destroy
   if( pxcArticle )
       pxcArticle->SendMsg( WM_CLOSE, 0, 0 );

   // Application was told to close, so post a QUIT message to the OS
   PostMsg( WM_QUIT, 0, 0 );
```

```
    // Debug
    pxcLog->Write( "NEWS:WM_CLOSE:End" );
    return FALSE;
}
```

MsgClose() first retrieves the current size of the window and writes this information to the OS2USER.INI files. In this way, if the user has moved the window, it can be repositioned the next time the program is executed.

```
    // Get all the savable parameters
    GetSizePosition( &iX, &iY, &iW, &iL );

    // Save parameters into the INI file
    C_INI_USER xcIni( "BookNews" );
    xcIni.Open();
    sprintf( szString, "%d", iX );
    xcIni.Write( "MainX", szString );
    sprintf( szString, "%d", iY );
    xcIni.Write( "MainY", szString );
    xcIni.Close();
```

Finally, MsgClose() ensures that all the child windows are closed. In the current version of news, only a single instance of each window can exist. This makes management of the closure much easier for the purposes of demonstration.

In a full news application, you would want to permit the user to have multiple message lists and article viewers open at any time. Closing the application would then become much more complicated because the program would be required to keep track of each window.

Listing Available Groups

In this section, we will add the capability of displaying a list of available newsgroups supported by the NNTP server. We need not review every method in the C_WINDOW_GROUP class because you have seen most of this code before. Instead, I will show only those items that differ from previous examples.

From the message diagram shown in Figure 10-4, we already know a great deal about the contents of the C_WINDOW_GROUP class. For example, we know that is it instantiated by the main window when the user selects the "Available Groups" menu item of the toolbar button. We also know that, when the user closes the group window, it issues a PM_GRP_CLOSE message to the instance of C_WINDOW_MAIN. Finally, if the user subscribes to a group, we know that this window generates a PM_GRP_SUBSCRIBE message.

The basic functions are all implemented in the message and command methods of the class. The message table for C_WINDOW_GROUP follows.

```
//----------------------------
// Group Window Message Table \
//---------------------------------------------------------------------------
//
DECLARE_MSG_TABLE( xtMsgGroup )
   DECLARE_MSG( PM_CREATE,          C_WINDOW_GROUP::MsgCreate )
   DECLARE_MSG( PM_PARENT,          C_WINDOW_GROUP::MsgParent )
   DECLARE_MSG( WM_CLOSE,           C_WINDOW_GROUP::MsgClose )
   DECLARE_MSG( WM_SIZE,            C_WINDOW_GROUP::MsgSize )
   DECLARE_MSG( WM_CONTROL,         C_WINDOW_GROUP::MsgControl )
   DECLARE_MSG( WM_PAINT,           C_WINDOW_STD::MsgPaint )
   DECLARE_MSG( PM_POPULATE,        C_WINDOW_GROUP::MsgPopulate )
END_MSG_TABLE
```

The C_WINDOW_GROUP class currently provides only two command handlers. These are shown in the following command table.

```
//----------------------------
// Group Window Command Table \
//---------------------------------------------------------------------------
//
DECLARE_COMMAND_TABLE( xtCommandGroup )
   DECLARE_COMMAND( DM_GROUP_SUBSCRIBE,     C_WINDOW_GROUP::CmdSubscribe )
   DECLARE_COMMAND( DM_GROUP_LOAD,          C_WINDOW_GROUP::CmdRefresh )
END_MSG_TABLE
```

The constructor and destructor for this class should look familiar by now. The constructor simply associates the instance with the message and command tables, while the destructor frees up the dynamic memory allocated by the child window objects when the instance was created.

```
//-------------
// Constructor \
//---------------------------------------------------------------------------
//
// Description:
//     This constructor assigns the message and command tables for this class.
//
C_WINDOW_GROUP::C_WINDOW_GROUP( void ) : C_WINDOW_STD( xtMsgGroup )
{
   // Enable the required handlers for this window
   CommandTable( xtCommandGroup );
}
```

```
//-------------
// Destructor \
//------------------------------------------------------------------------
//
// Description:
//     This destructor disposes of the memory used by the child
//     window classes.
//
C_WINDOW_GROUP::~C_WINDOW_GROUP( void )
{
   pxcLog->Write( "GROUP:Destructor:Start" );

   // Free up the child windows
   delete pxcTBar;
   delete pxcStatus;
   delete pxcCont;

   pxcLog->Write( "GROUP:Destructor:End" );
}
```

The MsgCreate() message handler retrieves any saved window size and position information for the group windows, as well as the previous window colors and font. It uses this data to restore the window to the exact state it was in during the previous execution of the program.

```
//-----------
// MsgCreate \
//------------------------------------------------------------------------
// Event:      WM_CREATE
// Cause:      Issued by OS when window is created
//
void *C_WINDOW_GROUP::MsgCreate( void *mp1, void *mp2 )
{
   char    szX[10];
   char    szY[10];
   char    szW[10];
   char    szL[10];
   char    szFont[80];
   char    szFontSize[10];
   char    szBColor[80];
   char    szFColor[80];

   // Create a status bar to display miscellaneous data
   pxcStatus = (C_STATUS *) new C_STATUS( this );

   // Create a toolbar control
   pxcTBar = (C_TOOLBAR_GRP *)new C_TOOLBAR_GRP( this, pxcStatus );
```

```
    // Create a new container to display group listing
    pxcCont = (C_CONTAINER_GRP *)new C_CONTAINER_GRP( this );

    // Load parameters out of the INI file
    C_INI_USER xcIni( "BookNews" );
    xcIni.Open();
    xcIni.Read( "GroupFont", szFont, "System Proportional", 80 );
    xcIni.Read( "GroupFontSize", szFontSize, "10", 10 );
    xcIni.Read( "GroupBColor", szBColor, "000,000,000", 80 );
    xcIni.Read( "GroupFColor", szFColor, "255,255,255", 80 );
    xcIni.Read( "GroupX", szX, "0", 10 );
    xcIni.Read( "GroupY", szY, "0", 10 );
    xcIni.Read( "GroupW", szW, "0", 10 );
    xcIni.Read( "GroupL", szL, "0", 10 );
    xcIni.Close();

    // Set the font in the window
    pxcCont->SetFont( szFont, atoi( szFontSize ) );

    // Set the window colors
    pxcCont->SetForegroundColor( atoi( &szFColor[0] ),
                            atoi( &szFColor[4] ), atoi( &szFColor[8] ) );
    pxcCont->SetBackgroundColor( atoi( &szBColor[0] ),
                            atoi( &szBColor[4] ), atoi( &szBColor[8] ) );

    if( atoi( szW ) != 0 && atoi( szL ) != 0 )
    {
        // Position and size the window
        SetSizePosition( atoi( szX ), atoi( szY ), atoi( szW ), atoi( szL ) );
    }

    // Make the window visible
    pxcCont->Focus();

    return (void *)TRUE;
}
```

By examining the code in the main window, we know that when a new instance of C_WINDOW_GROUP is created, the main window sends it a PM_POPULATE message. Processing of this message is managed by the MsgPopulate() method responsible for populating the group window with the list of available newsgroups.

Since loading a container control can be a very time-consuming task, MsgPopulate() begins executing a new thread to avoid blocking Presentation Manager.

```
//-------------
// MsgPopulate \
//----------------------------------------------------------------------------
// Event:      PM_POPULATE
// Cause:      Issued by OS during the initial creation of the groups window
//
// This method populates the container object within the group window. Since
// this is a time-consuming task, it will be done on a separate PM thread.
//
void *C_WINDOW_GROUP::MsgPopulate( void *mp1, void *mp2 )
{
   // Begin a thread to populate the group list
   xcPopulateThread.Create( PopulateGroupThread, 40000, this );

   return FALSE;
}
```

The PopulateGroupThread() function is executed on a separate thread to load the container information. This is the first time we have seen any interaction with the server, so I'll spend a bit more time on this code.

The first thing that the thread function does is to determine if the group file needs to be retrieved from the server. Since this list can contain in excess of 5000 groups for a typical server, it can take a significant amount of time to download. For this reason the list of available groups is maintained in the GROUPS.GRP. If this file does not exist, it must be downloaded from the server.

In the PopulateGroupThread() code you will see the following code:

```
// Get a network connection
iConnection = pxcMgr->Connect();
if( iConnection >= 0 )
{
    pxcMgr->Connection(iConnection)->List( "groups.grp" );
    pxcMgr->Disconnect( iConnection );
}
```

This code retrieves a free connection from the connection manager, and uses this connection to fetch a list of all available newsgroups from the server. This information is stored in the GROUPS.GRP file. The final step in the network task is to return the connection back to the connection manager by calling the Disconnect() method.

Once the GROUPS.GRP file exists, it is opened and each item is counted. This is done to improve the performance of the container load. Based on the item count, enough memory is allocated from the heap to store each container record.

Then the GROUPS.GRP file is reopened and each of the group strings is loaded into a container record, using the following code:

```
pRecord = (T_GRPRECORD *)pxcThis->Container()->Fill( pRecord, szString );
```

The code for the container load, and more specifically the Fill() method, will be described in more detail later in this chapter.

After each record has been populated, the records are inserted into the container window by placing a call to the Insert() method of the group container class.

```
// Perform the container insertion
pxcThis->Container()->Insert( 0, pFirstRecord, iCount );
```

Finally, the records are sorted and the container window is redrawn to show the list of available newsgroups.

```
    // Sort the records
    pxcThis->Container()->Sort( SortGroupByAlpha );
```

That is all there is to loading a container. It is not a very difficult concept to grasp as long as you remember that the container code within Presentation Manager is not very fast, so this code should always run on its own thread of execution. The listing for the PopulateGroupThread() function follows.

```
//----------------
// PopulateThread \
//--------------------------------------------------------------------------
//
// Description:
//     This thread loads the groups from the groups.grp file into the
//     container displayed by the group window. This is done on a separate
//     thread because it can be a very time-consuming task.
//
void _Optlink PopulateGroupThread( void *pvData )
{
   C_WINDOW_GROUP       *pxcThis;
   C_THREAD_PM          *pxcThread;
   char                 cChar;
   char                 szString[1024];
   FILE                 *hFile;
   int                  iCount;
   int                  iConnection;
   T_GRPRECORD          *pFirstRecord;
   T_GRPRECORD          *pRecord;

   // Get a point to the main window object
   pxcThread = (C_THREAD_PM *)pvData;
   pxcThis = (C_WINDOW_GROUP *)pxcThread->ThreadData();

   // Create a PM process for this thread
   pxcThread->InitializeThread();
```

```
// Look to see if the group file is here
if( access( "groups.grp", 0 ) != 0 )
{
    pxcThis->Status()->Text( "Loading groups from server..." );
    // Debug
    pxcLog->Write( "Loading groups from the server" );

    // Get a network connection
    iConnection = pxcMgr->Connect();

    // Debug
    pxcLog->Write( "Got connection:%d", iConnection );

    if( iConnection >= 0 )
    {
        pxcLog->Write( "Getting list" );
        pxcMgr->Connection(iConnection)->List( "groups.grp" );
        pxcLog->Write( "Disconnecting" );
        pxcMgr->Disconnect( iConnection );
    }
    pxcLog->Write( "Done loading groups from the server" );
}

// The first thing we need to do is determine the number of
// supported groups
pxcThis->Status()->Text( "Populating news groups..." );
iCount = 0;
hFile = fopen( "groups.grp", "r" );
if( hFile )
{
    while( !feof( hFile ) && fgets( szString, 1024, hFile ) )
    {
        // Get rid of any CR/LF
        if( strstr( szString, "\r" ) )
            *strstr( szString, "\r" ) = 0;
        if( strstr( szString, "\n" ) )
            *strstr( szString, "\n" ) = 0;

        // Get the support indicator character
        cChar = (char)toupper( szString[strlen( szString ) - 1] );

        // If this group is supported count it
        if( cChar != 'X' || ( cChar == 'X' &&
                              szString[strlen( szString ) - 2] != ' ' ) )
        {
            iCount++;
        }
    }
```

```
    fclose( hFile );
}

pxcLog->Write( "iCount =%d", iCount );

// Insert groups if there are any
if( iCount > 0 )
{
    // Allocate some container space, but keep track of where it starts
    pFirstRecord = (T_GRPRECORD *)pxcThis->Container()->Allocate(
                        sizeof( T_GRPRECORD ), (USHORT)(iCount+1) );
    pRecord = pFirstRecord;

    // Now insert each supported record into the container
    iCount = 0;
    hFile = fopen( "groups.grp", "r" );
    while( !feof( hFile ) && fgets( szString, 1024, hFile ) )
    {
        // Get rid of any CR/LF
        if( strstr( szString, "\r" ) )
            *strstr( szString, "\r" ) = 0;
        if( strstr( szString, "\n" ) )
            *strstr( szString, "\n" ) = 0;

        // Get the support indicator character
        cChar = (char)toupper( szString[strlen( szString ) - 1] );

        // If this group is supported count it
        if( cChar != 'X' || ( cChar == 'X' &&
                        szString[strlen( szString ) - 2] != ' ' ) )
        {
            if( strstr( szString, " " ) )
                *strstr( szString, " " ) = 0;

            // Insert this record
            if( strlen( szString ) )
            {
                pRecord = (T_GRPRECORD *)pxcThis->Container()->Fill(
                                        pRecord, szString );
                iCount++;
            }
        }
    }
    fclose( hFile );

    // Perform the container insertion
    pxcThis->Container()->Insert( 0, pFirstRecord, iCount );
```

```
        // Sort the records
        pxcThis->Container()->Sort( SortGroupByAlpha );

        // Tell the user how many groups there are in the list
        pxcThis->Status()->Text( "%d Groups loaded", iCount );
    }
    // Terminate the thread
    pxcThread->TerminateThread();
}
```

The last window message handler we will look at for C_WINDOW_GROUP is the MsgClose() method called by the window manager to close the group window. The code should be relatively obvious; the only thing I will mention is the presence of a line to send a message back to the news control panel window. This PM_GROUP_CLOSE message simply notifies the owner window that the groups window no longer exists.

```
//----------
// MsgClose \
//---------------------------------------------------------------------------
// Event:      WM_CLOSE
// Cause:      Issued by OS when window is closed
//
void *C_WINDOW_GROUP::MsgClose( void *mp1, void *mp2 )
{
    char    szString[80];
    int     iX;
    int     iY;
    int     iW;
    int     iL;
    BYTE    byR;
    BYTE    byG;
    BYTE    byB;

    // Get all the savable parameters
    GetSizePosition( &iX, &iY, &iW, &iL );

    // Save parameters into the INI file
    C_INI_USER xcIni( "BookNews" );
    xcIni.Open();

    // Save the window dimensions
    sprintf( szString, "%d", iX );
    xcIni.Write( "GroupX", szString );
    sprintf( szString, "%d", iY );
    xcIni.Write( "GroupY", szString );
    sprintf( szString, "%d", iW );
    xcIni.Write( "GroupW", szString );
```

```
    sprintf( szString, "%d", iL );
    xcIni.Write( "GroupL", szString );

    // Save the font
    pxcCont->GetFont( szString );
    if( strstr( szString, "." ) )
    {
        xcIni.Write( "GroupFont", strstr( szString, "." ) + 1 );
        *strstr( szString, "." ) = 0;
        xcIni.Write( "GroupFontSize", szString );
    }

    // Save the window foreground color
    pxcCont->GetForegroundColor( &byR, &byG, &byB );
    sprintf( szString, "%03d,%03d,%03d", byR, byG, byB );
    xcIni.Write( "GroupFColor", szString );

    // Save the window background color
    pxcCont->GetBackgroundColor( &byR, &byG, &byB );
    sprintf( szString, "%03d,%03d,%03d", byR, byG, byB );
    xcIni.Write( "GroupBColor", szString );
    xcIni.Close();

    // Kill any threads we own that are still running
    xcPopulateThread.Kill();

    // Commit suicide
    Destroy();

    // Tell the parent that the user told us to shut down. Our parent will
    // clean up our mess (i.e. call our destructor)
    pxcParent->PostMsg( PM_GROUP_CLOSE, 0, 0 );

    return FALSE;
}
```

The C_WINDOW_GROUP class supports two commands from the user. The first of these manages new subscriptions.

The user is free to select one or more groups from the available groups list and subscribe to them. When the Subscribe option is selected by the user, CmdSubscribe() uses the FirstSelected() method in the container class to determine if any groups have been chosen. For each selected group, this method sends a PM_GROUP_SUBSCRIBE message to the main news window, then deselects the item. CmdSubscribe() then uses the container method, NextSelected(), to find any additional group selections, and repeats the subscription process, if required.

```
//-------------
// CmdSubscribe \
//------------------------------------------------------------------------
// Event:       DM_SUBSCRIBE
// Cause:       User selects the subscribe option from the toolbar or menu
// Description:This method subscribes to all the currently highlighted
//              container items. It does this by sending a PM_SUBSCRIBE
//              message to its parent window (the news control panel).
//
void *C_WINDOW_GROUP::CmdSubscribe( void *mp1, void *mp2 )
{
   T_GRPRECORD *pRecord;

   // Get the first selected record in the list
   pRecord = (T_GRPRECORD *)pxcCont->FirstSelected();
   while( pRecord )
   {
       pxcLog->Write( "pRecord = %s", pRecord->szString );

       // Tell our parent that the user wants to subscribe to this group
       pxcParent->SendMsg( PM_GROUP_SUBSCRIBE, (void *)pRecord->szString, 0 );

       // Unselect as we go so the user knows something is happening
       pxcCont->SelectRecord( pRecord, FALSE );

       // Go to the next record
       pRecord = (T_GRPRECORD *)pxcCont->NextSelected( pRecord );
   }

   return FALSE;
}
```

The second command handler is responsible for refreshing the group list. CmdRefresh() removes any existing GROUPS.GRP file. Then, by issuing a PM_POPULATE message to the message manager for the instance, this method forces the list to be retrieved from the server.

```
//------------
// CmdRefresh \
//------------------------------------------------------------------------
// Event:       DM_REFRESH
// Cause:       User selects the refresh option from the toolbar or menu
// Description:This method removes the group file from the disk and forces
//              the news server to resend it.
//
void *C_WINDOW_GROUP::CmdRefresh( void *mp1, void *mp2 )
{
```

```
    // Force the groups file to go away
    DosForceDelete( "groups.grp" );

    // Say that we want to reload the groups from the server
    PostMsg( PM_POPULATE, 0, 0 );

    return FALSE;
}
```

Managing News Subscriptions

In this section, we will add the code for the subscription window to news. This window keeps track of what groups the user has an interest in, and displays the number of messages in each.

Since so much of the source code for the subscription window is similar to that found in the group window, we need only discuss a few key parts. However, the entire source for this window can be found on the companion disk.

The message table for the C_WINDOW_SUBSCRIPTION class is almost identical to that shown previously for C_WINDOW_GROUP.

```
//----------------------------------
// Subscription Window Message Table \
//------------------------------------------------------------------------
DECLARE_MSG_TABLE( xtMsgSubscription )
    DECLARE_MSG( PM_CREATE,          C_WINDOW_SUBSCRIPTION::MsgCreate )
    DECLARE_MSG( PM_PARENT,          C_WINDOW_SUBSCRIPTION::MsgParent )
    DECLARE_MSG( PM_POPULATE,        C_WINDOW_SUBSCRIPTION::MsgPopulate )
    DECLARE_MSG( PM_SUB_SUBSCRIBE,   C_WINDOW_SUBSCRIPTION::MsgSubSubscribe )
    DECLARE_MSG( WM_CLOSE,           C_WINDOW_SUBSCRIPTION::MsgClose )
    DECLARE_MSG( WM_SIZE,            C_WINDOW_SUBSCRIPTION::MsgSize )
    DECLARE_MSG( WM_CONTROL,         C_WINDOW_SUBSCRIPTION::MsgControl )
    DECLARE_MSG( WM_PAINT,           C_WINDOW_STD::MsgPaint )
END_MSG_TABLE
```

The command table for the class includes two entries. The function of both of these methods is described later in this section.

```
//----------------------------------
// Subscription Window Command Table \
//------------------------------------------------------------------------
DECLARE_COMMAND_TABLE( xtCommandSub )
    DECLARE_COMMAND( DM_SUB_UNSUBSCRIBE,
                             C_WINDOW_SUBSCRIPTION::CmdSubUnsubscribe )
    DECLARE_COMMAND( DM_SUB_READ,C_WINDOW_SUBSCRIPTION::CmdSubRead )
END_MSG_TABLE
```

The constructor and destructor for C_WINDOW_SUBSCRIBE are identical to those outlined for the groups window. The MsgPopulate() message handler is also similar, so I won't go into any further detail for it either, except to note that it loads the subscription window's container by starting the PopulateSubscriptionThread() function on a separate thread of execution.

PopulateSubscriptionThread() loads the contents of the GROUPS.SUB file into the container window, and does so in a manner similar to the technique used for loading the list of available groups. Once each record is loaded and displayed, this thread scans each group and, with the help of the server, populates the total number of articles stored in each newsgroup.

The code establishes a connection with the connection manager layer, and then issues a GROUP command to the server to fetch the total number of articles. This value is stored in the record for each group, and the container window is updated.

```
//---------------
// PopulateThread \
//---------------------------------------------------------------------------
//
// Description:
//     This thread function is used to populate the subscription window
//     container. It loads data from the subscription file, parses it, and
//     writes it to the container window.
//
void _Optlink PopulateSubscriptionThread( void *pvData )
{
   C_WINDOW_SUBSCRIPTION*pxcThis;
   C_THREAD_PM          *pxcThread;
   char                 szString[1024];
   FILE                 *hFile;
   int                  iConnection;
   int                  iCount;
   T_SUBRECORD          *pFirstRecord;
   T_SUBRECORD          *pRecord;
   ULONG                lFirst;
   ULONG                lLast;
   ULONG                lTotal;

   // Get a point to the main window object
   pxcThread = (C_THREAD_PM *)pvData;
   pxcThis = (C_WINDOW_SUBSCRIPTION *)pxcThread->ThreadData();

   // Create a PM process for this thread
   pxcThread->InitializeThread();

   // Remove any previous data because this could be an update
   pxcThis->Container()->RemoveAll();
```

```
// The first thing we need to do is determine the number of
// supported groups
iCount = 0;
hFile = fopen( "groups.sub", "rt" );
if( hFile )
{
    while( !feof( hFile ) && fgets( szString, 1024, hFile ) )
    {
        // Found a subscription
        iCount++;
    }
    fclose( hFile );
}

pxcLog->Write( "SUBS:iCount =%d", iCount );

// Insert groups if there are any
if( iCount > 0 )
{
    // Allocate some container space, but keep track of where it starts
    pFirstRecord = (T_SUBRECORD *)pxcThis->Container()->Allocate(
                        sizeof( T_SUBRECORD ), (USHORT)iCount );
    pRecord = pFirstRecord;

    // Now insert each supported record into the container
    hFile = fopen( "groups.sub", "rt" );
    while( !feof( hFile ) && fgets( szString, 1024, hFile ) )
    {
        // Get rid of any CR/LF
        if( strstr( szString, "\r" ) )
            *strstr( szString, "\r" ) = 0;
        if( strstr( szString, "\n" ) )
            *strstr( szString, "\n" ) = 0;

        // Insert this record
        pRecord = (T_SUBRECORD *)pxcThis->Container()->Fill(
                                        pRecord, szString );
    }
    fclose( hFile );

    // Perform the container insertion
    pxcThis->Container()->Insert( 0, pFirstRecord, iCount );

    // Redraw the container to show the subscriptions
    pxcThis->Container()->Redraw( 0 );

    // Get a network connection
    iConnection = pxcMgr->Connect();
```

```
    }
    else
    {
        // No records left, so clean up the file
        DosForceDelete( "groups.sub" );
    }

    // Terminate the thread
    pxcThread->TerminateThread();
}
```

C_WINDOW_SUBSCIPTION class is also responsible for adding newsgroups to the subscription list. As previously described, we know that the main window sends a PM_SUB_SUBSCRIBE message when a new group needs to be added to the list; the MsgSubSubscribe() manages this message.

The code first waits to ensure that the thread that populated the list is idle. It does this by invoking a call to WaitIndefinite(), a method in the C_SEM_EVENT class. This call points out a potential design and implementation problem.

Waiting for a semaphore is not the kind of thing you should normally do in a message handler. In this case, there should be no problem; however, depending on your design, the posting of the semaphore may well depend on the occurrence of some other Presentation Manager operation. This can result in deadlocking PM due to a violation of the 1⁄10 second rule. Take definite care when waiting for semaphores while executing on the main thread of a PM program.

```
//-----------------
// MsgSubSubscribe \
//-------------------------------------------------------------------------
// Event:      PM_SUB_SUBSCRIBE
// Cause:      Issued by parent window when a new subscription is sent;
//             mp1 contains a pointer to the group string being subscribed.
//
void *C_WINDOW_SUBSCRIPTION::MsgSubSubscribe( void *mp1, void *mp2 )
{
    char    *szGroup;
    FILE    *hFile;

    // Wait for any current subscription update to complete
    xcPopulateThread.WaitIndefinite();

    // Get the group that is being subscribed
    szGroup = (char *)mp1;
    pxcLog->Write( "PM_SUB_SUBSCRIBE:%s", szGroup );

    // Write the new group to the subscription file
    hFile = fopen( "groups.sub", "at" );
    if( hFile )
```

```
    {
        pxcLog->Write( "PM_SUB_SUBSCRIBE:Writing:%d",
        fprintf( hFile, "%s\n", szGroup ) );
        fclose( hFile );
    }

    // Repopulate the container
    PostMsg( PM_POPULATE, 0, 0 );

    return FALSE;
}
```

I previously described the UnsubscribeThread() function. This is activated by the CmdSubUnsubscribe() method when the user selects the "Unsubscribe" menu item or presses the toolbar button.

```
//-------------------
// CmdSubUnsubscribe \
//-------------------------------------------------------------------------------
// Event:       DM_SUB_UNSUBSCRIBE
// Cause:       User selects the Unsubscribe button or menu option
// Description: This method is called any time the user wants to unsubscribe
//              to newsgroup(s). The method finds each selected item and
//              removes it from the list.
void *C_WINDOW_SUBSCRIPTION::CmdSubUnsubscribe( void *mp1, void *mp2 )
{
    // Begin a thread to unsubscribe all selected items
    xcUnsubscribeThread.Create( UnsubscribeThread, 40000, this );

    return FALSE;
}
```

The second command implemented by the C_WINDOW_SUBSCRIPTION class is invoked when the user double-clicks the left mouse button while the mouse pointer is positioned over a group in the subscription list. Alternatively, the "Read" menu item or toolbar button may be selected to execute this code.

When CmdSubRead() is executed, it locates the first selected subscription groups and issues a PM_SUB_READ message to the main window. This subsequently displays a list of messages for this group in the message window. This will be the subject of the next section.

```
//------------
// CmdSubRead \
//-------------------------------------------------------------------------------
// Event:       DM_SUB_READ
// Cause:       User selects the Read button or menu option
// Description: This method is called any time the user wants to read the
```

```
//          message headers for a selected subscription. If more than
//          one subscription is selected when this command is invoked,
//          the first selected subscription is used and the remainder
//          are ignored.
void *C_WINDOW_SUBSCRIPTION::CmdSubRead( void *mp1, void *mp2 )
{
   T_SUBRECORD*pRecord;

   // Get the first selected group
   pRecord = (T_SUBRECORD *)pxcCont->FirstSelected();
   if( pRecord )
   {
      // Tell the parent to display the message list
      pxcParent->SendMsg( PM_SUB_READ, pRecord->szGroup, 0 );
   }

   return FALSE;
}
```

Displaying Message Lists

In this section, I will briefly describe the process involved in displaying lists of messages for newsgroups. These lists are displayed when a group is selected from the subscription window, and consist mainly of a message title and a message number that identifies the message.

The code to accomplish this window display is similar to what we have already seen for the group and subscription windows. Scan the following message table used to control the message window and you will see the commonality. The code is so similar to previous source code that you should have few problems understanding the program flow.

```
//-----------------------------
// Message Window Message Table \
//-----------------------------------------------------------------------
DECLARE_MSG_TABLE( xtMsgMessage )
   DECLARE_MSG( PM_CREATE,        C_WINDOW_MESSAGE::MsgCreate )
   DECLARE_MSG( PM_PARENT,        C_WINDOW_MESSAGE::MsgParent )
   DECLARE_MSG( PM_POPULATE,      C_WINDOW_MESSAGE::MsgPopulate )
   DECLARE_MSG( WM_CLOSE,         C_WINDOW_MESSAGE::MsgClose )
   DECLARE_MSG( WM_SIZE,          C_WINDOW_MESSAGE::MsgSize )
   DECLARE_MSG( WM_CONTROL,       C_WINDOW_MESSAGE::MsgControl )
   DECLARE_MSG( WM_PAINT,         C_WINDOW_STD::MsgPaint )
END_MSG_TABLE
```

```
//------------------------------
// Message Window Command Table \
//-------------------------------------------------------------------------------
DECLARE_COMMAND_TABLE( xtCommandMsg )
   DECLARE_COMMAND( DM_MSG_READ,C_WINDOW_MESSAGE::CmdMsgRead )
END_MSG_TABLE
```

There are some key features of the message list window that I will describe, however. These features include loading of messages from the server; since there are two different techniques for this, it is important to understand the variations.

We know, from the message diagram shown at the beginning of this chapter, that the main program window sends a PM_POPULATE to the message list window when the window is created. This invokes the MsgPopulate() method, which sets the window title to match the name of the subscription group and then creates a thread calling PopulateMessageThread() to load the message list container with information about the articles in the newsgroup.

```
//-------------
// MsgPopulate \
//-------------------------------------------------------------------------------
// Event:       PM_POPULATE
// Cause:       Issued by the main window whenever it wants us to display a
//              new message.
// Description:This method is invoked whenever the main window wants to
//              change the group for which this window is listing messages.
//              The mp1 parameter contains a string holding the name of the
//              new group.
//
void *C_WINDOW_MESSAGE::MsgPopulate( void *mp1, void *mp2 )
{
   char    szString[64];

   // Get the group name to populate
   strcpy( szGroup, (char *)mp1 );
   pxcLog->Write( "MESSAGE:MsgPopulate:%s", szGroup );

   // Set the window title to the first 56 characters of the group name
   // This is a limitation of OS/2
   memset( szString, 0, 64 );
   strncpy( szString, szGroup, 56 );
   SetTitle( szString );

   // Begin a thread to load the messages
   xcPopulateThread.Create( PopulateMessageThread, 40000, this );

   return FALSE;
}
```

The only other message processor I am going to mention in this chapter is the CmdMsgRead() command handler. It is called whenever the user selects an item from the message list indicating that the article is to be displayed for reading.

CmdMsgRead() simply starts a news thread, calling the LoadMessageThread() routine to load the requested message from the server and inform the main news window that it should display the article.

```
//------------
// CmdMsgRead \
//---------------------------------------------------------------------------
// Event:       DM_MSG_READ
// Cause:       User selects the Read button or menu option
// Description: This method is called any time the user wants to read the
//              article text for a specified message.
//              If more than one message is selected when this command is
//              invoked, the first selected subscription is used and the
//              remainder are ignored.
void *C_WINDOW_MESSAGE::CmdMsgRead( void *mp1, void *mp2 )
{
   T_MSGRECORD*pRecord;

   // Get the first selected group
   pxcLog->Write( "MESSAGE:CmdMsgRead:Start" );
   pRecord = (T_MSGRECORD *)pxcCont->FirstSelected();
   if( pRecord )
   {
      // Start a thread to load the article
      xcLoadThread.Create( LoadMessageThread, 40000, this );
   }
   pxcLog->Write( "MESSAGE:CmdMsgRead:End" );

   return FALSE;
}
```

The message window source code includes a thread to load the message list information from the server. PopulateMessageThread() performs similarly to the threads used to load the groups and subscriptions shown previously, but is required to implement some additional parsing to force the information into a format desirable for our client. As was described in the C_CONNECT_NEWS code, some servers support the XOVER command, which performs a quick load of the messages for a given group. Some servers, however, do not implement overview support, so a slower loading process must be used. We will look at both these loading techniques shortly.

The PopulateMessageThread() code attempts to load the overview by invoking the Overview() method for the current server connection. If the process fails to create an overview file, the code calls the SlowParse() procedure; otherwise, FastParse() is used. Once the list of messages from the server has been parsed, they are counted and inserted into the container.

```
//-----------------------
// PopulateMessageThread \
//---------------------------------------------------------------------------
//
// Description:
//     This thread function is used to populate the message window container.
//     It loads data from the message file, parses it, and writes it
//     to the container window.
//
void _Optlink PopulateMessageThread( void *pvData )
{
   char                  szString[1024];
   C_WINDOW_MESSAGE      *pxcThis;
   C_THREAD_PM           *pxcThread;
   FILE                  *hFile;
   int                   iCount;
   int                   iConnection;
   int                   iResult;
   T_MSGRECORD           *pRecord;
   T_MSGRECORD           *pFirstRecord;
   ULONG                 lStart;
   ULONG                 lLast;
   ULONG                 lTotal;

   // Get a point to the main window object
   pxcThread = (C_THREAD_PM *)pvData;
   pxcThis = (C_WINDOW_MESSAGE *)pxcThread->ThreadData();

   // Create a PM process for this thread
   pxcThread->InitializeThread();

   // Get a network connection
   iConnection = pxcMgr->Connect();
   if( iConnection >= 0 )
   {
       // Get the group information and article status
       iResult = pxcMgr->Connection(iConnection)->Group(
                               pxcThis->Group(), &lStart, &lLast, &lTotal );
       if( iResult >= 200 && iResult <= 300 )
       {
           pxcThis->Status()->Text( "Loading Overview..." );

           // Try to do an overview of the messages
           iResult = pxcMgr->Connection(iConnection)->Overview(
                                         lStart, lLast, "news.ovr" );
           if( iResult >= 200 && iResult < 300 )
           {
               // Overview supported, so do a quick parse
```

```
            iCount = pxcThis->FastParse();

            // Get rid of the overview file
            DosForceDelete( "news.ovr" );
        }
        else
        {
            // Overview not supported, so do the listing the slow way
            iCount = pxcThis->SlowParse( iConnection, lStart, lLast );
        }
    }

    // Free up the network connection
    pxcMgr->Disconnect( iConnection );

    // Remove any previous data because this could be an update
    pxcThis->Container()->RemoveAll();

    // Insert groups if there are any
    if( iCount > 0 )
    {
        // Allocate some container space, but keep track of where it starts
        pFirstRecord = (T_MSGRECORD *)pxcThis->Container()->Allocate(
                            sizeof( T_MSGRECORD ), (USHORT)iCount );
        pRecord = pFirstRecord;

        // Now insert each supported record into the container
        hFile = fopen( "news.msg", "r" );
        while( !feof( hFile ) && fgets( szString, 1024, hFile ) )
        {
            // Get rid of any CR/LF
            if( strstr( szString, "\r" ) )
                *strstr( szString, "\r" ) = 0;
            if( strstr( szString, "\n" ) )
                *strstr( szString, "\n" ) = 0;

            // Insert this record
            pRecord = (T_MSGRECORD *)pxcThis->Container()->Fill(
                                            pRecord, szString );
        }

        // Perform the container insertion
        pxcThis->Container()->Insert( 0, pFirstRecord, iCount );

        // Redraw the container to show the subscriptions
        pxcThis->Container()->Redraw( 0 );

        fclose( hFile );
```

```
            // Get rid of the message file
            DosForceDelete( "news.msg" );
        }
    }

    // Terminate the thread
    pxcThread->TerminateThread();
}
```

As mentioned earlier, the SlowParse() routine is called whenever the news client detects a server that does not support the XOVER server command. This code loops for each message that must be loaded, and issues a "HEAD" command to the server. Though the news protocol class C_CONNECT_NEWS implements a Head() method, it writes to a disk file; in order to improve performance somewhat, SlowParse() issues the "HEAD" command itself and reads the responses directly into memory.

Once the command has been issued from the server, each line of the header for the requested messages is returned from the server (even lines for which we have no need). SlowParse() extracts the information it needs by examining the beginning of each line. For example, if a line starts with "Subject:" then the code determines that this is the header line containing the subject text. The output below is an actual message header extracted from Usenet, which demonstrates some of the fields processed by the parser.

```
Path: stn.ns.ca!newsflash.concordia.ca!utcsri!utnut!isnews.csc.calpoly.edu!usenet
From: gutz@hookup.net (Steven Gutz)
Newsgroups: comp.os.os2.mail-news
Subject: NeoLogic Mail program ??
Date: 8 Sep 1995 20:51:07 GMT
Organization: NeoLogic Inc.
Lines: 17
Message-ID: <42qabr$73t@hookup.net>
NNTP-Posting-Host: mailer.hookup.net
X-Newsreader: NeoLogic News for OS/2 [version: 4.3]
```

After each field is parsed, a new line is written to the message list file containing all the information displayed by the message list window. Then SlowParse() fetches the next message header, and the process repeats.

It is not very difficult to see why this routine is call "SlowParse." The software must read in all sorts of useless information that needs to be parsed, and large portions of it are simply discarded. Still, until only a few years ago when some inventive person devised a fast method (XOVER), this is how every news reader retrieved message information from the server.

```
//-----------
// SlowParse \
//---------------------------------------------------------------------------
//
// Description:
//     This method is used to load message information from servers that
//     do not support the XOVER command. It loads the header for each message
//     using the HEAD command and parses the information into a format that
//     is acceptable to news.
//
// Parameters:
//     iConnection      - News connection to use for acquire
//     lFirst           - First message number in the range
//     lLast            - Last message number in the range
//
// Returns:
//     int              - The number of messages found in the specified range.
//
int C_WINDOW_MESSAGE::SlowParse( int iConnection, ULONG lFirst, ULONG lLast )
{
  char    szHeader[4096];
  char    szAuthor[256];
  char    szSubject[256];
  char    szLines[256];
  FILE    *hFile;
  int     iCount;
  ULONG   lCtr;

  iCount = 0;
  hFile = fopen( "news.msg", "wt" );
  if( hFile )
  {
      // go to the first article
      lCtr = lFirst;
      while( lCtr <= lLast )
      {
          // Tell the user what's going on with the loading process
          pxcStatus->Text( "Loading %ld of %ld", lCtr - lFirst + 1,
                                                   lLast - lFirst + 1 );

          // Get the header for the new article and return the result
          sprintf( szHeader, "head %ld\r\n", lCtr );
          pxcMgr->Connection(iConnection)->Send( szHeader );
          pxcMgr->Connection(iConnection)->Receive( szHeader );
          if( atoi( szHeader ) >= 200 && atoi( szHeader ) < 300 )
          {
              // Skip the path string
              pxcMgr->Connection(iConnection)->Receive( szHeader );
```

```
            // Initial data areas
            memset( szAuthor, 0, 256 );
            memset( szSubject, 0, 256 );
            memset( szLines, 0, 256 );

            while( strcmp( szHeader, "." ) != 0 )
            {
                // Parse Lines
                if( strncmp( szHeader, "Lines:", 6 ) == 0 )
                {
                    strncpy( szLines, szHeader + 7, 256 );
                    if( strstr( szLines, "\r" ) )
                        *strstr( szLines, "\r" ) = 0;
                }
                if( strncmp( szHeader, "From:", 5 ) == 0 )
                {
                    strncpy( szAuthor, szHeader + 6, 256 );
                    if( strstr( szAuthor, "\r" ) )
                        *strstr( szAuthor, "\r" ) = 0;
                }
                if( strncmp( szHeader, "Subject:", 8 ) == 0 )
                {
                    strncpy( szSubject, szHeader + 9, 256 );
                    if( strstr( szSubject, "\r" ) )
                        *strstr( szSubject, "\r" ) = 0;
                }

                pxcMgr->Connection(iConnection)->Receive( szHeader );
            }

            // Write this to the file and increment the message count
            sprintf( szHeader, "%ld\t%s\t%s\t%s",
                                lCtr, szLines, szAuthor, szSubject );
            fprintf( hFile, "%s\n", szHeader );
            iCount++;
        }

        // Go to the next message
        lCtr++;
    }
    fclose( hFile );
  }

  return iCount;
}
```

Of course, most servers do implement the XOVER command now, and it offers vast improvement over the previous technique. The news client can retrieve information from the server without needing to perform significant parsing, and none of the information retrieved is generally thrown away (though the limited news reader here does discard some data).

The FastParse() routine extracts its information from the overview file, which has been fetched from the news server using the Over() method in the C_CONNECT_NEWS class. This data has a known format, which was described in Chapter 7, and field information can be extracted in a known order.

Once extracted, data is written to a message list file in a format which the message window container recognizes.

```
//-----------
// FastParse \
//-------------------------------------------------------------------------
//
// Description:
//     This method is used to load message information from servers that
//     do support the XOVER command. It loads the headers in overview format
//     and parses the information into a format acceptable to news.
//
// Parameters:
//     none
//
// Returns:
//     int              - The number of messages found in the overview file.
//
int C_WINDOW_MESSAGE::FastParse( void )
{
   char    szString[2048];
   char    szHeader[4096];
   char    szAuthor[256];
   char    szSubject[256];
   char    szLines[256];
   char    *szPtr;
   FILE    *hFile;
   FILE    *hInFile;
   int     iCount;
   ULONG   lCtr;

   iCount = 0;
   hInFile = fopen( "news.ovr", "rt" );
   if( hInFile )
   {
       hFile = fopen( "news.msg", "wt" );
       if( hFile )
       {
           while( !feof( hInFile ) && fgets( szString, 2048, hInFile ) )
           {
```

```
// Get rid of any CR/LF
if( strstr( szString, "\r" ) )
    *strstr( szString, "\r" ) = 0;
if( strstr( szString, "\n" ) )
    *strstr( szString, "\n" ) = 0;

// Make sure every field has a value, even if it is blank
while( strstr( szString, "\t\t" ) )
{
    // Pad empty fields in the overview line with a space char
    szPtr = strstr( szString, "\t\t" ) + 1;
    memmove( szPtr + 1, szPtr, strlen( szPtr ) + 1 );
    *szPtr = ' ';
}

// Initial data areas
memset( szAuthor, 0, 256 );
memset( szSubject, 0, 256 );
memset( szLines, 0, 256 );

// Get next message number from overview file
szPtr = strtok( szString, "\t" );
if( szPtr )
    lCtr = atol( szPtr );

// Get the subject text
szPtr = strtok( NULL, "\t" );
if( szPtr )
{
    strncpy( szSubject, szPtr, 256 );
    if( strstr( szSubject, "\t" ) )
        *strstr( szSubject, "\t" ) = 0;
}

// Get the author text
szPtr = strtok( NULL, "\t" );
if( szPtr )
{
    strncpy( szAuthor, szPtr, 256 );
    if( strstr( szAuthor, "\t" ) )
        *strstr( szAuthor, "\t" ) = 0;
}

// Skip the date,Message-ID and Reference
szPtr = strtok( NULL, "\t" );
szPtr = strtok( NULL, "\t" );
szPtr = strtok( NULL, "\t" );
szPtr = strtok( NULL, "\t" );
```

```
                // Get the Line text
                szPtr = strtok( NULL, "\t" );
                if( szPtr )
                {
                    strncpy( szLines, szPtr, 256 );
                    if( strstr( szLines, "\t" ) )
                        *strstr( szLines, "\t" ) = 0;
                }

                // Write this to the file and increment the message count
                sprintf( szHeader, "%ld\t%s\t%s\t%s",
                            lCtr, szLines, szAuthor, szSubject );
                fprintf( hFile, "%s\n", szHeader );

                // Count the number of items written to the output file
                iCount++;
            }

            // Close the output file
            fclose( hFile );
        }

        // Close the overview file
        fclose( hInFile );
    }

    // Return the number of messages in the overview
    return iCount;
}
```

The second thread of execution in the message window is responsible for loading complete article text from the server. When the user determines that an article should be viewed, the desired message can be selected from the list. This initiates the LoadMessageThread(), which acquires a server connection from the connection manager and uses the C_CONNECT_NEWS::Article() member function to fetch the article into the ARTICLE.TXT file.

Once the article has been successfully loaded, LoadMessageThread() sends a PM_MSG_READ message back to the main window to tell the program that the article needs to be displayed.

```
//-------------------
// LoadMessageThread \
//----------------------------------------------------------------------------
//
// Description:
//     This thread function is used to load the text for a message into a
```

```
//     disk file on the local system. Once loaded, the code sends a message
//     back to message to display the article in an article window.
//
void _Optlink LoadMessageThread( void *pvData )
{
   C_WINDOW_MESSAGE        *pxcThis;
   C_THREAD_PM             *pxcThread;
   int                     iConnection;
   int                     iResult;
   T_MSGRECORD             *pRecord;
   ULONG                   lStart;
   ULONG                   lLast;
   ULONG                   lTotal;

   // Get a point to the main window object
   pxcThread = (C_THREAD_PM *)pvData;
   pxcThis = (C_WINDOW_MESSAGE *)pxcThread->ThreadData();

   // Create a PM process for this thread
   pxcThread->InitializeThread();

   // Find out which record is selected
   pRecord = (T_MSGRECORD *)pxcThis->Container()->FirstSelected();

   // Get a network connection
   iConnection = pxcMgr->Connect();
   if( iConnection >= 0 )
   {
       // Get the group information and article status
       iResult = pxcMgr->Connection(iConnection)->Group(
                           pxcThis->Group(), &lStart, &lLast, &lTotal );
       if( iResult >= 200 && iResult <= 300 )
       {
           pxcThis->Status()->Text( "Loading Article..." );

           // Try to load the article
           iResult = pxcMgr->Connection(iConnection)->Article(
                           atol( pRecord->szNumber ), "article.txt" );
           if( iResult >= 200 && iResult < 300 )
           {
               // Tell the parent to create an article window for this.
               pxcThis->Parent()->SendMsg( PM_MSG_READ,
                                   (void *)"article.txt", 0 );
           }
       }

       // Free up the network connection
       pxcMgr->Disconnect( iConnection );
   }
```

```
    // Terminate the thread
    pxcThread->TerminateThread();
}
```

As with the code shown in the previous sections, we need not review much of this code as it is similar to what has already been described. The complete source for the message window is included in the companion disk.

Viewing Articles

In this section, I will describe how article text is displayed so the user can read it. However, I am going to show you only two routines from the article code.

We have already seen most of the article code in other places. The article window uses a multiline edit control to display information, and the code for this is remarkably like that we have seen for the Enhanced System Editor in Chapter 8. In fact, the editor actually implements far more capabilities than the article window does, and you may want to transfer some of that code into this source if you are planning to enhance news. For example, the news article window does not implement clipboard operations for copying and pasting text, nor does it offer any way of saving articles to a permanent disk file.

The editor, however, implements all of this and more, and you should be able to transfer those features to the article window with some simple cut-and-paste. I wanted to keep the viewer as simple as possible, so I deliberately left out these features.

When the user selects an item from the message list window, the main news window creates a new instance of an article window and issues a PM_POPULATE message to the new window. This executes the MsgPopulate() method in the article code, which simply starts a new thread to load the possibly large message into the article viewer's multiline edit control.

```
//-------------
// MsgPopulate \
//------------------------------------------------------------------------
// Event:      PM_POPULATE
// Cause:      Issued by OS during the initial creation of the group window
//
//  This method populates the container object within the group window. Since
//  this is a time-consuming task, it will be done on a separate PM thread.
//
void *C_WINDOW_ARTICLE::MsgPopulate( void *mp1, void *mp2 )
{
    // Get the filename we're supposed to load
    strcpy( szArticle, (char *)mp1 );

    // Begin a thread to load the article text
```

```
   xcPopulateThread.Create( PopulateArticleThread, 40000, this );

   return FALSE;
}
```

The PopulateThread() thread function loads text from the ARTICLE.TXT file into the MLE. This is almost exactly the same as the code used in the Enhanced System Editor in Chapter 8.

```
//----------------
// PopulateThread \
//----------------------------------------------------------------------------
//
// Description:
//      This thread function loads the article window's MLE control with the
//      text from the message file.
//
void _Optlink PopulateArticleThread( void *pvData )
{
   C_WINDOW_ARTICLE     *pxcThis;
   C_THREAD_PM          *pxcThread;

   // Get a point to the main window object
   pxcThread = (C_THREAD_PM *)pvData;
   pxcThis = (C_WINDOW_ARTICLE *)pxcThread->ThreadData();

   // Create a PM process for this thread
   pxcThread->InitializeThread();

   // Load the multiline editor with the article file
   pxcThis->MLE()->Load( pxcThis->Status(), pxcThis->Article() );

   // Terminate the thread
   pxcThread->TerminateThread();
}
```

What's Missing?

This news reader application is naturally limited in features and scope. In this section, I will quickly overview some of the missing components; in many cases, I will outline some possible solutions to fill these voids. The point of this exercise is to give you enough knowledge of the weaknesses of this program so that you can extend it to meet your own specific needs. If you are looking for features to add, an excellent place to look is in other news reader applications. Do not limit your search to OS/2 readers—there are many excellent readers available on the Windows and UNIX platforms that offer comprehensive feature sets.

The first and most obvious limitation of this client is the lack of posting capability. The current news application is limited to reading news articles only. Virtually all commercial and shareware news readers allow the creation of articles, which are submitted to Usenet via the news server.

Many of the newsgroups supported on Usenet carry binary files encrypted in ASCII text form. This encryption is normally achieved through the use of a uuencode program. Many news readers supply the capability of reversing the encoding process to extract the binary information, allowing users to store this information on their own systems. An easy solution to allow support for binary files is to load the articles and then transparently start a uudecode program. There are many flavors of uudecode available as freeware or shareware, any of which will suit the task.

One final notable omission from news and other applications in this book is the capability of printing information to an output device, such as an ink jet or laser printer. I will not be discussing printing capability because it is beyond the scope of this book; however, there are several excellent sources of information regarding printing. One particularly useful source are the sample programs available in the OS/2 Programmer's Toolkit. One of these programs describes, in detail, the selection of print queues and page formatting. A more advanced news reader application should permit the user to print articles in a paged output format. Without this capability, the program becomes almost useless.

There are, of course, many other limitations to the news reader presented here, but I will leave it as an exercise for you to determine what features you deem important. The object-oriented approach used in the current implementation should permit significant enhancement without the existing code hindering your planned extensions.

Dealing with Code Inefficiency

Many times throughout this chapter I noted that I was omitting parts of the source because they were similar to code found in some other class. If you are a real object-oriented programming guru, then you have to be asking some questions about the efficiency of this. Duplication of code is not supposed to occur when building C++ applications. So I thought it prudent to take some time to justify this extra code, and to offer up a possible alternative object hierarchy to eliminate all this extra code.

I implemented a lot of identical code in each object in order to keep the number of objects to a minimum. By expanding on the number of classes, it is possible to simplify the coding; however, it does tend to complicate the design. I did not want to confuse new C++ programmers reading this book with a lot of very tight objects.

However, there is one possible solution to help eliminate as much as 40% of the code in the new application, simply by adding some additional objects. If you look at each of the window objects present in this chapter, you will note that all of them implement certain functions. So why not create an intermediate class that implements this common code once, and derive the window classes from it?

The C_WINDOW_NEWS class is derived from C_WINDOW_STD in the PMCLASS library. The new class contains all the code that has been duplicated in each of the existing classes—for example, the MsgParent() method, or the code used to read and write state information to the INI file. Much of the existing code can be pushed up into this new class and eliminated from the classes we have already seen.

Adding this one simple class can reduce the size of the code significantly; though the value of this is questionable in such a small application, if you plan to expand on this program, you may want to consider implementing this additional class as well as any other classes that either reduce the complexity of the design or the code itself. If you are building commercial applications, fewer lines equate directly with few bugs. Maintenance is a very real cost that must be factored into any commercial design, and if you can increase the code efficiency by even a few lines, maintainability will improve.

Chapter Summary

In this chapter, we have built a limited but functional NNTP news reader. Though it is not nearly as complete as a typical user would require, it can very quickly access news articles from any of the newsgroups supported by a given server.

Of course, many other features are required to make this a more usable application. For example, the program does not support posting new articles or replying to existing articles, but the C_CONNECT_NEWS class in the NETCLASS library does support these capabilities, so adding a posting feature should not be very difficult. With a little work, the application presented in this chapter can be extended to something functional enough for typical users. The purpose of this limited news reader is to demonstrate how to interface an advanced Presentation Manager application to TCP/IP and the Internet. To that end, the program should be functional enough to show you how to build a more advanced networking application.

In this chapter

- ✓ Implementing a limited FTP application
- ✓ Adding main window controls
- ✓ Suggested FTP enhancements

11

A Basic FTP Client

Goals for the FTP Client Application

Without a doubt, FTP is one of the most popular TCP/IP applications, rivaled only recently by Web browsers. FTP permits file transfer from one system to another at relatively high speeds, and is a great way to distribute shareware and freeware applications around the world. Anyone who owns OS/2 Warp V3.0 already owns a copy of two useful FTP applications, one for text mode use and one for Presentation Manager. There are a number of shareware and commercial FTP applications available which, for the most part, are great improvements over the programs shipped with Warp.

In this chapter, we will develop our own limited, but usable, FTP application that implements most of the commands described by RFC 959. The goal is to create an application that will help you to understand how FTP clients work, and allow you to modify the application to suit your own needs. If you are familiar with the command line FTP program, you will know about commands like DEL, CD, or GET. These commands are not defined by the RFC; rather they have been implemented as part of a command parser within the many FTP applications.

The FTP application presented here does not provide a parser to interpret standard client commands. Instead, its command set is that specified by the RFC, with only one or two additions. This client uses commands like DELE, CWD, and RETR rather than those from the typical FTP client command set; you can refer to RFC 959 for details on the commands and their syntax. Furthermore, a typical FTP application automatically prompts the user for a user name and password, while the FTP client in this chapter does not. The user must consciously enter a USER command, followed by a PASS command, after a connection has been established.

These limitations notwithstanding, the application presented in this chapter is powerful enough to do almost anything that the command FTP can do, with the exception of passive mode FTP. It can transfer files between the client and a specified host, and it can perform basic directory manipulation. It also does this within a Presentation Manager interface, which adds a certain flavor to the program not found in the text-mode FTP client. For example, since the whole session is written to a multiline edit control, the user can scroll back to the beginning of the FTP session if it is necessary to refer to a previous command response.

Figure 11-1 illustrates a sample session from the FTP client developed in this chapter. The large multiline editor window contains the session display, showing the commands from the user and the responses from the server. At the bottom of the application window is an edit line where FTP commands are entered and a button used to send the commands to the server. The application also implements a toolbar, but I have not provided code for the lone button it contains. It is my hope that you will extend this application to suit your own needs. For example, you may want to add a toolbar button to set a new server address or to toggle the transfer mode between ASCII and binary.

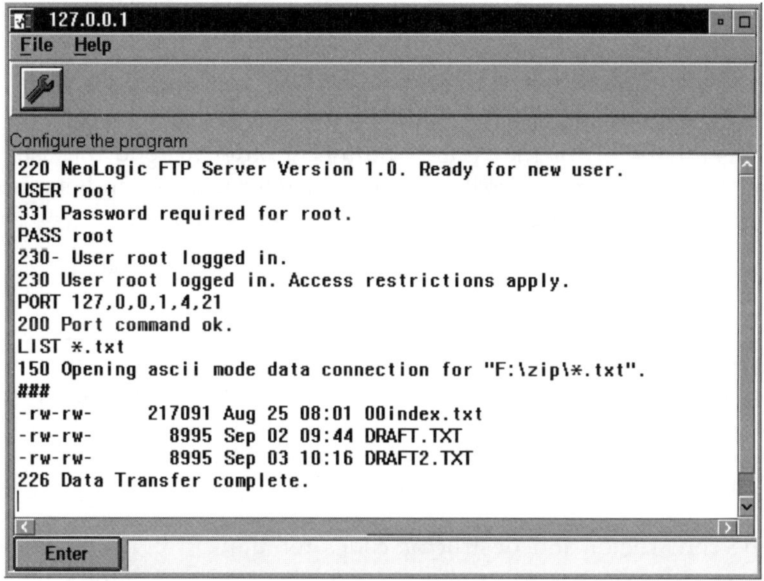

Figure 11-1 FTP sample program output

Coding the FTP Client

We've examined almost all the code in this application in the other programs in this book in one form or another. The complicated parts of this program are contained in the FTP network interface, shown in Chapter 7. For the most part, this application is the "glue" code to stick several objects together.

All of the FTP code is contained in a single file; if you study the FTP.CPP file you will see that this code is quite short. Compare this to the source for the text-mode FTP, which can be obtained from many sources on the Internet, and you will notice that the code in this chapter is much more straightforward.

Looking at the message table for the C_WINDOW_MAIN class, you will see only six message handlers; of these, only PM_CONNECT is new. The other handlers are similar to those implemented in the news and Ping applications.

```
//--------------------------
// Main Window Message Table \
//---------------------------------------------------------------------------
DECLARE_MSG_TABLE( xtMsgMain )
   DECLARE_MSG( PM_CREATE,                   C_WINDOW_MAIN::MsgCreate )
   DECLARE_MSG( WM_CLOSE,                    C_WINDOW_MAIN::MsgClose )
   DECLARE_MSG( WM_SIZE,                     C_WINDOW_MAIN::MsgSize )
   DECLARE_MSG( WM_CONTROL,                  C_WINDOW_MAIN::MsgControl )
   DECLARE_MSG( PM_CONNECT,                  C_WINDOW_MAIN::MsgConnect )
   DECLARE_MSG( WM_PAINT,                    C_WINDOW_STD::MsgPaint )
END_MSG_TABLE
```

The command table for the main FTP window object is also fairly simple. It implements a handler for the "Enter" button in order to send the user entered command to the server. The exit and product information handlers are almost duplicates of those used in the Ping application from Chapter 8.

```
//--------------------------
// Main Window Command Table \
//---------------------------------------------------------------------------
DECLARE_COMMAND_TABLE( xtCommandMain )
   DECLARE_COMMAND( ID_ENTERBUTTON,          C_WINDOW_MAIN::CmdCommand )
   DECLARE_COMMAND( DM_EXIT,                 C_WINDOW_MAIN::CmdExit )
   DECLARE_COMMAND( DM_INFO,                 C_WINDOW_MAIN::CmdHelpInfo )
END_MSG_TABLE
```

The constructor and destructor codes for the C_WINDOW_MAIN class should be familiar, since they are almost complete duplicates of the same methods in the news application. The constructor initializes the child classes and the command and message tables. The destructor frees up the dynamic memory allocated by these objects when C_WINDOW_MAIN was created.

```
//-------------
// Constructor \
//-----------------------------------------------------------------------------
//
// Description:
//     This constructor initializes the main window class for the editor.
//     It zeroes the class attributes and sets up the command handler and
//     server address.
//
// Parameters:
//     szServer    - Address of the news server
//
C_WINDOW_MAIN::C_WINDOW_MAIN( void ) : C_WINDOW_STD( xtMsgMain )
{
   // Initialize all child objects
   pxcTBar = 0;
   pxcStatus = 0;
   pxcConsole = 0;
   pxcCommand = 0;

   // Enable the required command handler for this window
   CommandTable( xtCommandMain );

   // Set the server address
   strcpy( szServerAddress, "" );
}

//-------------
// Destructor \
//-----------------------------------------------------------------------------
//
// Description:
//     The destructor frees up all of the dynamically allocated objects
//     and attributes used by this instance.
//
C_WINDOW_MAIN::~C_WINDOW_MAIN( void )
{
   pxcLog->Write( "~C_WINDOW_MAIN:Start" );

   // Free up dynamic window space.
   delete pxcTBar;
   delete pxcStatus;
   delete pxcConsole;
   delete pxcCommand;
   delete pxcEnterButton;

   pxcLog->Write( "~C_WINDOW_MAIN:End" );
}
```

The main() routine for the FTP application registers the main window instance and configures it as a standard PM application window, including a title, a menu, and the normal buttons for minimizing and maximizing the window.

```
void main( int argc, char *argv[] )
{
   // Create a debugging log file
   pxcLog = (C_LOG *)new C_LOG( "ftp.log", 1 );
   pxcLog->Open();

   // Register the application window
   xcWindow.Register( "OS/2 FTP" );
   xcWindow.WCF_SizingBorder();
   xcWindow.WCF_SysMenu();
   xcWindow.WCF_TaskList();
   xcWindow.WCF_ShellPosition();
   xcWindow.WCF_MinButton();
   xcWindow.WCF_MaxButton();
   xcWindow.WCF_Icon();
   xcWindow.WCF_Menu();
   xcWindow.WCF_TitleBar();
   xcWindow.Create( ID_WINDOW, "OS/2 FTP" );

   // Set the news server
   xcWindow.SetServer( argv[1] );

   // Start the message loop
   xcApp.Run();

   // Close and free the debug log
   pxcLog->Write( "FTP:Closing Log" );
   pxcLog->Close();
   delete pxcLog;
}
```

The SetServer() method is called only from the main() routine; it sets the server address that was specified by the user on the command line at run time. SetServer() sets the szServerAddress attribute, and then sets the title of the application window to indicate the name of the server to which it is attached.

```
//-----------
// SetServer \
//-------------------------------------------------------------------------
//
// Description:
//     This method sets the news server specified by the user on the command
//     line when the application was started
//
```

```
// Parameters:
//     szServer         - Address of news server
//
void C_WINDOW_MAIN::SetServer( char *szServer )
{
   // Set the server address
   strcpy( szServerAddress, szServer );

   // Set the window title
   SetTitle( szServer );
}
```

The MsgCreate() is called with the PM_CREATE message, as it is for every other application in this book. This method creates the MLE, edit line, and "Enter" button controls, as well as the status line and toolbar windows. The final line of code in MsgCreate() starts a new thread of execution to establish a connection to the selected FTP server.

```
//-----------
// MsgCreate \
//--------------------------------------------------------------------------
// Event:       WM_CREATE
// Cause:       Issued by OS when window is created
// Description:This method gets called when the window is initially created.
//             It initializes all of the visual aspects of the class.
//
void *C_WINDOW_MAIN::MsgCreate( void *mp1, void *mp2 )
{
   char    szX[10];
   char    szY[10];
   char    szW[10];
   char    szL[10];
   char    szFont[80];
   char    szFontSize[10];
   char    szBColor[80];
   char    szFColor[80];

   // Create a status bar to display miscellaneous data
   pxcStatus = (C_STATUS *) new C_STATUS( this );

   // Create a toolbar control
   pxcTBar = (C_TOOLBAR_TOP *)new C_TOOLBAR_TOP( this, pxcStatus );

   // Create a multiline edit control for the console window
   pxcConsole = (C_MLE *)new C_MLE( this, ID_CONSOLE );
```

```
    // Create a command entry window
    pxcCommand = (C_EDIT *)new C_EDIT( this, ID_COMMAND );
    pxcCommand->SetText( "" );

    pxcEnterButton = (C_PUSHBUTTON *)new C_PUSHBUTTON( this,
                                        ID_ENTERBUTTON, 0, "Enter" );

    // Load parameters out of the INI file
    C_INI_USER xcIni( "BookFTP" );
    xcIni.Open();
    xcIni.Read( "MainX", szX, "0", 10 );
    xcIni.Read( "MainY", szY, "0", 10 );
    xcIni.Read( "MainW", szW, "100", 10 );
    xcIni.Read( "MainL", szL, "100", 10 );
    xcIni.Read( "ConsoleFont", szFont, "System Monospaced", 80 );
    xcIni.Read( "ConsoleFontSize", szFontSize, "10", 80 );
    xcIni.Read( "ConsoleBColor", szBColor, "000,000,000", 80 );
    xcIni.Read( "ConsoleFColor", szFColor, "255,255,255", 80 );
    xcIni.Close();

    // Set the font in the MLE
    pxcConsole->SetFont( szFont, atoi( szFontSize ) );

    // Set the MLE colors
    pxcConsole->SetForegroundColor( atoi( &szFColor[0] ),
                              atoi( &szFColor[4] ), atoi( &szFColor[8] ) );
    pxcConsole->SetBackgroundColor( atoi( &szBColor[0] ),
                              atoi( &szBColor[4] ), atoi( &szBColor[8] ) );

    // Make the window look like a control panel
    SetSizePosition( atoi( szX ), atoi( szY ), atoi( szW ), atoi( szL ) );

    // Make the window visible
    Show();

    // Prevent the user from entering commands until we're ready
    pxcEnterButton->Enable( FALSE );

    // Start a thread to connect to the server
    xcConnectThread.Create( ConnectThread, 40000, this );

    return FALSE;
}
```

Creating FTP Connections

The ConnectThread() creates an instance of a C_CONNECT_FTP object and opens the connection. Once the connection is established, the thread issues a PM_CONNECT message to the main window. Note that this code performs no error checking—if you are developing an application for a typical user then this is a very dangerous prospect, and you should avoid it. I didn't want to confound the connection code with a lot of error checking since I wanted to produce code that was as obvious as I could make it.

```
//---------------
// ConnectThread \
//---------------------------------------------------------------------------
//
// Description:
//     This thread function creates a connection to the news server. If
//     successful, it sends a PM_CONNECT message back to the main window class.
//
void _Optlink ConnectThread( void *pvData )
{
   C_WINDOW_MAIN   *pxcThis;
   C_THREAD_PM     *pxcThread;

   // Get a point to the main window object
   pxcThread = (C_THREAD_PM *)pvData;
   pxcThis = (C_WINDOW_MAIN *)pxcThread->ThreadData();

   // Create a PM process for this thread
   pxcThread->InitializeThread();

   pxcThis->Status()->Text( "Connecting to %s...", pxcThis->ServerAddress() );

   // Create a instance of an FTP connection
   pxcThis->pxcConnection = (C_CONNECT_FTP *)new C_CONNECT_FTP(
                pxcThis->ServerAddress(), D_FTP_PORT, pxcThis->Console() );

   // Open a connection to the server
   pxcThis->pxcConnection->Open();

   // Send a connect message to the main window
   pxcThis->PostMsg( PM_CONNECT, 0, 0 );

   // Terminate the thread
   pxcThread->TerminateThread();
}
```

The PM_CONNECT message invokes MsgConnect(). This method enables the "Enter" button, which is normally disabled during network processing. This prevents the user from entering a new FTP command while the current command is being processed.

```
//-----------
// MsgConnect \
//------------------------------------------------------------------------
// Event:      PM_CONNECT
// Cause:      Issued by the connection thread when a connect is completed
//
void *C_WINDOW_MAIN::MsgConnect( void *mp1, void *mp2 )
{
   // We are ready to accept commands so enable the "ENTER" button
   pxcEnterButton->Enable( TRUE );

   return FALSE;
}
```

Processing FTP Commands

When the user presses the "Enter" button, Presentation Manager generates a WM_COMMAND message containing the ID_ENTERBUTTON command, which in turn invokes the CmdCommand() method. CmdCommand() first disables the "Enter" button to prevent further commands being issued by the user. It then starts a new thread of execution to process the FTP command typed by the user.

```
//---------
// CmdCommand \
//------------------------------------------------------------------------
// Event:      ID_ENTERCOMMAND
// Cause:      User presses the ENTER button on the main window
//
void *C_WINDOW_MAIN::CmdCommand( void *mp1, void *mp2 )
{
   // Disable the button to prevent commands from being entered
   // during processing
   pxcEnterButton->Enable( FALSE );

   // Start a thread to connect to the server
   xcParseThread.Create( InterpretFTPCommand, 40000, this );

   return FALSE;
}
```

The InterpretFTPCommand() thread function extracts the user enter command line from the edit control in the main window. The routine breaks this text up into a command and an option string. The command is compared to each of the supported FTP commands and, when a match is found, the appropriate C_CONNECT_FTP method is started.

The current code uses a long series of "if" statements which are adequate for the demonstration purposes of this application; however, if you are building a complete FTP client, you may want to implement this as a lookup table instead. In this way, adding new command support would be as simple as adding a new line in the lookup table.

```
void _Optlink InterpretFTPCommand( void *pvData )
{
   char             szData[256];
   char             szCommand[256];
   char             szFTPCommand[256];
   char             *szOption;
   C_WINDOW_MAIN    *pxcThis;
   C_THREAD_PM      *pxcThread;

   // Get a point to the main window object
   pxcThread = (C_THREAD_PM *)pvData;
   pxcThis = (C_WINDOW_MAIN *)pxcThread->ThreadData();

   // Create a PM process for this thread
   pxcThread->InitializeThread();

   // Get the contents of the edit line
   pxcThis->Command()->GetText( szFTPCommand, 256 );

   // Extract the FTP command
   strcpy( szCommand, szFTPCommand );
   if( strstr( szCommand, " " ) )
       *strstr( szCommand, " " ) = 0;

   // Get the remainder of the command line (options)
   szOption = szFTPCommand + strlen( szCommand );
   while( isspace( *szOption ) )
       szOption++;

   // Process the FTP commands using RFC 959 style
   if( strcmpi( szCommand, "SYST" ) == 0 )
       pxcThis->pxcConnection->SYST();
   if( strcmpi( szCommand, "SITE" ) == 0 )
       pxcThis->pxcConnection->SITE( szOption );
```

```
    if( strcmpi( szCommand, "ACCT" ) == 0 )
        pxcThis->pxcConnection->ACCT( szOption );
    if( strcmpi( szCommand, "USER" ) == 0 )
        pxcThis->pxcConnection->USER( szOption );
    if( strcmpi( szCommand, "PASS" ) == 0 )
        pxcThis->pxcConnection->PASS( szOption );
    if( strcmpi( szCommand, "TYPE" ) == 0 )
        pxcThis->pxcConnection->TYPE( szOption );
    if( strcmpi( szCommand, "PWD" ) == 0 )
        pxcThis->pxcConnection->PWD( szData );
    if( strcmpi( szCommand, "CWD" ) == 0 )
        pxcThis->pxcConnection->CWD( szOption );
    if( strcmpi( szCommand, "RMD" ) == 0 )
        pxcThis->pxcConnection->RMD( szOption );
    if( strcmpi( szCommand, "MKD" ) == 0 )
        pxcThis->pxcConnection->MKD( szOption );
    if( strcmpi( szCommand, "DELE" ) == 0 )
        pxcThis->pxcConnection->DELE( szOption );
    if( strcmpi( szCommand, "DIR" ) == 0 )
        pxcThis->pxcConnection->DIR( szOption, "dir.txt" );
    if( strcmpi( szCommand, "RETR" ) == 0 )
        pxcThis->pxcConnection->RETR( szOption, szOption );
    if( strcmpi( szCommand, "STOR" ) == 0 )
        pxcThis->pxcConnection->STOR( szOption, szOption );
    if( strcmpi( szCommand, "QUIT" ) == 0 )
    {
        // Send the QUIT command
        pxcThis->pxcConnection->QUIT();

        // Close the data connection
        pxcThis->pxcConnection->Close();

        // Since the connection is now dead, close the application
        pxcThis->PostMsg( WM_CLOSE, 0, 0 );
    }

    // Re-enable the ENTER button so the user can give us another command
    pxcThis->EnterButton()->Enable( TRUE );

    // Reset the command buffer to a NULL
    pxcThis->Command()->SetText( "" );

    // Terminate the thread
    pxcThread->TerminateThread();
}
```

Closing the Application

The last code we will review is the MsgClose() method. This code stores any INI data changes and posts the WM_QUIT message to Presentation Manager to terminate the program.

```
//----------
// MsgClose \
//------------------------------------------------------------------------
// Event:      WM_CLOSE
// Cause:      Issued by OS when window is closed
//
void *C_WINDOW_MAIN::MsgClose( void *mp1, void *mp2 )
{
   char     szString[80];
   int      iX;
   int      iY;
   int      iW;
   int      iL;
   BYTE     byR;
   BYTE     byG;
   BYTE     byB;

   // Get all of the saveable parameters
   GetSizePosition( &iX, &iY, &iW, &iL );

   // Save parameters into the INI file
   C_INI_USER xcIni( "BookFTP" );
   xcIni.Open();
   sprintf( szString, "%d", iX );
   xcIni.Write( "MainX", szString );
   sprintf( szString, "%d", iY );
   xcIni.Write( "MainY", szString );
   sprintf( szString, "%d", iW );
   xcIni.Write( "MainW", szString );
   sprintf( szString, "%d", iL );
   xcIni.Write( "MainL", szString );

   // Save the font
   pxcConsole->GetFont( szString );
   if( strstr( szString, "." ) )
   {
      xcIni.Write( "ConsoleFont", strstr( szString, "." ) + 1 );
      *strstr( szString, "." ) = 0;
      xcIni.Write( "ConsoleFontSize", szString );
   }

   // Save the window foreground color
```

```
    pxcConsole->GetForegroundColor( &byR, &byG, &byB );
    sprintf( szString, "%03d,%03d,%03d", byR, byG, byB );
    xcIni.Write( "ConsoleFColor", szString );

    // Save the window background color
    pxcConsole->GetBackgroundColor( &byR, &byG, &byB );
    sprintf( szString, "%03d,%03d,%03d", byR, byG, byB );
    xcIni.Write( "ConsoleBColor", szString );

    xcIni.Close();

    // Debug
    pxcLog->Write( "FTP:WM_CLOSE:Start" );

    // Applcation was told to close so post a QUIT message to the OS
    PostMsg( WM_QUIT, 0, 0 );

    // Debug
    pxcLog->Write( "FTP:WM_CLOSE:End" );
    return FALSE;
}
```

Possible Enhancements

As stated earlier, the FTP code presented here is very short and to the point. As such there are many places where the program can be improved. The most obvious improvement would be to implement a command set in keeping with typical FTP clients. This should not be a large chore; the only possible difficulty you may run into is the login process.

Normal FTP clients automatically display the "Username:" and "Password:" prompts when connecting to a server. The logical procedure to accomplish this is to create dialog box resource that can be displayed as part of the connection process. This dialog could prompt the user to enter a user name and password, then generate the appropriate USER and PASS commands to the FTP remote host.

If you want to do more extensive modification, you could parse the directory listing retrieved from the remote host and display the items using a container control. This involves a great deal of work, since there are many different directory formats for which a parser would be required. This is the level of code I had to create for the initial NeoLogic FTP client; as I discovered, there are dozens of server variations to be taken into account. However, if you adopt a logical, object-oriented approach, you can reuse much of the parser code for various servers.

The possible extensions are almost limitless. How about an FTP "agent" that searches a selected list of servers and downloads any file containing a given string? This is a pretty specific application, but it's just one of the possible applications that can be written using a modified version of the FTP client code.

Chapter Summary

In this chapter, I have shown a functional FTP client for TCP/IP. Though there are many limitations to this application, it will connect to any FTP server on the Internet, and allow both binary and ASCII files to be transferred from one end of the connection to the other.

Although I have not shown all the source code for the FTP client, the entire source is contained on the companion disk, accompanied by the files required to build the code, using either the Borland or IBM compiler. I encourage you to modify this application to suit your own needs, since that is the aim of this book.

• • •

I would like to congratulate you on arriving here—we've covered a lot of material and code; I hope I have succeeded in sharing my knowledge so that you may enhance the source code and add the extensions and modifications you desire.

Where can this knowledge take you? Many developers today are well versed in PM programming, but lack the experience to build TCP/IP sockets. One of the most appealing applications for TCP/IP is gaming. With the explosion of the Internet, Multi-User Dungeons (MUDs), which permit two or more players to play the same game in real time, are becoming the wildly popular.

If you are a MUD developer, you will not find much direct help in this book, as MUDs tend to be very specific to the game for which they were developed. What you will find, however, is the C_CONNECT class, which eliminates a lot of the low-level networking code necessary for implementing a MUD. If you want to develop a MUD server, you will have to be able to listen for and accept connections from remote hosts. Though C_CONNECT does not implement these functions, C_CONNECT_FTP does, and you should be able to adapt these routines with little or no difficulty.

IBM is working on a product called the "Entertainment Developer's Toolkit" which began appearing in beta form on the OS/2 Developer Connection Volume 8. This package includes some network interfaces specifically aimed at network game developers. If you are developing a MUD, you may want to evaluate that package in lieu of using the network code developed in this book.

This book also presented a simple set of classes that wrap much of the more common PM APIs. Although many people have failed in accomplishing this feat, I hope I have given you some insight into how to do this. Though these classes are for the most part incomplete, I will continue to enhance them, and I would expect you to do the same. If there are features you need or classes that you absolutely must have and are unable to implement yourself, please contact me via e-mail at nstn4064@fox.nstn.ca and we can work together to improve the libraries.

My goal for writing this book was to make smart people smarter. I hope you will begin writing applications for Presentation Manager and more specifically for the Internet — the world needs more OS/2 applications, so do get going!

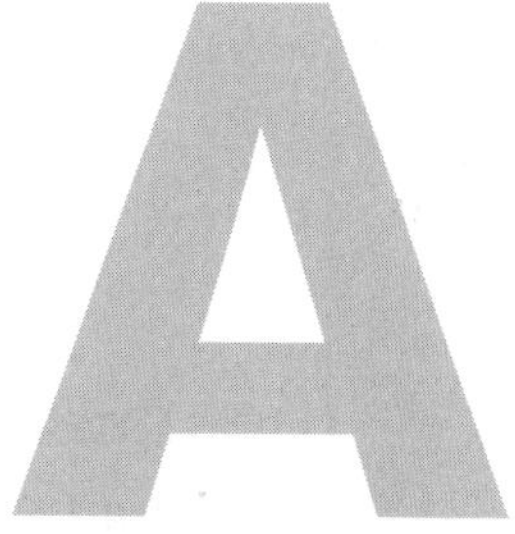

Nonvisual Class Library Reference

C_INI ini.hpp

The C_INI class is used for persistent storage. OS/2 provides a set of functions for reading and writing data to profiles or INI files. This class wraps the INI functionality into a portable set of methods.

Public Constructors and Destructors

- C_INI(char *szFile, char *szAppName);

  This constructor creates an instance of the C_INI class. It accepts a pointer to a filename that is the INI file to which profile data will be written and retrieved. The szAppName parameter points to a string containing the application name, which will be tagged onto the INI file. This string can contain any valid string.

Public Members and Attributes

- void Open(void);

  This method opens the INI file associated with the class instance.

- void Close(void);

  This method closes the INI file associated with the class instance.

- void Read(char *szField, char *szData, char *szDefault, int iLength);

  The Read() method accepts a field name from which data will be read. The szData parameter points to a buffer where the data will be written. The szDefault parameter points to a string representing the default value that will be placed in the szData buffer if the specified field is undefined; iLength is the maximum string length that will be inserted into szData.

- void Write(char *szField, char *szData);

  This method writes the string pointed to by szData to the specified field in the INI file.

C_INI_USER ini.hpp, iniuser.hpp

The C_INI_USER class is used for persistent storage specifically in the OS2.INI file. OS/2 supports this profile specifically for user application settings. This class is derived from C_INI.

Public Constructors and Destructors

- C_INI_USER(char *szAppName);

  This constructor creates an instance of the C_INI_USER class. The szAppName parameter points to a string containing the application name, which will be tagged into the OS2.INI file. This string can contain any valid string.

Public Members and Attributes

- void Open(void);

  This method opens the OS2.INI file associated with the class instance.

- void Close(void);

  This method closes the OS2.INI file associated with the class instance.

C_INI_SYSTEM ini.hpp, inisys.hpp

The C_INI_SYSTEM class is used for persistent storage specifically in the OS2SYS.INI file. OS/2 supports this profile specifically for system application settings; it should not be used by applications under normal circumstances. This class is derived from C_INI.

Public Constructors and Destructors

- C_INI_SYSTEM(char *szAppName);

  This constructor creates an instance of the C_INI_SYSTEM class. The szAppName parameter points to a string containing the application name which will be tagged into the OS2SYS.INI file. This string can contain any valid string.

Public Members and Attributes

- void Open(void);

  This method opens the OS2SYS.INI file associated with the class instance.

- void Close(void);

  This method closes the OS2SYS.INI file associated with the class instance.

C_THREAD **thread.hpp**

The C_THREAD class implements program threading in controlled way not normally supported by OS.2. The advantage of using the C_THREAD is portability. The NVCLASS library support two types of thread class. The C_THREAD class is used for normal non-PM threads or for PM threads that do not require interaction with the PM windowing system.

Public Constructors and Destructors

- C_THREAD(void);

  This constructor is used typically for creating an instance of the C_THREAD class without requiring the immediate creation of the thread itself. For instances constructed with this void constructor, the Create() method must be subsequently called to create the actual thread. This constructor creates a C_THREAD place holder only.

- C_THREAD(void (*ThreadFunction)(void *), unsigned int iStackSize, void *pvData);

  This constructor creates an instance of the C_THREAD class and immediately starts the supplied thread function. The iStackSize parameter is the size of the thread stack in bytes, and the pvData parameter contains an optional pointer to any data to be passed into the thread function.

Public Members and Attributes

- void *ThreadData(void);

  This method returns a pointer to the user defined data buffer initially passed into the thread function. This value can be casted to the appropriate data type.

- void Create(void (*ThreadFunction)(void *), unsigned int iStackSize, void *pvData);

  This method starts execution of the supplied thread function. The iStackSize parameter is the size of the thread stack in bytes, and the pvData parameter contains an optional pointer to any data to be passed into the thread function.

- void Kill(void);

  Kill() immediately terminates execution of the thread function.

- void WaitIndefinite(void);

  This method is used to flag execution of the thread. The process that created the thread can call this method to place itself in sleep mode until the thread terminates.

C_THREAD_PM **threadpm.hpp**

The C_THREAD_PM class implements program threading that is specific to Presentation Manager. This class will be used to create any thread which must send messages to windows in the application. The thread function of a PM thread class is distinguished by the creation of a message queue.

Public Constructors and Destructors

- C_THREAD_PM(void);

  This constructor is used typically for creating an instance of the C_THREAD_PM class without requiring the immediate creation of the thread itself. For instances constructed with this void constructor, the Create() method must be subsequently called to create the actual thread. This constructor creates a C_THREAD_PM place holder only.

- C_THREAD_PM(void (*ThreadFunction)(void *), unsigned int iStackSize, void *pvData);

  This construct creates an instance of the C_THREAD_PM class, and immediately starts the supplied thread function. The iStackSize parameter is the size of the thread stack in bytes, and the pvData parameter contains an optional pointer to any data to be passed into the thread function.

Public Members and Attributes

- void InitializeThread(void);

  This method must be called by the C_THREAD_PM thread function in order to create a message queue. This should appear as the first line of code within the thread function.

- void TerminateThread(void);

  This method must be called by the C_THREAD_PM thread function in order to destroy the thread function's message queue. This should appear as the last line of code within the thread function.

C_SEM_EVENT semev.hpp

The C_SEM_EVENT class wraps the event semaphore functionality supplied by OS/2 into a portable C++ class. This type of semaphore can be used to control the synchronization of events occurring within an application.

Public Constructors and Destructors

- C_SEM_EVENT(void);

  This constructor provides a default void construction mechanism. The method actually contains no code at all, and has been provided only to adhere to convention.

Public Members and Attributes

- void Create(void);

  This method creates and opens a new semaphore for use by the program. If the semaphore does not already exist within the operating system, then this method must be called.

- void Open(void);

  This method opens a previously defined semaphore for use by the program.

- void Close(void);

  This method closes a semaphore in use by the program.

- void Reset(ULONG *plPostCount);

  This method resets the semaphore flag, returning a count representing the number of times the semaphore has been posted since the last reset.

- void Post(void);

  This method posts the semaphore flag.

- void WaitIndefinite(void);

  This method places the current thread on "hold" until the semaphore flag gets posted. Use this with caution, since it is possible to "hang" your application in a situation where the current thread is waiting for a semaphore that can be posted only by code within the same thread.

B

PM Class Library Reference

C_APPLICATION **app.hpp**

The C_APPLICATION class is responsible for controlling the execution of a PMCLASS-based program. It contains all the methods required to start up and terminate applications, as well as containing code to return the values of system metrics and constants.

Public Constructors and Destructors

- C_APPLICATION(void);

  This constructor creates an instance of the C_APPLICATION class. It calls the operating system specific code to initialize the Presentation Manager display engine, and creates a message queue for the application.

- ~C_APPLICATION(void);

  This destructor destroys the application message queue, and shuts down the window manager before returning control to the operating system.

Public Members and Attributes

- void Run(void);

  This method starts the PM application message loop, allowing the application to begin executing.

- HAB AnchorBlock(void);

  This method returns a handle to the Presentation Manager specific handle to the application anchor block. This HAB does not play an active role in OS/2 programs, but has been provided to allow the implementation of "safe" applications.

- int DesktopHeight(void);

  The DesktopHeight() method returns the system constant containing the pixel height of the desktop window.

- int DesktopWidth(void);

  The DesktopWidth() method returns the system constant containing the pixel width of the desktop window.

- int MenuHeight(void);

  The MenuHeight() method returns the system constant containing the pixel height of the action menu bar used by all applications.

- int TitleBarHeight(void);

  The TitleBarHeight() method returns the system constant containing the pixel height of the caption (title bar) displayed by applications running on the desktop.

- int DialogBorderHeight(void);

  The DialogBorderHeight() method returns the system constant containing the pixel height (thickness) of thick borders used when displaying dialog boxes.

C_WINDOW **window.hpp**

The C_WINDOW class is the base for all other windows in the PMCLASS library. It contains all the code common to standard application, child, and dialog windows.

Public Constructors and Destructors

- C_WINDOW(void);

  This constructor initializes the window class attributes.

- C_WINDOW(T_MSG_TABLE *pxtMsg);

  This constructor initializes the window class attributes and assigns a message table for the window object.

- ~C_WINDOW(void);

  This destructor destroys the window object.

Public Members and Attributes

- HWND ParentWindow(void);

  This method returns a PM handle to the parent/owner window.

- void Window(HWND hNewWnd);

  This method sets a PM handle to the window. This is normally done as part of the construction process. Changing the PM window handle after the window has been created is not recommended.

- HWND Window(void);

  This method returns a PM handle to the window.

- void *SendMsg(ULONG lMsg, void *mp1, void *mp2);

  This method sends a message to the window.

- void PostMsg(ULONG lMsg, void *mp1, void *mp2);

  This method posts a message to the window.

- void SetText(char *szString);

  This method sets the text contents for the window. This message is commonly used to set the initial strings for edit controls.

- void GetText(char *szString);

  This method retrieves the text contents for the window.

- void Show(void);

  This method makes the window visible.

- void Hide(void);

  This method makes the window invisible.

- void Update(void);

  This method updates the window, forcing any pending paint messages to be processed.

- void ClassName(char *szClass);

  This method sets the name of the window class. This method should be called as part of the object construction process.

- char *ClassName(void);

  This method returns the name of the window class.

- void GetSizePosition(int *piX, int *piY, int *piCX, int *piCY);

  This method returns the values of the X,Y location of the window, as well as the width and height. These values are measured in pixels relative to the owner window.

- void GetSize(int *piCX, int *piCY);

  This method returns the values of the width and height of the window. These values are measured in pixels.

- void GetPosition(int *piX, int *piY);

  This method returns the values of the X,Y location of the window. These values are measured in pixels relative to the owner window.

- void SetForegroundColor(BYTE byRed, BYTE byGreen, BYTE byBlue);

  This method sets the foreground (text) color of the window.

- void SetBackgroundColor(BYTE byRed, BYTE byGreen, BYTE byBlue);

  This method sets the background color of the window.

- void SetFont(char *szFont, int iSize);

  This method sets the font and size of text within the window.

- void GetForegroundColor(BYTE *pbyRed, BYTE *pbyGreen, BYTE *pbyBlue);

  This method returns the foreground (text) color of the window.

- void GetBackgroundColor(BYTE *pbyRed, BYTE *pbyGreen, BYTE *pbyBlue);

  This method returns the background color of the window.

- void GetFont(char *szFont);

  This method returns the font of text within the window. The font is returned as a string with the format "size.font".

- void SetForegroundColor(BYTE byRed, BYTE byGreen, BYTE byBlue);

  This method sets the foreground (text) color of the window.

- void SetBackgroundColor(BYTE byRed, BYTE byGreen, BYTE byBlue);

  This method sets the background color of the window.

- void Invalidate(void);

  This method causes the window to generate a paint message to force a redraw.

- void Focus(void);

  This method forces the PM window focus to be set to the window object.

- void Register(char *szClass);

  This method registers a new window class with Presentation Manager.

- void Create(HWND hFrameWnd, HWD hWnd);

  This method associates the window object with the PM window, hWnd, and its owner, hFrameWnd.

- void Destroy(void);

  This method destroys the window.

- void MessageTable(T_MSG_TABLE *pxtMsg);

  This method associates the specified message table with the window object.

- void CommandTable(T_MSG_TABLE *pxtCommand);

  This method associates the specified command table with the window object.

C_WINDOW_STD window.hpp, winstd.hpp

The C_WINDOW_STD class is used to create application windows. These windows are owned by the Workplace Shell desktop.

Public Constructors and Destructors

- C_WINDOW_STD(void);
  This constructor initializes the window class attributes.
- C_WINDOW_STD(T_MSG_TABLE *pxtMsg);
  This constructor initializes the window class attributes and assigns a message table for the window object.

Public Members and Attributes

- void WCF_Standard(void);
  This method sets the standard windows attributes.
- void WCF_SysMenu(void);
  This method sets the system menu window attribute.
- void WCF_Menu(void);
  This method sets the menu window attribute to display an application menu to the window.
- void WCF_Icon(void);
  This method sets the icon window attribute to add an icon to the window object.
- void WCF_MinButton(void);
  This method sets the minimize button window attribute.
- void WCF_MaxButton(void);
  This method sets the maximize button window attribute.
- void WCF_TitleBar void);
  This method sets the title bar window attribute to add a caption to the top of the window.
- void WCF_Border(void);
  This method sets the thin border window attribute.
- void WCF_DialogBorder(void);
  This method sets the dialog border window attribute.
- void WCF_SizingBorder(void);
  This method sets the sizable border window attribute.

- void WCF_ShellPosition(void);

  This method sets the shell position window attribute, which causes the window to be automatically sized and positioned when it is first created.

- void WCF_TaskList(void);

  This method sets the task list window attribute, which forces the window caption to be added to the task list window.

- void GetSizePosition(int *piX, int *piY, int *piCX, int *piCY);

  This method returns the values of the X,Y location of the window, as well as the width and height. These values are measured in pixels relative to the desktop.

- void GetSize(int *piCX, int *piCY);

  This method returns the values of the width and height of the window. These values are measured in pixels.

- void GetPosition(int *piX, int *piY);

  This method returns the values of the X,Y location of the window. These values are measured in pixels relative to the desktop.

- void SetSizePosition(int iX, int iY, int iCX, int iCY);

  This method sets the values of the X,Y location of the window, as well as the width and height. These values are measured in pixels relative to the desktop.

- void SetSize(int iCX, int iCY);

  This method sets the values of the width and height of the window. These values are measured in pixels.

- void SetPosition(int iX, int iY);

  This method sets the values of the X,Y location of the window. These values are measured in pixels relative to the desktop.

- void SetTitle(char *szTitle);

  This method sets the window caption for the application window.

- void GetTitle(char *szTitle, int iLength);

  This method sets the window caption for the application window.

- void Create(int iID, char *szTitle);

  This method creates a new application window.

- void *MsgPaint(void *mp1, void *mp2);

  This method provides a generic window painter that can be used by any application derived from C_WINDOW_STD.

C_WINDOW_CHILD **window.hpp, winchild.hpp**

The C_WINDOW_CHILD class is used as the base for all child window classes. This includes such objects as list boxes, edit controls, and pushbuttons.

Public Constructors and Destructors

- C_WINDOW_CHILD(void);

  This constructor initializes the window class attributes.

- C_WINDOW_CHILD(T_MSG_TABLE *pxtMsg);

  This constructor initializes the window class attributes, and assigns a message table for the window object.

- C_WINDOW_CHILD(C_WINDOW *pxcParentObj, T_MSG_TABLE *pxtMsg);

  This constructor initializes the window class attributes, and assigns a message table for the window object. The pxcParentObj parameter specifies the owner window.

Public Members and Attributes

- void ParentObject(C_WINDOW *pxcParentObj);

  This method sets the owner window object of the window. This is normally performed as part of the construction process; use of this method after the window has been instantiated is not recommended.

- void Create(int iID, int iMode, char *szTitle, int iX, int iY, int iCX, int iCY);

  This method creates a new child control window.

- void Create(int iID, char *szTitle);

  This method creates a new application window.

- void SetSizePosition(int iX, int iY, int iCX, int iCY);

  This method sets the values of the X,Y location of the window, as well as the width and height. These values are measured in pixels relative to the owner window.

- void SetSize(int iCX, int iCY);

  This method sets the values of the width and height of the window. These values are measured in pixels.

- void SetPosition(int iX, int iY);

  This method sets the values of the X,Y location of the window. These values are measured in pixels relative to the owner window.

C_DIALOG window.hpp, dialog.hpp

The C_WINDOW_DIALOG class is used as a C++ wrapper for dialog boxes stored within application resource files. This allows the PMCLASS classes to interact with traditional PM resources.

Public Constructors and Destructors

- C_DIALOG(C_WINDOW *pxcParentObj, T_MSG_TABLE *pxtMsg);

  This constructor initializes the window class attributes, and assigns a message table for the dialog object. The pxcParentObj parameter specifies the owner window.

Public Members and Attributes

- void Create(int iID);

  This method associates the dialog resource having the specified resource identifier with the parent window.

- void Process(void);

  This method processes the dialog box.

- void Close(void);

  This method closes the dialog window.

C_LISTBOX window.hpp, winchild.hpp, listbox.hpp

The C_LISTBOX class implements the code required to support the list box control.

Public Constructors and Destructors

- C_LISTBOX(C_WINDOW *pxcParentObj, int iID, int iMode);

  This constructor initializes the list box class. The pxcParentObj parameter specifies the owner window.

- C_LISTBOX(C_WINDOW *pxcParentObj, int iID);

  This constructor initializes the list box class. The pxcParentObj parameter specifies the owner window.

- C_LISTBOX(C_DIALOG *pxcParentObj, int iID, int iMode);

  This constructor initializes the list box class. The pxcParentObj parameter specifies the owner dialog resource.

Public Members and Attributes

- void Insert(char *szText, int iHow);

  This method inserts a test item into the list box; iHow specifies how the item is inserted (i.e., at the end of the list).

- void Delete(int iItem);

  This method removes the specified item from the list box control.

- void DeleteAll(void);

  This method removes all items from the list box control.

- void Select(int iItem, BOOL bBoolean);

  This method selects or deselects the specified item.

- int Selection(int iFrom);

  This method returns the item number of the current selection.

- int ItemCount(void);

  This method returns the number of items in the list box control.

- void ItemText(int iItem, char *szString, int iBufferSize);

  This method returns the text associated with the specified item number.

C_STATUS window.hpp, winchild.hpp, status.hpp

The C_STATUS class implements the code required to support the status line control.

Public Constructors and Destructors

- C_STATUS(C_WINDOW *pxcParentObj);

  This constructor initializes the status class attributes. The pxcParentObj parameter specifies the owner window.

Public Members and Attributes

- void Text(char *szFormat, ...);

  This method inserts a printf-style string of text into the status line.

C_MENU window.hpp, winchild.hpp, menu.hpp

The C_MENU class implements the code required to support the menu control.

Public Constructors and Destructors

- C_MENU(C_WINDOW *pxcParentObj);

  This constructor initializes the menu class attributes. The pxcParentObj parameter specifies the owner window.

Public Members and Attributes

- void EnableItem(int iIDItem);

  This method enables the specified menu item.

- void DisableItem(int iIDItem);

  This method disables the specified menu item.

- void SetItemText(int iIDItem, char *szText);

  This method sets the text for the specified menu item.

- void GetItemText(int iIDItem, char *szText, int iSize);

  This method returns the text for the specified menu item.

C_SLIDER window.hpp, winchild.hpp, slider.hpp

The C_SLIDER class implements the code required to support the slider control.

Public Constructors and Destructors

- C_SLIDER(C_WINDOW *pxcParentObj, int iID, int iMode, int iIncrements, int iScale);

  This constructor initializes the slider class attributes. The pxcParentObj parameter specifies the owner window. The iIncrements and iScale values specify the number of increments on the slider and the spacing between increments.

- C_SLIDER(C_DIALOG *pxcParentObj, int iID);

  This constructor initializes the slider class attributes. The slider control is located within a dialog resource.

Public Members and Attributes

- void Scale(int iIncrements, int iSpacing);

  This method sets the scale and increment for the slider. This is normally performed as part of the construction process.

- void Value(int iValue);

  This method sets the slider position value.

C_BUTTON window.hpp, winchild.hpp, button.hpp

The C_BUTTON class implements the code required to support the toolbar button control.

Public Constructors and Destructors

- C_BUTTON(void);

  This constructor initializes the toolbar button class attributes.

- C_BUTTON(C_WINDOW *pxcParentObj);

  This constructor initializes the toolbar button class attributes. The pxcParentObj parameter contains a pointer to the owner object—typically a toolbar window.

Public Members and Attributes

- void Initialize(int iButtonID, int iXPos, int iYPos, int iUp, int iDn, int iDis, char *szText);

  This method initializes the toolbar button class attributes. Typically this is called only during the construction process.

- void State(int iNewState);

  This method sets the state of the button (i.e., Up, Down, or Disabled).

- void Toggle(void);

  This method toggles the state of the button from up to down, or vice versa.

C_TOOLBAR window.hpp, winchild.hpp, tbar.hpp

The C_TOOLBAR class implements the code required to support the toolbar control. The toolbar window is essentially a regular child window, with some additional visual components, such as a chiseled border.

Public Constructors and Destructors

- C_TOOLBAR(C_WINDOW *pxcParentObj, int iTBarID, iTBarHeight);

  This constructor initializes the toolbar class attributes. The pxcParentObj parameter contains a pointer to the owner object—typically an application window.

- ~C_TOOLBAR(void);

  This destructor deallocates the class and resets the button count.

Public Members and Attributes

- void Status(C_STATUS *pxcStatusWindow);

  This method sets the internal pointer to the status line window used to display the fly-over toolbar text.

- void CreateButtons(T_BUTTON_TABLE *pxtButtonTable);

  This method creates button objects for each item in the supplied button table, adding them to the toolbar window.

- void ButtonData(int iID);

  This method returns a pointer to the button object for the specified button identifier.

- void ButtonToggle(int iID);

  This method toggles the button for the specified button identifier.

- void ButtonState(int iID, int iState);

  This method sets the state for the button with the specified identifier.

- void ButtonEnable(int iID, int iValue);

  This method enables/disables the button with the specified identifier.

C_MLE **window.hpp, winchild.hpp, mle.hpp**

The C_MLE class implements the code required to support the multiline editor bar control. This includes all the functionality supported by Presentation Manager, plus the ability to save or load the contents of the MLE to disk.

Public Constructors and Destructors

- C_MLE(C_WINDOW *pxcParentObj, int iMLEID, iMode);

  This constructor initializes the MLE class attributes. The pxcParentObj parameter contains a pointer to the owner object—typically an application window. The iMode parameter specifies any additional operating system specific control parameters.

- C_MLE(C_WINDOW *pxcParentObj, int iMLEID);

  This constructor initializes the MLE class attributes. The pxcParentObj parameter contains a pointer to the owner object—typically an application window.

Public Members and Attributes

- void ReadOnlyStatus(short iBool);

  This sets or resets the read-only status of the MLE.

- void WordWrap(int iBool);

  This method sets or resets the word wrap status of the MLE.

- void ResetDirtyBufferFlag(void);

  This method resets the flag that keeps track of changes to the contents of the editor control.

- int IsBufferDirty(void);

  This method returns the value of the flag that keeps track of changes to the MLE buffer.

- void Copy(void);

  This method copies the current MLE selection to the clipboard.

- void Cut(void);

  This method cuts the current MLE selection to the clipboard.

- void Paste(void);

  This method pastes the clipboard contents to the insertion point of the MLE buffer.

- void Clear(void);

  This method clears the current selection from the MLE buffer.

- void UnDo(void);

  This method undoes the last change to the MLE buffer.

- LONG BufferLength(void);

  This method returns the number of characters contained within the MLE buffer. This includes all tabs, carriage controls, and other invisible characters.

- void DisableRefresh(void);

  This method disables updates to the edit control.

- void EnableRefresh(void);

  This method enables updates to the edit control.

- void Insert(char *szString);

  This method inserts the supplied text into the MLE at the current insertion point.

- void Delete(LONG lStart, LONG lCount);

  This method removes text from the MLE buffer, starting at the specified buffer offset and spanning the number of characters supplied in lCount.

- void Select(LONG lStart, LONG lEnd);

  This method selects MLE text within the specified range.

- void QuerySelection(LONG *pAnchor, LONG *pCursor);

  This method returns the current selection range within the MLE.

- void TransferBuffer(char *szString, LONG lSize);

  This method is specific to OS/2, and sets the transfer area to which MLE text will be imported or exported.

- void ExportBuffer(LONG *ipStart, LONG *ipEnd);

  This method exports the specified range of MLE text into the transfer area.

- void FindFirst(char *szString);

  This method searches for the first instance of the specified text within the MLE buffer.

- void FindNext(void);

  This method searches for the next instance of the specified text within the MLE buffer.

- LONG Line(LONG lPointer);

  This method returns the line number containing the specified offset.

- LONG Column(LONG lLine);

  This method returns the column number on the supplied line containing the cursor.

- LONG NumberOfLines(void);

  This method returns the number of lines within the MLE buffer.

- void Load(C_STATUS *pxcStatus, char *szFileName);

  This method loads the specified file into the MLE buffer.

- void Save(C_STATUS *pxcStatus, char *szFileName);

  This method saves the contents of the MLE to the specified file.

C_CONTAINER window.hpp, winchild.hpp, contain.hpp

The C_CONTAINER class implements the code required to support the CUA'91 container control.

Public Constructors and Destructors

- C_CONTAINER(C_WINDOW *pxcParentObj, int iID, iView, int iFlags, int iMode);

  This constructor initializes the container class attributes. The pxcParentObj parameter contains a pointer to the owner object—typically an application window. The iMode parameter specifies any additional operating system specific control parameters.

- C_CONTAINER(C_WINDOW *pxcParentObj, int iID, iView, int iFlags);

  This constructor initializes the container class attributes. The pxcParentObj parameter contains a pointer to the owner object—typically an application window. The iMode parameter specifies any additional operating system specific control parameters.

- C_CONTAINER(C_DIALOG *pxcParentObj, int iID, iView, int iFlags);

  This constructor initializes the container class attributes. The pxcParentObj parameter contains a pointer to the dialog object.

- ~C_CONTAINER(void);

  This destructor removes all items from the container and destroys it.

Public Members and Attributes

- void Setup(int iView, int iFlags);

  This method sets up the view used for the container.

- void Allocate(ULONG iLength, USHORT iCtr);

  This method allocates a number of container records of a specified size.

- void Insert(void *pParent, void *pRecord, int iCount, int iUpdate);

  This method inserts one or more container records into the container.

- void Insert(void *pParent, void *pRecord, int iCount);

  This method inserts one or more container records into the container, and forces the container to update.

- void Remove(void);

  This method removes all records from the container and frees the memory used for the record structure.

- void Remove(void *pvData, short iCount);

  This method removes a selected number of container records, starting with the record specified in pvData.

- void Redraw(void *pRecord);

  This method forces the specified record to be redrawn; a value of zero forces all records to be redrawn.

- void Sort(void *SortFunc);

  This method sets the sort function used by the PM container manager to sort the container records.

- void Search(void *pStart, char *szString, unsigned int iType);

  This method searches the container for the specified string. The iType parameter is used to specify which container view is searched.

- void *ParentRecord(void *hCurrent);

  This method returns a pointer to the parent record of hCurrent. This method is used only for tree view containers.

- void *FirstRecord(void);

  This method returns the first record in the container.

- void *NextRecord(void *hCurrent);

  This method returns the next record in the container. A return value of zero indicates the end of the container.

- void *PreviousRecord(void *hCurrent);

  This method returns the previous record in the container. A value of zero indicates that the first record has been reached.

- void *MemoryFirstRecord(void);

  This method returns the first record in the container's linked list.

- void *MemoryNextRecord(void *hCurrent);

  This method returns the next record in the container's linked list. A return value of zero indicates the end of the container.

- void *FirstChild(void *hCurrent);

  This method returns the first child record of a specified parent in a tree view container.

- void *LastChild(void *hCurrent);

  This method returns the last child record of a specified parent in a tree view container.

- void *FirstSelected(void);

  This method returns the first record in the container that is selected.

- void *NextSelected(void *hCurrent);

  This method returns the next record in the container that is selected.

- void ExpandTree(void *pRecord);

  This method expands the specified parent record in a tree view container.

- void CompressTree(void *pRecord);

  This method compresses the specified parent record in a tree view container.

- void SelectRecord(void *pRecord, short sBool);

  This method selects or deselects the specified record.

C_LOG window.hpp, winchild.hpp, log.hpp

The C_LOG class implements the code required to support the debugging capabilities of PMCLASS.

Public Constructors and Destructors

- C_LOG(char *szLogFile, int iLogMode);

  This constructor initializes the debugging log class. Output is written to the specified file and optionally to a multiline editor window.

- ~C_LOG(void);

  This destructor removes the dynamic MLE object used by C_LOG, if that object was created.

Public Members and Attributes

- void Open(void);

  This method opens the debug log.

- void Write(char *szFormat, ...);

  This method closes the debug log.

- void Write(char *szFormat, ...);

  This method writes a printf-style string to the debug log.

Network Class Library Reference

C_CONNECT net.hpp

The C_CONNECT class is used as a base class to derive more advanced classes to implement the hierarchy of TCP/IP protocols. It acts as the insulator between the native TCP/IP API and network applications. Much of the functionality in this simply wraps functions from the native API.

Public Constructors and Destructors

- C_CONNECT();

  This constructor simply calls the Initialize() method to initialize the class attributes to default values.

Public Members and Attributes

- void Initialize(void);

  This method is normally called before the network connection is established. It initializes the internal class attributes to their default values.

- int FindHost(void);

  This method builds a host structure that will be used to connect a socket to a remote host. This member function returns D_NET_HOST if there was an error determining the host, or D_NET_OK if the operation was successfully completed.

- int Protocol(char *szProtocol);

  This method builds a protocol structure based on the protocol string passed into the routine in the szProtocol parameter. These protocol strings are defined in the PROTOCOL file in the TCP/IP installation. If there was an error setting the protocol, this member function returns D_NET_PROTOCOL, or D_NET_OK if the operation was successfully completed.

- int StreamSocket(void);

  This method sets the socket interface to stream type. This member function returns D_NET_SOCKET if there was an error selecting stream type or D_NET_OK if the operation was successfully completed.

- int RawSocket(void);

  This method sets the socket interface to raw data transfer type. This member function returns D_NET_SOCKET if there was an error selecting raw type, or D_NET_OK if the operation was successfully completed.

- int Open(void);

  This method opens a stream mode socket and creates a connection to the remote host. This member function returns D_NET_CONNECT if there was an error connecting to remote host, or D_NET_OK if the operation was successfully completed.

- void Close(void);

  This method closes the connection to the remote host and shuts down the socket.

- int Send(char *szString);

  This method writes the NULL terminated string passed in szString to the remote host, using the protocol currently in use. This member function returns the number of bytes written to the remote host.

- int ReceiveBuffer(char *szBuffer, int iSize);

  This method retrieves lines of text from the remote host. The text is written to the supplied szBuffer and is limited to the number of bytes specified in the iSize parameter. This member function returns the number of bytes read from the remote host.

- void Receive(char *szBuffer);

  This method reads the next complete line of text received from the server. Line termination is stripped from the string. Care must be taken when using this method in conjunction with the ReceiveBuffer() method, because C_CONNECT double buffers received text from the remote host. ReceiveBuffer() operates outside the buffering code at the lowest level, so it can extract text before this data gets buffered. This will result in data loss. It is best to use the Receive() method for most interactions with the remote host.

- void ReceiveFrom(char *pbyBuffer, short sLength, struct sockadr *pxsFrom);

  This method reads UDP packets from the specified socket. Any data received from the socket specified in pxsFrom is written to the buffer pbyBuffer. The method is a simple code wrapper for the TCP/IP API function recvfrom().

- void SendTo(char *pbyBuffer, short sLength);

  This method writes UDP packets to the socket defined for the instance. The data written is sourced from the buffer pbyBuffer. The method is a simple code wrapper for the TCP/IP API function sendto().

- void LoadFile(char *szFilename);

  This method reads any data arriving from the remote host and writes it to a file. The process terminates and the file closes when an "\r\n.\r\n" character sequence is detected. This type of data is used so frequently with TCP/IP protocols that it has been implemented as a top-level method.

C_CONNECT_PING net.hpp, netping.hpp

The C_CONNECT_PING class implements the Ping segment of the ICMP protocol, as specified by RFC 795. It has the capability of sending pings to a host and receiving them back, accompanied by a time delay.

Public Constructors and Destructors

- C_CONNECT_PING(USHORT iIdentity, char *szConnectServer);

  This constructor initializes the C_CONNECT_PING class. It accepts an identity byte tagged onto every Ping packet and is used as an identifier. szConnectServer contains the address of the host being pinged.

Public Members and Attributes

- int Open(void);

  This method creates and opens a Ping connection to the address specified when the object was instantiated.

- int PingTx(BYTE *pbyPacket, int iLength);

  This method transmits a ping packet of the specified size to the connected host. This member function returns a D_NET_OK if the packet was transmitted correctly.

- int PingRx(BYTE *pbyPacket, char *szString);

  This method receives a ping packet from the connected host. The member function returns the number of bytes received.

C_CONNECT_NEWS net.hpp, netnews.hpp

The C_CONNECT_NEWS class implements the NNTP news protocol, as specified by RFC 977. It implements the entire client specification for news, including some extensions, such as overview support.

Public Constructors and Destructors

- C_CONNECT_NEWS(char *szConnectServer, int iConnectPort);

  This constructor initializes the C_CONNECT_NEWS class. It accepts a server address and a port number for the connection.

Public Members and Attributes

- int Open(void);

  This method opens a connection to the news server.

- int Close(void);

  This method closes the connection to the news server.

- int OpenPost(void);

  This method initiates the posting of a new message.

- int ClosePost(void);

  This method ends the posting of a new message. The new message is submitted to the server for posting.

- int List(char *szFilename);

  This method returns a list of news groups from the server.

- int ListNewGroups(char *szDate, char *szFilename);

  This method returns a list of new news groups added to the server since the specified date/time. szDate is specified as "YYMMDD HHMMSS". See RFC 977 for additional specifiers.

- int Overview(ULONG lStart, ULONG lEnd, char *szFilename);

  This method returns a message list overview for the current news group. The overview spans the message range from lStart to lEnd.

- int Group(char *szGroup, ULONG *plFirstArticle, ULONG *plLastArticle, ULONG *plTotal);

  This method selects the specified news groups, and returns the first and last article numbers for the group, along with the total number of articles.

- int First(ULONG lArticle);

  This method sets the internal server pointer to the specified article.

- int Next(ULONG *plArticle);

  This method sets the internal server pointer to the next successive article, and returns the article number.

- int Article(ULONG lArticle, char *szFilename);

  This method retrieves the specified article from the news server.

- int Body(ULONG lArticle, char *szFilename);

  This method retrieves the specified article body from the news server.

- int Head(ULONG lArticle, char *szFilename);

  This method retrieves the specified article body from the news server.

C_CONNECT_FTP net.hpp, netftp.hpp

The C_CONNECT_FTP class implements the FTP file transfer protocol, as specified by RFC 959. It implements much of the specification for the client side of the connection.

Public Constructors and Destructors

- C_CONNECT_FTP(char *szConnectServer, int iConnectPort, C_MLE *pxcConsole);

  This constructor initializes the C_CONNECT_FTP class. It accepts a server address and a port number for the connection. pxcConsole contains a pointer to an optional multiline edit control used to display commands and server responses.

Public Members and Attributes

- int Open(void);

  This method opens a connection to the FTP server.

- int Close(void);

  This method closes the connection to the FTP server.

- int Send(void);

  This method sends a command to the FTP server.

- int Receive(void);

  This method receives a response from the FTP server.

- int SYST(void);

  This method sends a SYST command to retrieve the system server information.

- int SITE(char *szString);

  This method sends a SITE command to send any site specific commands to the server.

- int ACCT(char *szString);

  This method sends an ACCT command to send any account information to the server.

- int USER(char *szString);

  This method sends a USER command to set the user name information.

- int PASS(char *szString);

  This method sends a PASS command to send the user password to the server.

- int TYPE(char *szString);

  This method sends a TYPE command to set the mode used for file transfers.

- int PWD(char *szString);

  This method sends a PWD command to return the current working directory from the server.

- int CWD(char *szString);

  This method sends a CWD command to set the current working directory on the server.

- int RMD(char *szString);

  This method sends an RMD command to remove a directory from the server.

- Int MKD(char *szString);

  This method sends an MKD command to create a new server directory.

- int DELE(char *szString);

  This method sends a DELE command to remove the specified command from the server.

- int DIR(char *szString);

  This method sends a DIR command to retrieve a directory listing from the server.

- int ABOR(char *szString);

  This method sends an ABOR command to abort a file transfer.

- int RETR(char *szSrcFile, char *szDstFile);

  This method sends a RETR command, retrieves the specified source file from the server, and stores it on the local drive as szDstFile.

- int STOR(char *szSrcFile, char *szDstFile);

  This method sends a STOR command to transfer the specified file from the local drive to the server.

- int QUIT(char *szString);

  This method sends a QUIT command to terminate the connection.

- int NOOP(char *szString);

  This method sends a NOOP command to perform a "no operation."

Index

A

Anchor block 27, 95
API
accept 303, 306
DosKillThread 56, 80
DosSleep 56
DosWaitThread 55
getprotobyname 262
ioctl 8
listen 301
recv 49, 303
recvfrom 270
select 316, 392
send 49, 306
sendto 269
shutdown 305
sock_init 48, 259
soclose 305
WinBeginPaint 141
WinCreateMsgQueue 27, 94
WinCreateStdWindow 28, 140
WinCreateWindow 24
WinDefDlgProg 152
WinDefWindowProc 29
WinDestroyMsgQueue 95
WinDispatchMsg 28
WinEnableMenuItem 167
WinEndPaint 141
WinInitialize 27, 94
WinInvalidateRect 118
WinPostMsg 107
WinQueryPresParam 117
WinQueryWindowPos 112
WinQueryWindowText 109
WinRegisterClass 27
WinRegisterWindow 120
WinSendMsg 107
WinSetPresParam 116
WinSetWindowPos 110
WinShowWindow 110
WinTerminate 27, 95
WinUpdateWindow 111
ARPANET 39

B

Barnes, David 14
Bitmaps 91, 166, 221, 241
Buttons 91, 99
Enabling, disabling 109
Minimize, maximize 129
System menu 129

C

Child window
Creating 145
Getting parent object 145
Setting parent object 144
Setting size, position 146–147
Class libraries 11
Code reuse 67
Command tables 91
Common User Access 32
Action bars 33
Edit menu 34
Help menu 35

Keyboard accelerators 35
Compilers xii, 4–5, 7
Connections
Closing 266
Finding host for 260
Initializing 259
Loading text file from 271
Opening 264
Raw socket interface 263
ReceiveFrom method 270
Receiving data 268
Sending data 266
SendTo method 269
Setting protocol for 262
Streaming socket interface 263
Containers
Allocating record space 228
Columns in detail view 243
Compressing trees 242
Example sort function 233
Expanding trees 241
Extended selection in 225
Fast record manipulation 237
Finding child records 238
Inserting records 229
Parent records in tree view 234
Redrawing records 232
Removing records 231
Searching for data 233
Selecting records 242
Sorting 232
Style flags (CCS_) 224
Views 226

D

Datagram sockets 263
Debugging 245
DEF File
DATA 328
DESCRIPTION 328
HEAPSIZE 329
PROTMODE 329
STACKSIZE 329
Desktop
Height 96
Width 97
Dialog boxes
Border height 98
Closing 151
Creating 149
Creating with parent 150
Processing 150
Dynamic link libraries 10

E

E (OS/2 system editor) 327
Edit controls 201
Event semaphores 84

F

Files
DEF 328
RC 337
RES 337
FTP 262, 295, 322, 467
FTP connections
ABOR 316
Accepting data connection 303
ACCT 309
Closing 299
Closing data socket 305
CWD 313
DELE 314
DIR 315
Listening for data connection 301
MKD 314
NOOP 319
Opening 298
Out-of-band messaging 306
PASS 310
Putting file 306
PWD 312
QUIT 319
Receiving data 300
RETR 317
RMD 313
Sending data 300
Sending FTP commands 308
SITE 309
STOR 318
SYST 308
TYPE 311
USER 310

G

Games, TCP/IP development for 467
Gopher 322
Gwinn, Ray 6

H

HAB 27
HTML 14
Hungarian notation xi
Hypertext Markup Language 14

I

IBM
  Developer Assistance Program 14
  Developer Connection for OS/2 4, 467
  Employee Written Software Library 14
  Entertainment Developer's Toolkit 467
  OS/2 Redbooks 4
  TCP/IP Programmer's Toolkit 4, 7
  TCP/IP utilities 4
ICLUI xii, 5, 69, 254
ICMP 259, 262–263, 272
Icon 130, 132, 140, 174, 177, 179, 181, 186, 221
ICONEDIT utility 174, 339
INI File 70
  Closing 72
  Opening 71
  Reading from 73
  Sample program 74
  System 76
  User 74
  Writing to 73
INT 21 interface 20
International Standards Organization 40
Internet
  OS/2 newsgroups 12
  Useful FTP sites 13
  Useful Gophers 13
  Useful Web pages 14
Internet Relay Chat 321
IOCTL 20
IP Protocol 263
ISO/OSI 40

L

Listbox
  Counting items 162
  Deleting all items 160
  Deleting items 160
  Inserting items 159
  Querying item text 163
  Querying selections 162
  Selecting items 161
  Style flags (LS_) 157
Logging debug information 245

M

MAKE 8–9
Menus
  Disabling items 168
  Enabling items 167
  Getting item text 169
  Height 98
  Setting item text 168
Message tables 90
Microsoft
  DOS 19
  Windows 19
  Windows 3.1 8, 322
  Windows 95 254
  Windows NT 8, 16–17, 254
MLE Style flags (MLS_) 204
Moskowitz, David 31
Motif 254
MPTS 3
Multiline edit controls
  Clearing text 210
  Clipboard operations 208
  Deleting text 212
  Detecting changes in 207
  Enabling, disabling refresh 210
  Getting buffer length 210
  Inserting text 211
  Insertion point column number 216
  Insertion point line number 216
  Loading from file 218
  Number of lines 217
  Querying text selections 212
  Read only 206
  Saving to file 219

Searching for text 215
Undoing changes 209
Word wrap 207
Multi-Protocol Transfer Services 3
Multithreading 54
Multi-User Dungeons 467

N

NeoLogic Network Suite viii, 4, 322
NETCLASS
C_CONNECT 256
C_CONNECT_FTP 295
C_CONNECT_PING 272
C_NEWS_CONNECT 278
NETSTAT 6, 50
Network File System 263
News
Global memory use 405
Object message flow 403
Uudecode 452
News connections 286
Closing 282
End posting 284
Getting newsgroups list 284
Listing new newsgroups 286
Loading article body 293
Loading article header 294
Loading articles 292
Loading newsgroup descriptions 285
Loading newsgroup overview 288
Opening 281
Selecting newsgroups 289
Server responses 281
Start posting 283
NFS 263
NMAKE 8
NNTP 264, 278, 295, 322, 393
NVCLASS
C_INI 70
C_INI_SYSTEM 76
C_INI_USER 74
C_SEM_EVENT 84
C_THREAD 77, 380
C_THREAD_PM 81
NVCLASS library 69

O

1/10 second rule 6, 57, 63, 436
Object Windows Library 69
OpenDoc 393
OS/2
Architecture 20
Common User Access 32
Development tools 6
Memory management 19
Multitasking 18
Single message queue 17
Structure 20
Threading 18, 54
Useful FTP sites 13
Useful Gophers 13
Useful newsgroups 12
Useful Web pages 14
Virtual memory 19
Warp Bonus Pack 3, 17
What is it? 16
OS2.INI 75
OS20Memu 4, 6
OS2SYS.INI 76
OWL xii, 31, 69

P

Ping 44, 272
Ping connections
Opening 274
Packet checksum 278
Receiving packets 275
Transmitting packets 274
PM Message
WM_CHAR 367
WM_CLOSE 151
WM_COMMAND 91, 123, 152, 154, 192, 198
WM_CONTROL 188
WM_CREATE 28, 187, 409, 459
WM_INITDLG 153
WM_PAINT 29, 91, 141, 179
WM_QUIT 465
WM_SIZE 379
PMCLASS
C_APPLICATION 93
C_BUTTON_TBAR 174

C_CONTAINER 221
C_DIALOG 148
C_EDIT 199
C_LISTBOX 156
C_LOG 245
C_MENU 166
C_MLE 202
C_PUSHBUTTON 154
C_SLIDER 169
C_STATUS 163
C_TOOLBAR 183
C_WINDOW 99
C_WINDOW_CHILD 142
C_WINDOW_STD 126
Command tables 91
Message tables 90
Minimal example 30
Pointer Image 186
POP 271
Portability 68
PPP 41
Presentation Manager
Anchor block 27
C Source minimal example 24
Child windows 23
Control windows 24
Goals for applications 31
Header file minimal example 24
How does it work? 23
Initializing threads 83
Message model 17
Single message queue 17
Terminating threads 83
What is it? 21
PRJ2MAK 8
Pstat 6
Pulse 4, 6

R

Raw sockets 263
Reich, David 36
Resource Compiler 337
RFC 14, 38, 40
RFC 1055 41
RFC 768 44
RFC 791 43
RFC 795 44, 272
RFC 826 44
RFC 959 45, 295, 454
RFC 977 287, 294

S

Semaphores 84
Closing 87
Creating 86
Opening existing 86
Posting 88
Resetting 87
Waiting for activation 88
Simonyi, Charles xi
SIO drivers 6
Sliders
Setting scale 173
Setting value 173
Style flags (SLS_) 170
SLIP 41
SMTP 271
Sockets
Datagram 263
Raw 263
Streaming 262
Status line 165
Streaming sockets 262
System Application Architecture 32

T

Taligent 393
TCP 41, 262, 266
TCP/IP
ARPANET 39
FTP 295, 322
Gopher 322
ICMP 263, 272
IP 263
IRC 321
Minimum programming example 46
NNTP 264, 278, 295, 322, 393
Ping 272
POP 271
PPP 41
SLIP 41
SMTP 271
TCP 41, 262, 266

UDP 41, 263, 266
Utilities 4
Theseus/2 6
Threads
Creating 79
Killing 80
Use in PM programs 81
Waiting for completion 81
Toolbar buttons
Initializing 177
MsgBMButton1Down method 180
MsgMouseMove method 178
MsgPaint method 179
Setting state 181
Toggling 181
Toolbars
Associating status line 192
Creating buttons 193
Enabling and disabling buttons 197
MsgBMButton method 188
MsgBMButton1Down method 189
MsgBMText method 189
MsgCreate method 187
MsgMouseMove method 190
MsgPaint method 190
Sample code 198
Setting button state 196
Toggling buttons 195

U

UDP 41, 263, 266
UNIX 18–19, 68, 254

V

Visual development tools 5
VisualAge xii, 5
VisualBuilder 5

W

Warp Connect 3, 16
WatchCat 4, 6
WebExplorer 3
Window
Adding border 133
Adding icon 130
Adding maximize button 132
Adding minimize button 131
Adding titlebar 132
Creating 120, 140, 145
Destroying 121
Enabling, disabling 109
Getting background colors 117
Getting font 117
Getting foreground colors 117
Getting size, position 113–114, 135–137
Getting text 109
Getting window title 140
Handles 105
Hiding 110
HWND_DESKTOP 62, 105
HWND_OBJECT 62
Inserting into task list 134
Invalidating 118
MsgPaint method 141
Parent window 105
Posting messages 107
Registering 120
Retrieving class name 112
Sending messages 107
Setting background color 115
Setting class name 111
Setting command table 122
Setting focus 119
Setting font 116
Setting foreground color 114
Setting message table 122
Setting size, position 137–139, 146–147
Setting text 108
Setting window handle 106
Setting window title 139
Showing 110
Standard creation flags 129
Updating 111
Window procedure 123
Workplace Shell viii, 16, 135, 327, 332

X

X Windows 68, 254

About the Companion Disk

The companion disk contains the complete source code for all the libraries and applications described in the text. The code should compile with most OS/2 C++ compilers. MAKE files have been provided for Borland C++ and IBM VisualAge C++, but adapting these to other compilers should be relatively easy.

To install the source, insert the companion disk into a floppy drive and run the INSTALL program provided.

The code contained on the disk is subject to periodic changes and updates to correct programming errors and add new features.

To report a coding error, get the latest version of the source, or to suggest new features, send e-mail to Steven Gutz at nstn4064@fox.nstn.ca.